Workers' Culture in Weimar Germany

Workers' Culture in Weimar Germany
Between Tradition and Commitment

W.L. Guttsman

BERG
New York / Oxford / Munich
Distributed exclusively in the US and Canada by
St. Martin's Press, New York

First published in 1990 by
Berg Publishers Limited
Editorial Offices:
150 Cowley Road, Oxford OX4 1JJ, UK
165 Taber Avenue, Providence RI 02906, USA
Westermühlstraße 26, 8000 München 5, FRG

Library of Congress Cataloging-in-Publication Data
Guttsman, W.L.
Workers' culture in Weimar Germany Between Tradition and Commitment /
W.L. Guttsman.
p. cm.
Includes bibliographical references.
ISBN 0–907582–59–1
1. Germany—Popular culture—History—20th century. 2. Arts and
society—Germany. 3. Working class—Germany—History—20th century.
I. Title.
NX180.S6G88   1990
700'.1'03—dc20   89–38853
                                                              CIP

British Library Cataloguing in Publication Data
Guttsman, W.L. (Wilhelm Leo *1920–*)
Workers' culture in Weimar Germany Between Tradition and Commitment
1. Germany. Working classes. Social conditions, history
I. Guttsman, W.L. (Wilhelm Leo) *1920*
305.5'62'0943
ISBN 0–907582–59–1

Printed in Great Britain by Billing and Sons Limited, Worcester

To the British Library of Political and Economic Science, London School of Economics and to the Library of the University of East Anglia; to my friends and colleagues 1948–1962 and 1962–1985; and to the memory of Tony Holloway and John Kimber, librarians and scholars.

Contents

Contents

Contents

List of Tables and Figures

Tables

Figures

Abbreviations

ABTD	Arbeiter Theater Bund Deutschlands
ADGB	Allgemeiner Deutscher Gewerkschaftsbund
AfSG	Archiv für Sozialgeschichte
Arb. Bldg.	Arbeiter Bildung
ARB	Arbeiter Radio Bund
ARBKD	Assoziation revolutionärer Bildender Künstle
or ASSO	Deutschlands
ATSB	Arbeiter Turn und Sport Bewegung (Sport Bund)
AIZ	Arbeiter Illustrierte Zeitung
BPRS	Bund revolutionärer Schriftsteller Deutschlands
DASB	Deutscher Arbeiter Sängerbund
DATB	Deutscher Arbeiter Theater Bund
DASZ	Deutsche Arbeiter Sänger Zeitung
F & R	W. Fähnders and M. Rector, Literatur im Klassenkmpf. Munich 1971
IAH	International Arbeiter Hilfe
Ifa	Interessengemeinschaft für Arbeiterkultur
INPREKOR	Internationale Presse Korrespondenz
IWK	Internationale Wissenschaftliche Korrespondenz zur Geschichte der Arbeiterbewegung
KdAS	Kampfgemcinschaft der Arbeitersänger
KM	Kampfmusik
KPD	Kommunistische Partei Deutschlands
KW	Kulturwille
MASCH	Marxistische Arbeiter Schule
MdVA	Mitteilungen des Vereins Arbeiterpresse
NG	Neue Gesellschaft
NZ	Neue Zeit
RF	Rote Fahne
SM	Sozialistische Monatshefte
SPD	Sozialdemokratische Partei Deutschlands
SPD Pttg	SPD Parteitag (Annual, later biennial, Conference – Report)
SAJ	Sozialistische Arbeiterjugend
Soz. Bldg.	Sozialistische Bildung
USPD	Unabhängige Sozialdemokratische Partei Deutschlands
VFV	Volks Film Verband
WgdW	Wem gehört die Welt (published by the Neue Gesellschaft für Bildende Kunst, Berlin, 1977)

Preface

The seeds of this book were sown during my researches into the history of the German Social Democratic Party from its inception to its destruction in 1933, which were published as a book in 1981; but its roots go deeper. In the last years of my childhood in Berlin I received some fleeting and inchoate impressions of the political culture of the Weimar Republic, which was soon to collapse into the Nazi dictatorship. As an adolescent I could henceforth only furtively, and in the security of home or of a circle of friends, absorb some of the culture which was now defamed and proscribed. Later in London during the war and in the immediate post-war period I had some contact with members of German socialist *émigré* groups, and hence with the history and aspirations of that other Germany. I did not follow their example and return to Germany; but I am grateful for their friendship and appreciative of their influence on my thinking.

My work *The German Social Democratic Party, 1875–1933* owed much to previous research in the field of political sociology; and some of the material then collected and contacts then established helped in the preparation of this book. Research in German libraries and archives was assisted by the German Academic Exchange Services, the British Council, the British Academy and the Akademie der Wissenschaften der Deutschen Demokratischen Republik, whose grants and academic exchange schemes facilitated research visits to West Germany and to the German Democratic Republic. I am most grateful to them and to their officers.

I would like to thank Professor Peter Feist and Dr Ursula Horn of the Institut für Aesthetik und Kunstwissenschaft of the Akademie der Wissenschaften, and colleagues at the Lehrstuhl Kulturtheorie of the Humboldt University, Berlin, and especially Dr Horst Groschopp, for help and advice. Dr Groschopp kindly read one of the chapters of the MS, as did Dr Christa Hempel-Küter of Hamburg and Professor Richard Evans of Norwich and London. The MS also benefited from the editorial skills of Mr Justin Dyer and Mr David Phelps.

Above all, I would like to put on record the debt which I owe to the many institutions and libraries in which I collected material for this book. They are listed here in no particular order; and my deep-felt thanks go to the many librarians, archivists and others who helped me to find and utilise material, welcomed me, and advised me, whether or not I have named them here.

Geheimes Staatsarchiv Preussischer Kulturbesitz, West Berlin
Bundesarchiv, Koblenz
Staatsarchiv Hamburg
Staatsarchiv Bremen
Arbeiterliedarchiv, Deutsche Akademie der Künste, Berlin, GDR. Dr Inge Lammel
Akademie der Künste, West Berlin. Professor Walter Huder
Institut für Marxismus-Leninismus, Berlin, GDR. Herr Heinz Sommer
Zentralbibliothek der Gewerkschaften beim Bundesvorstand der Freien Gewerkschaften, Berlin, GDR
Staatsbibliothek Preussischer Kulturbesitz, West Berlin
Fritz Hüser Institut für deutsche und ausländische Arbeiterliteratur, Dortmund. Dr R. Noltenius
Institut für Zeitungsforschung, Dortmund
Bibliothek zur Sozialgeschichte und Arbeiterbewegung, Hamburg
Institut zur Erforschung der europäischen Arbeiterbewegung. Ruhr Universität Bochum. Dr Peter Friedemann
Bibliothek der sozialen Demokratie, Friedrich Ebert Stiftung, Bonn. Herr Horst Ziska
Deutsche Bibliothek, Frankfurt.

Two libraries are missing from this list because my debt to them over the whole of my professional life could only be adequately acknowledged in the dedication of this book. Posts in the libraries of the London School of Economics and of the University of East Anglia span my professional career. Their books and other material on their shelves educated me more than lectures and seminars. Their collections provided most of the basic literature and much of the more specific material for this work and for earlier books and articles. My colleagues gave me their friendship and their comradeship, which helped to sustain me spiritually. For all this I am immensely grateful.

Last but not least I am most grateful to my wife for her continuous support and to my journalist daughter for reading and commenting on the text of this book.

For all the infelicities and inaccuracies that may remain I alone am to blame.

W.L. Guttsman

Introduction: Labour Movement and Workers' Culture

This book sets out to explore the creation and diffusion of the cultural activities and of the leisure time pursuits of the members of the German working class who saw in the labour movement their political and economic representation, and, in many individual cases, their spiritual home. With the exceptions of large sections of the agricultural labour force, who mostly followed the politics of landowners and peasant employers, and of a significant but gradually declining number of catholic workers, who tended to support the Catholic Centre Party, the manual working class identified with the labour movement, and increasingly supported first the German Social Democratic Party (SPD), and after 1918 the SPD and the Communist Party (KPD), in elections. Indeed, both class and movement grew almost simultaneously, and it is the strength of the class commitment which gave to the social-democratic organisation before 1914 its uniquely powerful position; although the governmental system of the German Empire prevented this internal strength from being translated into political power.

The forward march of the political labour movement in Germany started in the 1860s, and led to the founding of the Social Democratic Party in 1875. The SPD arose out of the fusion of two earlier movements, the General German Workers' Association, established in 1863 under the leadership of Ferdinand Lassalle, and the Social Democratic Workers' Party, which was influenced by Marx and Engels, and was established a few years later. The new party could count on the support of about 25,000 members and nine deputies in the Reichstag. At the election of 1877 the SPD polled nearly half a million votes, and gained twelve seats in the Reichstag.

The new, united party, which had secured 9.1% of the popular vote based on adult male suffrage over 25, was perceived by the Conservative government as a clear threat to the existing system. The government feared the power of ideas less than the efficiency of the organisation. The Prussian State Prosecutor, Tessendorf,

-1-

argued that he was not concerned with mass meetings but with mass organisations. 'Social Democrats could call meetings of hundreds of thousands, but they should not be allowed to centralise their activities or to organise themselves. They should not be allowed to form "a state within the state". Without such organisation and centralisation Social Democracy would be dead.'[1]

The government first tried to destroy the social-democratic movement by applying the existing laws; and when this failed it took drastic action by securing in 1878 a law which virtually proscribed the SPD, permitting only electoral activities. The party now found itself without a formal organisation, and was forced into a state of partial illegality. It operated frequently, and significantly in our context, in the disguise of choral societies, gymnasts' associations or hiking clubs, but even these were subject to harassment by the police and dissolution by the courts.[2]

Ingenuity and a deep feeling of injustice helped the socialist working class to circumvent the restrictions and partly nullify the effects of the prohibition, and the legislation thus had the effect of encouraging greater solidarity. As the socialist deputy, Hasenclever, told the Minister of the Interior 'your anti-socialist law has created another bond for us, the bond of all the prosecuted. This bond unites us. Herr von Putkamer, you have made us into a true party.'[3]

After the government had failed to obtain a renewal of the punitive legislation in January 1890, the SPD was set on a course of rapid expansion. Within a few weeks it polled 1.4 million votes – almost twice its 1887 vote – and secured 35 Reichstag seats. In the next two decades the party expanded its base nearly everywhere in the country.[4]

Its membership reached around 100,000 soon after the repeal, and a million by 1914. The trade union movement, which in 1891 had become united under the umbrella of the Generalkommission der Gewerkschaften – an umbrella-type of structure with about 350,000 members in its affiliated organisations – expanded quickly after the turn of the century. By the outbreak of war it had a membership of nearly 2.5 million. The social-democratic press,

1. P. Kampfmeyer and B. Altmann, *Vor dem Sozialistengesetz*, Berlin, 1928, p. 142.
2. Between 1878 and 1886 246 associations, mainly of this type, were dissolved following police prosecution.
3. Quoted in R. Höhn, *Die Vaterlandlosen Gesellen*, 2 vols, Cologne, 1964, vol. 1 p. xxx.
4. The discrepancy between the relative size of the vote and of party strength in the Reichstag was due to the inequitable distribution of the electorate, which greatly benefited rural constituencies as against urban, where the SPD had its support.

too, expanded rapidly after 1890. By 1914 there were 94 party-controlled newspapers, of which all but a handful appeared daily. Their combined circulation was almost 1.5 million, and their total readership was considerably larger. Although the SPD enjoyed greater freedom, the general political hostility against this allegedly insurrectionist party remained. So did the personal animosity shown by officials and other representatives of the authorities and by the bourgeois public in general towards known social democrats. Social democrats remained *Reichsfeinde* – enemies of the state – who were allegedly seeking the violent overthrow of existing institutions. Successive governments were urged from time to time by the parties on the right to re-introduce the legal prohibition of the SPD and restrict the economic and political freedom of the organised working class.

Social-democratic and trade union activities continued to be the target of restriction and prohibition. They were subject to police chicanery, and known social democrats were often blacklisted by employers. Social democrats were banned from government service, the party was refused meeting places, and censorship and legal action against the socialist press under such general headings as 'lèse-majesty', continued.[5] Discrimination and persecution helped to strengthen the feeling of solidarity within the labour movement; but such feelings were also strengthened by the SPD organisation, coupled with intensive socialist agitation.

During the period between 1890 and 1914 the SPD developed a dense organisational network and a legal framework for democratic decision-making. The units for administration and policy-making were the Constituency parties, which existed in most of the 397 electoral districts.

Regular public meetings of local parties to hear speakers, often of national renown, generally drew large crowds; but more domestic events were also well attended. Thus participation in routine events such as the monthly members' meetings, the *Zahlabende* – where dues were collected – was often high. In Neukölln, a strongly proletarian district of Berlin where in 1912 the SPD had polled 83% of the vote, every fourth voter was a party member, and out of a total of over 15,000 members, including 3,600 women, 4,019 attended the average *Zahlabend*.[6] Political issues were discussed and voted on in mass meetings of members, or in specially called smaller meetings in the districts. Equally impressive was the large

5. Between 1890 and 1912 the courts imposed a total of 1,410 years' imprisonment and over half a million marks in fines on social democrats for political offences.
6. SPD Neukölln, *Bericht*, 1912.

attendance at demonstrations, such as the huge May Day celebrations, and at fêtes organised by the local parties.

The local parties generally had full-time secretaries, and sometimes other paid staff. In addition there were federations of constituency parties and organisations at state level. To this organisational structure we must add the cultural organisations closely linked to the SPD, and often referred to as ancillary organisations of that party.

Beginning in the 1890s workers' sports clubs and choral societies came gradually into existence throughout Germany. Some had started life under the anti-socialist laws and continued once these were repealed; but the majority owed their rise to the antagonism to Social Democracy which the bourgeois Gymnastic and Music associations displayed, and to the corresponding wish of many workers to be independent of middle-class tutelage and to spend their leisure among members of their own class.

Before 1914 the socialist working class moved, in the political sphere and in the field of leisure-time activities, largely in a social ghetto. This ghetto had a self-maintaining function, in that it gave the socialist worker a basis for self-expression. It has been said with some exaggeration that the labour movement mobilised the German worker 'from the cradle to the grave'. Beginning with the organisation of children and youth, and ending with the cremation arranged by the proletarian freethinkers, the politically committed worker could satisfy his spiritual and emotional needs, and, with the development of Consumers' Co-operatives and of trade unions, even some of his material needs, within the orbit of institutions and facilities established by the movement.

After some years the individual clubs and societies, which gave scope for the exercise of leisure-time interests, combined into national associations concerned with the development of workers' culture. Their membership was largely politically committed, but the associations proclaimed a party-political neutrality, mainly to escape police interference with their activities. By the outbreak of war these organisations had a combined membership of almost 600,000, but their audience and sphere of interest was much greater.

After 1906 their work was paralleled by an extensive network of educational activities set up by the SPD under the direction of a newly created Central Education Committee. This committee also had the task of organising general cultural activities. This created a potential conflict. It was felt that the cultural and recreational activities might detract from political commitment. For many, cultural activities were to be only a handmaiden to the political struggle,[7] an emotional stimulus to the essentially political task. However, when, after defeat in war and a partial revolution, working-class status improved, and when the labour movement began to occupy a position of greater power, workers' cultural activities also assumed a generally undisputed position.

The November Revolution of 1918, unlike its Russian predecessor in October a year before, owed its impetus more to the effect of military defeat, wholesale desertions, widespread hunger and a general collapse, which forced a radical change of government, than to an act of deliberate leadership on the part of the SPD. In spite of the party's commitment to a social revolution its leaders did not seek to bring about fundamental economic and social changes. After the abdication of the Kaiser and the resignation of the last Imperial government the leaders of the SPD and of the Independent Social Democrats (USPD) took over the reins of government. Formally their power rested on a symbolic handover of power from the last Imperial Chancellor; *de facto* the 'Council of People's Representatives', the name given to the new government, received its authority from the Berlin Councils of Soldiers and Workers' Councils, who endorsed the new government on the very next day.

While this might be seen to embody the logic of the revolution, the new government, from which the Independent Social Democrats were soon to secede, did not seek to follow a revolutionary road. It rejected from the outset the Council model of direct democracy. Instead it aimed at the early establishment of a parliamentary democracy via elections to a constituent National Assembly. This commenced work in Weimar in January 1919, and produced a new constitution six months later – the liberal democratic state which, following its origins, was to go under the name of the 'Weimar Republic'.

Large sections of the SPD saw in the new state, and in the relatively progressive social legislation which it had passed, the realisation of many of the goals for which the party had fought; and its leaders urged their followers to identify with the new state. During the Weimar years the SPD, together with the newly founded German Communist Party, which in 1922 united with a section of the USPD, the Independent Social Democrats, continued

---

7. The Düsseldorf socialist paper, the *Volkszeitung*, told its readers in 1910 that 'a good comrade is not someone who joins the workers' singing, athletics, stenography, health and other organisation . . . but only someone who is an active member of the party and the trade union'. Cited by M. Nolan, *Social Democracy and Society. Working Class Radicalism in Düsseldorf, 1890–1919*, Cambridge, 1981.

to represent the bulk of the working class. Indeed, the reformist policies of the SPD even attracted a section of the growing white-collar strata, and the party even made some inroads into the new middle class. Of the combined vote of the left the KPD succeeded in mobilising nearly a third in 1924, and even increased its share after the onset of the depression in the autumn of 1929. In the two fateful elections of summer and autumn 1932 it mobilised between 40% and 45% of the vote of the two parties.

Yet this powerful party co-operated during those years with the state and its institutions only to a very limited extent. For the Communist Party the State of Weimar, in which, especially after 1930, the forces of nationalism and fascism were growing in power and influence, was a reactionary and fascist state. Social Democrats, as its supporters, were attacked as 'Social Fascists'.

The attitude of the two parties to the state and to each other also showed itself in their view of workers' culture and in their attitude to the cultural organisations. These will be discussed in the separate chapters on the cultural ideals and practices of the two parties, but also form a major theme of the chapters which examine specific areas of cultural activities.

As far as the SPD was concerned we find that in the new political and social climate some of the energy which had previously been devoted to the fight for political and legal emancipation was now directed to the expansion of workers' cultural activities. These certainly came to their fullest expansion in these years. The workers' cultural movements directed their appeal to all sections of the working class and beyond, and communist workers as much as social democrats sang under the aegis of workers' choral societies or swam with the workers' athletics clubs. Only after 1928 did the Communist Party, in effect, foster their own cultural organisations with policies which were specifically opposed to the SPD and to the institutions which identified with the Social Democracy. The communist organisations, as we shall see, were much smaller and less developed in the range of activities which could be pursued in them; but they were kept on a high level of political action through a largely covert control by the KPD.

The middle years within the Weimar period saw the greatest activity in the field of workers' culture. The period between the end of inflation in the autumn of 1924, which marked the beginning of Germany's economic recovery, and the onset of the Great Depression, constituted years of relative prosperity for the German workers. Unemployment was relatively low, and real wages were for the first time back at their pre-war level. The expansion in the

Table 1 Total membership of workers' cultural organisations in 1928

Workers' Sports Movement	1,220,000
Workers' Choral Movement	440,000
Socialist Workers' Youth	*c.* 100,000
Volksbühne – Workers' Theatre Movement	*c.* 500,000
Total	2,260,000

field of workers' culture thus went hand in hand with a growth in the self-confidence of the labour movement. At the general election of 1928 the SPD polled over nine million votes, its highest since 1919. The combined vote of the two working-class parties, of over 40%, almost equalled that of the revolutionary period. At the same time nearly five million workers were organised in social-democratic trade unions, and 2,260,000 were organised in workers' cultural organisations. (Trade unionists, voters for the parties of the left, and the members of other workers' organisations do, of course, overlap, not counting the overlap in the membership of the major cultural organisations.)

On the other hand the influence of these movements extended outwards from the individual member and from the local organis-ation to groups, families and friends. Through public displays and performances, and through participation in political meetings and celebrations, the influence of sports clubs and choral societies extended from their immediate circle into the wider labour move-ment and the whole of the working-class community.

The links between the workers' cultural organisations and the SPD and other organisations of the labour movement were strengthened by the formal organisations of the workers' cultural movements themselves. The major cultural associations had now become mass organisations with memberships often well in the hundreds of thousands, and they had their own bureaucracies at national, regional or local level. They were generally organised on a pyramidical pattern similar to the internal structure of the Social Democratic Party, which, following the shift from an electoral system based on constituencies to one based on a list system, now had a hierarchy of deliberating and decision-making bodies. Local athletics and choral societies were co-ordinated at the provincial or regional level in so-called *Gaue* (Districts), which held regular conferences and events, and decision-making went on from these to the biennial or triennial assemblies or the national councils or executives. Leaders and functionaries were frequently active Social

Democrats, often occupying party office or other representative positions. At the local level the various organisations co-operated through local co-ordinating committees (Kulturkartelle), in which SPD, unions and socialist youth organisations might also participate; but communist organisations were *de facto* excluded.[8]

Apart from such local organisational influences the SPD sought to stimulate cultural policy through the establishment of small departments and agencies at party headquarters or through conferences on cultural themes, such as 'Film and Radio', 'Festivals' and 'Libraries'. Thus the intermeshing of a number of workers' organisations and the system of delegation gave considerable power to officials and functionaries, and this in turn strengthened the influence of the full-time bureaucracies. The smaller communist cultural organisations did not develop equally powerful bureaucracies; but the strong party discipline made up for this, and ensured that the day-to-day activities of these bodies were in line with the policies and tactics of the KPD.

In spite of the breadth of the cultural activities organised in clubs and societies which were closely linked to the labour movement, a study of their institutions and activities alone cannot throw light on many aspects of working-class culture. Not only does it not help us to understand the cultural life of the workers before the rise of their political and economic organisations, nor the culture of the part of the German proletariat outside the influence of the labour movement: 'The identification of workers' culture with the culture of the socialist workers' movement', wrote the German historian, Gerhard A. Ritter, in a survey of Workers' Culture in 1978, '. . . obscures many central features of workers' cultural development . . . it is also inapplicable to many features of workers' lives – like material culture and the social history of day to day existence, which cannot be understood by investigating workers' associations alone.'[9]

The argument for making such a distinction between workers' culture and 'labour movement culture' has received further impetus from new trends in social history. Here we have seen a move away from an emphasis on institutions and their causal connections to an interpretative and narrative approach. In the case of Germany, in particular, there was dissatisfaction with the historiography of the working class via the history of the labour movement, its organis-

---

8. Cf. R. Stübling, *Das Kulturkartell der modernen Arbeiterbewegung*, Offenbach, 1983.
9. Gerhard A. Ritter, 'Workers' culture in Imperial Germany', *Journal of Contemporary History*, vol. 13, 1978, pp. 165–89, at p. 180.

ation, politics and personalities.[10] We are now encouraged to look at the social and group relationships in the working class outside the formal organisation, and recognise the importance of the informal groupings within the social and economic strata. At the same time the concept of culture is no longer confined to art, science and high culture in general, but has widened to include virtually all aspects of the satisfaction of human needs.

For the historical anthropologist, for the student of 'folk culture', and recently also for the social historian, workers' culture is thus rooted in the pattern of the workers' everyday lives, their families, and their workplaces and their residential communities.

The study of this *Alltagskultur*, and of the lives of ordinary folk, like that of the folklore of the lower classes, can, of course, easily turn into the merely anecdotal, and into the nostalgia of a cultural conservatism. On the other hand, an understanding of workers' culture in the above sense should help us to understand the mentalities, attitudes and preferences of whole groups and sections of the population, which may then express themselves in common action, be this strikes, or electoral behaviour, or possibly looting or violent protest.[11] For Jürgen Kocka, introducing another collection of papers on our theme, the uncovering of workers' culture would help to 'fill in some of the blank areas which lie between the economy, social structure and politics' because it is just 'the mentalities, attitudes and patterns of thought and action which generally are not captured in the hypotheses and the frame of reference of Social History'.[12]

In this connection, the material aspects of workers' life, e.g. food habits and living conditions, or their technical skills, are less relevant than the social environment and the community relations which have an influence on the labour movement and are, in turn, influenced by it.[13]

The lifestyle and material conditions of the German working class have recently been studied in considerable detail by historians and ethnographers. Through these studies we have gained insight into the working-class home and the institutions of the lodger and boarder, and their influence on family life. Changes in the diet of

10. Cf. Introduction to D. Langewiesche and K. Schönhoven (eds), *Arbeiter in Deutschland*, Paderborn, 1986, pp. 7–9.
11. Cf. J. Reulecke and W. Weber (eds), *Fabrik, Familie, Feierabend. Beiträge zur Sozialgeschichte des Alltags im Industriezeitalter*, Wuppertal, 1978.
12. J. Kocka, 'Arbeiterkultur als Forschungsthema', *Geschichte und Gesellschaft*, 1979, pp. 5–11.
13. K. Tenfelde, 'Anmerkungen zur Arbeiterkultur', in W. Ruppert, *Erinnerungsgabe. Geschichte und demokratische Identitaten in Deutschland*, Opladen, 1982.

the working class during the nineteenth century have been investigated in detail, with special attention to the consumption of alcohol and the role of drinking in the domestic and social life of the male worker.[14] Recent studies of workers' sport have paid more attention than previously to the importance of informal ties, and to the cultural symbolism of athletics, seeking to use anthropological techniques and oral history to link institutional and cultural history.[15]

The life and the working conditions of the industrial worker had been studied as early as the beginning of the century in the *Enquête* of the Verein für Sozialpolitik on the *Arbeiter in der Großindustrie*.[16] A series of historical studies of the industrial worker and the environment of the factory have been published recently, but they, too, are mainly concerned with the period before 1914.[17]

For the Weimar period we are so far much more dependent on studies based on oral history which have been undertaken belatedly during the last decade. They are inevitably based on selective evidence, and, because of the timelag, more informative on the later years of the period. We also have some contemporary interview- or questionnaire-based studies, mainly of adolescents, as well as some limited autobiographical material.[18]

Chapter 4 uses some of this material in an attempt to describe aspects of the culture of everyday life, and here the area of the workers' private leisure and commercially provided leisure-time activities is of particular importance. It is here that the influence of older traditions, as well as the impact of modern commercial culture, touch and often clash with the culture of the labour movement, and this area is discussed further in Chapter 10, dealing with the 'new media'.

Such clashes are a regular feature of the history of the workers'

14. Cf. Reulecke and Weber (note 11); G. Huck (ed.), *Sozialgeschichte der Freizeit*, Wuppertal, 1980.
15. Cf. H.J. Teichler (ed.), *Arbeiterkultur und Arbeitersport*, Clausthal-Zellerfeld, 1985; H.J. Teichler and G. Hauk (eds), *Illustrierte Geschichte des Arbeitersports*, Berlin–Bonn, 1987.
16. Verein für Sozialpolitik, *Auslese und Anpassung der Arbeiterschaft in den verschiedenen Zweigen der Großindustrie*, various volumes, Berlin, 1904–9.
17. Recent studies of industrial work and of the industrial worker include M. Grüttner, *Arbeitswelt an der Wasserkante. Sozialgeschichte der Hamburger Hafenarbeiter, 1886–1914*, Göttingen, 1984; H. Schomerus, *Die Arbeiter der Maschinenfabrik Esslingen*, Stuttgart, 1977; Klaus Tenfelde, *Sozial-Geschichte der Bergarbeiterschaft an der Ruhr*, Bonn, 1977.
18. Cf. W. Emmerich, *Proletarische Lebensläufe. Autobiographische Dokumente zur Entstehung der Zweiten Kultur in Deutschland*, 2 vols, Reinbeck, 1975, especially vol. 2, 1914–45.

cultural movements; but this is not surprising. The daily life of sections of the working class was for long an expression of the culture of poverty. The labour movement had come into being to do away with the degrading and impoverishing living conditions of the German worker and the *Arbeiterkulturbewegung*, the movement for workers' culture, sought to liberate the working class from conditions of spiritual and emotional deprivation.

We can observe such conflicts in the early years of the labour movement. Thus Vernon Lidtke, in his recent study of the social-democratic sub-culture of the years of the Empire, argued that 'social democrats did not seek to draw on the existing working-class culture, on the workers' total way of life as a source for cultural endeavour of the labour movement'. However, when the workers entered the socialist cultural milieu, as with socialist festival culture, they inevitably brought their working-class culture with them. Hence the forms of behaviour and customs which were part of the simple and traditional manifestations of working-class sociability influenced the actual forms of labour-movement culture, without however determining it.[19]

The history of the cultural organisations linked to the labour movement, especially those connected with the Social Democratic Party and its institutions, provides many examples of conflict between the cultural patterns established in the social milieu of everyday life and the values and ideals which the workers' cultural movement sought to establish.

However, if we look at the margins and the interstices of organised culture and everyday culture, and attempt 'to trace the germs of labour movement culture in the culture of the *Arbeiteralltag*' and 'to discover the *Arbeiteralltagskultur* in the field of labour movement culture' a more complex picture would seem to emerge.[20] This would seem to modify the idea of a clear distinction between 'Labour Movement Culture' and 'Workers' Culture'. It suggests that over some areas these two influence each other, and that conflict may be resolved or avoided through adjustment or compromise.

To illustrate such processes I have abstracted examples from material dispersed throughout the book and presented them here in a more systematic form. The instances which I have adduced are

19. V. Lidtke, *The Alternative Culture. Socialist Labor in Imperial Germany*, Oxford/New York, 1985, pp. 19–20.
20. Cf. H.J. Althaus, 'Das rote Mössingen', in H. Fielhauer and O. Bockhorn (eds), *Die Andere Kultur* (a fuller version of this study is referred to elsewhere in this book).

neither exhaustive, nor do they claim to provide proof for a new theory of working-class culture; but I hope that they will help readers to see the diverse elements of this book more in perspective.

As the working class constituted itself in the middle of the nineteenth century we find that reading for knowledge and for pleasure was an important element in workers' culture. The labour movement had stressed its importance from the beginning; it saw in the book a vehicle for the workers' self-improvement and for the political education of his class. To assist in both, individual trade unions and local trades councils began towards the end of the century to establish libraries. Their aim was the provision of popular scientific and above all socialist literature, popular history and serious literature. Popular taste, alas, showed a strong and disproportionate desire for popular fiction, adventure stories and the like, which was generally borrowed much more heavily than the more serious literature. The organisations responsible for the workers' libraries deplored this development; but they were generally forced to accept the trend and adjust their bookstock accordingly.[21]

Workers' sport was one of the areas in which the labour movement sought to pursue new goals and develop new attitudes by rejecting traditional competitiveness and record-beating. Instead it advocated co-operation and group performance, and stressed the importance of training the whole body, looking at fitness as an important attribute of the working-class struggle. Thus although football became, after 1900, rapidly popular, especially among the young, the rowdiness and aggressiveness often connected with the game made it at first unpopular with the workers' sports movement. But popular pressure, coupled with the fear that the youth teams would be absorbed by the bourgeois German Football Association, made the leaders of the movement propose the integration of football in workers' sport, although trying to stress its athletic as against its competitive element. In 1921 football was recognised as a distinct branch of sport; by 1932 there were some 130,000 football-playing members, although the 'football only' members were still looked at askance.[22]

The 'new media', especially film and radio, form another area

---

21. In a large and old-established library in Leipzig the percentage of social science literature in the bookstock dropped from 25% in 1898 to 8.1% in 1907. Cf. D. Langewiesche and K. Schönhoven, 'Arbeiterbibliotheken und Arbeiterlekture', *AfSG*, vol. 16, 1976, pp. 135–204, at pp. 169–71.
22. G. Hauk, 'Fußball, eine proletarische Sportart im Arbeiter Turn und Sportbund', in Teichler and Hauk (note 15) pp. 160–8.

where we can trace the influence of the customary lifestyles of the German worker on labour-movement culture. They soon became very popular throughout the working class – as far as the film is concerned particularly so among the young and among women. Here was a major instrument of relaxation and entertainment. Yet the attitude of the labour movement towards these media was originally one of suspicion, if not of outright hostility. The film above all was regarded as 'unserious', and the cinema was seen as having a corrupting influence on the working-class audience. Attempts at curbing the popularity of the film failed, and thus the parties of the left, as well as some specialist working-class cultural organisations, sought to mobilise the new media for more positive ends. 'Progressive' films were imported, mainly from Russia, for showing to workers' audiences, and there were partially successful attempts to create the German working-class film and to persuade the broadcasting companies to broadcast programmes by workers or with themes of special interest to working-class audiences.

The area of general entertainment and of leisure-time customs provides other examples of the take-over of popular customs into the 'events' culture of working-class organisations. Thus the dance and the social have long been practised within the working-class milieu. They were frequented particularly by the young, for whom they offered the opportunity of meeting members of the opposite sex.[23] Dances, like variety, ceilidhs and similar entertainments, at one time part of spontaneous village culture, became increasingly commercially organised and provided in pubs and restaurants. In Hamborn, a working-class community in the Ruhr which had virtually grown overnight from a small town into a heterogeneous working-class community of 100,000, two hundred and fifty-three dance licences were issued in 1910 – on average four per pub.[24] In the face of the general popularity of such entertainments, working-class organisations could not stand aside. In spite of the widespread criticism of such 'philistine' and petty-bourgeois customs, dances and 'entertainments' were often part of the celebrations not only of anniversaries but also of political events like the first of May, or were organised independently as an expression of socialist sociability.

But the interrelationship of workers' culture and labour-movement culture, of the traditional working-class milieu and

23. See S. Bajohr, *Vom bitteren Los der kleinen Leute*, Cologne, 1984.
24. E. Lucas, *Zwei Formen von Radikalismus in der deutschen Arbeiterbewegung*, Frankfurt, 1976, p. 94.

socialist ideology, can also be seen working in the opposite direction. Daily habits of workers and their families were subject to ideas created in the cultural organisations, and, at times, subject to some change.

The great importance of alcoholic drink as a personal stimulus and as a lubricant of social intercourse for the German worker has been widely attested. Its consumption clearly separated the adult male worker from the rest of his family. Official social-democratic opinion tended to disapprove of heavy drinking, and there was a small workers' abstainers' (*Arbeiterabstinenten*) movement; but, as Karl Kautsky pointed out in 1891, 'without the "local" the German proletariat not only had no social life, it had no political life either'.[25] After the war we can observe some changes in attitudes and practices. Largely under the influence of the youth movement, young workers would often give up drink or moderate their consumption considerably. Moreover, the growing importance of the largely trade-union-run *Volkshäuser* or *Gewerkschaftshäuser*, which had established lounges and refreshment rooms, welcomed and encouraged the patronage of the whole family. Social drinking was thus no longer entirely linked to the male presence in the pub, but began to be associated with an outing for the whole family.[26]

The activities and cultural ideals of the workers' youth movement had also some repercussions on the practices of marriage and family life. The traditions of most workers' cultural organisations did little to dispel the ethos of a male-dominated society, or to question the validity of the traditional gender-specific roles in family life.[27] Social-democratic attitudes to the 'Women's Question' and to sex and love (coyly referred to as the *Intimsphere*) were largely limited to demands for equality between the sexes in the political and the economic field. The SPD's sex-specific theory of emancipation did not seek fundamental changes in the role of the sexes in marriage and family life. The co-educational education which after 1918 was practised in the socialist youth movement, and the freer discussion of sex, led to demands for the full equality between the sexes. This was to influence the form and content of the marriages of some members of the younger generation, culminating in the years of the Weimar Republic in the practice of the 'partnership marriage' (*Kameradschaftsehe*), as well as in a freer and more egalitarian attitude to sex.

---

25. Cf. K. Kautsky, Der Alkoholismus und seine Bekämpfung. *NZ*, vol. 9, 1891 – pt. ii, p. 107.
26. S. Reck, *Arbeiter nach der Arbeit*, Lahn-Giessen, 1977, pp. 146 et seq.
27. Virtually all officials and functionaries in socialist and communist organisations, with the exception of the women-dominated Arbeiter Wohlfahrt, were men.

The examples of cultural practices and ideas presented here are discussed more fully and descriptively throughout the book. By treating them more systematically here I have tried to probe the validity of the distinction which has been made between workers' culture as *Alltagskultur* and of the labour-movement culture as the organised culture promoted by thousands of individual clubs and societies generally linked to the political and economic organisations of the left.

This is not to suggest that the material culture of the working class and the 'high culture' which the organisations of the labour movement sought to present to the German workers, form a continuous web, nor that they were co-extensive in respect of the groups which they covered. There were clearly breaks and asymmetrical developments in respect of time and place. There were some sections of the working class who were outside the influence of the labour movement, and there were also sections of the labour movement which rejected its cultural ethos and whose everyday lifestyle was not consonant with that of the majority of the organised working class.

We have an example of such deviant patterns of behaviour in casual workers, such as the Hamburg dock and harbour workers, among whom violent and riotous behaviour and the pilfering of goods were accepted forms of conduct, in contrast to trade union practices which insisted firmly on legal and peaceful action in the industrial struggle.[28]

Thus the traditional picture of a working class which, during the nineteenth century, moved from a culture of poverty to a culture of respectability, must be qualified.[29]

Any definition of workers' culture, as of culture in general attempted earlier, must allow for such variations in the culture of the everyday life of the proletariat on the one hand and of the cultural practices and ideals of the specific organisations which were developed under the influence of the labour movement on the other.

For many the link and determining factor was the socialist, and especially the Marxist, ideology which united members of the working class through a shared understanding of the reasons for their social and economic situation and an agreement on the action

28. Cf. M. Grüttner, 'Arbeiterkultur und Arbeiterbewegungskultur', in A. Lehmann (ed.), *Studien zur Arbeiterkultur*, Münster, 1984, pp. 244–82 and his *Arbeitswelt an der Wasserkante . . . 1886–1914*, Göttingen, 1984.
29. Cf. W. Conze, 'Vom Pöbel zum Proletariat', in H.U. Wehler (ed.), *Moderne Deutsche Sozialgeschichte*, Cologne, 1970, pp. 111–36.

needed to effect a change in it. In this view the gradual emergence of the capitalist system of production in its purest form leads to the disappearance of the intermediate strata and the emergence of a proletariat. 'The worker therefore develops a class consciousness . . . and a labour movement.'[30] The inherent logic of this process would lead to the social revolution, through which the oppressed class first become the dominant class, thereupon to bring about the abolition of all classes. The view of the purpose of organised workers' culture held by the SPD before 1914 can be seen as an expression of this ideology. This was to ensure that in the course of their emancipation the workers would be enabled to attain a high level of education and culture, and that the victorious proletariat would take over from the bourgeoisie the latter's role as the principal bearer of all culture.

Against such a determinist view, according to modern theorist of culture and cultural historians, such as E.P. Thompson, the institutions of the labour movement are facets of the whole culture, which in its widest definition is a way of life. Thus Williams speaks of 'the theory of culture as the study of the relationship between elements in a whole way of life' and Thompson puts attitudes, feelings and beliefs at the centre of history. History is not determined by the operation of social and economic institutions, but experientially, by the way people live. Observed over a certain period, this will establish certain patterns of relationship. Culture is 'a system of beliefs which shows a consistent structure of feeling, a whole way of comprehending the world'. Formal institutions would then be the expression of a system of attitudes and beliefs which are widely shared by sections of the population or by the population as a whole.[31]

Writing more specifically about the culture of the British working-class, Williams makes certain general statements which could also be applied to the Western working class in general, even if the industrial and political experience of German workers differed from that of their English contemporaries. According to Williams the distinctive element of British workers' culture did not lie in

30. E.J. Hobsbawm's paraphrasing of the argument developed by Engels in *The Condition of the Working Class in England*, (Panther edn, London, 1958), quoted by R. Johnson in 'Three problematics, Elements of a theory of working class culture', in J. Clarke *et al.* (eds), *Working Class Culture*, London, 1979, pp. 201–37, p. 205.
31. R. Williams, *The Long Revolution* (Penguin edn), Harmondsworth, 1963, p. 63: E.P. Thompson, *The Making of the English Working Class*, (Penguin edn), Harmondsworth, 1968, p. 11; Thompson, 'Historical Context', *Midland History*, vol. 1, no. 1, 1971, p. 54.

specific aspects of everyday life and customs. Dress, language and leisure-time habits, he argued, *tended* to a great extent to uniformity throughout the population. But this was not so in respect of social relationships. What characterised the social thinking of the working class was class loyalty, and the conviction that the improvement of its material lot was not a matter of individual advancement but of collective action, and that it was linked to the movement of the whole society.[32] Hence the great importance which workers attach to their collective and democratic institutions, trade unions and political parties, which translate this feeling into action. They, perhaps more than any other institution, represent the unique cultural achievement of the working masses.

Underlying this interpretation of working-class institutions is the fundamental importance of the expression of solidarity as a major unifying element in workers' culture. It stands in stark contrast to the bourgeois belief in the mechanism of competition and of personal advancement. The intensity of this sentiment, and the range of social and occupational sub-groups to which it is applied, will clearly vary with place and time. It will be influenced by the rigidity and fluidity of the social structure, the pattern of social esteem or deference between social classes, and the real or perceived level of opportunity for upwards social mobility. For the period from the SPD's Marxist programme of 1891 (the Erfurt programme) to the World Economic Depression and the triumph of fascism in 1933 it was undoubtedly the dominant sentiment throughout the labour movement.[33]

Solidarity was to be the main trigger for social intercourse and group formation within the working class. This emphasises the importance of workers' culture at the level of everyday activities, rather than of the labour-movement culture and the practices of 'high days and holidays'. It would urge on us the study of the 'culture' of the community of the tenement block and of the industrial community at trade union branch or local party level, in preference to that of the workers' cultural movements, which only appealed to an – admittedly sizeable – minority of workers. It would also suggest that the ideal way to study organised workers' culture would be via the membership and activities of local clubs and societies, and through the medium of life histories and personal

32. R. Williams, *Culture and Society*, (Penguin edn), Harmondsworth, 1963, pp. 312–15.
33. Cf. M. Vester, 'Was dem Bürger sein Goethe ist, das ist dem Arbeiter seine Soldiarität. Zur Diskussion der Arbeiterkultur', *Aesthetik und Kommunikation*, no. 24, 1976, pp. 61–72.

experience. The destruction of the bulk of the records and archives of the German labour movement, especially for the Weimar period, and the intervening gap of more than half a century severely limits this approach.[34] And paucity of material also makes it very difficult to reconstruct today the actual leisure-time customs and interests of the individual worker and his family.

In Chapter 4 I have discussed some aspects of the *Alltagskultur* of the working class, to set it against the more formal culture with which the book is mainly concerned. For this latter the study uses an institutional approach, coupled with an attempt to set the organised and some of the more informal cultural activities of the workers' cultural movement in the context of the contemporary political discussion within the labour movement and relate them to the politics of the two parties of the left. Its sources include the printed records of the various workers' cultural movements, as well as those of the SPD and the KPD and of some of their local organisations. Equally important was the documentation of the contemporary discussion of the practice and the theory of workers' culture in journals such as *Kulturwille*, and in more formal presentations of socialist and communist theory. Finally, we have for some of the fields, notably workers' sport and workers' theatre, a growing volume of secondary literature, and I have used this material.

In one sense I thus see the book as a contribution to the social history of the German labour movement and of the German working class, especially during the period of the Weimar Republic. But I hope also that it will help our understanding of the cultural history of the period. Although the contents of much of the workers' culture were borrowed from the general, mainly bourgeois, culture of the past and the present, there were also original and innovative developments. One such was the *Sprechchor*, the declamatory chorus, and another the Mass Festival. The agitprop theatre pioneered new techniques of acting and staging by small groups of mainly amateur actors, with impromptu speeches, caricature, song and mime; a forerunner of later-day street theatres. The working-class youth movement, especially the social-democratic Kinderfreunde movement for the under-fourteens, with its annual Children's Republic camps, pioneered a democratic pedagogic

---

34. Partial exceptions are some documentary accounts of workers' sport and reminiscences of former members of the Socialist Workers' Youth. But see also the pioneering study of social-democratic life at the grass roots in Göttingen, based on the preserved minute-books of the local party, in A. von Saldern, *Auf dem Wege zum Arbeiter-Reformismus*, Frankfurt, 1984.

system which was far ahead of its time.

The socially critical and controversial political art which we associate with the Weimar period was a product of the political conviction of individual artists; yet some of them received an impetus for their art through organised groups of committed artists, such as the Political Constructivists and the ASSO, the Association of Revolutionary Visual Artists. In weekly newspapers such as the AIZ, the *Arbeiter Illustrierte Zeitung*, or in satirical magazines such as *Der Knüppel* or *Der Wahre Jakob*, the labour movement had created original examples of photo-journalism or of political satire.

These and other original contributions of workers' culture to the general cultural achievements of the period of the Weimar Republic may well turn out to be its most lasting memorial.

–1–

The German Proletariat and the Cultural Heritage

The Foundations

At the 1896 conference of the German Social Democratic Party held in Gotha a banner at the back of the hall proudly proclaimed that 'Socialism is the bearer of all Culture'. This sentiment was undoubtedly widely shared among the politically conscious sections of the German working class. In concrete terms the slogan alluded to the expanding network of organisations catering for the leisure-time interests of the German workers, which had been established largely under social-democratic influence. On a more intangible plane it found its expression in the claims of the socialist section of the German working class to be the inheritors of the cultural achievements of the past, and to be the force which was destined to break the shackles of bourgeois dominance in the cultural sphere – a consummation which would be achieved with the victory of socialism. 'Culture in this context was essentially the 'High Culture' of the past, and it denoted primarily the arts and the expression of the wider creative activities of man.

In this chapter I examine the role of culture in the discussions and in the practice of the German labour movement in the three decades from 1890 to 1920. The period began with Social Democracy on the road to becoming a mass party with a marxist programme; and it ended with the aftermath of the 1918 revolution. After this the two separate and for most of the time mutually hostile political parties, Social Democrats and Communists, each also followed its own path as far as thoughts and policies on culture were concerned; and these separate developments form the theme of the next two chapters.

The importance which almost all sections of the social-democratic movement attached to the creative activity of the past and to that of their own time must be seen in the wider context of socialist ideology and the role it assigned to culture in the emancipatory struggle of the working class. Even in the days when the young labour movement was still linked to the bourgeois radical movement it had already looked forward to the spiritual as much as to the material and political emancipation of the worker. Art in its widest sense was seen as one of the most sublime expressions of the human spirit. It was one of the most powerful elements of the cultural heritage to which German socialism had laid claim from its earliest days.[1]

As the socialist movement developed its own ideology it laid claim to being the only progressive moral force in society. According to that ideology the socialist working class was destined to advance and to be victorious because of the sense of moral responsibility of its members and because the long-term interests and goals of the proletariat were identical with the true interests of mankind in respect of its political, its economic and its cultural progress. 'It was of the greatest importance for the course of [social] development that today the interests of the working class coincided with those of culture and of progress', wrote Karl Kautsky, the editor of the *Neue Zeit*, the SPD's principal theoretical journal, in the first volume of the periodical.[2]

The aims of the economic and social struggle had always been clear. They included the abolition of wage slavery, the replacement of private capitalism by public enterprise and the full enjoyment of all civic rights by all, especially by the workers, who had hitherto been excluded from political power. The *cultural* aspirations of the German workers were not as unambiguously formulated. Even in its incipient form the socialist movement had recognised that the intellectual oppression of the working class went hand in hand with bourgeois economic power. In order to make the national cultural heritage its own, the working class needed education, which the universal system of elementary education, instituted as early as the beginning of the nineteenth century, had failed to give them. The German Volkschule was recognised by the workers as an agency for the dissemination of the ruling ideology, or at best as a training of the workers for their role in the economy, not as providing *Bildung* in the way in which the latter was conceived by the German

---

1. In a speech at the opening of the Berlin Arbeiterbildungsschule in 1891 Wilhelm Liebknecht said that in the course of emancipating themselves the workers would also emancipate the arts. Cf. V.L. Lidtke, *The Alternative Culture. Socialist Labor in Imperial Germany*, New York, 1985, p. 162.
2. Quoted in B. Emig, *Die Veredlung des Arbeiters. Sozial-demokratie als Kulturbewegung*, Frankfurt, 1980, p. 193. Kautsky's thinking best expressed the belief in the natural progression of the working class following the laws of evolution. On Kautsky see also E. Mathias, 'Kautsky und der Kautskyanismus' in *Marxismus studien*, II, pp. 151–97.

bourgeoisie. An expansion and improvement of workers' education was necessary the better to conduct the emancipatory struggle, and the 'cultural question' as it affected the German proletariat is best considered in connection with the educational and cultural practices of the labour movement and its organisations.

In the 1860s Workers' Educational Societies, often founded with the help of middle-class radicals or as part of bourgeois philanthropy, sprang up all over Germany 'like mushrooms after a warm summer day', as August Bebel observed in his *Memoirs*. Originally these societies were largely concerned with the provision of elementary education which would help the skilled worker in his drive for self-improvement and vocational advance. These aims continued to be pursued, but under the influence of the early leaders of the German socialist movement these societies increasingly turned to the task of using education for the advancement of new social and democratic ideas.[3] In doing so they parted company from their bourgeois sponsors, who thought in terms of personal advance and support for democratic middle-class radicalism.

The political parting of the ways did not mean that the socialist movement also rejected the culture which the bourgeoisie sought to transmit to it. Ferdinand Lassalle, at that time the most outstanding, and for long after his early death in 1864 the most popular of the socialist leaders, argued that the purpose of workers' education was not to develop the cultural identity of the worker as distinct from that of the bourgeoisie, but to enable the proletariat to fulfil its objective role as the bearer of cultural progress – as it was of social progress – in a conscious and subjective sense also.

The self-improvement through education which Lassalle urged on the skilled and responsible artisans and workers to whom he principally addressed himself was a service to all workers. The struggle of the *Arbeiterstand* was a moral as well as a material one. As Lassalle put it in his 'Workers' Programme', 'once the sovereignty of the fourth estate over the state had been achieved there would be a flowering of morality, of culture and of science such as the world had never seen![4] Here were the roots of a *Kultursozialismus* which came to fruition half a century later.

Like Lassalle, the members of the first generation of social-democratic leaders came mostly from the ranks of the German middle class and petty bourgeoisie. Their upbringing and their

3. S. Na'aman, *Demokratische und soziale Impulse in der Frühgeschichte der deutschen Arbeiterbewegung der Jahre 1862/63*, Wiesbaden, 1969, p. 17.
4. Cf. Emig, *Veredlung* pp. 60–1 (from Lassalle's *Arbeiter-Programm*).

lifestyle reinforced the tendency to accept the attainment of the national culture as a goal of education for the working class. Wilhelm Liebknecht, who, together with August Bebel, led the SPD for a quarter of a century, had himself received a university education, and was a strong believer in the classical ideals of education and of the view of the ideal human being held originally by the philosophers of the German Enlightenment. He demanded that the workers should enjoy to the full the fruits of this tradition. He and other socialist writers claimed that the German bourgeoisie, the original guardian of these ideals, had abdicated its responsibility by its political compromise with the German aristocracy. It had surrendered its claims for democracy, and as a result the German educational system was not an instrument for the spread of universal *Bildung*, but, together with the Army and the popular press, one of the 'agencies of stupefaction' (*Verdummungsanstalten*) of the state. In his famous address 'Wissen ist Macht – Macht ist Wissen' on the relationship of education and emancipation Liebknecht argued that only in a free German state could genuine *Bildung* be achieved, and that only the working class, through its emancipatory struggle, could attain such a state. Hence the slogan to follow was not 'through *Bildung* to freedom' but 'through freedom to *Bildung*'.[5]

But already even now the aspirations of the social-democratic working class embodied all the ideals of humanity: 'it was the rock which stood above the tossing waves, and', Liebknecht told the Reichstag on 28 November 1888, 'on that rock European culture would save itself'.[6] In practice the Social Democratic Party was beginning to mount educational activities as soon as conditions permitted. In 1891 it started the Berlin Workers' College (Arbeiterbildungsschule). This provided both elementary instruction – German, book-keeping, stenography and courses in public speaking to complement elementary education and to fit workers for the organisational and agitational tasks of the party, as well as education in more theoretical and cultural subjects.[7]

Such central and party-directed activities were from the beginning paralleled by formally independent Education Societies, such as the Leipzig Arbeiterverein, the model for the Arbeiterbildungsschule. It dated back to the 1870s, and in 1892 it was, with 2,000 members, the largest working-class organisation in the city,

---

5. W. Liebknecht, *Wissen ist Macht – Macht ist Wissen*, 1872 and subsequent editions. Modern edition by H. Brumme, Berlin, GDR, 1968. Cited by Lidtke, *Alternative Culture*, pp. 161–2.
6. Cited in Emig, *Veredlung*, p. 193.
7. Cf. Lidtke, *Alternative Culture* pp. 162–4.

and was clearly regarded by the police as a social-democratic body. It provided both instruction and entertainment in the form of recitations, and, by the end of the century, the performance of plays, mainly by Schiller and Lessing.[8]

It was the literature of the German classical period which was urged on the working class by its leaders as an example of the cultural heritage which it should make its own. And this not only because it was held to be a pinnacle of artistic achievement, but because poets and dramatists such as Lessing and Schiller had made the struggle of the bourgeoisie against the shackles and prohibitions of feudalism and the injustices of aristocratic privilege a major theme in their work. Franz Mehring, the historian and literary critic who had joined the SPD after a journalistic career in the bourgeois press, and who was to become one of its authorities on cultural matters, held up the classical dramas as signposts for the German workers in their own emancipatory struggle. And among the classical dramatists it was above all, Schiller, the 'poet of freedom' and the author of *William Tell*, the drama of resistance against tyranny, who occupied a central place.[9]

Another group of artists who were accorded special recognition were bourgeois radical writers, such as Freiliggrath and Herwegh, connected with the unsuccessful revolution of 1848. Some socialist intellectuals, however, wished to hitch the social-democratic cultural wagon to the rising star of naturalist drama and narrative literature.[10] Some of the resulting controversy was over the choice of plays for the *Volksbühne*, the new people's theatre movement; another ground of dispute was the place and value of naturalist literature in workers' reading and in the socialist press. Edgar Steiger, the editor of *Neue Welt*, the social-democratic Sunday magazine taken in many workers' households, argued that Naturalism was the appropriate art for the proletariat, and the right vehicle to make workers sensitive to art as such.[11] Like the microscope in the study of nature, naturalism, he argued, was capable of showing up the subtlest stirrings of the human psyche. In doing so it showed up dialectically the dependence of consciousness on social reality.[12]

8. Cf. H.J. Schäfers, *Zur sozialistischen Arbeiterbildung in Leipzig 1890–1914*, Leipzig, 1962.
9. On the place of Schiller in the German labour movement see W. Hagen, *Die Schillerverehrung in der deutschen Sozialdemokratie*, Stuttgart, 1977.
10. The novels of Emile Zola were popular among those workers who read serious literature.
11. With a circulation which reached nearly 600,000 in 1914 the *Neue Welt* was clearly a most influential publication.
12. Cf. G. Fülberth, *Proletarische Partei und bürgerliche Literatur*, Neuwied and Berlin,

Steiger, who saw his task as an educational one, had practised his theories by serialising in the *Neue Welt* novels which dealt with working-class life in a frank and unadorned fashion, and at times used coarse and indelicate language. Many readers took exception to this and felt let down by the fact that the standards of behaviour of the proletarian characters were often unheroic, and even, in their eyes, immoral. This was not only a gut reaction. For the socialist *Hamburger Echo* it was an expression of healthy class-consciousness and of a wish for a literature which would extol virtues and altruism, love of freedom, and a feeling of solidarity.[13]

When the issue was discussed at the 1896 party conference the leading Hamburg Social Democrat, Karl Frohme, said that he was not concerned with decorous behaviour and moralising attitudes; but the new literature offended against good taste and common decency. And even less sensitive delegates attacked the publication of this kind of literature because it did not entertain the reader, and only depressed workers who were already experiencing unhappiness and misery. Edgar Steiger countered this by warning that the party was stepping on to the slippery slope which led to the printing of literature without value. The heroes of classical literature did not always behave heroically, and it would be wrong to 'show workers in dinner jackets'.[14]

Mehring did not share the prudish attitude of the ordinary party member; but he pointed out that they had recognised an inherent weakness of naturalist literature, namely that, while it described life at the lowest levels of society, it prescribed no solution to the problems which it uncovered. It thus failed to give the workers hope and support in their struggle. 'Naturalist art did in no way measure up to the historic magnitude of the proletarian struggle for emancipation', he wrote; it only knew how to criticise existing society, and not how to point the way to the society of the future.[15]

If the discussion on the content and literary policy of the *Neue Welt* forms one of the significant points of reference for our discussion of the meaning of workers' culture and of working-class aesthetics in the Wilhelmine period, the assessment of the person

---

1972, pp. 96–7.

13. Cf. Fülberth, *Proletarische Partei*, pp. 94–5.

14. For the *Neue Welt* debate, which lasted for a day and a half, see Fülberth, *Proletarische Partei* pp. 97–100 and *SPD Parteitag 1896 Protokoll*, pp. 78 ff. The debate ended inconclusively but the magazine did not continue with the experiment.

15. Cf. Franz Mehring, *Gesammelte Schriften*, 11, p. 448, *Geschichte der deutschen Sozial Demokratie*, 3 vols., Berlin, 1898, vol. 2, pp. 542–6.

and work of Friedrich Schiller forms another. It raises questions about the meaning of the bourgeois heritage for the proletariat, and it shows up some differences in the way in which the marxists and the revisionists within the social-democratic movement regarded that heritage.

Before 1914 Friedrich Schiller was clearly the central classical author in the pantheon of the working class, as he was for the nation at large. But, following Lassalle, the German worker sought above all the pure aesthetic experience which could be derived from classical literature, and, beyond all others, from the author of the 'Hymn to Joy'.[16] Schiller was revered mainly as a great poet and an admirable human being, not as the historian of the emancipatory struggle of the bourgeoisie, destined, in its turn, to provide ideological ammunition for the fight of the proletariat as the disadvantaged class of their own day.[17]

We have evidence of this interpretation of Schiller from the widespread celebration of the hundredth anniversary of the poet's death in 1905 held by social-democratic organisations throughout Germany. These demonstrated a great longing for culture, and showed the veneration in which the poet was held; but what moved audiences was not so much Schiller's ideological role or his political message, but 'its transformation into art, in the aesthetic form of beautiful poetry with its intoxicating pathos'.[18]

The Berlin memorial celebrations were, in the words of the *Vorwärts*, a tribute to Schiller as the mighty advocate of 'Art as the great educator of mankind'. Beneath a bust of Schiller, and following on the performance of the funeral march from Beethoven's Third Symphony, the veteran Austrian socialist August Pernersdorfer referred to Schiller as the beloved poet, the embodiment of a humanist and aesthetic ideal of a human being. In his plays he had shown the ideals of strong and daring personalities, rebellious by nature. To realise such ideals, to create a society in which a harmonious, confident personality could arise, was the task of socialists.[19]

A strongly positive view of Schiller's contemporary significance

16. The fraternal and pantheistic sentiment of the poem was further emotionalised by its musical rendering in the final chorus of Beethoven's Ninth Symphony, in itself a seminal work for the workers' cultural movement.
17. Cf. Hagen, *Schillerverehrung*, pp. 164–79.
18. Cf. M. Rector 'Wozu der Arbeiter die bürgerliche Kultur braucht', in E. Stüdemann and M. Rector (eds), *Arbeiterbewegung und kulturelle Identität*, Frankfurt, 1983, pp. 74–101, p. 97.
19. From the report in the *Vorwärts* of 9 May 1905, reprinted in Rector (note 18) pp. 75–6.

was also expressed in a Jubilee brochure issued by *Vorwärts*, to which leading revisionists contributed. They stressed Schiller's revolutionary idealism, which was still relevant for the labour movement. His failure to identify with the French Revolution was explicable in terms of his courtly surroundings.[20] Even more positive was the article by Friedrich Stampfer, one of the authors of the pamphlet, which was widely reprinted in the social-democratic press. He suggested that the enjoyment of works of art, and, naturally, Schiller's own writings, proceeded irrespective of their actual intellectual content, because they gave a pure, deep and true happiness. The admiration which the masses had for Schiller, which had shown itself in their pressure for the production of his plays, was for Stampfer a sign of a deeper understanding of the poet, which even his critical views on the contemporary masses and his rejection of the French Revolution could not undo. The slogan was thus not 'back to Schiller', but forward to Schiller, forward with him.[21]

Against such an idealistic interpretation of Schiller's significance the marxist assessment of the poet and of his work, expressed in Mehring's biography and in a special issue of the *Neue Zeit*, sought to put Schiller in a historical context. His failure to appreciate the meaning of the French Revolution could not just be explained by his environment, it was rooted in his general mentality. Schiller was not even a bourgeois revolutionary, and the contemporary worker could only receive a psychological impetus from the ideals of freedom and the mood of rebelliousness of the early plays, which it must re-interpret for its own ends.[22]

Rosa Luxemburg made a similar point in her contribution to the discussion. She wrote that 'the working class must look at all manifestations of the political and the aesthetic culture in their strictly objective historical and political context. It must see them as part of the general social development which is pushed ahead by its own revolutionary struggle. Schiller could be judged objectively as a mighty figure of bourgeois culture, instead of letting oneself be absorbed in him subjectively', as Stampfer had advocated.[23]

The extent and the solemnity of these anniversary celebrations and the enthusiastic reception of the poet and of his work symbol-

20. Cf. Fülberth, *Proletarische Partei*, 1972, pp. 76–7.
21. Cf. Hagen, *Schillerverehrung*, 1977, p. 173.
22. Cf. Fülberth, *Proletarische Partei*, 1972, pp. 77–83.
23. R. Luxemburg, review of Mehring's biography of Schiller in her *Gesammelte Werke*, vol. 1, part ii, Berlin, 1979, pp. 533–6, p. 534. Cf. M. Rector (note 18), pp. 81–2.

ised the strength of the workers' desire for culture. It also demonstrated the ability of the working class to give concrete expression of their commitment to culture. At the same time the differences in the assessment of Schiller's meaning for the workers reflect the ideological controversy in the SPD over the road to socialism, which had begun at the turn of the century. For the revisionists, who believed in society growing gradually into socialism, the value of the traditional culture for the working class was not in doubt. Schiller the idealist and the fighter was a good model of commitment to the struggle in general terms. Marxists, on the other hand, with their belief in tactics which would eventually bring about a social revolution, wished to judge the culture of the past more in terms of its didactic influence on the preparation of the proletariat for such a struggle.

The Labour Movement and Cultural Practice: The Education Guidelines of 1906

Questions about the relevance of the bourgeois heritage for the emancipatory struggle of the working class, which were raised in the interpretation of Schiller's work, emerged at about the same time in connection with the discussion of the party's educational programme. Although the SPD had long been concerned with problems of education, the issue was first raised at the party conference in Jena in 1905. This led to the acceptance of a set of 'Guidelines on Educational Policy' (*Leitsätze zum Thema Volkserziehung und Sozialdemokratie*), and to the setting up of the Central Education Council (Zentral Bildungsausschuß) at the next conference held in Mannheim in the following year.[24]

The background to this decision was a discussion in the columns of *Die Gleichheit*, the party's paper for women, edited by Klara Zetkin. This centred on the inadequate educational background of young workers, and on the need for a politically more knowledgeable membership. Zetkin and Heinrich Schulz, a former teacher, and now editor of the socialist *Bremer Bürgerzeitung*, were charged by the Party Executive with the preparation of an education programme. This spoke of the need to achieve for the working class 'the highest scientific and cultural ideals of our time, but to do so in clear distinction to bourgeois ideology and to bourgeois science and

---

24. On the education debate see K. Christ *Sozialdemokratie und Volkserziehung*, Diss., Erlangen–Nürnberg, 1975.

art'.[25] Those concerned with education in the SPD would be expected to identify with the aims of the party. Instruction, especially in the economic and social field, should be closely related to the workers' struggle, and, in the words of Klara Zetkin, 'promote the combative character of the proletariat'.[26]

The education proposals received comparatively little attention at the SPD Conference, which was overshadowed by the issue of the political strike; but the discussion of the underlying question was carried on in the socialist journal press of the period. The marxist point of view was put mainly in the *Neue Zeit*, while the group of revisionist intellectuals wrote mainly in *Die Neue Gesellschaft*. The latter rejected the assumption that bourgeois society corrupted the worker by its claims of a value-free art and science, as Heinrich Schulz had asserted.[27] They attacked the idea of a marxist science, claiming that there was only one great and all-embracing science, neither bourgeois nor proletarian, although they conceded that concessions might be made with regard to economics.[28] Bourgeois art and science were admittedly not free from prejudices and from conservative notions; but more recently scholars had begun to free themselves from such shackles. In any case 'the task of proletarian education was not to create a new science, let alone a new art, but to bring the old science and the old art to its fullest (and purest) development'.[29]

What the revisionists wanted in particular was to give workers a liberal, humanist education which would not be committed in a party-political sense, although they accepted an exception for education in socialist theory and policy. By contrast Schulz and his colleagues believed bourgeois science and scholarship in general to be perverted by political views, and cited the exclusion of known Social Democrats from teaching posts as an indicative example. If faced with such teaching the workers would not have the critical faculties to absorb it selectively. Those who were to give lectures to socialist workers must themselves be socialists.[30]

The discussion on the role of the arts in the life of the working class was differently focused from that on the education issue. Art,

25. From the *Leitsätze*, SPD *Parteitag 1906*, p. 122.
26. Klara Zetkin quoted by Lidtke, *Alternative Culture*, p. 167.
27. H. Schulz, 'Arbeiterkultur' *NZ* 24, 1905–6 vol. ii, pp. 263–66.
28. E. David, 'Volkserziehung und Sozialdemokratie', *NG* 1906, p. 459.
29. M. Maurenbrecher, 'Die bürgerliche Wissenschaft', *NG* 1906, pp. 54–55.
30. An original draft of the 'Guidelines' had actually proposed that because of the shortage of suitably qualified lecturers within the party the employment of bourgeois teachers should be considered. This proposal raised strong opposition, and was dropped from the final report.

literature and music were widely accepted as the creation of men of genius, transmitting beauty and elevated feelings. This meant that they were not so easily seen in class terms. The guidelines stated that, given the historical mission of the proletariat, it could not 'simply take over the spiritual culture of the bourgeoisie', but that it had to 'evaluate it according to its own basic ideology'.[31]

To do so was to prove difficult in practice. If the party sought to dismiss 'bourgeois' science and all other knowledge as biased, and interpret it according to its theories, it could do so comparatively easily in the formal sense by employing only party members as lecturers and teachers. For the arts, however, this implied not interpretation, but selection, and the possible discarding of all that had gone before. The paragraph which dealt with the organisation of the arts within the labour movement is, by implication, aware of the dilemma. It stated that 'within the party we must awaken and foster the artistic sensitivity through illustrated publications. The party should publish valuable works of fiction and issue reproductions of masterpieces of art. It should organise concerts . . . guided tours of museums or introductory lectures, publish reviews in the press and apply high aesthetic standards for the staging of festivals.'[32]

It was hardly possible to seek the highest values in respect of transmitted art while rejecting the mass of the art of the past and of the present as the product of a bourgeois society with its false values. Especially so, because apart from some examples of workers' poetry the German proletariat could not lay claim to a solid body of cultural and artistic achievement. Yet it was feared that too great a dependence on bourgeois culture, as on bourgeois science, could lead to ideological corruption, and weaken the fighting spirit of the proletariat. A resolution put to a Bremen SPD meeting by Heinrich Schulz in 1905 summed up the issue as follows:

Art and science are . . . influenced by the bourgeois capitalist basis of the contemporary social order. When seeking to satisfy their needs in respect of science and the arts the class conscious workers must be on their guard lest, under the pretext of a 'free' science and a 'free' art they let themselves be misused for the political interests of their bourgeois opponents.[33]

In the more theoretical discussion the objections to restrictions in

---

31. *SPD Parteitag 1906*, p. 122.
32. Ibid. p. 123.
33. H. Schulz, *Politik und Bildung*, Berlin, 1931, p. 90.

respect of art were more widespread than those in respect of bourgeois science. Max Maurenbrecher argued that as far as art was concerned it was not a question of origin but of quality. It was the task of the labour movement to bring the culture of the past to its fullest flowering – something that the bourgeoisie was prevented from doing.[34]

While the sciences were to serve the needs of the intellectual preparation of the working-class struggle, and hence the eventual victory of that class, the role of the arts was seen to be more direct and immediate. Their practice within the sphere of working-class activity was already seen by some as a visible signal of working-class emancipation. At the same time the arts were expected to give emotional support to the workers in their fight, and fill their life with greater meaning. 'Art should help in the class struggle by giving the worker a respite from the noise of battle – but neither too much nor too often to weaken his political resolve.'[35]

The cultural aspirations of the proletariat grew during the first decade of the century. This is shown in the growth of its own organisations, as well as in the demands for higher standards and a richer cultural fare.[36] Otto Rühle had noticed this in 1904, when he wrote that 'the labour movement's performance and achievement is in part at least determined by the intellectual capacity and the moral integrity of its members. Hence apart from the fight for material gains a good deal of the struggle must be directed at satisfying the general and deeply felt desire for higher intellectual and moral culture.'[37]

To satisfy this need the working class, it was argued, could not wait until its own art was born. 'It was more important that the workers should achieve a strong feeling for life and for victory' here and now.[38] The practice of the SPD seemed to heed such suggestions. In the following years local social-democratic organisations organised a considerable and slowly-growing number of cultural, and particularly artistic, events. Statistics based on reports by local Education Committees to the central organisation suggest that attendances at such events was counted in tens and, for theatre performances, in hundreds of thousands; and these figures do not

34. Maurenbrecher, 'Bürgerliche Wissenschaft'.
35. Schulz, *Politik und Bildung*, p. 88.
36. It is not surprising that this desire should have shown itself at that time. The first decade of the twentieth century saw a rise in real wages as well as some reduction in working hours.
37. Otto Rühle, 'Ein neuer Weg zur Volksbildung', *NZ* 1903–4 vol. ii, pp. 92–6.
38. L. Berg, 'Die Feste des Proletariats', *NG* 1906, p. 81.

Table 2 Cultural events promoted by local associations of the SPD, 1911/12

22 Dichterabende (Poetry Evenings)	with	11,572 participants
97 Concerts	with	58,115 participants
212 Rezitationen und Kunstabende (Poetry Recitals and other artistic events)	with	94,825 participants
742 Feiern (Festivals)	with	40,669 participants
42 Lieder und Märchenabende (Song and Fairy-tale recitals and readings)	with	94,825 participants
848 Theater Vorstellungen (Theatre Performances)	with	599,199 participants

Source: Figures from the annual report of the Zentral Bildungsausschuß to the national conference of the SPD in 1912 (*SPD Parteitag 1912*, p. 46). Figures for that year were a little lower than in earlier years because of the elections of 1912.

take account of many local parties which did not report to the centre.

The proposals for cultural and artistic activities which the Central Education Committee of the SPD published regularly show how far the movement relied on music and literature from the bourgeois cultural heritage. Between 1908/09 and 1910/11 the Bildungsausschuß issued some twenty such programmes for so-called *Kunstabende* ('art evenings') whose titles read like a roll-call of the great figures in the arts. There were programmes devoted to Beethoven, Chopin, Goethe, Heine, Mendelssohn, Mozart and Schiller, in addition to Folksong Evenings, Christmas matinees and Spring Festivals; and only the May Day celebrations, the Worker Poets Evenings and the *Freiligrath Feiern* were specially orientated towards the politics of the audience. The committee also produced proposals for more general forms of entertainment, programmes for an evening devoted to Ballads, or to the theme of Art and Revolution, or simply for anniversary celebrations. The works whose performance is implied by the programmes for these events include some that convey radical or socially critical sentiment; but many are just well-known songs, or popular music, or slides reproducing classical works of art – which, together with the appropriate music and poetry, were to accompany a lecture on the place of dance in literature, music and art.[39]

In seeking to satisfy the desire for greater enjoyment and enter-

---

39. SPD Zentral Bildungsausschuß, *Winterprogramm für das Jahr 1910/11. Winke und Ratschläge*, Berlin, 1910.

tainment those charged with the organisation of the events were generally more concerned with the preservation of standards of performance than with ideological probity, although sometimes both were achieved. To present Beethoven's ninth symphony, with its concluding appeal to universal brotherhood, to a three-thousand-strong working-class audience was a great achievement indeed. Kurt Eisner, until recently a journalist on the staff of *Vorwärts*, took this as a sign of the maturity of the proletariat, which 'everywhere sought to attain the highest and was reaching out to the stars'.[40] On the other hand there was also a growing concern about the lowering of the cultural level, especially in respect of the so-called 'Entertainment Evenings'.

An example of this can be seen in the work of the Education Committee (Bildungsausschuß) for Greater Berlin, the largest such body in the country. In its annual guide to educational and cultural activities, which gave detailed proposals for fêtes and festivities, it argued that art performed an elevating and enthusing function. 'It must become a vehicle to give workers new courage for their struggle.' Art could not be neatly divided into bourgeois and proletarian compartments. It appealed to the emotions and it should be cultivated so that the rebelliousness of the individual, and hence that of the masses, should be strengthened. 'When we educate the masses to derive joy from art we stimulate the desire for improvement in the material aspects of life.'[41]

The report noted that in the winter of 1913/14 the committee had arranged 133 artistic events and fêtes for 81 organisations; but it admitted that the majority had been of the music-hall type. It argued that 'less might have been more' and that they should really concentrate on events of a high quality. The committee saw it as their task to lead the worker gradually to the appreciation of more serious art and to the understanding of more difficult works. The celebrations of the working class should be 'dignified', and they should demonstrate that the working class endeavoured to raise all culture to the highest level of attainment possible. 'Art must become a source of genuine enthusiasm and this enthusiasm must in turn become a source of strength for the mighty struggle of the working class.'[42]

The discussion of the role of art, and, in particular, bourgeois art, in the life of the socialist movement received after 1910 a new impetus in the context of a discussion of contemporary literature

40. Kurt Eisner, 'Die Heimat der Neunten', *NG* 1906, p. 10.
41. SPD Groß Berlin, Bildungsausschuß, *Leitfaden*, 1913/14, p. 8.
42. Ibid. pp. 40–42.

and of the artistic policy of the *Volksbühne*. Although primarily concerned with the issue of tendentiousness in the bourgeois literary heritage, the aesthetic and ideological issues raised would naturally also be applicable to other arts.

It was generally recognised that there was as yet no socialist art, or at least little art of high quality which could also be seen as contributing to the strengthening of socialist principles. Even anthologies of poetry published at the instigation of the SPD and issued under such political-sounding titles as *Vorwärts* ('Forward') and *Buch der Freiheit* ('Book of Freedom') contained much naturalist verse, but relatively few explicitly political poems. As to the so-called *Arbeiterdichtung* ('workers' poetry') few of the authors were manual workers, and the literary quality was generally low. Librarians of workers' libraries urged their readers to read the classical authors and the poets of naturalism, rather than such 'working-class' writers.[43]

Apart from such limited efforts the SPD did not develop a *positive* literature policy. Faced with widespread concern about the corrupting influence of some trashy and politically or religiously bigoted literature for the young the party issued for a time lists of recommended juvenile reading. These were largely based on selections made by progressive Hamburg teachers; and the social-democratic leadership resisted attempts, made at successive party conferences, to foster socialist literature, arguing that there were no socialist authors in the field of youth literature.[44]

The paucity of this literature clearly lent support to the view that literature and politics were separate entities: that aesthetically socialist literature was below the high level attained in classical literature, and also inevitably tendentious, and so to be condemned on these grounds. But some critics, notably the Dutch playwright Hans Heijermanns, writing under the pseudonym Heinz Sperber, argued against this separation of literature and politics. Sperber thought that by rejecting tendentious art as part of bourgeois art, because it tended to fall below the high standard of the classics, some critics rejected all 'tendentiousness' in art and literature, even that which supported socialist aims. Even left-wing critics, he argued, were failing to recognise the internal tendentiousness of even the most highly artistic bourgeois art. He was particularly critical of the commercialism and uncritical dramatic policy of the *Volksbühne*. Even the masterpieces of dramatic literature were not

---

43. Cf. Lidtke, *Alternative Culture*, pp. 144–7.
44. Cf. Fülberth, *Proletarische Partei*, pp. 114–19.

without their 'bias'. For Sperber it was the task of socialists to oppose the old tendentious literature with a new socialist art. He wanted the workers, guided by their class-consciousness and following their class instincts, to decide what art they would accept or reject.[45]

Against this argument the traditionalists among the social-democratic critics asserted that over and above all questions of political tendency there were issues of artistic form and standards of perfection which made a work attractive, and that the judgement on these should not be determined by popular choice. Franz Mehring, who had been a champion of the radical plays of the classical authors, rejected the suggestion that a judgement based on the feelings of the working masses, 'the aesthetics of the horny hand of toil' should decide what literature was relevant.[46]

Another critic, Heinrich Ströbel, took up the case against Sperber by accusing him of seeking to further pro-socialist literature at the expense of artistic quality. It was wrong to make the feeling of the average worker a criterion for what is socialist art. A critical proletariat would receive the art of the past selectively, and would separate the chaff of its obnoxious politico-social attitudes from the grain of the poetic worth of the work, which would co-incide with its overall ideology. Socialists would judge bourgeois art also by its social content; but there were also aesthetic criteria which meant that art could not be judged purely in ideological terms.[47] According to Friedrich Stampfer, writing in *Vorwärts*, bourgeois aesthetics should be accepted. For 'as long as art exists people will judge an artist and his work on the basis of connoisseurship, not class instincts'.[48]

Such a positive reception of bourgeois art and literature, advocated by Ströbel and others, was seen by the reformists in the SPD as a necessary corollary to their anti-revolutionary attitude; so that in parallel to the reformists' belief in the gradual social integration of the working class into wider society we find a similar belief in integration in the cultural sphere. As a writer in the revisionist *Sozialistische Monatshefte* wrote in 1910, 'the experience of great art and of all that was beautiful would in a measure anticipate for the worker the better society for which he was fighting'.[49] The dis-

---

45. For an account of Sperber's arguments and of the ensuing debate see Fülberth, *Proletarische Partei*, pp. 123–50.
46. Ibid. pp. 137–9.
47. H. Ströbel, 'Kunst und Proletariat', *NZ* 30, 1912, vol. ii, pp. 785–90.
48. Cf. *Vorwärts*, 9 June 1911.
49. Wally Zeppler, 'Die psychischen Grundlagen der Arbeiterbildung' *SM* 1910, pp. 1551–9.

cussion on the link between political ideology and culture and the arts received a new impetus from the revolution of 1918.

The Impact of the November Revolution

The November Revolution brought with it a considerable amount of discussion and re-assessment of cultural and artistic policies, and of the relationship of the working class to culture and the arts. The impetus for this came both from within the German labour movement and from the intellectual and artistic community. Among the latter sentiments which, until now, had only been expressed in artistic creation assumed a more direct political character. The approach which Ludwig Rubiner had forecast before the war in his essay 'Der Dichter greift in die Politik',[50] that politics was based on moral considerations and that the heightened sensitivity of the artist made him identify with all sufferers and deprived, was now shared more widely. Artists were more willing to engage themselves outside the narrow confines of their art. And in respect of their art they could now also expect to work in a freer and more liberal atmosphere, shorn both of the restrictions of the Wilhelmine censorship regulations, and, at least for a time, of the more overt opposition of academic art and bourgeois philistinism.

The German working class seemed at the end of the war to be on the threshold of the longed-for power. This hope was not to be fulfilled; but some tangible gains, notably the eight-hour day introduced in 1918, remained. The scope of working-class existence was thus widened, and cultural questions became both a matter of personal lifestyle and of working-class power.[51]

The leadership of the SPD noted in 1919 that there was a widespread interest in intellectual and cultural matters. During the war the educational activities of the party had come virtually to a standstill. This had left a vacuum, and there existed now 'a much increased desire for a purifying spiritual sustenance'. The Party executive, together with the Social Democratic parliamentarians and the Party Council, meeting in joint session in Weimar in March 1919, declared that 'it was one of the most urgent tasks before the party to embark on a comprehensive and sensibly based programme of cultural activities'.[52] Criticism came from within the

50. *Die Aktion*, 1912, vol. 2, nos. 21 and 23.
51. Cf. Paul Kampfmeyer, *Arbeiterbewegung und Sozialdemokratie*, Berlin, 1921.
52. SPD. Parteikonferenz, Weimar 1919. Reprinted in *Protokolle der Sitzungen des Parteiausschusses der SPD, 1912–1921* (Reprint 1980), vol. 2, p. 646.

extreme left of the movement, from the ranks of the Independent Socialists and of the followers of the newly established Communist Party, and in particular from some of the adherents of anarcho-syndicalist groups and the Oppositional Communists. The relationship of the proletariat to the cultural inheritance, with its strong connection with the bourgeoisie, was the subject of scrutiny and of renewed debate.

Parallel with the organisational and intellectual movements within the working-class left, we have significant developments among radical artists. These had generally identified with the basic political aims of the revolution. Many of them had shared in the growth of pacifist sentiment, and they now wished to make a contribution to the development of a new, more egalitarian, more liberal and more pacific society; and they naturally believed that the arts could contribute towards such an aim. The artists who proved to be most open to 'revolutionary' influences were those associated with the expressionist movement. Not only were they the artistic opposition group *par excellence*, they were also often libertarians in their general attitude. At the heart of expressionist art was human experience and conflict. The impact of modern technology and of the tremendous turbulence of city life was a theme close to the centre of their interest.[53]

Expressionist artists were moved by the suffering which they saw around them. They were sympathetic to a search for new lifestyles and new experiences; the pathos of human existence moved them, and they 'hoped for a change in man's humaneness. What they desired was the fraternity of all mankind.'[54] Such basic sentiments were challenged and strengthened by the war and by the spirit of the upheaval and change engendered by the revolution, which chimed in with some of the underlying feelings of the expressionist artists.

Already during the war, which many young artists experienced at the front, some expressionists felt drawn towards the political left. Some became pacifists and allied themselves with the Independent Social Democrats. And those on the political left who supported expressionist art hoped that links with the proletariat would bring their art more down to earth. Franz Pfemfert, publisher and editor of *Die Aktion*, and other contributors, argued that expressionist artists should give up their utopian beliefs and attitudes and

53. Expressionism was essentially an urban movement. Cf. R. Samuel and R.H. Thomas, *Expressionism in German Life, Literature and the Theatre*, Cambridge, 1971.
54. E. von Sydow, *Die deutsche expressionistische Kultur und Malerei*, Berlin, 1920.

devote their art wholeheartedly to the democratic and radical cause. Tied to the earthiness of the proletarian revolutionaries their art would become more realistic and more related to the issues of the struggle.[55]

At the same time it was widely believed that the art of the revolutionary movement and of the newly invigorated proletariat could only be an expressive and expressionist art. Such art was thought to be 'the art of the aspiring classes', and expressionist artists were generally very prominent among those who in the wake of the revolution formed themselves into groups and societies in many centres of artistic activity in Germany.[56]

Soon after the outbreak of the revolution, Ludwig Meidner, painter and poet, issued his call 'to all artists' urging them to join the socialist movement and to identify with the cause of the working class.

> We must finally make a start and help so that a just order should reign in state and society. We artists, poets must do our share. There must be no more exploiters and exploited . . . We must decide in favour of social-ism for [a general and continuing and irresistible] process of socialisation of the means of production. This will give every person work, leisure, bread, a home, and the intimation of a higher goal. Socialism should be our new credo.
>
> We painters and poets are linked to the poor by a bond of sacred solidarity. After all, many of us have experienced misery and shameful hunger . . . Are we not like beggars dependent on the whims of the art-collecting bourgeoisie . . . The bourgeoisie will again seize power . . . it knows no love, only exploitation . . . Those of you whom the bourgeoisie pays, out of vanity, snobbery and ennui, high wages for their work, listen to me: this money is tainted with the sweat and blood . . . of thousands of poor and exhausted people . . . Painters, poets and all artist comrades, we must become strong: socialism is at stake . . . that means justice, freedom and love among all men for the sake of God's order in the world.[57]

55. H. Stern in *Die Aktion*, 1919, col. 779–80.
56. Sentiments in favour of Expressionism as the dominant art form of the post-revolutionary period were shared by some representatives of the labour move-ment. Richard Schaefter wrote in the *Rote Fahne* that 'if Expressionism would advance along the road of greater objectivity and if the expressionist artist were to succeed in elevating the subjective and unique into the impersonal, principled and enduring and thus advance from a style to a representation then it would become what we all hope for: art of the masses, art out of the masses and art for the masses'. *RF* 24 February 1921, no. 92.
57. L. Meidner, 'An alle Künstler', *Kunstblatt*, 1919, reprinted in U.M. Schneede (ed.) *Die Zwanziger Jahre. Manifeste und Dokumente deutscher Künstler*, Cologne, 1979, pp. 41–3.

Looking back we must conclude that the utopian sentiments expressed here had little basis in reality, and that the hopes for the future of the arts were largely unfulfilled. On the other hand it is a tribute to the strength of feeling held by many artists that they were prepared to join organisations of like-minded colleagues to advance their ideas.

In the wake of the revolution such groups of radical artists arose all over Germany. The largest and best known were the *Arbeitsrat für Kunst* and the *Novembergruppe*, which were founded in Berlin early in 1919. For them, as for smaller groups in the provinces, the policies of the revolution form the starting base. The members of the *Novembergruppe* saw themselves as 'revolutionaries of the spirit' uniting expressionists, cubists and futurists in the belief in the beneficial influence of the visual arts on the whole population. They claimed to stand squarely 'on the fertile grounds of the revolution'.[58]

The Central Working-Committee of the *Novembergruppe* began its appeal to prospective members with the statement that '[our] long-established challenge to the established order has finally been followed by a struggle, and the political upheaval has decided in our favour.' But they emphasised at the same time that they represented neither a class nor a political party. They merely regarded it as their most important duty to gather together all artistic talent, and to use it for the well-being of the whole community.[59]

The *Arbeitsrat für Kunst*, an organisation with a largely overlapping membership with that of the *Novembergruppe*, put forward a programme which sought to allow art to reach the mass of the population. Some days before the appeal of the *Novembergruppe* it issued a circular: 'In the conviction that the political system should be used for the liberation of art from age-long wardship a circle of like-minded artists has been founded.' Its principal object was to ensure that 'Art and the People should be one and that art should no longer be for the enjoyment of a few, but that it must become the life and happiness of the masses'. Its aim was to 'unite all arts under the wings of great architectural projects'. This architecture was to be a communitarian enterprise and to serve a social purpose. Through it 'the brotherliness which will blossom forth from the common effort in the service of a flourishing architecture would create in the souls of men what we all desire, the true socialist spirit'.[60]

58. Cf. H. Kliemann, *Die Novembergruppe*, Berlin, 1969, pp. 55–7.
59. Ibid.
60. Akademie der Kunste (Berlin West), *Der Arbeitsrat für Kunst, 1918–1921*, Berlin, 1980, p. 87.

Other groups of artists also stressed the communitarian aspects of socialism and frequently saw it linked to the role of the artist as an artisan-craftsman. The *Hallische Künstlergruppe* declared in its programme that '[we] [i.e. the artists] would help to educate for the state a mature and spiritually sound people. We shall create with the people, a people's art . . . we want to raise the crafts to be art'; and the *Vereinigung für neue Kunst und Literatur* in Magdeburg set themselves even higher goals.

> Art will again become religion. No longer the arcana of a closed circle . . . Art advances freely and purposefully. Across the battlefields of France and Russia brother clasps the hand of brother. What politics has destroyed, art will make good. Through art one man will find the way to the other . . . No longer slaves, hostile peoples of a Europe in conflict, but brothers, men and women of one world. We believe in a great and liberated art and in the salvation of mankind through it.[61]

There was a widespread desire to make art more popular and more workmanlike. Max Pechstein, one of the early members of the *Brücke* group of artists, a leading member of the *Arbeitsrat* and a sympathiser of the SPD, envisaged that the socialist republic would lead to a state of affairs in which artistic activities were widely shared and art would occupy a much more prominent place than hitherto. The career of an artist would be open to all, instead of being restricted to members of the middle class, as it had tended to be until now. The training would start off with the learning of a craft, leading thus to a closer link between people and art.[62] The artist whom Pechstein drew for the cover of a collection of essays with the title 'An alle Künstler' was not a bourgeois aesthete but a muscular worker, his right arm raised as if to show the way upwards, and holding his flaming heart like a palette.

The spirit which created the *Bauhaus* in Weimar, encompassed a longing for community, an attempt to break down the division between artist and craftsman, and, last but not least, the hope for a new and almost religious spirituality. The school was to educate designers and executants in building-related crafts, and the basic

---

61. D. Schmidt (ed.), *Manifeste, Manifeste, 1905–1933*, Dresden, 1964, pp. 180–1.
62. Similar sentiments were expressed by many of the respondents to an enquiry conducted by the *Arbeitsrat* and published as a kind of manifesto for the new trends in the visual arts under the title *Ja, Stimmen des Arbeitsrats für Kunst* (Berlin 1919). One of the questions related to the attitude to socialism, and in the replies there is talk of artists' communities, of apprenticeship and of 'Masters', of new settlements for artists, of the artist as a worker and of the building of new and beautiful towns.

training was as much concerned with practical skills as with artistic principles. Its Director, Walter Gropius, who had been Chairman of the *Arbeitsrat*, sounded a clarion call in his *Bauhaus Manifesto*, which showed on its cover a woodcut by Lyonel Feininger which had been given the title 'The Cathedral of Socialism'. It concluded:

> Architects, Sculptors, Painters, we must return to the craft. There is no vocation called art, there is no substantial difference between the artist and the craftsman. God's grace makes it possible that in some rare moment art will blossom forth from the work of his hands – it cannot be forced, and the workmanlike creation forms the basis for all artistic endeavour. In it there is the fountainhead of creative activity. Let us form a new guild of craftsmen without the class-dividing pretensions which have sought to create a high wall between artists and craftsmen. Let us will, devise and create together a new monument for the future, an edifice which will be all and everything: Architecture and sculpture and painting, which formed by millions of craftsmen's hands, will rise against the sky as a crystalline manifestation of a new faith.[63]

The ideological affinities between the utopianism of radical artists and the parties of the left resulted in comparatively few formal links, and these are discussed in the chapter devoted to the role of the visual arts and their influence on the life of the German workers and their organisations. Here I only discuss one organisation which sought to re-interpret the relationship between the working class and culture, namely the Bund für proletarische Kultur, which came into being in the summer of 1919. Founded by Arthus Holitscher and Friedrich Natteroth, it included a number of well-known writers and artists, but the membership also comprised some working-class organisations, Shop Steward Committees and Education Committees of enterprises in Berlin and its surroundings, most of them with an Independent Socialist background. In its manifesto the association pleaded the cause of culture and urged a response to the spiritual needs of the people. 'There was a clamour for a new culture, for a revolution of the spirit . . . which demands that the struggle for the most noble goals of the revolution be based on a moral conscience and dignity.'[64]

The manifesto condemned the trivialisation of culture and its subordination to the economic and political interests of the bourgeoisie. For the latter 'the last war had been an encouragement. Its

---

63. From Walter Gropius 'Das Endziel', in the *Manifest* of the Bauhaus, reprinted in Schneede, *Zwanziger Jahre*, pp. 144–5.
64. 'Aufruf zu einem Bund für proletarische Kultur', in W. Fähnders and M. Rector (eds), *Literatur im Klassenkampf*, Munich, 1971, pp. 155–7.

philosophers, poets and clerics had blessed and praised the war, but for us workers this was an occasion to be ashamed of our culture; we fought against it and we have not yet shaken off the shackles of the bourgeois century.' In opposition to this trend we 'must lay the foundations for a new proletarian culture . . . and no one is going to gainsay it, not even the artists themselves'.[65]

The culture which they wished to create was to mirror the thoughts and feelings of the proletariat, and to 'reflect back on the economic and the political struggle and strengthen it'. Yet not all traditional culture was to be rejected. This group of bourgeois intellectuals wished to distinguish between ideologically tainted creation and those 'eternal values and works which a select few among the spirits of the past had given to mankind'. The latter were exemplary creations and mostly the outcome of a fight against 'established' values. The former were the products of an evil class society, and deserved to be destroyed with it.[66]

The ideology and the expressed sentiments of the Bund für proletarische Kultur derived in many respects from the Russian *Proletkult* experiment. *Proletkult* policies sought to incorporate cultural activities firmly within the organisational structure and political function of the proletariat. To be effective and accepted, culture must come from within the workers' daily experience, and the artist would have to submerge himself in the general proletarian struggle.[67]

Thus for Wieland Herzfelde, the founder of the Malik Verlag, the artist had to accept his position as a bourgeois, who could not change his status but who recognised that he was a bourgeois in a stage of the bourgeoisie's historical superfluousness. He must devote all his talents and his energies, his brush and his pen, to the service of the party which identified with the cause of the proletariat, and this was for Herzfelde the Communist Party. Only as one of its members could the bourgeois artist make his contribution to the development of proletarian culture.[68]

The *Bund* did not go as far as that. It would seek to operate largely at factory level. In its activities, and especially through its proposed programme of lectures on artistic, political and scientific

65. Ibid.
66. Bund für proletarische Kultur, 'Grundsatze und Programm', in Fähnders and Rector, *Literatur*, p. 160.
67. On *Proletkult* see P. Gorsen and E. Knoedler-Bunte, *Proletkult*, 2 vols, Stuttgart, 1974–5.
68. W. Herzfelde, 'Gesellschaft, Künstler und Kommunismus', in Fähnders and Rector, *Literatur*, pp. 124–49.

subjects, or through music, drama or exhibitions, its members wished to ensure that they would remain in close emotional contact with the workers. At the same time the *Manifesto* of the *Bund*, unlike other similar programmatic declarations on the role of the artist *vis-à-vis* the proletariat, did not demand that the artist should actually join the organised ranks of the working class. It was not the membership card, but socialist conviction that created the committed artist.[69]

Compared with the high expectations aroused by the programme of the association, the reality that followed was disappointing. Only in the field of the theatre do we find institutions created especially for workers. In the Tribüne Theater, and later in the Proletarische Theater, the Bund put on plays with a definite ideological slant.

Even more important was the *Proletarische Theater – Bühne der revolutionären Arbeiter*, the creation of Erwin Piscator, an immediate successor to the *Proletarische Theater* of the Bund. Something resembling *Proletkult* practice was here in existence. It operated as a peripatetic theatre which took its plays to the working-class districts. It also attempted to bridge the gulf which tended to separate actors and spectators, by bringing workers on to the stage as amateurs, and by attempting to establish a dialogue between players and audience.[70] This theatre also created a popular support organisation, the Arbeitsgemeinschaft der Berliner Arbeiterorganisationen für Proletarisches Theater, which had a membership of 5,000 – 6,000, and put on some fifty performances of plays.

The company was banned after half a year – allegedly on technical grounds; but one wonders whether it would have been possible to continue to maintain working-class support. The traditional working class preferred the more anodyne plays put on by the *Volksbühne*, and the official communist line tended to be hostile, so that the support for such experiments in proletarian culture came at that time largely from the small organisations on the extreme left.[71]

The attempt to create a new proletarian culture from above through a medium such as the Bund für Proletarische Kultur could probably not succeed because the thoroughly bourgeois literateurs and artists who comprised the active membership were not really accepted by their working-class audiences.[72] Käthe Kollwitz, when

69. Fähnders and Rector, *Literatur*, p. 157.
70. Cf. Fähnders and Rector, *Literatur*, pp. 24–5.
71. See also Gertrud Alexander's views on propaganda plays reprinted in Fähnders and Rector, *Literatur*, pp. 196–9.
72. See the letter of a woman worker to the *Räte Zeitung* suggesting that while

asked for her support for the *Bund*, touched on a raw point. She was sceptical of its claim to be able to create a new culture. 'To my mind', she wrote, 'proletarian culture is nonsense. There is no such thing. There will be a socialist culture once we have socialism. Then the culture which will belong to it will grow. The proletariat, however, is a transitory phenomenon, a state of things which we must overcome. It seems quite wrong to me, if a speaker really asserts that proletarian culture is the culture of mankind. *Socialist culture* – conceived in its highest development – yes, that may well be called the culture of mankind'. [73]

Käthe Kollwitz went on to ask whether the emphasis on proletarian culture was not all very artificial, an act of 'thoughtless following of fashion, because a bourgeois culture was condemned unseen. Does the proletariat not find nourishment in bourgeois culture, bourgeois art?' She cited music as a bourgeois creation by members of the bourgeoisie. 'Art could well become a spokesman for those who cannot express themselves adequately but the purest creations don't spring out of a partisan spirit but out of a general humanist spirit. They tower above the passionate but short-sighted struggle of the parties'. [74]

Bourgeois Heritage and Committed Art

At the heart of any discussion about revolutionary art and culture and the cultural practices of the working class, lie questions about the significance of the art of the past (and in particular that part of it which had been created or assimilated by the bourgeoisie). The intellectual atmosphere of the post-revolutionary period encouraged a questioning and critical attitude to cultural traditions, and the discussion of what was termed the 'bürgerliche Erbe' ('the bourgeois heritage') thus became more significant after 1918. The reasons were manifold. The power and the self-confidence of the middle class had suffered under the impact of defeat. Artists and writers had frequently turned against the ethos of their bourgeois background. In the words of Siegfried Lenz they had moved from

workers gladly 'lent eye and ear to the beautiful', they could not express their admiration because they lacked the opportunity, in Fähnders and Rector, *Literatur*, p. 102.

73. Letter to Max Barthel, one of the leading members of the Bund. See his *Kein Bedarf an Weltgeschichte. Geschichte eines Lebens*, Wiesbaden, 1950, p. 52. Also Fähnders and Rector, *Literatur*, pp. 223–4.
74. Fähnders and Rector, *Literatur*, pp. 223–4.

the library or the studio out on to the barricades. At the same time, the German working class was now a greater political and cultural force than it was before the war. It was more able and more willing to challenge bourgeois claims to hegemony in cultural as well as in other areas. In addition, the Russian Revolution had made the issue of proletarian culture a prominent one, and its discussion had had some influence on thinking within the German labour movement.

The movement's political and cultural organisations were now often anxious to relate their cultural activities more closely to the socialist ideals and the aims of the political parties. Questions about relevance and commitment to the revolution emerged in the policy-making and the practice of virtually all the cultural organisations of the left; but they usually did so in a diluted and pragmatic form. It is in the immediate post-revolutionary period that we find a more substantial, more penetrating, and more theoretically founded discussion.

The discussion on the relevance of the bourgeois heritage as we can observe it in the controversies of these years, centres on three connected issues. The significance of traditional – that is, largely, bourgeois – art for the German workers; the extent of the corrupting influence of bourgeois culture, and in particular of the emotion-transmitting works of art and literature of the past on proletarian conduct and revolutionary commitment; and the place of the contemporary artists in the cultural life and activities of the proletariat.

Bourgeois tradition tended to elevate art, at least established art, stamped as the work of genius, into the realm of the sacred and the inviolable, In the post-war era the idea that there was an art 'above classes and nations', and that the recognition of it was widely accepted throughout the working class, became a matter for debate. One such debate was occasioned by the slight damage done, in 1920, to a painting by Rubens in the Dresden Zwinger, which housed the principal art gallery of the city. During the fighting in Central Germany, which developed after the eventually unsuccessful right-wing insurrection known as the 'Kapp Putsch', this painting, 'Bathsheba at the fountain', was grazed by a bullet.[75] Oskar Kokoschka, then Professor at the Dresden Academy of Art, regarded this as an act of sacrilege, and issued a broadsheet in which he sought to persuade the local population to desist from fighting in the vicinity of such art treasures. He suggested that the fighting

---

75. In the Dresden fighting on 15 March 1920 ninety-five persons were killed and 151 injured. Cf. L. Fischer, *George Grosz*, Reinbeck bei Hamburg, 1983, p. 69.

would better take place at the local shooting ranges on the heath outside the town, where works of human genius would not be endangered. 'The preservation of such majestic works of art', he argued, would be of greater long-term significance than any political action, 'because the German people would later derive more happiness from the viewing of such pictures than from all the political opinions of today'.[76]

In response to Kokoschka's 'heartfelt request', John Heartfield and George Grosz fired a salvo in the May issue of *Der Gegner* under the title of 'Der Kunstlump' ('the Art-rascal'). In it they attacked this crass overvaluation of works of art 'which had long gathered dust in museums and galleries, and which had now not the slightest significance for the people as against the life and happiness of the workers of today'. Art was today an object of bourgeois commercialism and of the collectors' instinct of the rich. Kokoschka's sentiments were typical of the attitude of the bourgeoisie, which 'valued its art more than the life of the working class'. We are overjoyed, they wrote, 'that the bullets should have landed in galleries and palaces and in Rubens' masterpieces rather than in the dwellings of the poor in the working class quarters of the city'.[77]

Grosz and Heartfield, moreover, drew more general conclusions from the incident, and initiated a controversy which became known as the '*Kunstlump* debate'. They argued that the workers, so heavily involved in their daily struggle and suffering, had little interest in art, let alone in classical art, and, by an extension of the argument, any art which was not created with a desire to advance the cause of the revolutionary struggle. Such works had no place in the art which should be placed before the working class for its education or enjoyment. The so-called art without tendentiousness (*Tendenzlose Kunst*), or 'art for art's sake', had no place in workers' culture. It had always implied a flight from reality, an attempt to create the '*schöne Schein*' – 'the beautiful apparition' – which 'would conjure up a world of peace and order'.

Traditional art is, in effect, criticised on two points: The great tradition of religious art was really a vehicle through which a 'false consciousness' was being created through a displacement of the

---

76. From Kokoschka's appeal cited in George Grosz and John Heartfield, 'Der Kunstlump', *Der Gegner*, vol. 1 1919/20, pp. 10–12, reprinted in Schneede, *Zwanziger Jahre*, pp. 50–1 and 54–8; also in Fähnders and Rector, *Literatur*. See also E. Siepmann, *Montage: John Heartfield, vom Klub dada zur Arbeiterillustrierten*, Berlin, 1977.
77. Grosz and Heartfield, 'Der Kunstlump' (note 76).

everyday reality by focusing on an otherworldly future. Secular art served the purpose of satisfying the bourgeois sentiment of ostentatiousness and the longing for possession. Hence such art must seek to mollify; it cannot carry any message which would run counter to bourgeois ideology.

Thus the art of the past, as transmitted by the bourgeoisie, only distracts the proletariat from its emancipatory struggle, 'sabotages its class-consciousness and saps its will to power'. The claim by the bourgeoisie, of which Kokoschka was for Grosz and Heartfield a mouthpiece, that the sacred inheritance must be preserved for posterity, really meant only that the Rembrandts and Rubenses would be preserved for the enjoyment of the rich and for the benefit of capitalist speculators in works of art. Veneration of the artists of the present was as misplaced as veneration of the art of the past. Present-day artists were identified with the bourgeoisie, and this only increased their self-esteem and distanced them from the workers.

Thus the virtual rejection of all art in favour of the pursuit of political aims, which permeates the essay, takes us back to the stances of the dadaist movement, in which the two authors were so intimately involved. It also leads us to the expression of their belief that 'the workers will surely create their own culture unaided, in the way in which they had created the organisations needed for their class struggle, out of their own strength'.

Of the visual artists, Grosz and Heartfield were not alone in their negative attitude to the bourgeois inheritance, querying both its present-day relevance and its inherent contradiction of the aspirations of the working class. Franz Seiwert, a Cologne painter and an adherent of an anarcho-syndicalist group, the Allgemeine Arbeiter Assoziation, stressed that the art which Kokoschka wished to preserve so fervently was really dead and spiritless. 'For centuries we had here enormous frames surrounding enormous holes'.[78] To put the preservation of such art higher than concern for the loss of life which had brought about the threat to its survival was a perversion of values.

It was also inimical to the development of a true contemporary art. The spirit of the great artists of the past, Seiwert argues, is indestructible, but the burden of their creations weighs heavily on the present, and takes from us the courage to act. It was for the sake of the future that the works of the past ought to be destroyed.

---

78. F.W. Seiwert, 'Das Loch in Rubens' Schinken', in Schneede, *Zwanziger Jahre*, p. 60.

There should be an end to the veneration of all this bourgeois culture. Destroy the old idols in the name of the future proletarian culture.[79] And this new proletarian art, Seiwert recognised, could not just be the use of bourgeois art forms in the service of proletarian ends. To do this was only to continue in a social-democratic tradition. For him and his colleagues in the Cologne group of *Political Constructivists* both content and form must be proletarian in character.[80]

What was rejected in the art of the past was not individual creativeness, however great, but the overall role of bourgeois art in the oppression of the working class. And this role was performed inevitably, even by art which had no particular political or social message. Art could not be judged in purely formal terms. Citing the example of Goethe's poetry, Max Herrmann-Neisse, the left-wing communist poet, argued in 1922 that a purely aesthetic assessment would be wrong at a time 'when the proletariat was still so deeply involved in its fiery final struggle'.[81] Once that struggle had been successfully brought to a conclusion, a selective appraisal of bourgeois art and culture could commence. For the moment it was important to resist the covert and insidious world of ideas of the bourgeoisie, which was as hostile and dangerous as the influence of the economic world. Art, Herrmann-Neisse argued, should not be judged in emotional terms, but rather in terms of 'whether it serves the needs of the proletariat or not'. Whoever absorbs even the smallest morsel of the capitalist-bourgeois spirit', he argued, 'is no longer of use for the cause of the proletariat.'[82]

Such a didactic attitude to art implies for Herrmann-Neisse that within the art of the past, and among the formally bourgeois artists of the present, there are those who are essentially anti-bourgeois, and whose work strengthens the worker in his struggle.[83] But in the end a new proletarian culture cannot arise until there is a spiritually unified working class, united by a common feeling of community. As bourgeois art arose with the formation of the bourgeoisie as a class, so would proletarian art arise with the rise of

79. F.W. Seiwert, 'Offener Brief an den Genossen Bogdanov', in Fähnders and Rector, *Literatur*, pp. 114–16.
80. Ibid.
81. Max Herrmann-Neisse, 'Die bürgerliche Literaturgeschichte und das Proletariat' in Fähnders and Rector, *Literatur*, p. 73.
82. Ibid. p. 84.
83. Herrmann-Neisse mentions in particular Francois Villon, Charles-Louis Phillippe, Anatole France, Martin Anderson-Nexö, Conrad Felixmüller, George Grosz and Frans Masareel as artists who sought to explore and describe in detail the world of the proletariat and denounce its opponents in their work.

universal working class solidarity: 'only then will there be an art which is the art of the propertyless for the propertyless'.[84]

Yet if the critical assessment of the bourgeois heritage came from the left, and the extreme left of the political spectrum, so did voices in support of the traditional culture and its expression in works of art. The official communist line, speaking through the *Rote Fahne*, the party's national newspaper, did not agree with proposals for the wholesale rejection of bourgeois culture and art. Thus Gertrud Alexander, who was the paper's principal literary critic and reviewer in the early 1920s, maintained that in the end a truly proletarian culture would inevitably arise to take the place of 'that bloodless and ascetic art', the expressionist culture of the present, which stood in such contrast to the human values of the works of the old masters; and that therefore the workers would at best be fools, and at worst vandals, if they were to throw away the whole of the cultural achievement of the past in favour of a transitory movement which represented no more than a flight from contemporary reality. In doing so, they would destroy masterpieces 'which will always be objects of beauty and admiration also for workers'. Not only was the art of the past of historic interest, and possibly even a stimulus to revolution, but 'in spite of capitalism and exploitation there existed a culture in which immortal works were created. A new culture could not arise so quickly that the workers . . . could not, and should not, derive joy from past beauty.'[85]

The question was, however, not only an aesthetic one. In the view of communist politicians it also involved wider political issues. August Thalheimer, at one time editor-in-chief of the *Rote Fahne*, wrote at the end of the debate, that it was wrong and shortsighted to reject and discard the cultural inheritance, any more than one would destroy deliberately the material achievements of the bourgeoisie. The latter had already destroyed many of its own material and spiritual achievements, and the fight against it would inevitably destroy more. 'The slogan of the destruction or rejection of the art of the past, which claims to be ultra-revolutionary and anti-bourgeois is, in reality, a bourgeois slogan, a mirror image of the practice of a bourgeoisie in a state of decline and self-destruction.'[86]

The political struggle of the proletariat, Thalheimer suggested,

84. Herrmann-Neisse, 'Die bürgerliche Literaturgeschichte', p. 78.
85. Gertrud Alexander, 'Herrn John Heartfield und George Grosz' in Fähnders and Rector, *Literatur*, pp. 50–3.
86. August Thalheimer, 'Proletarische Kunst', in Fähnders and Rector, *Literatur*, pp. 60–1.

would absorb all its energies, and the drive to conquer and acquire for its use the cultural heritage of the past 'was a strong force, which pushed things along in this political struggle'. To abandon that drive would not only weaken the proletarian struggle, it would also alienate the still healthy sections of the bourgeois world.[87]

The widespread participation of communist workers in the early years of the Republic in non-communist workers' cultural institutions suggests that sentiments in favour of the incorporation of much of the cultural tradition of the bourgeoisie extended beyond the SPD, which had maintained a largely positive attitude towards the cultural heritage. Such opposition as there was came largely from the extreme left, although communists within the organisation sought to push through policies in favour of radical political measures.[88]

The difficulty of creating 'islands of proletarian culture' was not entirely internal to the movement. It was also due to the absence of artists who were not only drawn emotionally towards socialism, but who would also identify fully with the proletariat and its organisations in a political sense. With relatively few exceptions, the artists who before, during, and after the revolution identified with the working class were almost all bourgeois by origin and upbringing. Their political decisions tended to be motivated by feelings of revulsion and empathy, rather than by close identification with socialist or communist ideology.

Rather, they held an almost religious belief in the possibility of achieving a perfected, humanitarian society 'through a change in the human psyche'. Their view of revolution was a view of a libertarian rather than an economic event; and if they expressed admiration for Russia, it was on account of the innate religiosity and the communitarian belief of its people.[89]

Idealist attitudes and bourgeois pasts alike prevented the artist from becoming a genuine proletarian. He could not easily dedicate thought and action to a role whose highest aim was to destroy the basis for egocentric materialism and separatist individualism. Wieland Herzfelde wrote that 'the only role for the bourgeois artist

---

87. Ibid.
88. This agitation is dealt with in the respective chapters.
89. Cf. D. Mayer, *Linksbürgerliches Denken. Untersuchungen zur Kunsttheorie, Gesellschaftsauffassung und Kulturtheorie in der Weimarer Republik*, Munich, 1981, pp. 180–1. In the preface to the 1955 Hamburg reprint of his seminal anthology of expressionist verse, *Menschheitsdämmerung* (1920), Karl Pinthus wrote that the socialist or utopian demands of Expressionism did not come from Marx but from humanist thought.

who wishes to identify with the cause of the working class and its politics, is to create art which will be understood by the working class and serve its needs'. That meant that in his work he must seek to depict the bourgeoisie in such a way that 'everyone would recognise it as what it is: the force that destroys all happiness, all justice, and all freedom', and through the effect of that portrayal to become a means towards the eventual success of the revolution. As for himself, the bourgeois artist must accept the fact that he will lose his existing social ties without acquiring new ones. That he will be 'a bourgeois who has recognised his eventual but inevitable historical demise.'[90]

In Herzfelde's view, it is the artist's lack of roots in the proletariat and his role in the political struggle which determines the character of his art; but Herzfelde is less specific about the mechanism of the artist's creativity. There was no 'art which stood above the classes', and it was futile to speculate on how far the art of the present could provide nourishment for a future society. 'In the mean time the Communist can do no more than put his faculties wholly and unreservedly at the service of the revolutionary present.'[91]

Some years later Herzfelde returned to the theme in an essay, 'Die Kunst ist in Gefahr', written together with George Grosz. They ask whether there is still a place for the arts in the revolutionary struggle, or whether the artist should not cede his place to the photographer, while on the other hand concentrating all his energies on the political fight. Realising that art need no longer describe reality – 'if you wish to know what the world is like you go to the cinema, not to an art exhibition' – and rejecting the metaphysics of expressionism, the artist of today can only become a technician. As such, Grosz argues, he must choose between mere mechanical competence as draughtsman, architect or illustrator in the service of industry, and propaganda for the class struggle. If he chooses the latter he must 'as narrator and critic, reflect the images of the times . . . [and] as defender of the revolutionary idea and of its followers, rank himself in the army of the oppressed'.[92]

The significance of the views of Grosz, Heartfield and Herzfelde lies less in their account of the role of the artist in the political struggle of the proletariat than in their assessment of bourgeois and workers' culture. The subordination of personal creativity to the

90. Wieland Herzfelde, 'Gesellschaft, Künstler, Kommunismus' in Fähnders and Rector, *Literatur*, pp. 124–49, p. 136.
91. Ibid., p. 141.
92. Ibid.

demands of political service to the Communist Party, for which they argued, was practised by many organised artists and intellectuals.[93] It was institutionalised in the organisations of 'revolutionary visual artists' and 'revolutionary writers' discussed in later chapters.

Their challenge to the workers to base their struggle on their own cultural roots was answered neither by the working class nor by the leadership of the Communist Party. Their outright rejection of bourgeois culture as the expression of class hatred and exploitation was countered 'officially' on aesthetic as well as on political grounds. More importantly, there is no evidence that the workers, to whom these 'bourgeois' artists addressed themselves, heeded the proposal to reject the bourgeois heritage and foster their own culture independently. Indeed, it is doubtful whether workers regarded their own indigenous lifestyle, which was so closely linked with the poverty and deprivation which they so wished to escape, as culture.[94]

The fact that from Ferdinand Lassalle via Wilhelm Liebknecht and Franz Mehring to Valtin Hartig and Leo Kestenberg socialist renegades from the bourgeoisie acted as champions of 'High Culture' encountered little if any opposition from the socialist rank and file.[95] Middle-class intellectuals formed the core of the teachers engaged in the social-democratic educational system, and after 1918 working-class choirs welcomed conductors from the ranks of professional musicians and of teachers of music, and the bulk of the membership fell in with their wishes to perform musically demanding but generally politically neutral pieces from the classical repertoire.[96]

Throughout the workers' cultural movement there was widespread agreement on the importance of achieving in the performances of works of art high standards of technical and artistic competence. These were regarded as proof that the working class in the Weimar state had achieved also in the cultural field a position which could command esteem, and that workers, who had long

93. Heartfield and Herzfelde were members of the KPD throughout the Weimar period, but George Grosz distanced himself from the party in 1923, though he continued to be sympathetic to the cause for some years.
94. Cf. M. Rector (note 18), p. 100.
95. Leo Kestenberg was a high-ranking social-democratic Civil Servant in the Prussian Ministry of Education and Science who was a regular speaker on art and music at social-democratic cultural conferences. See his *Bewegte Zeiten*, Zurich, 1961.
96. Thus the great majority of the teachers at the Berlin Party School (1906–1914) came from bourgeois families and were University-educated. See also Chapter 6.

been culturally deprived, were now attaining what was rightfully their own. Conversely, we find that outside choral music, where high standards could be achieved by non-professionals, social-democratic cultural policy did not encourage amateurism, as the critical attitude towards workers' amateur dramatics before 1918 shows.[97]

The practice of the KPD in encouraging workers to write, draw and photograph, and the development of the Agitprop Theatre to be discussed in Chapters 3 and 8, followed a different course, but one that was strictly linked to the political battle and its needs. The *Proletkult*-type ventures discussed earlier remained isolated and relatively unsuccessful experiments.

We saw that the actual content of the culture which labour-movement organisations were to transmit had been the subject of discussion largely among the intellectual élite within the SPD, and this discussion was to continue in the Weimar period; but there is no evidence to suggest that the mass of organised workers rejected the generally positive attitude towards 'High Culture' advocated by most of the mainly middle-class educationists and others who absorbed such culture themselves.

97. Cf. Chapter 8.

–2–

Emancipation Through Culture: Social-Democratic Theory and Practice

The Social-Democratic Discussion in the Weimar Years

The discussion within the German Social Democratic Party about the role of culture in the life of the working class and in its emancipatory struggle, whose origins and early development were discussed in the last chapter, widened during the years of the Weimar Republic. War and revolution had politicised large sections of the population, including workers who had until now been apolitical.[1]

To meet this expansion there was now much greater scope for workers' cultural endeavour than there had been under the Empire. The new state was built on liberal principles: the constitution had abolished censorship and other restrictions on cultural and political activities. Culture and leisure-time organisations allied to the SPD, such as Workers' Sports Organisations or Workers' Choral Societies, were no longer subject to the 1908 *Vereinsgesetz* (the 'Law relating to Association') which had forbidden them to engage in political activities or even to discuss political issues. Such discussions now took place in virtually all branches of the social-democratic cultural movement, and the relevant issues are raised in the chapters devoted to the individual areas of workers' culture.

This chapter aims to deal with some of the more general aspects of this discussion, which centred on the political role of workers' culture in the wider society and on the content of that culture in the context of social-democratic thinking and of the political practices of the SPD.

As we shall see, many of the workers' cultural organisations reached, after 1918, a high level of perfection in their field. This is

---

1. At the first election after the revolution based on adult suffrage the SPD and the Independent Social Democrats polled 45% of the vote, compared with 34% in 1912. As throughout the Weimar period the female vote was less radical than that of men an election based on male voting only might have given the left an absolute majority.

exemplified in the standards of performance attained by workers' choirs in their musical offerings, or, in the case of the Workers' Theatre movement, in the quality and originality of the Berlin Volksbühne. Much of this was facilitated by the SPD's involvement in the new state, and its participation in government at municipal, state and national level. This new status and the newly-found 'respectability' of the party helped to give these organisations an entrée into the ranks of performing artists, and, in particular, helped the workers' choral societies to find badly needed conductors, which had not been easily possible during the years of the Empire.

The awareness of this apparent equality in the level of performance of working-class and bourgeois institutions was taken by many socialist politicians as proof of the integration of workers into the national community. The social and cultural emancipatory struggle had thus led to the 'respected position which the working class now occupied in state and society.'[2] Hence, the cultural equality of the workers in the Weimar period, it was thought, became an element in their identification with the new state. There was a parallel here with some thought on the development of the economy which was then current. The traditional socialist view had always been that society was deeply and fundamentally split, and that the conflict between capital and labour could only be solved through a political and social revolution. But during the 1920s the view gained ground within the SPD, and, above all, in the trade union movement, that the institutionalised system of industrial relations established in the Republic was a portent of growing equality between employers and labour. This, it was thought, would gradually lead to an economic democracy (*Wirtschaftsdemokratie*), a kind of tamed capitalism, on which the advance to socialism could be based. Equal achievement in the cultural field would increase the workers' feeling of equality with the bourgeoisie, and would lead eventually to a full incorporation in the state.[3]

In spite of the greater prominence of the activities of social-democratic leisure-time organisations after 1918, cultural aims and policies received generally less discussion within the SPD than economic and social issues, which were widely debated within the

---

2. Cf. R. Weimann, 'Sozialismus als Kulturbewegung', *Unser Weg, Monatsschrift der Berliner Sozialdemokratie*, vol. 2, 1928, p. 35.
3. On the concept of *Wirtschaftsdemokratie* see F. Naphtalie, *Wirtschaftsdemokratie*, Berlin, 1928, and reprint, Frankfurt, 1968. Also H.A. Winkler (ed.) *Organisierter Kapitalismus, Voraussetzungen und Anfänge*, Göttingen, 1974.

party. After the 'Education Guidelines' of 1906, referred to in the last chapter, no official statement on educational and cultural policy was issued, and the two party programmes of 1921 and 1925 pay scant attention to cultural policy. The earlier Görlitz programme only mentions the right of all citizens to the whole of culture, while the Heidelberg (1925) programme deals largely with educational policy.[4]

To understand what might be regarded as the official attitude of the SPD in this field we must look at the views expressed by permanent officials of the SPD and by the *Referenten* – the experts appointed by the party to speak at conferences and meetings on specific topics. Equally important are the views expressed in the party press, and especially in *Vorwärts*, the central organ of the party, and in the specialist press, above all in the *Kulturwille* (1924–33), which more than any other journal can be identified with the ideas and aspirations of *Kultursozialismus*. And, unlike the discussion in the pre-war period, which had centred on educational issues, the post-war discussion was now more clearly focused on cultural questions. After 1918 the SPD divested itself of many of its responsibilities in the educational field, especially where liberal education was concerned. It did so through a policy of co-operation with the Volkshochschulen, the Adult Education Colleges, which after the war grew greatly in numbers and size. They were now no longer linked with bourgeois institutions and ideals, and they generally welcomed the opportunity to provide education for the working class. Heinrich Schulz, the Secretary of the SPD's Central Education Committee, told the 1920 Party Conference that 'except in so far as it does not concern the innermost subject of our work – the education of workers to socialism – the party could co-operate with educational institutions or with organisations of other ideological persuasions'.[5] In any case, now that the party and the trade unions were increasingly involved in public life, the so-called 'socialist education policy' was primarily concerned with the training of party and trade union officials and activists, and those who were engaged in it stressed the need to prepare people 'for positive collaboration in the state, in the economy and in legal matters.'[6]

Given the more restricted role of the SPD in the field of edu-

---

4. For the text of the Görlitz and Heidelberg programmes see S. Miller and H. Potthoff, *A History of German Social Democracy*, Leamington Spa, 1986, pp. 253–64.
5. *SPD Parteitag*, 1920, p. 77.
6. Cf. *Arbeiter Bildung*, 1929, pp. 21–3 (from an article on the Workers' College in Harrisleefeld by E. Marquart.) See also A. Braunthal, 'Die Arbeiterhochschule Tinz', *Arb. Bldg*, 1926, pp. 53–6; and, in general, H. Feidel-Merz, *Zur Ideologie der Arbeiterbildung*, 2nd ed., Frankfurt, 1972.

cation the party and its organisations turned increasingly to the propagation of cultural events. In 1926 the party launched the Sozialistische Kulturbund ('Socialist Culture League') to develop, strengthen and co-ordinate cultural activities which had previously been the responsibility of the Central Education Committee. The League organised conferences which became platforms for the discussion of the place and purpose of culture in the life of the working class. The first of such conferences took 'Socialism and Culture' as its theme. All the speakers agreed that in as much as 'socialism was not a matter for sermons on high days and holidays, so cultural activities were not Sunday afternoon entertainment but an integral part of the political and economic work of the social democratic movement'.[7]

The criteria by which the importance of this culture was to be judged were psychological as well as social. The enjoyment of culture was seen in part as compensating for the strains and hardships of monotonous manual work, but its wider social role was equally important. In spite of the fact that the workers' living standards in the immediate post-war period were below the pre-war level it was widely held that socialism was no longer a 'bread and butter' question. The political and economic work of Social Democracy was really only working towards the better enjoyment of the cultural life.[8] As *Vorwärts* wrote in 1921 'all the struggle of the working class for their material improvement was not the ultimate goal but the means to achieve a truly human communal life so that the Social Democratic Party would become even more a party of culture'.[9] By this not only would the working class demonstrate its equality with all other social groups, but by the sincerity and devotion of its cultural endeavours it would show its high moral purpose. Thus if, in the 1920s, it became customary for the SPD to celebrate the passing of the old year with a performance of Beethoven's great Choral Symphony, in contrast to the jollifications of the middle class, this was evidence of the seriousness of purpose and the moral superiority of the socialist working class.[10]

7. Alexander Stein in *Sozialismus und Kultur*, Report of the Conference of the Sozialistische Kulturbund 1926, 1927.
8. Ibid.
9. *Vorwärts*, 18 August 1921 cited in C. Rülcker, 'Arbeiterkultur und Kulturpolitik im Blickwinkel des Vorwärts', *ASG*, vol. 14, 1974, 115–55. See also Paul Kampfmeyer, *Arbeiterbewegung und Sozialdemokratie*, 1921, p. 290 ('Nicht für eine Messer- und Gabelfrage setzt der Arbeiter seine Existenz auf das Spiel, sondern für die Frage der körperlichen und geistigen Vollmenschlichkeit.').
10. *Vorwärts*, 5 January 1928. But note that the *Kulturwille* complained in 1924 that in the previous year the performance in Leipzig had only been half full.

In claiming that the workers were equal to the members of the bourgeoisie in their role as audience or spectators the party also tended to accept the importance of the national cultural heritage, and to recognise that its work had to be judged by the criteria of artistic achievement. Such emphasis on the reputation and achievement of the established culture led many socialists back to the great creative figures of the German past. Thus for the masses of socialist youth who met in Weimar at the end of August 1920, the twenty-eighth of the month, the date of Goethe's birth, was 'the holiest date of this great cultural epoch'; and the Frankfurter Kulturkartell der modernen Arbeiterbewegung celebrated the bicentenary of Lessing's birth 'in veneration and as a tribute to the great forerunner of classical literature'.[11] *Vorwärts* did not doubt that the whole of artistic creation was potentially relevant for workers, and demanded only that the conditions under which it was purveyed, performed or displayed should be such that cost and conditions of access did not present obstacles to its enjoyment by workers.[12]

Compared with the criterion of artistic perfection, ideological factors were thought to be of lesser importance, and *Vorwärts* argued that the workers' cultural movement must in the last resort remain independent in order to maintain its 'purity'. The paper regarded it as an act of cultural vandalism when freethinkers prevented the performance of Mozart's *Ave Verum* at a secular memorial service because of its Christian text.[13]

Ideological issues were of course raised in the discussion of cultural policy, but much of it was on an abstract and rhetorical level, if only because of the dearth of material with a socialist content. At a conference of the Bezirksbildungsausschüsse in 1927 the Frankfurt delegate, Konrad Brosswitz, argued that 'cultural activities were part of the class struggle and not a preserve of an intellectual élite'.[14] But this meant only two things, a certain selectivity in respect of the transmitted culture, and attempts to bring workers themselves more into the area of cultural activities.

Social-democratic thinking about culture and its effects on the working class during the Weimar period failed to produce a new aesthetics, or to continue the discussion of fundamental issues of workers' culture which we found in the pre-war SPD, and which flourished after 1918 among some more independent artists and

11. For the meeting of the Socialist Workers' Youth in Weimar see Chapter 11. See *Kulturkartell der modernen Arbeiterbewegung* Frankfurt, 1929, pp. 20–1.
12. Rülcker, Arbeiterkultur, pp. 144–7.
13. Cf. *Vorwärts* June 1, 4, 8, 1928.
14. *Arb. Bldg.* vol. 2, 1927, p. 85.

intellectuals, as was discussed in the last chapter. Within the movement and its cultural institutions and organisations there was little
consistent critical assessment of the artistic and literary heritage, or
of bourgeois culture in general. Nor was there any parallel to the
attempts, found in the communist camp, to develop a body of
social-reportage literature, concentrating on working-class life.
Only in respect of workers' poetry and in the socialist choral drama
can we trace the beginnings of a new art more organically linked to
the working-class milieu and to workers' aspirations.

On the face of it this is surprising. Given the sympathy for some
of the basic ideals of socialism shown in particular by expressionist
artists and writers, some of whom openly identified with the SPD,
one might have expected some reciprocity on the part of the
organisation or its spokesmen and its writers on cultural matters.
Yet the discussions within the party showed no particular enthusiasm for the modern movement in art and literature.[15] Nor,
with a few exceptions, do the public expressions on artistic matters
by social-democratic organisations, especially trade unions, show
much evidence of a positive attitude towards new art.

The labour movement, including the unions, was in a limited
way a patron of art, especially in respect of new building; but this
rarely manifested itself in original, innovatory architecture. The
majority of *Volkshäuser* or trade union headquarters were not
'spontaneously growing edifices . . . buildings shaped into clear
and sacred vision'. They were built in a traditional style, 'histor-
icist' rather than modernist in form.[16] It is only in the field of public
housing, with its simple, unadorned and rational style of architecture, and in the propaganda for functional furniture for workers'
homes that we find the influence of modern architecture and design
at work.[17] It is likely that the bulk of the German working class
would not have shown great sympathy or understanding for
reality-distorting painting and sculpture or abstract art; but there
were no attempts, on the part of the social-democratic organisations or their press, to interpret this art or to awaken support for
its ideas. 'The worker looks at art in the same way in which he
looks at everyday life . . .' wrote a contemporary critic. 'He looks

15. But see Klara Bohm-Schuch's contribution to the discussion at the first confer-
    ence of the Sozialistische Kulturbund (see note 7), when she drew attention to
    the architecture of Bruno Taut and Ludwig Hoffmann.
16. One, pre-1914, example was the Hamburg Gewerkschaftshaus (1906 extended
    1913) discussed by E. Domansky, 'Der Zukunftsstaat am Besenbinderhof' in
    A. Herzig *et al.* (eds) *Arbeiter in Hamburg*, Hamburg, 1983, pp. 373–85.
17. Cf. Chapter 7 on the Visual Arts.

for the obvious, for that which can be readily understood. In art he looks for the concrete, for the things which he finds around him. He is satisfied with it if it merely mirrors the customary surroundings.'[18]

There was clearly no congruence between radical thinking in economic and political matters and sympathy with radical if not revolutionary styles in art and literature. Only in the USPD, the independent social-democratic party which had split off from the main party in 1917, and which later split again into a communist wing and a section which returned to the SPD, do we find aesthetic judgements showing sympathy and understanding for the modern movement. This showed itself in the USPD's weekly magazine, *Freie Welt*, which printed examples of avant-garde literature and contemporary revolutionary art. Writing about the *Große Kunstausstellung* in Berlin in 1919 the reviewer admitted that working-class taste tended to be petty-bourgeois, and that the modern and ultra-modern art was alien to it. It was their task, however, 'to show the workers that modern art was essentially revolutionary and that one can already predict that in due course this art would become an ally of the proletariat'.[19]

Instead of looking critically at the culture of the past and making a rigorous selection from it to form the basis of a new workers' culture, socialist educators and cultural critics envisaged new cultural forms. They thought in terms of a participatory culture through which a new socialist community would be created. The aim was to activate the ordinary worker not only as a passive listener and spectator but as a participant in the events themselves. 'An appreciation of art . . . as the passive reception in respect of the works of the great masters in museums and concert-halls should be taught at school', a report by the Berlin SPD argued in 1928. 'Social-democrats had to embark on something bigger. We must make everyone active and awake, in and through the masses, a growing people's culture.'[20]

The exhortation to workers to be creative was linked especially to the workers' choral movement, which was just then trying to find socialist cantatas and oratorios, and, above all, to the new

---

18. A. Kreiter, 'Was bedeutet dem Arbeiter die Kunst', in *Arbeiterkulturwoche und Gewerkschaftsfest*, Leipzig, 1924, p. 12, reprinted in R. Kober, *Die Verhältnisse von Leipziger Arbeitervereinen und Vereinen für Arbeiter zur bildenden Kunst*, Leipzig, 1970.
19. *Freie Welt*, no. 39, 1919.
20. Leo Kestenberg at the Leipziger Kulturwoche, 1924, cited in Erich Winkler, 'Bericht über die Kulturwoche' *Die Tat*, 1924, pp. 892–90, p. 902.

practices of the *Sprechchor* and the *Bewegungschor*, declamation by massed voices in the style of a Greek chorus, on the one hand, and miming and rhythmical movement *en masse* on the other. Its advocates hoped that the creation of these new forms of cultural activity would in themselves create a community where 'the verbalisation (*Wortbild*) of the massed proletarians was being transformed into the live and lively picture of the masses'.[21] Such choruses, combined with music, gymnastics and other forms of visual display, formed the basis of the Mass-Festivals which became popular in the German labour movement in the early 1920s. It was hoped that such practices would create a collective experience which would enthuse all the participants, and awaken and sustain a feeling of solidarity.[22] Often organised in the form of *Proletarische Feierstunden* – a kind of socialist equivalent to the Sunday services of the established religions – they were seen as 'the first step towards the creation of *Lebensgemeinschaft*, an 'everyday community' which carried within it the seeds of socialism.[23]

This emphasis on collective actions and performances and the resulting mass-experience through cultural events, uniting ideally both 'actors' and audience, was in marked contrast to the cultural ideals of the mature and rounded individual personality which the bourgeoisie had taken over from antiquity via the Renaissance. It was however consonant with the emphasis on solidarity which was at the heart of the socialist struggle. The SPD as the first socialist mass party had frequently demonstrated its strength and the devotion of its members by the vast numbers who attended its meetings, demonstrations and funeral processions. It seemed only natural to institutionalise this solidarity in a formally less combative situation and to forge it into a lifestyle at a time when, as some thought, the political and social struggle was less fierce.

Gustav Radbruch, a social-democratic academic and one of the party's theoreticians on cultural questions, also saw the organised collectivity of the socialist workers as the basis of its cultural activities. To be effective the appeal to mass sentiment through cultural events did naturally assume 'the community of a common cause, a common task and a common struggle'.[24] For Radbruch the

21. SPD Bezirksverband Berlin, *Jahresbericht 1928*.
22. Cf. Chapter 9 on *Festkultur*.
23. Leo Kestenberg, 'Die Aufgaben der Kunst', in *Sozialismus und Kultur* (see note 7), pp. 38–44, p. 40.
24. G. Radbruch, *Kulturlehre des Sozialismus*, Berlin, 1927 – extracts cited in W. Van der Wills and R. Burns (eds), *Arbeiterkulturbewegung in der Weimarer Republik, Texte, Dokumente, Bilder*, Frankfurt am Main, 1982, p. 42.

socialist worker was a member of a subordinate and defensive group whose life was already lived largely collectively. The cultural experience of the workers was therefore almost naturally a communal culture, both in its presentation and its purpose.[25] According to Theodor Leipart, the leader of the German Federation of Trade Unions (ADGB) 'leisure time and leisure-time culture for the working class must seek to give physical and spiritual health to the individual worker, but the latter must serve the wider aim of elevating the working class as a whole'.[26]

Radbruch saw signs of the rise of a new communal culture in the socialist workers' youth movement. Their culture was not simply a revolt against accepted bourgeois lifestyles and a search for freedom; this could become mere self-indulgence, unless it was linked to a greater ideal. In the socialist youth movement the new lifestyle was subordinated to the pursuit of socialism. 'At the meeting point of youth movement and labour movement there was the spring of new life; only the *Arbeiterjugend* could give to the new lifestyle of youth culture a strong new content.'[27] Other workers' organisations, like the workers' sports movement, less strongly culturally committed, were also concerned with the moulding of the masses, and thus 'with the formation of a socialist culture coming into being'.[28]

Radbruch was aware that such a moulding of the masses could lead to an undesirable suppression of individuality; but he argued that, although acting *en masse* could pervert the individual, the masses could also elevate him above his ordinary self and enable him to act with enthusiasm and even heroism of which he would not ordinarily be capable. The most supreme expression of this Mass Culture was for Radbruch and for most of the Cultural Socialists the *Feier*, the celebration and Festival. 'In the few years of the German Democracy we have already learnt to create Mass Assemblies, Mass Demonstrations and Mass Celebrations which were impressive for the spectator and deeply moving for the participants. In such celebrations the people – the source of all political power – assumed physical and spiritual form.'[29] For Radbruch such communal acts clearly implied a political affirmation of the democratic state and of the national community. With the

25. Ibid. p. 47.
26. Th. Leipart, 'Die Gewerkschaften und die Kultur der Arbeiterschaft', *KW* 1924, no. 7, p. 108.
27. G. Radbruch, *Die Kulturlehren des Sozialismus (1927)*, 1949, p. 27. The socialist youth movement is discussed more fully in Chapter 11.
28. Ibid.
29. Radbruch, *Kulturlehren*, p. 28.

advent of democracy a new 'unified intellectual stratum' had developed, and the new socialist culture which would arise in the new state would be an amalgam of an indigenous proletarian culture and of the surviving bourgeois culture.[30]

Another root of social-democratic thinking about the realisation of a communal culture was the idea of a revived *Volkskunst* (folk or popular art) which was to form the basis of a new proletarian culture. For Valtin Hartig, the editor of the *Kulturwille*, folk art combined the idea of a people's art with that of the 'popular arts' which would speak to the ordinary man in a language which he could understand. 'To ordinary people', he wrote, 'a work of art must be comprehensible in terms of content as well as form and it must take as its subject themes from the actual experience of the masses.' Popular arts, rooted in the traditions of the countryside, while not immediately applicable to the worker's own experience, could help him to appreciate beauty.[31]

In a wider sense, the argument went on, *Volkskunst* contained not only the 'folk' element, but also that of a communal art whose traditions were shaped in the Middle Ages, when overarching beliefs created harmony in the cultural field. Then art, which found its highest expression in the building of the cathedrals, was a collective enterprise, uniting artists, craftsmen and the admiring and supporting populace.

As we saw, some radical artists and architects had already expressed similar ideas after the revolution. Lyonel Feininger's woodcut of 'The Cathedral of Socialism', and Bruno Taut's idea of the *Stadtkrone*, the crowning edifice of the city, serving the whole community, refer back to the medieval community.[32] But the discussion of *Volkskunst* in the *Kulturwille* does not refer overtly to the utopian and quasi-religious views which underlay that earlier discussion, and it is more likely that the practices of the Socialist Workers' Youth, with its revival of old folk customs such as folksong and the celebration of the solstices, had greater influence here. In any case, we have here earlier examples of a participatory culture which, so Hartig and others thought, could serve as models of the future proletarian culture, provided it was adapted to the life of the working class in the big cities.[33]

30. Ibid. pp. 24–6.
31. Valtin Hartig, 'Volkskunst', *KW* 1924, vol. 1, no. 5.
32. Cf. Chapter 7 on the Visual Arts.
33. Cf. M. Bauer, 'Kunst und Leben', *KW* 1925, no. 8. The discussion makes no reference to the survival of older popular customs in the daily life of the working class into the twentieth century.

They recognised that a proletarian folk art still lacked an economic foundation, but thought that something could already be done to bring beauty into the daily life of the proletariat. Young workers, influenced by the spirit of the youth movement, were urged to bring colour into their homes and surround themselves with beautiful objects.[34]

In stressing the importance of creating culture with a broad popular appeal and in encouraging mass participation in cultural events, sections of the Weimar SPD followed a potentially fruitful path towards the creation of a workers' culture. But in concentrating on individual and collective experience through new forms its protagonists neglected questions of content and of the strengthening of ideological conviction. The propagation of old works hallowed by tradition, the performance of the *chefs d'oeuvre* of German culture of the past especially for workers, remained high on the agenda of the relevant organisations.[35] They were supported by a leadership whose fight for the emancipation of the German working class included the ideal of 'art for the people', but did not generally question its content, provided that it was good art and well presented.[36]

The Structure of the 'Third Pillar of the Movement'

The years of the Weimar Republic saw the development of a very extensive network of working-class cultural and recreational organisations and of intensive activity to support them by the party organisations. The cultural area was now, next to the political and the economic, conceived as the 'third pillar' of the movement, and it received the support of a substantial bureaucracy at the national and at the local level. This trend had, of course, already come into being before 1914. To translate the principles of social-democratic educational policy, agreed at the 1906 party conference, into practical politics the SPD had set up the Zentral Bildungsausschuß (Central Education Council) to oversee policy and to assist with the organisation of educational and cultural activities. The Council consisted of six members, appointed by the Party Executive, which

---

34. Cf. W. Eschbach, 'Kunst und Volkskunst', *Proletarier Jugend*, no. 16.
35. The Hanover Social Democratic organisation reported with obvious pride that lectures were given by eminent academics, and that musical performances could bear comparison with the best that was offered elsewhere (SPD Hanover, *Bericht des Unterbezirksvorstandes*, 1928).
36. For a related discussion of folksong and political songs cf. chapter 6.

endeavoured to make it representative of the various tendencies within the movement.

The status of the Central Council was that of a department of the Party Executive. It was initially staffed by a full-time Secretary, who was also the party's expert on educational matters, with some clerical assistance. The first Secretary was Heinrich Schulz, co-author of the 'Guidelines on Education'; the post of second secretary was created in 1910, and Wilhelm Pieck was appointed to it.

This central model was mirrored at the local level of party organisation. Parties and trade unions, operating through their own co-ordinating committees, the local Gewerkschaftskartelle (Trades Councils), of which 684 were in existence by 1910, formed local Bildungsauschüsse (Education Committees), which operated independently of the centre, and in many cases had no regular contact with the party leadership.[37] Given the many small local parties – by 1912 the SPD had 5,122 local branch organisations – local education committees covered only a minority of localities; but these included most larger towns and cities. Indeed, in the larger cities the local institutions had generally a full-time Secretary and other staff, and the scope of their operations extended beyond educational activities deeply into serious or popular entertainment.

The Central Council did not see itself as a central bureaucratic authority but rather as an 'advisory body, ready to help all types of working-class organisations'.[38] In addition to giving specific pieces of advice and as well as exercising a general oversight the Council assisted through the formulation of model programmes for educational or cultural activities. It published plans for the establishment of libraries, and arranged conferences for the training of officials. Through the publication of guides to plays and to music it sought to assist the growing interest in drama and in opera among German workers. The principal task of the Bildungsausschuß was, however, the education of party members, especially functionaries, who, it was hoped, would then influence the bulk of the membership. Their role was not the transmission of general knowledge, but of 'theory which would act as a compass in the high seas of practical politics'.[39] This the Bildungsausschuß did through

---

37. The number of local Bildungsausschüsse rose rapidly from 281 in 1908 to 410 in 1910 and 854 in 1913. The Central Council had however regular contact with less than half of them, despite repeated requests for information. Cf. D. Fricke, *Zur Organisation und Tätigkeit der deutschen Arbeiterbewegung, 1890–1914*, Leipzig 1962, p. 168.

38. *SPD Parteitag* 1910, p. 48.

39. *SPD Parteitag* 1908, p. 221 (from the Annual Report of the Zentral-Bildungs-ausschuß).

arranging lecture courses and by employing peripatetic teachers
(*Wanderlehrer*) who were able to offer a variety of courses, and were
mostly active in places which did not have enough local talent.
Participants in the centrally-arranged courses and lectures numbered only 72,000 just before the war; but then the courses
addressed themselves only to a minority of the total membership of
the SPD of nearly one million, many fewer than the 800,000 or so
who, as we saw, took part in cultural and recreational events
organised by the local Education Committees. All these activities
were largely self-financing, and remained so even after the war.
Admission charges were levied not only for public performances,
but also for lectures; and they ranged before 1914 from 20 pfennigs
for a single lecture or 0.30–0.50 marks for a concert or a poetry
reading to one Mark for a course of lectures – and this at a time
when the average hourly wage in industry was less than 0.50
marks.[40]

In the years after the war the educational work undertaken by the
SPD further declined in scope and in the range of subjects that it
covered. In general the social-democratic movement accepted the
role of the Adult Education system in the provision of general
liberal education; and, as an addition to this, the trade unions,
which before the war had been jointly responsible with the party
for educational activities at the local level, and whose members had
tended to take part in its ideologically-based system of instruction,
built up their own educational system after 1918. This operated
partly under the auspices of the local Gewerkschaftskartelle, which
had their own bureaucracy, and partly through the individual
unions, either in their own residential education institutions, as in
the case of the powerful Metal Workers' Union, or by sending
officials and activists to local part-time courses or to full-time
residential courses in political or neutral institutions, such as the
Berlin Gewerkschaftsschule (until 1923), special courses in local
Technical Colleges, and, at the apex of the system, the Akademie
der Arbeit attached to Frankfurt University. This range of educational activities was now directed less at preparation for the
political and industrial struggle. The industrial and social-welfare
system which had been created in the new state, and in particular
the Betriebsräte (Works Council) system, gave the unions new
rights to representation and consultation; and the education sought
by them was now increasingly oriented towards service in these

40. The financial support for educational and cultural activities from central funds
    was quite low – less than 20%.

institutions, and to practical work in state and industry in general.[41]

For the broad masses which were organised in the SPD the 'Central Education Council', now renamed Reichsausschuß für sozialistische Bildungsarbeit, was now concerned principally with the training of party functionaries; and some of this was now undertaken full-time by the residential colleges in Schloss Tinz and Harrisleefeld. The Volkshochschulen succeeded in satisfying the general educational needs of most of the working class. This was particularly so in the large centres of social-democratic activities such as Hamburg, Leipzig and Frankfurt, where the local party organisation co-operated closely with the local Adult Education Institution.

Here and elsewhere cultural and recreational activities became increasingly important, and the Reichsausschuß took account of this when in 1925 it sponsored the foundation of the Sozialistische Kulturbund as an initiating and co-ordinating body for cultural activities within the wider social-democratic movement. The 'Socialist Culture League', whose central organisation was supported by the SPD, had as its member organisations, apart from the Education Council, the Association of Socialist Teachers, the Socialist Workers' Youth, the Kinderfreunde organisation for the under-14-year-olds, and the Arbeiterwohlfahrt (Workers' Welfare Organisation). Other leisure-time organisations such as the Workers' Sports Organisation, the Workers' Music Movement, and the Volksbühne were represented on its Council, and collaborated at the local level.

The Kulturbund was organised as an independent organisation, whose task was 'to stimulate and strengthen the creative artistic forces of the working class in the field of science, art education, youth welfare and physical training and assist through this in the expansion and the deepening of the socialist cultural consciousness'.[42]

The Kulturbund was naturally concerned with cultural questions on a national level. It would take a stand on issues such as the proposed censorship law for juvenile literature and films contained in the *Schmutz und Schundgesetz*, and fight against reactionary cultural policies. It also set up a number of advisory bodies on workers' music and on broadcasting, the Arbeiter Musik Kommis-

---

41. The educational activities of the German Trade Unions have so far not been extensively documented, but see H. Feidel-Merz, *Zur Ideologie der Arbeiterbildung*, Frankfurt, 1972; F. Gumpert *Die Bildungsbestrebungen der Freien Gewerkschaften*, Diss. Jena, 1923.
42. *Der Führer*, 1925, no. 6, p. 24

sion and the Freie Rundfunk Zentrale, as well as a Zentrale Film Kommission, 'to develop film production in the spirit of the movement'.[43]

The bulk of the work of the Socialist Culture League was, however, the encouragement of local endeavour, and assistance with the techniques of cultural production. Again, the national organisation was reflected in the local organisation of education and culture, which underwent major changes as the result of the radical re-casting of the electoral system in 1919. The latter was now based on the list system, instead of the 397 constituencies, each of which used to have a social-democratic political association. The new national system was reflected in the party organisation, now based on the local branch (Ortsverein), and on the newly re-drawn and more powerful thirty-three party districts (*Parteibezirke*). The latter became the principal decision-making bodies for political districts and for the selection of candidates for Parliament and of delegates to the Party Conference. They, the sub-districts, and lower down the Ortsvereine tended to establish their own co-ordinating committees for education, and later their own co-ordinating committees for cultural affairs (Kulturkartelle). Even the party districts came into play as the organisers of conferences on educational or cultural matters. Indeed, in the large cities, especially where the party organisations were coterminous with municipal or state boundaries, they would be the predominant organisation. They offered scope for the large-scale organisation of cultural events.

The Hamburg social-democratic organisation, whose territory extended over the whole of the *Land*, as well as the powerful trade-union Ortsausschuß (local committee), organised an extensive programme of educational and cultural events. The Bildungsausschuß of the SPD had two separate departments, one concerned with 'political-scientific' matters, i.e. education, and the other covering the 'artistic'. In the latter area the unions, who arranged their own training programme as well as a general educational programme for the trade union youth, comprising general lectures and discussions as well as highly popular film shows, co-operated with the SPD's Education Committee. In 1928 party and unions joined forces to form a Zentral Kommission für Bildungswesen, with remits for four areas of leisure-time activity – Education and Training; Libraries; Artistic Events; and Travel, the demand for which, small though it was, grew during these years.[44]

---

43. Cf. *SPD Handbuch für Ortsvereine*, 1930, and the relevant sections in the SPD Jahrbücher, which were published between 1927 and 1930.
44. Cf. ADGB Ortsauschuß Hamburg, *Bericht 1924–1930*; SPD Landesorganisation

A similar picture could be drawn in other areas of cultural or quasi-cultural activity and Figure 1 seeks to illustrate the network of social-democratic organisations in the cultural field, whether directly under SPD auspices or in parallel to it. Thus apart from local Education Committees and Kulturkartelle the Central Sports Committee too had co-ordinating Committees at the local level in the form of Sportskartelle. These would not only unite the sports organisations, . . . but other workers' organisations, such as the socialist youth organisations, would also affiliate to them in their capacity as 'consumers' of sport. Similarly, the organisations of socialist teachers had local groups in major centres, and they and other bodies interested in youth welfare were represented in local Jugendausschüsse (Youth Committees), set up by the party organisations.

Occasionally a wide range of organisations involved in cultural activities came together in Days of Culture (*Kulturtage*) or Cultural Weeks (*Kulturwochen*) which some of the larger Kulturkartelle or similar bodies tended to organise in the middle and hopeful years of our period. Thus the *Leipziger Kulturwoche* brought together partly on successive days and partly in overlapping fashion a number of different organisations and a series of cultural events as such. Held in the first week of August, and coinciding with the tenth anniversary of the outbreak of the First World War, it saw the national conference of the Kinderfreunde and the Reichskonferenz of the Bezirksbildungsausschüsse, the national conference of the socialist students and of socialist teachers. The *Mitteldeutsche Jugendtag* – a meeting of socialist youth from Central Germany – took place at the same time, as well as the national meeting of the Council of the Socialist Workers' Youth. On the Tuesday there was a *Kulturkonferenz* with national speakers.[45] There were a series of performances of plays and of music, culminating in the *Gewerkschaftsfest*, a large out-of-doors festival. An exhibition of social and political art was held to coincide with these events.[46]

The formal structure of the organisations involved directly or indirectly in workers' cultural activities cannot tell the whole story. If we look at the operation of local organisations we find a great complexity together with evidence of some dysfunctional aspects of the arrangements which sought to ensure the propagation of

---

Hamburg, *Bericht, 1920/21–1929/30*; J. Schult, *Die Hamburger Arbeiterbewegung als Kulturfaktor*, Hamburg, 1954.
45. For a programme of the events see *Arbeiter Jugend*, 1924, p. 231, as well as the special brochure mentioned in Chapter 9 on *Festkultur*.
46. For the exhibition see Chapter 7 on the Visual Arts.

Figure 1 Cultural organisations within the social-democratic orbit
c. 1928

SPD

Organisations close to the SPD

Arbeitsgemeinschaft
sozialistischer Lehrer

Zentralkommission für
Arbeitersport und Körperkultur

Deutscher Arbeitersängerbund
(DASB)

Arbeiterturn und Sport Bund
(ATSB)

Arbeitertheaterbund

Arbeiterlichtbildbund

Verband für Filmkunst
(Volksfilm-Verband)

Arbeiterwohlfahrt

Sozialistische Arbeiter Jugend
(SAJ)

Naturfreunde
Kinderfreunde

Volksbühnenverband

Bücherkreis

Büchergilde Gutenberg

Arbeiter Radio Klubs

Organisations set up by the SPD

via Reichsausschuß für sozialistische
Bildungsarbeit or Sozialistische
Kulturbund:

Zentralstelle für die arbeitende
Jugend (SAJ, Kinderfreunde)

Film und Lichtbilddienst

Beratungsstelle für Festgestaltung

Arbeitermusikkommission

Kommission für Filmfragen

Freie Rundfunkzentrale

Sozialistischer Kulturbund

(Member Organisations:
Reichsausschuß für Sozialistische
Bildungsarbeit; Arbeitsgemeinschaft
sozialistischer Lehrer; SAJ;
Kinderfreunde; Arbeiterwohlfahrt).
ATSB and DASB willing to
co-operate.

Local Kulturkartelle (e.g. in
Frankfurt, with the following
membership: SPD – local; Trades
Council, Jungsozialisten,
Arbeiterabstinenten, Elternbeiräte –
Parent School Governors; Worker
Choristers, Arbeitsgemeinschaft
sozialistischer Lehrer)

Local Sportskartelle
Composed of representatives of the
various Sports Organisations, SAJ.

socialist cultural life. With the expansion in party functions more power devolved from the group of party officials to a lower level of party functionaries, the actual party activists.

In many places it became customary to hold a meeting of functionaries before each general members' meeting to discuss topical, but possibly problematic, issues. The party advised local organisations to invite the representatives of ancillary and friendly organisations, including trade unions, to such meetings. The Hamburg SPD, one of the largest and best organised local parties, was, in effect, run as 'a closed society of party functionaries'.[47]

At the same time the multiplication of organisations and the overlap of membership was thought to lead to a dissipation of energies. Critics argued that less time and effort should be devoted to all of them, or party activities, above all, would suffer. Otto Wels, the Party Chairman, sounded a warning note at the SPD's national conference in 1927. After enumerating the great number of ancillary organisations, especially in the cultural field, he added 'I counted over 40 different types of such societies and associations in which members could be active. All these groups seek to attract more men and women members of the party . . . and while these organisations also attract new members to the party, they get hold of the person in the first instance for their own ends.'[48]

All this affected general cultural activities particularly strongly, because individual organisations would tend to stage their own events. A middle-sized town may have had thirty or forty societies, with perhaps three hundred functionaries, who easily became preoccupied with the development of the organisations for their own sakes.[49] The local Kulturkartelle became primarily concerned with the co-ordination and the prevention of overlapping activities, instead of with initiating new developments.[50] In the smaller places, especially, the officers of these organisations formed very often a stage army, the members of which were all the time meeting together, but wearing different hats on each occasion. It was in the larger centres, for example Hamburg, Leipzig and Berlin, that the Bildungsausschüsse, and later the Kulturausschüsse

47. Cf. F.W. Witt, *Die Hamburger Sozialdemokratie in der Weimarer Zeit*, Hanover, 1971.
48. *SPD Parteitag* 1927, pp. 34–5.
49. Frankfurt had 157 workers' cultural societies, including 35 workers' sports clubs and 37 workers' choirs. Cf. J. Wickham, 'The Working Class Movement in Frankfurt during the Weimar Republic', Ph.D. Sussex, 1979, n. 121 (based on the *Merkbuch* published by the Union Druckerei). See also Paul Franken, *Vom Werden einer neuen Kultur*, Berlin, 1930.
50. Cf. F. Bieligk *et al.*, *Die Organisation im Klassenkampf*, Berlin, 1931.

Table 3 SPD Hamburg cultural activities, 1927/28

	No.	Attendances
Evening courses	53	2,213
Residential courses	7	117
Cultural-political lectures	9	4,547
Film shows	96⎫	
Slide shows	193⎭	70,220
Guided lecture-tours of museums, etc.	303	7,150
Meetings of young members	23	2,180
Artistic events	111	77,971
Christmas exhibition	1	13,000
Total	796	177,398

Source: Annual Report (*Bericht der Landesorganisation*) of the SPD Hamburg, 1927/28

or other specific local co-ordinating bodies carried out effective activities. Over the whole field we find that in the second half of the 1920s formal education inside the SPD tends to decline, while cultural events become more important – until they too suffered in the deteriorating economic conditions. The Hamburg Bildungsausschuß covered nearly the whole of the cultural field – with theatre, opera and other musical events occupying pride of place. But more humdrum activities, such as Christmas exhibitions, also received support.[51]

It is difficult to know how far the local cultural activities were in tune with the interests of the majority of members. A report from the Berlin Social Democratic organisation throws some doubt on this. It stated that the bulk of the membership was, as yet, not sufficiently attuned to the importance of the new cultural movement while, at the same time, 'there was a tendency for the cultural organisations to isolate themselves from the workers' economic and political movements and to lead a self-sufficient existence *at the margin of the labour movement*.'[52]

The Central Education Council, and the experts who advised it, sought to direct the attention of the membership at large to new developments in the cultural field and to stimulate expertise in the arts throughout the country. This was done through *ad hoc* meetings of specialists and local officials, and, even more influentially, through articles in the journals published by the Reichausschuß or

51. SPD Hamburg, Landesorganisation, *Bericht für 1927/28*.
52. SPD Berlin, Bezirksverband, *Bericht, 1925/26* (emphasis added).

by the Kulturbund.[53] The latter devoted one conference to the future of workers' music, and another in 1930 to 'Film and Radio', and it sought to direct the attention of the party at large to the importance of the new media and to influence radio programmes through action at the level of the Advisory Committees attached to the regional companies.[54]

At the time of its greatest strength, between 1926 and 1930, the SPD also attempted to further culture and education by central action to help libraries, and by seeking to put the distribution of films on a proper footing. It founded the Zentralstelle für Arbeiter Büchereiwesen (Agency for Workers' Libraries), with the central purchasing of books and the training of librarians as its task, and helped by establishing an agency for the hire of films and equipment. More indirectly, the SPD was involved in the founding of the Bücherkreis book-club, originally allied to the Dietz Verlag, the party's official publishing house.

The SPD, as the largest workers' party in Europe, with a highly developed organisational structure, has been attacked for its allegedly excessive bureaucracy, and for the oligarchic tendencies of its leadership cadres. Socialist cultural organisations were not free from bureaucratic elements, and at the local level a great number of clubs and societies do show some signs of that preoccupation with the minutiae of internal administration which the Germans call *Vereinsmeierei*. Yet the party had helped to create expertise and new forms of cultural activities, without which the sphere of workers' culture would not have developed so vigorously during this decade and a half.

53. These journals were *Arbeiterbildung* (1920–2); continued as a supplement of *Bücherwarte* 1926–8 and as *Sozialistische Bildung*, with *Bücherwarte* as a supplement, 1929–33.
54. For film and radio in the labour movement see Chapter 10 on the New Media.

-3-

Towards a Fighting Culture: The Case of the German Communist Party

Culture as a Weapon

Even though the German Communist Party laid down certain policies on cultural issues at an early stage, these issues and the considerations of cultural policy were initially less important in Communist Party theory and practice than they were in the discussions and activities of the SPD. It was only towards the end of the 1920s that the KPD began to foster specific organisations for cultural activities, and serious discussion of cultural questions occured only after the foundation of associations of 'revolutionary artists and writers' in 1928.

As the SPD had done in 1906, the Communist Party proclaimed in 1921 a set of guidelines on educational policy. These stated that the struggle of the proletariat was not only an economic and political struggle, but that it was an essential part of the intellectual and emotional formation of the communist worker that he shake off the superseded forms of bourgeois ideology and lifestyle.[1] The programme also aimed to fight for 'a higher socialist culture', without explaining what was meant by that phrase. To achieve an understanding of what it meant we shall therefore have to look both at theoretical statements and at evidence from the party's tactics.

From the general discussion within the wider communist movement it is clear that there was considerable doubt about whether a socialist or a communist culture could be attained before the proletariat had actually achieved political power.[2] Germany saw only a very limited echo of the Russian *Proletkult* experiment, which had gained considerable support in Russia in the early 1920s.

1. Cf. 'Leitsätze zur Bildungsarbeit der KPD', in L. Hoffmann and D. Hoffmann-Ostwald (eds), *Deutsches Arbeitertheater, 1918–1933*, 2 vols, Berlin, 1972, vol. 1, pp. 99–102. Also in *Die Internationale* vol. 3, no. 18/19, pp. 682–3.
2. The issue had agitated the Russian Communist Party before and after the revolution.

Proletkult sought to stimulate artistic expression of, and by, the workers, based on class-related solidarity within the formal organisations or in the communal structures of the working class. The underlying idea was that instead of an outside culture imported into the working class, the working class itself should become articulate.[3] The *Proletkult* experiment was criticised from within the movement, and later abandoned; but its sentiments persisted. In Germany, as we saw, it found expression in the activities of organisations such as the *Bund für proletarische Kultur* discussed earlier; and its ideas also had some influence later in the decade on attempts to establish a proletarian literature.

A different view about socialist culture came from Trotsky. He not only held that existing bourgeois culture contained much that was of great permanent value, but also believed that a proletarian art and culture could not arise while the working class was still in the midst of a continuing struggle which absorbed most of its energies. Hence a socialist culture – the first truly human culture – would not arise until the classless society had been achieved. At that stage, Trotsky suggested, 'there is no proletarian culture; there never will be and there is no reason to regret it. The proletariat comes into power in order to do away with class culture forever.' With this long-term view, Trotsky did not worry overmuch about the character of the culture to be imparted to the proletariat in the transitional period. What was needed was 'to impart to the backward masses the essential elements of the culture which already existed'. In addition there should be a fair measure of freedom of artistic creation.[4]

Trotsky's theories gained little support within the German communist movement, where antagonism to bourgeois culture was strong. There was a belief that it might be possible to take some steps towards creating a proletarian culture during the period of political struggle, but 'only the annihilation of the capitalist world will offer a firm foundation for the creation of a proletarian culture', wrote the *Rote Fahne* in 1922.[5]

It is a clear sign of the subordinate position which the German Communist Party attached initially to the implementation of its

3. On the *Proletkult* in Germany see P. Gorsen and E. Knoedler-Bunte, *Proletkult*, 2 vols, Stuttgart, 1974–5.
4. Cf. Leon Trotsky, *Literature and Revolution*, quoted in B. Knei-Paz, *The Social and Political Thought of Leon Trotsky*, Oxford, 1978, p. 294.
5. M. Kerschenzew, 'Die internationale Revolution und die proletarische Kultur', *RF* 1 March 1922, no. 116, reprinted in M. Brauneck, *Die Rote Fahne*, Munich, 1973, p. 139.

cultural programme that for some years to come it made virtually no effort to translate it into any kind of practical activity. The party was content to leave the propagation of culture for workers to the old-established, essentially social-democratic organisations. It hoped to exercise political influence on them through its members, and, if possible, to change the political direction of such organisations. The KPD did, of course, from the beginning, stress the importance of the ideological education of all party members; but it did not regard it as its task to provide a general liberal education. It feared that such training would only detract from the demands of the economic and political struggle.

Apart from agitation and the training of party officials the party initially did no more than organise acts of political commemorations and dedication, using the talents of sympathetic artists largely for agitation and propaganda.[6] As the guidelines mentioned earlier suggested, popular propaganda, including artistic display and representation, was expected to assist in the mobilisation of the uncommitted broad masses of the working class.[7] When in 1925 cultural work within the party was handed over to the agitprop department, this clearly indicated that cultural activity was to be subordinated to political aims, and in particular to the fight against the so-called *Kulturreaktion*, the reactionary cultural policy of the bourgeois parties, with whom the SPD was increasingly being numbered. Organisations formally concerned with workers' leisure-time activities, mostly splinter groups from social-democratically oriented associations which had been brought into the communist orbit, were urged to subordinate their cultural activities to the demands of the general political struggle, and to engage in political agitation. The Ifa, the Interessengemeinschaft für Arbeiterkultur – the communist co-ordination body for workers' culture, set up in 1929 – urged member organisations to 'relate [their] work to the crust of bread, the wage cuts and the struggle for the most elementary human needs.'[8] Cultural work proper was to take second place.

Towards the end of the 1920s, with the communist agitation growing increasingly hostile to the Social Democratic Party, such sentiments grew in strength. Franz Dahlem, the head of the KPD's Agitation Committee and a member of the Central Committee, declared at the 1929 Party Conference that 'the treasonable policies of the Social Democracy have caused the mass organisations to

6. The visual art of committed communists is discussed in Chapter 7.
7. From the 'Leitsätze' (see note 1).
8. *Ifa Rundschau*, vol. 3, nos. 2–4, March–April 1931.

engage in a life-and-death struggle between Social Democracy and Communism'.[9]

Within the social-democratic cultural organisations the KPD conducted an oppositional policy, forming factions to operate cohesively against the established leadership; while organisations under communist control devoted their energies increasingly to agitation in support of the general demands of the party. If the latter were to be the overriding considerations then those appointed to positions of leadership in the cultural organisations need not have to be particularly interested in the area of activity covered by the organisations.[10]

The policy of mobilising all organisations for the political struggle was not appreciated by all organisations or by all sections of their membership. The party had to admit that some of its followers still preferred to pursue personal cultural enrichment, rather than subordinating their activities primarily to political goals and propaganda.[11] In smaller places in particular there was a tendency to stress the social aspect and ignore the class-struggle aspect. Thus while the Breslau KPD could report on the existence of a number of theatre groups working within the communist orbit, it had to admit that some showed little willingness to engage in the performance of propagandist plays, and were still concerned with the staging of amateur dramatics.[12]

The underlying issue was closely linked to the general analysis of culture and of its political function. Culture, as experience, was sought by loyal communists also in the celebrations and commemorative events which the party had long held to be of importance. In the view of the leadership this could lead to situations where artists and artistic considerations 'had more influence on the arrangements and content of an event than was good, in terms of its political function', so that these celebrations became literary events instead of inculcating revolutionary fervour.[13]

For the KPD celebrations such as the annual Liebknecht, Luxemburg, and Lenin memorial meetings were not meant to create a festive mood among the participants or to arouse enthusiasm in

9. *KPD Parteitag Berlin-Wedding, Bericht,* Berlin 1929, p. 173.
10. The local direction of cultural activities should not be left entirely to those connected with the cultural organisations. 'On no account should only intellectuals be charged with the task. In this area in particular it was important not to lose contact with the daily struggle of the workers . . .'. 'Die kulturpolitischen Aufgaben der KPD', *Der Kampf um die Massen,* 1929, no. 5, p. 6.
11. 'Massenorganisation und Einheitsfront', *Der Parteiarbeiter,* 1929, p. 342.
12. KPD, Bezirksleitung Schlesien, *Bericht,* 1931, Breslau, 1931.
13. *Der Parteiarbeiter,* vol. 2, no. 5, 1929, pp. 99–100.

their spectators. Their purpose was to strengthen the feeling of solidarity and heighten political awareness. 'The proletariat has as yet no grounds to celebrate' wrote the *Ifa Rundschau*, 'for us there is only the demonstration and the manifestation of our preparedness to carry on the struggle.'[14]

The communist view on culture rejected contemporary bourgeois culture, although the party sought to attract bourgeois intellectuals and artists into its midst. In the past this culture might have had a progressive face; but, as Klara Zetkin, since 1919 a member of the KPD, wrote in 1927, it now showed all the symptoms of commercialism, and was used purely as 'a tool of bourgeois domination.'[15] The KPD naturally also rejected the kind of community culture which the SPD sought to foster. It argued that the latter spread bourgeois cultural domination, that it lulled the worker into a false sense of security, by making culture perform a compensatory role for the shortcomings of his material life and the hardship of his physical environment. The KPD was prepared to acknowledge the emotional needs of the worker, but it argued that 'the undernourished worker, exhausted by his job, could not fully enjoy the culture which was offered to him.'[16]

The task of the party was to show the worker the connection between the satisfaction of his economic and his cultural needs. It had to show him that 'while technical progress created the material basis to satisfy his growing cultural demands, increased exploitation deprived him (at the same time) of the opportunities for actually doing so'.[17] The opportunities to create a proletarian culture of a high standard seemed therefore to be limited, not least because of the ideological test to which this culture was to be subjected. For the KPD proletarian culture, including art, had to be a fighting culture, born out of dialectical thinking and 'representing the deepest truth accessible to the epoch'.[18] Art must therefore not only expose all that is bad in the existing society, as 'the literature of social misery' did, but it must identify with the proletarian struggle and praise the heroism of the workers.[19]

14. *Ifa Rundschau*, vol. 3, 1932, nos. 1–2.
15. Cf. K. Zetkin, 'Über bürgerliche Kultur', *RF* 5 July 1927 reprinted in Brauneck (see note 5) pp. 267–71; K.A. Wittfogel, 'Zur Frage einer marxistischen Aesthetik', *Linkskurve*, May–November 1930, reprinted in *Aesthetik und Kommunikation*, 1971, no. 3.
16. 'Massenorganisation und Einheitsfront', *Der Parteiarbeiter*, 1929, p. 340.
17. 'Die Kulturpolitischen Aufgaben der KPD und die Arbeit in der Ifa', *Kampf um die Massen*, 1929, no. 5, p. 5.
18. Wittfogel (see note 15) p. 72.
19. Ibid.

Given the communist assessment of the social position of the proletariat it was recognised that it would be difficult even for the gifted worker to acquire the necessary artistic or literary skills. It required a great effort on the part of the ordinary worker to overcome both the material difficulties which he experienced and escape the intellectual obfuscation which bourgeois cultural policies created.

Yet it was precisely in the field of propaganda and agitation that the communist movement sought to develop working-class talent. One of the initiating factors was the perceived need to enliven the communist press and bring it and other forms of agitation closer to the everyday experience of the working class. Imitating Russian practice the party sought to mobilise voluntary help with the work of written and visual communication. Operating largely through its press it fostered the establishment of groups of worker-illustrators, worker-photographers and, especially, worker corre-spondents – probably the most active of these groups.

They were all expected to devote their skills to the production of didactic and propaganda material, be it writing, drawing or pho-tography. Working mainly through contributions to the commu-nist press and through news-sheets and leaflets produced at factory or street-cell level, these partly trained amateurs were expected to assist the professional journalists or local organisers in the pro-duction of lively and topical newspapers, or in the work of agi-tation and communication at the grass-roots level.[20]

Through pictures and by using apposite captions or the new technique of photomontage, these ordinary amateurs were ex-pected to illuminate the intrinsic and often contradictory relation-ships which underlay reality. The worker photographers were working mainly for the AIZ, the popular communist illustrated, which encouraged them to make their picture-taking serve the needs of the press for accurate visual information and help with political propaganda. The worker photographers were urged to take pictures in factories where press photographers had no right of entry and make their work show the harshness of working class life and reveal the realities of the class struggle. The Arbeiterfotografen were to be the eyes of their class and through their cameras they were expected to raise class consciousness.[21]

20. On the Arbeiterkorrespondenten see C. Hempel-Küter, 'Die kommunistische Presse und die Arbeiterkorrespondenten Bewegung. Das Beispiel der Hambur-ger Volkszeitung.' Phil. Diss., Hamburg, 1987 (MS), and articles by the author cited below (notes 27 and 28).
21. Cf. *Der Arbeiterfotograf – Dokumente und Beiträge zur Arbeiterfotografie, 1926–1932*, Cologne, 1978.

Basic communication skills were important for these tasks, and newspaper staff and the Marxist Workers' School (MASCH) helped to train the small bands of interested and dedicated workers in them.[22] But equally or even more important for the success of their work was political conviction and an understanding of communist ideology, as well as a training in dialectical thinking through which to interpret to themselves, and to their audiences, their daily experience of the reality of proletarian life in the community, and, above all, on the factory floor. The contribution to literature by worker correspondents and by worker writers in general was not just related to their specific experience of working-class life; their ideological-political point of view was even more important.[23] In treating their material dialectically they sought to persuade the reader to engage in similar argumentation and abstraction, and to interpret his own situation as an example of the general situation of his class.[24] The effect should be twofold, to challenge the individual's own, and possibly mistaken, interpretation of events, and to attempt to convince him of the correctness of the ideology which interpreted it for him.

Based on these assumptions the work of these small groups was only an extension of normal party work, and a contribution to the political struggle. It was not looked on as an attempt at self-expression. Undoubtedly, the party raised levels of expectation and a desire for independent creativity on the part of some of the worker correspondents. But, as the Berlin *Rote Fahne* found, there was fortunately only a slight danger that 'all the work of the worker correspondents for the newspaper would develop into a slight dilettantism, a literary plaything, which would alienate the writer from party work instead of linking him ever closer to it'.[25] The worker correspondents would not be prevented if they were to develop in this way; but their principal task was that of reportage.[26]

Nevertheless, the tendency to write 'literary prose', to produce poetry showed itself among workers' correspondents and seems equally to have been resisted by the papers for whom they wrote, who looked for facts, not *feuilletons*. As an editor of the communist

---

22. On the MASCH see G. Gerhard-Sonnenberg, *Marxistische Arbeiterbildung in der Weimarer Republik*, Cologne, 1976.
23. Cf. A. Klein (ed.), *Im Auftrag ihrer Klasse. Beiträge zur Geschichte der deutschen sozialistischen Literatur im 20. Jahrhundert*, Berlin 1972, p. 410.
24. Cf. H. Möbius, 'Der Rote Eine Mark Roman', *AfSG*, 13, 1974, pp. 157–212.
25. F. Lux, 'Die Erste Konferenz der Arbeiterkorrespondenten der Roten Fahne', *INPREKOR*, 1925, no. 5, 1925, pp. 57–61, p. 57.
26. Cf. the resolution for the conference cited above.

Hamburger Volkszeitung wrote to a contributor, workers' correspondents should 'describe the fact concisely and pointedly, without much lyrical adumbration'.[27]

We know that a number of proletarian writers with literary gifts or ambitions turned into professional writers. Their membership of the *Arbeiterkorrespondentenbewegung* was coincidental with their literary careers; the movement itself did not act as an organ for the socialisation of worker-authors into a literary career.[28] Given the movement's immediate political aim, in its role as a handmaiden of the communist press, this is not surprising.

Neither worker correspondents nor worker illustrators were national movements with their own organisations. They were groups of workers with fluctuating memberships, generally held together by the local communist newspaper or by the party's agitational organisation, under whose auspices they had been assembled and trained, and who made use of their contributions. The significance of these movements cannot be measured in terms of their numbers; they must be seen in the way in which they reflect communist thinking on workers' culture. Here was a development which stressed the creation of culture by the workers themselves as against its reception – even if the whole activity was subordinated to a political aim. The primary purpose was not the education of future visual artists or writers, but to produce art in the service of a political organisation. But such a policy could not help but produce, in an admittedly embryonic form, art *by* workers, as well as 'art for workers'. And this showed itself in the discussion of more theoretical issues.

The more active of the worker correspondents or of the worker illustrators were nevertheless involved in considering issues relating to workers' culture through their membership of the national organisations of 'Proletarian-Revolutionary' artists and writers, which were both founded in 1928, and which combined professional and amateur writers or artists in one organisation.[29] These associations, which, though communist-sponsored, also had a

27. C. Hempel-Küter, Introduction to a collection of poems submitted to the *Hamburger Volkszeitung* (not yet published); the same, 'Darum höret mich Genossen/ zum Kampf ruf ich Euch', *Hamburger Zustände, Jahrbuch zur Geschichte der Region Hamburg*, vol. 1, pp. 145–159.

28. Cf. C. Hempel-Küter, 'Arbeiter schreiben für 'ihre' Zeitung, eine Studie zur Organisation der Arbeiterkorrespondenten Bewegung in Hamburg während der Weimarer Zeit', in P. Assion (ed.), *Transformationen der Arbeiterkultur*, Marburg, 1986, pp. 137–48.

29. The activities of the second organisation, the ARBKD or ASSO, are discussed in Chapter 7.

membership of non-communist sympathisers, came into being out of communist cells which had existed for some time in the national organisations of writers as well as of visual artists; and they also received stimulation and some support from the corresponding Russian organisations.[30]

Neither of the two organisations succeeded in establishing clearly defined aims; but of the two it was the 'League of Proletarian-Revolutionary Writers' (Bund proletarisch-revolutionärer Schriftsteller – BPRS for short) which attracted a larger workers' membership through its appeal to members of the Worker Correspondents movement. At the same time the League had attracted bourgeois writers, generally sympathetic to the cause and often committed members of the Communist Party.[31] In contrast to the organisation of visual artists the BPRS was from the beginning more involved in the discussion of such basic questions as what literature could do to help in the propagation of communist ideas, and to help to involve its worker-readers more in the revolutionary struggle. It set itself the task of creating a literature which was appealing to the broad masses of the working class, while at the same time carrying a political message. Its activities and discussion offer us a suitable case study of communist theories of proletarian culture. And against the background of this discussion we should be able to understand better the way in which cultural and leisure-time activities in the communist movement were directed and organised.

Literature and Ideology

The foundation of the BPRS followed quickly on the international conference of proletarian-revolutionary writers held in Moscow in 1927. A small German delegation under J.R. Becher had attended the conference, and after their return they formed a preparatory committee. Through the publication *Proletarische Feuilleton Korrespondenz* they sent out a manifesto through which they sought to mobilise support for the formation of an organisation along the

30. The two national organisations were the Schutzverband deutscher Schriftsteller and the Reichswirtschaftsverband Bildender Künstler Deutschlands. For the Russian organisations of writers see H. Möbius, *Progressive Massenliteratur*, Stuttgart, 1977, pp. 9–15.
31. Of the membership of the BPRS some 30% were workers, while 60% were classified as petty-bourgeois. One quarter were described as journalists, and only 1% were full-time writers who lived from their pen. Members of the KPD accounted for 40% of the membership, but only 1.5% belonged to other parties of the Left.

lines of the Russian writers' organisation RAPP (later VAPP). Help for the launch also came through the Arbeitsgemeinschaft kommunistischer Schriftsteller, a communist caucus in the German Writers' Defence Society' (Schutzverband deutscher Schriftsteller). Figures for the national membership of the BPRS vary from 500 to 800; but only Berlin had any sort of formal organisation, and it was also Berlin which furnished the national leadership'.[32]

Following the example of the Russian association the BPRS saw it as one of its main tasks to create imaginative literature for the German working class which would be consistent with the party's ideological position, and to counter the 'false values' of bourgeois writing. In the view of the league the proletariat needed literature which would lay bare the evils of existing society and fill the masses with revolutionary fervour, while at the same time engaging the hearts and the minds of its readers, schooling them to prepare for the revolution.[33]

From the start leading members of the organisation were concerned about the nature of this literature and what group of writers were best qualified to produce it. These two topics became the group's most important subjects for discussion, and they were dealt with extensively in the *Linkskurve*, the journal started by the BPRS in 1929 and published until 1932, with financial assistance from the Russian International Bureau for revolutionary literature. The discussion had already started among members of the 'Action Committee' of the communist writers within the German Writers' Union. To show the talents of the new working-class authors to a wider public the 'Action Committee' organised a *Literarische Morgenfeier* in which six proletarian authors read from their works. Commenting on the experiment the *Rote Fahne* wrote that 'the workers need no longer order their songs and poems from the bourgeoisie. Today the proletariat has its own poets, and where once the sympathising bourgeois enthused audiences there stands today the man from the shop floor.'[34]

Whether the work of budding proletarian poets and novelists was the only relevant literature for the working class, and whether bourgeois authors, especially non-communists, still had a place in the cultural tradition of the proletariat, was one of the underlying issues which concerned the 'proletarian-revolutionary' writers. In

32. Cf. E. Simons, 'Der Bund proletarisch revolutionärer Schriftsteller Deutschlands', in A. Klein (ed.), *Literatur der Arbeiterklasse*, Berlin, 1974, pp. 110–91.
33. From the *Aktionsprogramm* of the BPRS in *Zur Tradition der deutschen sozialistischen Literatur*, 4 vols, Berlin, 1979, vol. 1, p. 138.
34. *RF* of 31 March 1928, cited in Simons, (note 32), p. 165.

political terms the discussion never reached a clear-cut conclusion, and the League, which only met twice during its short life – at the inaugural meeting in 1928 and at a 'Working Conference' in 1932, which was however not formally representative of the membership – never agreed on a substantive programme. A series of ideas on the subject were published in a paper called 'Guidelines for communist writers', which had been submitted to the League's inaugural meeting; but its tenets did not meet with general approval.[35] Despite this the 'Guidelines' are an important statement of communist cultural policy, and their basic approach is probably in accord with the views of the KPD.

The guidelines rejected the view, expressed most strongly by Trotsky, that a proletarian culture could arise only when the working class had attained power. No doubt 'the victorious proletarian revolution conquers the whole of the arts [and] raises them to a level undreamt of in capitalist countries'.[36] This, it was argued, had already been largely achieved in the Soviet Union; but even outside Russia the proletariat, thanks to the vigour with which it had conducted the class struggle, had by now reached a stage at which it could, in some areas, pursue cultural activity independently. And this not only as the consumers of culture but also as possible producers. The organisation and the economic power of the proletariat was not sufficiently strong to engage in the production of cultural media which required large capital investments; but there were cultural areas where the working class could be active as producers. Literature was one of these areas.

Bourgeois literature, contaminated by the capitalist and imperialist spirit in which it developed, could not provide this need, despite its protestations about its political neutrality. It was unable to deal fully with current economic and social problems, and where it was not reactionary it was weak and divorced from reality, a fact for which it sought to compensate by an apparent richness in colour and content and by a verbal radicalism.[37] In addition the workers' literary needs could not be met by professional writers who sympathised with the proletariat however critical or 'objective' they might claim to be. The author who writes for a working-class audience at a time when the class struggle is becoming more and

---

35. Simons (note 32), p. 169. For the partly critical reception of the guidelines in the communist *Fraktion* of the BPRS see the report of the BPRS (for 1929) in *Zur Tradition* (note 33) pp. 180–194, p. 182.
36. BPRS Entwurf von Richtlinien, in Klein (see note 33), vol. 1, pp. 630–41, p. 631.
37. Ibid. pp. 634–5.

more accentuated must 'without reservation rest on the standpoint of the avant-garde of the proletariat.' The great proletarian literature could therefore only be created from within the working class, although this could include in its ranks members of other classes who had identified fully with the revolutionary proletariat and had put their artistic talents fully at the service of the class struggle.[38]

At the same time the BPRS realised that mere membership of the working class coupled with literary skills was not enough to create a revolutionary author, and that a correct class-consciousness was an essential prerequisite. The League hoped that the great proletarian writers would arise from the group of Workers' Correspondents and those active in the workers' theatre movement.[39]

The strict application of communist ideology as the criterion of proletarian literature, and the rejection of the work of all bourgeois authors, unless they had completely identified with the party, became a matter of some disagreement during the discussion of the guidelines. The two issues run like a red thread through the discussions of literary policy within the BPRS, and the debate was continued after 1933 among the communist *émigrés* and within the international communist writers' movement.

The BPRS appealed above all to 'Workers' Correspondents', who formed a significant part of its early membership. The 'Correspondents' expected therefore that the League would be an organisation which would not be dominated by the *Prominenz* – established and widely praised communist writers like J.R. Becher. They expected help to get out of their isolation, strengthen their self-confidence, help them improve their literary skills and in general offer encouragement and comradeship. 'The proletarian-revolutionary novel, poem or drama', wrote Karl Grünberg, himself on the road to becoming a full-time writer, 'cannot flourish in the closet. We wish to be printed and read – and criticised' – a task which the organisation was expected to perform.[40]

Some of these writers saw in the act of reporting from the centre of the struggle in the factories or elsewhere something which already constituted an example of proletarian literature. Such literature, it was claimed, was already 'developed by tens of thousands of workers who need no publisher or presses . . . they have only stencils and duplicating machines'. The factory news-sheets

---

38. Ibid. p. 636.
39. Ibid. p. 637.
40. Cf. Karl Grünberg, 'Was erwartet der proletarisch-revolutionäre Schriftsteller vom Bund', in *Zur Tradition* (see note 33), vol. 1, pp. 124–8, p. 127. Grünberg was one of the founder-members of the League.

which they produced, and their exposures relating to the daily life of the class were in this view the foundation of the new literature, a combatant's literature to strike out at the enemy. 'The proletarian revolutionary literature can be no more, no less than the struggle of the working class is.' And it could only be created by those who were engaged in that struggle – that is, the proletariat itself.[41]

Such a populist view of proletarian literature was not widely shared. It was generally agreed that the worker-author should seek to described all facets of working-class life and register all its emotions. The would-be proletarian writer must learn his craft just like other writers, learning from the revolutionary literature of the past, whether bourgeois or working class.[42] But the workers' correspondents would have to unlearn some of the practices used in reporting, and describe events and persons in a natural popular language, discarding the didactic approach they had used until then. 'A straightforward report of a strike for the factory news-sheet can be more significant for the class struggle than a master-piece of proletarian literature, but that did not elevate such a report to the level of proletarian literature and the proletarian reporter does not suddenly become a proletarian writer.'[43]

Literature for the working class was not just the didactic pieces produced by the workers' correspondents for the communist press. The working class would not reduce its aesthetic and emotional demands for literature to such a narrow field. The discussion on the character and role of proletarian literature assumed that even the tired but politically strongly committed worker wished for a higher level of culture, and the satisfaction of this kind of demand should not be left to (classical) bourgeois literature. 'Our new literature can only arise when the writer not only seeks to get to know proletarian science but when he is convinced of it . . . and feels involved and able to participate in the class struggle as his own struggle.'[44]

The Hungarian *émigré* author and critic, Andre Gabor, who was one of the editors of the *Linkskurve*, stressed that the proletarian writer would only be able to carry out his task as a *full-time* author. This would be the only way to enable him to combine the experience of the workers' struggle from the standpoint of the revol-

41. Cf. Erich Steffen, 'Die Urzelle proletarischer Literatur', *Linkskurve*, 1930 no. 2, reprinted in Klein (see note 23), pp. 649–52.
42. Cf. N. Kraus (i.e. Josef Lenz), 'Gegen den Oekonomismus in der Literatur', *Linkskurve*, 1929 no. 3, pp. 10–12, reprinted in Klein (note 23), pp. 652–5.
43. Ibid. p. 654.
44. Cf. Andor Gabor, 'Über proletarisch-revolutionäre Literatur', *Linkskurve*, 1929 no. 3, pp. 3–6.

utionary class with a knowledge of revolutionary theory in all its ramifications.[45] This did not imply that literature should replace revolutionary theory; but it meant that the task of the revolutionary writers' movement was 'to educate poets, writers and novelists who in their work have digested and absorbed the writings of Marx, Engels and Lenin, so that they forge their *belles lettres* into a weapon of the class struggle.'[46] They should do so 'without turning such literature into political pamphlets because then the very readers who read it as fiction will put it down in favour of that [bourgeois] literature which works against us without the reader noticing it'.

This concept of the role of the proletarian writer became more widely accepted within the BPRS as it, and the policy of the KPD, moved to the left. It meant that the bourgeois writer, however strong his political commitment, was increasingly cast in the role of the midwife whose task was merely to assist in the creation of proletarian literature by helping the budding worker-author to develop literary skills and establish himself as a professional writer.

Although the size of the proletarian literature which had been created by that time was small, its very existence instilled great confidence in some. Aladar Komjat and Karl Biro argued that proletarian literature was superior to bourgeois writing even in absolute terms. In the draft platform for the BPRS they argued that although the new working-class literature was 'still young, its quality was today already much higher than bourgeois or social-democratic literary and artistic production. The latter distorts and falsifies reality while proletarian literature and art reflects reality in the light of dialectical materialism and seeks to change it.'[47]

Komjat's and Biro's statement was circulated within the BPRS in September 1931; but it never became the official policy of the League. It was soon attacked by the KPD leadership, and, following them, by the communist cell within the BPRS. It was also attacked by the International Bureau for Revolutionary Literature in Moscow.[48] The criticism was directed at the bland and unself-

45. Ibid.
46. BPRS *Bericht* (see note 35), p. 192.
47. From an unpublished draft of the Platform for the BPRS cited from the original MS by S. Roshnowski, 'Die Dialektik von Parteilichkeit und Realismus', in Klein (note 32), pp. 442–541, p. 527.
48. Cf. F. Albrecht and K. Kandler, *Der Bund proletarisch-revolutionärer Schriftsteller Deutschlands, 1928–1935*, Leipzig, 1978, pp. 76–82; H. Gallas, *Marxistische Literaturtheorie*, Neuwied, 1971, pp. 56–64. The Russian criticism was in line with the Communist Party's attitude towards the RAPP, the Soviet counterpart to the BPRS. This led to the dissolution of the latter in 1932.

critical and 'ultra left' assertions about the superiority of existing proletarian literature, and at the excessively negative attitude towards the work of bourgeois authors.

What was now demanded was a greater sympathy towards bourgeois 'sympathisers'. writers who were as yet outside the League. Conversely, excessive praise for the work of the worker correspondents was to be avoided.[49] The official line now called for an end to the overestimation of the artistic standards and of the political sophistication of the workers' literature which had been produced so far. The 'official' proposal of a programme for the League drawn up by a Programme Committee, which was strongly influenced by the poet J.R. Becher, laid considerably less stress on the earlier assertions of the superiority of proletarian writing as such.[50] It admitted that proletarian literature had not yet managed to influence the masses to any great extent, and that, although the Marxist-Leninist ideology was clearly superior to that of the bourgeoisie, 'the inferior weapon of the latter is handled [by the bourgeoisie] better than we handle ours'.[51]

Furthermore, the Programme Committee concluded that the literature so far produced had not really satisfied the objective needs of the masses. The new Communist tactics promulgated in 1931 were now developed in terms of the concept of a 'people's revolution', which was to be extended to include peasants and members of the petty bourgeoisie within its ambit. And consequently it was to be one of the tasks of the new literature now called for to convince these newly revolutionary strata that their future, too, lay in an alliance with the revolutionary proletariat.

In general proletarian literature still lacked this power of persuasion. Individual works combined ideological clarity with artistic truthfulness, but in many cases they failed 'to present the troubles, hopes and wishes, the sufferings and the struggles of the members of present-day society in such a way that the horizon of the reader is widened and that the questions which he had already put to himself, but was unable to answer, are answered clearly and convincingly'. Instead the literature was too often narrow and dull. 'It photographed the events instead of creating them, it comments in the style of resolutions instead of letting the conclusions develop

49. From the 'Resolution des Sekretariats des Z.(entral) K.(omité) der KPD zur Arbeit des Bundes . . .', in *Zur Tradition* (see note 33), vol. 1, pp. 40–3.
50. Cf. H. Gallas (see note 48), pp. 61–2.
51. 'Entwurf zu einem Programm des Bundes . . .', in *Zur Tradition* (see note 33), vol. 1, pp. 414–39, p. 429.

[naturally] out of the narrative.'[52]

This self-criticism did not really come to grips with the problems of providing a mass literature, which was now considered of major importance by the BPRS, and, following its new tactics, by the Communist Party itself.[53] The proletarian writers had hitherto not succeeded in providing a counter-attraction to the widely popular but trashy 'popular' literature published by bourgeois presses in vast editions. The latter included romantic fiction and detective and adventure stories which were produced by giant publishing houses such as Scherl and Ullstein. Apart from its low literary value, this literature was held to corrupt the worker emotionally and intellectually, by portraying a world of glitter and success, or by telling stories of self-made men which the poor but industrious need only emulate, or by implicitly or explicitly extolling nationalist and militarist values.[54]

The new mass literature which was to be created was expected to counter the ideological threats from mass editions. At the same time the BPRS regarded it as essential that the new literature should have a widespread popular appeal, encompassing the whole family, and that it should deal with a wider range of topics and heroes than had so far been the case with the proletarian novel.

Not that proletarian writers should imitate the low standards of pulp literature. The proletariat was thought to be capable of absorbing more demanding reading, and to provide them with 'trash and pulp dyed red', said Johannes Becher, underestimated the capabilities of the masses.[55]

The clamour for mass-produced popular fiction had two consequences – an experiment in mass publishing, and, following on this experiment, a sustained discussion about the appropriate form for such a literature. The publishing enterprise took the form of a series of cheap novels, the *Rote Eine Mark Romane*, issued in editions of 20,000–25,000 copies in paperback, and, as the title of the series suggest, sold for one mark.[56] The publishers, the *Neue Deutsche*

52. Ibid. p. 431.
53. Resolution (see note 49). See also J.R. Becher's speech at the Russian Writers' Congress at Charkow, in *Zur Tradition* (see note 33), vol. 1, pp. 291–3.
54. Otto Biha, 'Der proletarische Massenroman', *RF* 2 August 1930, reprinted in M. Brauneck (see note 5), pp. 404–6.
55. J.R. Becher, 'Unsere Wendung', *Linkskurve*, 1931, no. 10, pp. 1–8, in *Zur Tradition* (see note 33), vol. 1, pp. 409–23, p. 418.
56. The *Neuer Deutscher Verlag* was part of the successful Münzenberg publishing empire, which also published the AIZ. It was difficult to sell these titles. Booksellers were unwilling to stock them, and they were generally distributed

Verlag, issued a total of nine novels before Hitler's rise to power. All but one of the nine dealt with contemporary themes, with life at the factory floor, in the mines, and in the tenement block. The authors were found in a talent-scouting expedition by Becher and by Kurt Kläber, the editor of the series, and they came mainly from the ranks of the Workers' Correspondents.

We know little about the impact made by the series. There are reports that criticism evenings took place in Berlin in connection with the 'Month of the Proletarian Book'; but no record exists. Kläber hoped that the novels would be regarded as 'literature for the proletarian struggle and agitation'; but he had to admit that the bulk of the one to two million potential purchasers would look at the books as mere recreational reading. Indeed, he thought that many were probably bought for show or even as collectors' items, 'to be put into the imitation oak bookcase behind polished glass doors'.[57] He admitted that in order to create a mass public for the proletarian novel the prejudices and misconceptions of the traditional reader would have to be overcome. He would have to learn to identify, not with individual heroes or with the tribulations of a particular human psyche, but with the collective will and the collective action of the fighting proletariat.[58]

The ultimate aim of the new literature was the creation of the great proletarian work of art, 'which sought to describe the everyday of the proletariat in conjunction with that of the other classes in such a way that in [and through] an account of everyday life it outlined the major forces of social developments as they emerge and are made obvious.'[59] This did not mean, however, that such a work should necessarily take a form similar to the nineteenth-century social novel; but it was to be a sign that the proletariat was claiming a predominant place in the field of literature. Such a claim should equally apply to what was termed the 'little open form' of literature, such as reportage or the short story, comment or sketch, used either singly or in a series of loosely-connected scenes, or of documentary pieces, as distinct from the 'large closed form' of the traditional novel. This 'little open form' was the kind of writing

---

through the organisations of the KPD. They were thus acquired more by activists than by the non-committed.

57. Kurt Kläber, 'Der proletarische Massenroman', *Linkskurve*, May 1930, p. 23, cited in F. Schonauer, 'Die Partei und die schöne Literatur', in W. Rothe (ed.), *Die deutsche Literatur in der Weimarer Republik*, Stuttgart, 1974, pp. 114–42.
58. Cf. J.R. Becher's Introduction to the Russian edition of his *Levisite oder der einzige gerechte Krieg*, quoted in H. Gallas (see note 48).
59. Entwurf (as note 51), p. 423.

which the workers' correspondents had practised, and which had been used in the plays produced by the Agitprop Theatre.[60] The alleged veracity and persuasiveness of this literature, and the scope which it gave for ideological commentary had put it high in the canon of literature advocated in the BPRS.

In general the theories of literature developed by the BPRS stressed the importance of content as against form. Preoccupation with the latter was regarded as typical of the obfuscating tendencies of bourgeois literature. But in widening the potential audience, and working towards the creation of mass literature, questions of form and presentation came to be discussed. The documentary form, which emerged from the daily struggle and referred to it, seemed here the most appropriate means to interest and engage the masses. Dialectical materialism called for an emphasis on the factual, as against the psychologising techniques of bourgeois literature, which only aimed to create a fiction of reality. The dialectical realism of proletarian literature, using the techniques of documentation, on the other hand, would justify what is narrated and make it verifiable. By such means, generally combined with a commentary, the literature sought to inform and to activate the reader.[61]

The League was not unaware of the difficulties and possible shortcomings of these techniques, especially in respect of the short-story type of literature, which, it was admitted, could so easily decline into the superficial and the banal.[62] It urged authors not to overlook the wider context of the subject of their writing. The novels produced by the majority of proletarian writers, and by bourgeois writers addressing a proletarian audience, however, used the documentary form. The failure to use the techniques of the social novel, and the shortcomings of documentary forms of literature, caused the literary critic Georg Lukács to attack the new proletarian literature. The attack, from a literary as well as from an ideological point of view, came in a series of articles in the *Linkskurve* at the end of 1931 and during 1932. In these Lukács analysed the work of two authors in the new 'One-Mark Novels' series, Willi Bredel and Ernst Ottwalt.[63]

In the documentary character of Willi Bredel's novels, and, by implication, those of other writers, Lukács objected not to the use

60. Gallas, (see note 48), pp. 94–95. For the Agitprop theatre see Chapter 8.
61. Ibid. pp. 128–9.
62. Entwurf (as note 51) p. 433.
63. The novels in question were Willi Bredel's *Maschinenfabrik N & K* and *Die Rosenhofstraße*, and Karl Ottwalt's *Denn sie wissen nicht was sie tun*. For Lukács' articles and Bredel's reply see reprint in Klein (note 32).

of formal material (reports, resolutions) as such, but to the fact that the same formal language is used in the description of personal relationships and in the conversations of the actors. He praised the structure of the novels, the fact that the relationships of the proletariat and the other classes were described in real-life situations, but condemned a narration that was cast in part as reportage and which reads, in part, like press reports of meetings. 'The skeleton of the action remains a skeleton; that which could make it come alive, real people and changing relationships between them, is completely lacking', he added.[64] For Lukács this was not primarily the result of inadequate literary skills but rather the lack of dialectical insight, and of the insight that changes do not occur suddenly but slowly, as the result of changing human relationships and as the outcome of a gradual learning process. Bredel short-circuited this process showing the results and not the process itself.[65]

Lukács made a more generalised criticism of the literary form of documentary techniques by comparing it with the techniques of narrative fiction. He saw these new forms as inartistic, and linked to a petty-bourgeois understanding of the world. Their persuasive powers were related to the sciences, because their power to convince was working analogously to that of the sciences, by relying on comparability and reasoning.[66] He contrasted this method with the creation of fictional characters, where the interrelationships of individuals' fates complement and illuminate each other. Although details may be incorrect, the whole becomes 'typical and significant'.[67] Truth in respect of the individual character thus becomes a kind of essential truth. Unlike the truth of reportage, which relies on the fact that it may be verified, it may be incorrect in every detail, yet realistic and true in terms of the total process. Lukács admitted that a 'realistic' account of the basic processes in society called for the writer to have a proletarian-revolutionary background. Thus only the working-class author can write the great proletarian novel; but the progressive writers of the great social novels of the revolutionary period of the bourgeoisie had demonstrated a less developed form of insight. The reportage novel, on the other hand, is appropriate to the petty-bourgeois

64. Cf. G. Lukács, 'Willi Bredel's Romane', *Linkskurve*, 1931 no. 11, pp. 23–7, reprinted in Klein (see note 32), pp. 715–27, p. 722.
65. Ibid. p. 725.
66. 'Science' in the German sense of the word relates to all disciplines, not only the natural sciences.
67. Cf. G. Lukács, 'Reportage und Gestaltung', *Linkskurve*, 1932 nos. 7 and 8, pp. 23–30; 26–31; and in *Zur Tradition*, (see note 33), pp. 499–523, p. 506.

writers whose opposition to capitalism is limited by their inability to understand the totality of social processes.[68]

Lukács' argument is a strong assertion of the value of fictional narrative and of the creation of rounded and developing characters for the proletariat. He expected the reader to understand these characters by a process of empathy, and he rejected the 'fetishism of facts', however formally objective, which, by giving formal political statements to the reader, was meant to persuade him to action. Lukács did not disagree with this as an aim; but he thought that literature which followed the techniques of realistic description, especially in the form of the novel, would uncover historical processes in depth. This was consonant with a dialectical understanding, which was 'the recognition and representation of the historical process as the . . . totality of its real determining forces, as a constant and elevated reproduction of its innate dialectical contradictions.'[69] In this connection Lukács quoted with approval Friedrich Engels, who credits Balzac with the intention of praising the disappearing class of the *Ancien Régime*, but being forced against his own class sympathies and political prejudices to give an exhaustive and correct picture of contemporary society.[70]

These discussions would not warrant resurrecting if they had not led to further discussions and controversies and if they had not raised fundamental problems of aesthetics and of communist cultural policy. The discussion of the appropriate cultural forms for the ideological persuasion of the working class and for the preparation of the revolutionary struggle was continued after 1933 in the so-called *Expressionismusdebatte*, conducted by *émigré* communist writers and others in the communist journal *Das Wort* (Moscow 1936–38).[71] It was a debate on whether expressionism had contributed to the rise of fascism, and a discussion on the value of experimental and introspective literature as such.

At this point literary theory became linked with the question of the appropriate constellation of forces to resist the spread of fascism and counter the danger of war. At the same time literary theory becomes related to Soviet, and later to other communist, literary

---

68. Lukács was thinking here in particular of writings by nineteenth-century authors, such as Eugène Suë and Victor Hugo, who had used such documentary techniques. Cf. Gallas (note 48), pp. 152–3.
69. Lukács, 'Tendenz oder Parteilichkeit', *Linkskurve*, 1932 no. 6, pp. 13–21, p. 20, reprinted in *Zur Tradition* (see note 33), pp. 479–99.
70. Ibid.
71. The relevant articles are reprinted in H.J. Schmitt (ed.), *Die Expressionismusdebatte. Materialien zu einer marxistischen Realismuskonzeption*, Frankfurt, 1978.

policy. In 1932 Stalin had proclaimed 'the advent of Socialism in Russia', and with it the alleged end to class antagonism and factional conflict. Translated into the field of literature this meant that the demand for a literature with a revolutionary message was to be replaced by the literature of Socialist Realism, which was henceforth seen as the criterion by which the literature past and present was to be judged. This change of ideological direction meant that on the social plane it was not the social background of a writer, but his willingness to support and extol the party line, which was the criterion of correctness for literary creation.

In Western Europe a similar widening of the circle of writers and other intellectuals whose writings were accepted into the canons of communist literary orthodoxy occurred as the result of the movement's Popular Front policy. This sought to unite men and women of different backgrounds and following different literary styles under the banner of a broad anti-fascist cultural movement.

Popular-front tactics and the identification of the interests of the working masses with the interests of the Soviet Union led to the abandonment of the doctrine, to which even Lukács had seemed to subscribe, that only the writer who through his background and formative experiences was firmly anchored in the proletariat was capable of creating a socialist literature. Proletarian-revolutionary writing was now conceived politically rather than sociologically, and became dependent on the political identification of the writer with the cause of the proletariat rather than on his class background.

This politically-inspired change in communist thought, which came into being essentially as the result of tactical considerations, was naturally strengthened by the literary critique developed by Georg Lukács and others, which brought the great social-realist novelists of the nineteenth century into the canon of literature which was suitable for the working class.[72] Thus in a strange way the discussion about the bourgeois heritage returns to its point of departure within the German social-democratic movement.

The Cultural System of Democratic Centralism

We have looked at the communist attitude to culture in its theoretical aspects; we must now look at the organisational framework

---

72. Lukács developed his theories and made them more concrete in his *Studies in European Realism*, London, 1950 (reprinted 1972).

and at the changing tactics employed by the KPD. Here too the new party was to strike out in new directions. The roots of German communism were within Social Democracy. Soon, however, the organisation and the policy-making process began to follow that of the Russian Communist Party.[73] Following it, the KPD adopted the model of Democratic Centralism for its organisational structure. Although the party built up a mass membership, which peaked at 359,000 in 1927, it was absolutely and relatively never as large as that of the SPD.[74] Moreover, the KPD membership was subject to considerable fluctuation. This hindered the rise of strong local organisations, and made the central direction of party activities easier.

Instead of locality-based organisations the party sought to build up stronger organisations at factory, street, or block level. These were subject to control by local or district leaderships, which were themselves largely appointed and controlled by the centre.[75] There was therefore less scope for the development of the cultural pluralism which we find within the SPD, especially if we include trade union influence and activities. And in accord with this it is not surprising that the formal structure of cultural activities within the German Communist Party and its ancillary organisations and their control was more politicised and more centralised than elsewhere in the German labour movement.

Although the KPD formulated a cultural policy in very general terms fairly early in its existence, it did not establish cultural or leisure-time organisations until much later. By that time the pyramidal structure of the party had been well established, and the power of the party centre, of the Central Committee, or ZK (Zentral-Komité), and, controlling it, the Polbüro (Political Bureau), and, finally, the power of the Secretariat, consisting of only three or four persons, was gradually strengthened until it became virtually dictatorial. Party statutes laid down that the lower authorities were strictly subordinated to the higher ones, and this was reinforced by a rigid system of party discipline. This control applied not only to the descending levels of party leadership, but

---

73. On the structure of the German Communist Party see H. Weber, *Die Wandlungen des deutschen Kommunismus*, 2 vols, Frankfurt, 1969, vol. 1, pp. 249–359.
74. The membership figures for the two parties between 1922 and 1932 show the following maxima and minima: SPD 1,180,000 and 806,000; KPD 359,000 and 127,000.
75. The total number of persons employed by the KPD in 1927 was 2,348. Of these the majority were employees of the communist press. Political employees were estimated at *c*. 500. Cf. Weber (note 73) (one-vol. edn) pp. 266–7.

also to its major functional subdivisions, the departments – of which the *Agitprop* (Agitation and Propaganda) division is particularly relevant in our context – and to the ancillary and formally independent organisations discussed below.

The comparatively late (1928–) establishment of more specific cultural organisations under the direction of, or in close association with, the Communist Party must be seen in the context of changing views on the role of education and culture in the whole field of party activities described earlier.[76] In its early years the KPD acquiesced in the fact that the existing working-class cultural organisations, which had traditionally identified with the SPD, continued to attract communist members. This was in line with the party's general policy of creating a 'united front from below'. The general political discussion which took place inside the left during these years therefore found an echo in the political discussions within these organisations. The Communist Party believed that this discussion, and the application of pressure from communist members in these organisations, would bring about a realignment of policies, and, eventually, an alliance of them with the communist movement.

Such a policy was based on the assumption that popular pressure would force the SPD to shed its reformist wing and adopt a more radical course.[77] The grass-roots movement would then be paralleled by a policy of a 'united front from above'. The KPD did not therefore, during these early years, encourage the secession of ancillary organisations or the splitting-off of groups from them. Indeed, in the only instance where a section of an existing organisation – namely of the Arbeiter Samaritaner Bund (The Workers' Samaritans) – seceded as the result of communist opposition, the new body, the Proletarische Gesundheitsdienst (Proletarian Health Service) proved to be too small to be viable.[78] Future communist policy in the cultural field followed the party's general strategy closely. Thus in its new 'left' line after 1926/7 the KPD abandoned

76. The details of this development and its application at the local level have as yet only been partially covered in the literature. But see H. Wunderer, *Arbeitervereine und Arbeiterparteien. Kultur und Massenorganisationen in der Arbeiterbewegung, 1890–1933*, Frankfurt, 1980. In spite of its title the book deals largely with communist organisations since *c.* 1923.
77. On Communist policy and practice see also Weber (note 73); O. Flechtheim, *Die KPD in der Weimarer Republik*, Frankfurt, 1969 and later edns.
78. The Proletarische Gesundheitsdienst was mainly concerned with the provision of first aid at meetings, etc. It was founded in 1921 and dissolved in 1924. Cf. A. Labisch, 'The Workingmen's Samaritan Federation, 1888–1933', *Journal of Contemporary History*, 1978, pp. 297–322.

its 'unity from below' policy and started to develop mass-membership organisations in the cultural field.

Under the slogan 'into the masses' the party attempted to mobilise and convert workers who were organised in bourgeois or social-democratic cultural or leisure-time organisations, and to encourage them to join separate communist-inspired bodies. In the words of A. Kuusinen, a leading official of the Communist International, what was needed was the creation of 'a whole solar system of organisation around the communist party itself'.[79] What kind of organisation did not seem to matter too much to the party leadership.

When the party discussed the problem of the ancillary organisations at its eleventh National Conference in Essen in 1927 W. Schneller, the principal speaker, drew attention to the fact that the membership of bourgeois cultural organisations vastly exceeded that of the organisations identified with the working class. He argued that it was essential to draw the workers away from those organisations, with their insiduous influence on the political consciousness and commitment of the working class. Schneller suggested that the importance of joining the relevant kind of organisation was not always recognised even by committed communists. He pointed to the discrepancy between the size of the party membership and that of the communist youth organisation.

On the other hand there was a danger that cultural activities would cause workers to neglect their political duties. There were party members, even functionaries, who regarded themselves as sportsmen or freethinkers in the first instance and as communists only after that. Such attitudes had to be changed. Comrades active in the cultural organisations of the Social Democracy must recognise that these organisations should not concern themselves only with sport. They should politicise them, and work against the reformist ideology which permeated them. 'No subject was too small or too old-fashioned not to be cultivated by the party and for the working-class adherents in the 'bourgeois' organisations to be won over to the new organisations.'[80]

The Essen conference proposed the establishment of a *Rote Kulturkampffront*, but, as the name 'cultural fighting front' indicates, the thrust was directed as much at what the KPD regarded as the 'reactionary' cultural policies of the SPD – let alone those of the bourgeois institutions – as at the establishment of their own cultural

79. INPREKOR, 6 April 1926, p. 275.
80. Cf. KPD 11. Parteitag, *Thesen und Resolutionen*, Berlin, 1979, p. 64.

organisations.[81] It is also significant that the reference was to cultural *policy* rather than to cultural activities, and the decisions of the conference were implemented only slowly. It was only in November 1928 that a circular urged the districts to establish cultural secretariats 'to maintain the connection with the Central Committee and to deal with all matters pertaining to educational and cultural policy'.[82]

The Essen Conference also resolved that communists in the new cultural organisations should bear in mind the realisation of the organisations' aims as well as of the need to create 'a direct link between these tasks and the struggle of the whole of the proletariat and of all those who work'.[83] In this dual approach it was, however, the political struggle rather than the cultural pursuits which gained the upper hand, and the political element gradually came to overlay the purported cultural purpose of these organisations.

The struggle generally began inside the social-democratic organisations, where the oppositionist policies of committed communists brought about their control of individual clubs and of some local organisations. Such bodies seceded or were expelled from the larger organisations by the latter's social-democratic leadership – a process which the KPD decried as 'splitting'.

Thus the Hamburg district of the KPD reported in 1929 that 'the Workers' Radio Club was in the hands of the SPD', and the current communist policy consisted only in attempting to ensure that its members should be represented in the weekly broadcasts addressed to workers. The 'Worker-Photographers' Organisation' (Arbeiterfotografen), on the other hand, 'was in the hands of the KPD' – hardly surprising, as it had been started under communist auspices. Elsewhere the situation was more fluid. Thus among the group of 'Worker Guitar Players' (Arbeiter-Mandolinisten Klub), the report went on, 'our influence is comparatively strong. The leadership of the organisation is in the hands of party members or sympathisers.'[84] The means for securing communist influence was generally the result of the establishment of communist *Fraktionen* – 'formally organised factions' of Communist Party members inside the organisations. Their task was to ensure that these bodies pursued a policy which was in opposition to that of the social-

---

81. Ibid. p. 69.
82. Cf. D. Heinemann, *Proletarische Kulturvereine in der Weimarer Republik*, Diss. Halle, 1981. The districts (*Parteibezirke*) were the largest territorial units of the KPD below the national level.
83. *Thesen und Resolutionen* (see note 80) p. 65.
84. KPD Bezirk Wasserkante, *Bericht 1929*, p. 77.

democratic leadership, and that, in cases where a society had already seceded, the policy of the new organisation followed the Communist Party line as closely as possible. The *Fraktionen* constituted effective voting blocks, and sought to take over the leadership of the organisations. They were possibly even more important in the new communist-inspired cultural organisations. On the other hand, their repeated failure to work effectively was cited by local Communist Party organisations as a reason why the power of the SPD leadership had not been broken. In the Hamburg district the 'factional' activities, even in the cultural organisations in sympathy with the KPD, were described in 1932 as 'completely unsatisfactory', and there were widespread complaints about the inadequate work of communists in the social-democratic sports organisations, although, as we shall see, it was in this area that the communists could claim most success.[85]

We can only assume that the membership of the new oppositional groups was still interested in athletic pursuits and in the establishment of social ties. The leadership of the KPD, on the other hand, saw these new ancillary organisations primarily as additions to the political troops of the movement. This policy was in line with that established in the older mass organisations of the party. Apart from the communist youth movement – the KJVD or Kommunistischer Jugend Verband Deutschlands, later known simply as Kommunistische Jugend – we are primarily concerned with three bodies: the IAH, the Internationale Arbeiter Hilfe (International Workers' Aid), whose task was to render social assistance to workers, and in particular to combat hunger in Russia; the Rote Hilfe or 'Red Aid', the communist support-organisation for those charged with political offences and to provide help for the victims of strikes and for political prisoners and their families; and finally the Rote Frontkämpfer Bund (RFB) – the 'Red Fighters' Front'. The official function of this last was to act as guards for political meetings and demonstrations; but its members were equally attracted by the social life of the organisation.

These older organisations were set along a course running in parallel with the party. Their specific tasks would serve some of the interests of the KPD; but, being less obviously political in character, they could also attract the support of people who would not readily join the party. The IAH, in particular, was very successful in this, thanks largely to the organising and publicising genius of its Secretary, Willi Munzenberg. It formed the basis for public ven-

85. KPD Bezirk Wasserkante, *Bericht 1932*, p. 149.

Table 4 The membership of communist mass organisations during the
Weimar period

ASSO	350–800
BPRS	800
Rote Hilfe	44,347ª–307,971[+]
Rote Frontkämpferbund	44,450ª–127,000
IAH	12,000ª– 45,000ª
Rotsport	100,000 –113,542ª
Kampfgemeinschaft der Arbeitersänger	15,000 – 20,000[b]
Arbeiterfotografen	2,400ª
Arbeiter Theaterbund	no individual members
Freier Arbeiter Radio Bund	3,000
Kommunistischer Jugendverband (KJVD)	18,377ª– 40,000

Notes: Figures are generally subject to considerable fluctuation. Maximum and
minimum figures are given in case of considerable variation.
   [+] Includes collective affiliations
   a Figures derived from Weber and Wunderer
   b According to I. Lammel, *Arbeiterklasse und Musik*, 1974 p. 56

tures in the entertainment and publishing fields which reached far
beyond the narrow circles of the KPD. While much of this was
concerned with propaganda for the Soviet Union, itself the main
beneficiary of IAH help, it eventually ranged much more widely in
the cultural field. Above all, it was raising mass support from the
ranks of the working class and beyond which would not otherwise
have identified with the communist cause. The hope of the KPD
was that such affiliators to formally independent mass organisations
would in time become its direct supporters.[86]

   The second wave of foundations of communist ancillary organisations, covering the cultural field, was also expected to follow this
pattern. They sought to recruit and mobilise the oppositional forces
within the existing cultural associations, wean their members away
from social-democratic thinking, and give them a formal status
within the communist orbit. As Table 4 shows, the new cultural
organisations were generally small, and the membership figures of
the larger associations were often swollen through collective affiliations by other organisations. Membership dues were low, if only
to enable the unemployed, particularly numerous in the KPD, to
join. But this in turn meant that funds for actual cultural activities
were limited.

   Compared with some of the older 'communist' mass-organis-

86. KPD Parteitag 1927, *Bericht*, p. 263.

ations, and compared with their social-democratic parent bodies, these new organisations were really quite small. They sometimes comprised only a number of specialists in their particular fields, rather than an open and active membership organisation. Formally the new foundations did indeed form a 'planetary system' around the communist sun; but by comparison with the dense network of cultural organisations on the socialist side their movement was less vigorous.

Only the Kampfgemeinschaft für Arbeitersport, the communist sports organisation, managed to attract a mass membership, although small by comparison with the social-democratic sport and athletics organisations from which the communist sports clubs drew their support. The old organisation had contained oppositional elements, who in one or two areas had already seized control of the organisation. For the KPD 'the time was now ripe to act . . . Everywhere where worker athletes were under oppositional leadership they should be organised in the Kampfgemeinschaft to form the basis for the re-establishment of unity on the basis of the class struggle.'[87]

The communist ancillary organisations also operated in a different organisational framework from that of the social-democratic bodies. The activities of the latter were supported by the SPD through its central bureaucracy and integrated in the Sozialistische Kulturbund. They had their own national bureaucracies, and they were co-ordinated at the local level through cartels and committees. The communist cultural organisations were inevitably poorer, and activities were concentrated in relatively few localities. After 1929 they were held together mainly at the national level by a newly-established co-ordinating and agitating body, the Ifa, the Interessengemeinschaft für Arbeiterkultur, best translated as 'Association for Workers' Culture'.[88] Its foundation followed hard on the meeting of the twelfth National Conference of the KPD in Berlin-Wedding in June 1929. A resolution passed there called for the fight against the 'cultural reaction' to be intensified, and it was followed by a circular to the District Leaderships, the Bezirksleitungen, informing them of the foundation of Ifa. It was accompanied by an 'Eight-Point Programme' on the 'political content of the cultural work of the party'.

Much of this programme was taken up with an attack on the existing workers' cultural organisations, emphasising the need to

87. Franz Dahlem at the 1929 Parteitag of the KPD.
88. Literally 'Interest Community for Workers' Culture'.

fight against their petty-bourgeois ideology, their arbitrary bureaucracies, and the 'reformist splitters', and the need for the revolutionary unity of the Arbeiterkulturorganisationen, which should be co-ordinated by the Ifa. But the programme stresses also the need to 'make the membership more active and to awaken their creative cultural forces'.[89] What reveals itself in this programme is one of the underlying contradictions and conflicts in the field of communist cultural activities: how to subordinate the work of the movement to the political struggle while maintaining interest in the subjects pursued, which was what had caused most members to join.

The Ifa sought from the beginning to encompass a wide range of organisations, from ideologically oriented associations, such as the 'Proletarian Freethinkers' or various educational pressure groups, to workers' hobby clubs, such as chess enthusiasts or guitar players. Indeed, there seems to have been no working-class organisation which might not be brought under the umbrella of the Ifa.[90] Thus in Saxony the Ifa endeavoured to organise worker philatelists on a *Land*-wide basis, and an organisation of peripatetic singers (who sang in the courtyards of tenement blocks) and of street musicians was also planned. 'There was an inexhaustible field for the activities of the Ifa and the many small organisations which are now mobilised by the Ifa constitute a link in the chain of the Red United Front.'[91]

The Ifa argued that socialist and bourgeois organisations should not be left in a monopoly position in the cultural field, especially as 'the SPD-led workers' cultural organisations are today the supporting pillars of the cultural reaction' and the fight on the cultural front was therefore as much a fight against the SPD as against the bourgeoisie. The Ifa had been founded to encourage local co-operation, found local cartels, and, above all, to transform the individual organisations into 'agencies of the class struggle against the *Kultur Reaktion*'.

The Ifa saw itself as the organisation and political leadership of the 'Section Culture' on the 'Fighting Front of the Revolutionary Class Struggle'. It was led by communist functionaries whose names had been put up as a slate at the first Ifa Congress. Its first

89. Cf. G. Ihlow, *Genesis, Intention, Struktur und Wirkungsweise . . . der Ifa*, Diss. Halle, 1983, pp. 128–9.
90. The *Ifa-Rundschau*, Jan.–Feb. 1931 lists the affiliated bodies. Many were clearly locality-based, such as 'Marxist Parents' School Committees' (*Elternbeiräte*) and 'Esperanto Study Circles'.
91. KPD Bezirksleitung Sachsen, *Bericht (1930)*.

chairman was Horst Frölich, a former communist journalist and head of the Agitprop Department of the Berlin party district.[92]

During its relatively short life the organisational strength of the Ifa was largely Berlin-based. It encouraged, and to some extent achieved, the formation of local cartels and of Ifa organisations at the party-district and sub-district level. A national report of the Ifa listed thirteen local groups whose membership ranged from 600–800 (Frankfurt and Halle) to 25,000 (Berlin). The local organisations were largely concerned with political activities, but some organised exhibitions – and in Düsseldorf the local Ifa organised a garden fete.[93]

The largest and most active constituent body of the Ifa was the Association of Proletarian Freethinkers, and local activities often drew on the strength of this element. It was at the Chemnitz and Southern Saxony district conference of the Freethinkers that the local Ifa organisation was founded.[94]

Ifa organisations also existed elsewhere in Saxony, with local cartels reported in the Leipzig district, as well as in Hamburg and in the Ruhr. There is, however, little evidence of regular cultural activities being carried out under Ifa auspices; it was rather a political agency whose task was to initiate and co-ordinate local campaigns. The report of the KPD District Leadership in Saxony to the Third District Party Conference in December 1932 lists campaigns taught by the Freie Arbeiter Radio Bund – the communist oppositional organisation concerned with broadcasting; the mobilising of parents in the *Schulkampf*, the struggle for the schools; the organisation of festivities for school-leavers; activities against the *Filmreaktion*; and others. But the report from the *Fraktion* in the Ifa admitted candidly that most of these campaigns only brought out those who were already organised, and that, although the campaign in the field of cultural policy was very important, it had hitherto found little resonance even in the bigger towns.

Yet the organisers seem to have left no stone unturned to use 'cultural' activities for political ends. One of these projected activities was a tour by a 'magician', 'a comrade who by means of the projection of "occult" practices and a subsequent lecture "revealing" what had taken place, was to lift the veil of the occult

---

92. Cf. 'Massenorganisation und Einheitsfront, die kulturpolitischen Aufgaben der KPD und die Ifa', *Der Parteiarbeiter*, 7 October 1929, pp. 316–18.
93. From a national report of the Ifa-Leitung in the Staatsarchiv in Bremen. See also *Ifa Rundschau*, vol. 2, nos. 4–6, 1930.
94. Cf. *Proletarische Freidenkerstimme*, vol. 3, no. 12, 1930 (report on the Bezirkskonferenz Erzgebirge-Vogtland).

obfuscation of the masses'. The events which had so far taken place were attended largely by sections of the working class and of the lower middle class remote from the party, and 'the venture showed that it was possible by such means to approach new groups with our ideology and gain their support for the Red United Front'.[95]

In Hamburg the communist opposition in the workers' sport movement had succeeded in wresting control of many clubs; but only 10–15% of the membership of those affiliated to the Kampfgemeinschaft were party members, and the attempts at the political education of the rest met with little success.[96] In addition to local activities the Ifa organised its constituent bodies into subject sections, covering Religion (i.e. Freethought); Art; Film and Radio; Education; Nationalities; Language; and Lifestyles. Thus at the second National Conference of the Ifa (Reichs-Kultur-Kongress) in 1931 the sections met on the eve of the Congress to consider their specific problems and to decide how to respond to the tasks which they had been set. The leadership did not wish these partial interests to become too strong, and the report on the meeting stated with obvious satisfaction that the sectional interests were giving way to 'the great central task, the struggle over issues of cultural policy'.[97]

The Congress discussed some concrete policy issues such as educational policy in schools and the policy with regard to film and cinema. They advocated the founding of local *Film-aktivs*, sections which were to mobilise public opinion against anti-proletarian films, and to bring public pressure to bear on local cinema-owners to show proletarian films. The main thrust of the political pressure remained general and propagandist. In the face of a fierce political struggle on the left in the concluding years of the Republic, and in the face of stricter controls and prohibitions of communist activities, the Ifa put the emphasis on political action. The political resolutions of the Congress echoed those of the KPD closely. They emphasised in particular the need for members to be active in the Red Trade Union Opposition, the Rote Gewerkschafts Opposition (RGO). During the Berlin Metalworkers' strike in 1930 the *Ifa Rundschau* wrote that 'the Ifa must become a voice of the communist opposition within the trade unions, help the fighting workers [and] the million of unemployed. It must not be a wallflower of cultural fads in the manner of the left of the SPD.'[98]

95. KPD Bezirk Sachsen, *Bericht der Bezirksleitung an den 3. Parteitag* 3–4 Dec. 1932.
96. KPD Bezirk Wasserkante, *Bericht 1931*.
97. *Ifa Rundschau*, vol. 3, nos. 1–2 Jan.–Feb. 1931.
98. Wunderer (see note 76) pp. 165–8 and *Ifa Rundschau*, vol. 2, nos. 7–8 p. 56 and vol. 3, nos. 2–4 p. 28.

The Ifa urged independent mass actions by cultural organis-ations, and urged that they should be closely co-ordinated with the economic and political struggle of the working class. 'If we succeed in this task the cultural organisations would create the base for a mass movement throughout the country which would sweep away the oppressive capitalist system and replace it with a socialist society.' Its slogan was 'Form the storm battalions of the red cultural front.'[99]

The Reichskulturkongress also stressed the need to increase the membership of the affiliated organisations; to mobilise groups not yet strongly represented, such as peasants and intellectuals and other members of the middle class, and to expand activities among women and young people. It suggested that the sympathetic groups of the *Naturfreunde* should combine their hikes with agi-tation in the countryside, and that oppositional groups of the worker singers should make it a principal task to sing political songs at factory gates.

There seems little evidence that such calls were heeded, and there was no growth in the membership of the relevant organisations. The leadership of the Communist Party district of Silesia noted that the masses still displayed a widespread lack of enthusiasm and support, and they saw little evidence of a vigorous and organised communist opposition in the 'reformist', that is, in the social-democratic workers' cultural organisations.[100]

The Ifa seems to have pursued political goals largely to the exclusion of cultural practice, and where it organised events it looked at the latter mainly in terms of their ideological and propa-gandistic content. One of the events which it undertook was the so-called *Ifa Schau*, formally the Reichs Arbeiter-Kulturausstellung, held in conjunction with the National Congresses in Berlin in 1930 and in Leipzig in 1931. In these Ifa-Shows the workers' cultural organisations, and, above all, the communist media, displayed their wares and made propaganda. The Berlin exhibition, which ran for four weeks in the Pschorr Beerhalls, consisted of nineteen exhibition booths with the following themes: The Soviet Union, Freethinkers, Ifa Sales, Radio and Records, Film, Theatre, Visual Art, Workers' Music, Workers' Sport, MASCH (Marxistische Arbeiter Schule), Left-Wing Publishers and the Universum Bücherei, (five sections), Esperanto, and Workers' Abstainers.[101]

99. *Ifa Rundschau*, vol. 3, nos. 2–4, p. 31.
100. KPD. Bezirksleitung Schlesien, *Bericht an den 17. Bezirksparteitag.*
101. Cf. R. May, 'Unterhaltung und/oder Bewußtseinsbildung? zu Intentionen und praktischen Aktivitätsformen kultureller Organisationen der kommunisti-

The Ifa also sponsored some concerts; but such activities met with criticism from the party. In the view of the KPD the Ifa was created to politicise the cultural organisations. By organising events of its own it was getting away from the difficult tasks of political and organisational work in the cultural organisations and of the strengthening of its own organisation in the districts and localities.[102]

The new communist policy in the field of workers' culture was introduced in a period of growing economic difficulty and rising unemployment, which was particularly strongly reflected in the membership of the KPD. Although voting for the Communist Party increased absolutely and relatively after 1928 – mainly at the expense of the SPD – the membership of the Communist Party and its ancillary organisations declined rather than grew at the same time. Above all, the deepening of the political conflict engendered by the economic (and the consequent political) crisis of the Weimar Republic was reflected in the politicisation of communist cultural activities. Thus the sometimes original and innovatory ideas about the role and content of culture for the working class which have been described in this chapter, and will be further discussed in the chapters on individual areas of culture, were widely and increasingly put to the service of political agitation and persuasion.

The political campaign was directed increasingly at the SPD, whose leaders were attacked as 'Social Fascists'; through this campaign it was hoped to prise large masses away from the SPD and cause a realignment of political forces on the left. This attempt largely failed. After the initial secessions from the workers' cultural movements of 1928–30 the frontiers re-set and hardened. The goal of a united front was nowhere achieved. Just as the Nazis came to power Losowski, the Secretary of the Red Trade Union International, remarked with bitterness that 'the organs of a revolutionary united front only succeeded in creating a united front with themselves.'[103]

---

schen deutschen Arbeiterbewegung nach 1925', *Mitteilungen aus der kulturwissenschaftlichen Forschung*, no. 22, 1987, pp. 143–151; Ihlow (note 89) p. 88.

102. Cf. Ihlow (see note 89) pp. 52–3. The Besucherorganisation which the Ifa had created did not exist long. The second Reichskongress in March 1931 was told that it had been dissolved.

103. INPREKOR, 31 January 1933, p. 523, quoted in Wunderer (see note 76) p. 227.

–4–

Working-Class Milieu and Workers' Leisure: The Culture of Everyday Life

Labour, Living Standards and Leisure Time

Before we embark on the account of the individual areas of workers' culture and of their organisations we must look at some aspects of the material conditions of the working class in the process of industrialisation. Working conditions and the domestic economy of the working-class family, especially the length and intensity of work and the material environment of the home, are major influences on the quantity and quality of leisure; and they, in turn, affect the cultural life of the worker. This applies, in varying degree, to all societies; but it is of particular relevance to the modern industrial societies in which the socialist labour movement developed.

In traditional societies, especially in the system of peasant agriculture and handicraft production, which was based largely on the family as an economic unit, production and consumption, work and leisure, are not as clearly separated as we find them in the system of wage labour. In the pre-industrial economy the process of physical reproduction which affects the individual worker is related to the social reproduction process of the economy in which he works. Furthermore, the exchange mechanism between workers and their employers, and between rulers and ruled, is to some extent influenced by custom and tradition.[1]

In the modern wage economy such organic traditional ties are cut, and the production and the pattern of consumption of the working-class family rests largely on the cash nexus. It is this which provides the link between work, income, consumption and leisure. And these four aspects of working-class life are closely interrelated.

---

1. As an example see the account of bread riots and the fixing of the price of corn in the eighteenth century in E.P. Thompson, 'The Moral Economy of the English Crowd in the Eighteenth Century', *Past and Present*, no. 50, February 1971, pp. 76–136.

This does not mean that leisure time and its uses are simply residual categories, determined by hours of work, income, prices, and the 'loose' cash in workers' pockets. Work and leisure are linked in a qualitative sense too. The intensity of work and the growing complexity of the industrial task change the demand for leisure. The 'reproduction of the worker's labour power' must therefore be seen not purely in material terms – food, rest, psychic equilibrium, and what is necessary to attain these – but also in intellectual terms. The worker in a modern highly mechanised industry expends skills as much as nervous energy. To be able to respond to the demands made on him by his work he requires in addition to food and clothing, sleep and shelter, educational accomplishments at one end of the scale as much as undemanding recreational pursuits at the other.[2]

If we look at this process we can observe two trends which over time became mutually reinforcing, namely, a rise in real incomes, and a reduction in the length of the working day – and later also of the working year. As a result, the average worker in employment need spend progressively less time and effort on the mere restoration of his physical stamina and well-being, in regenerating the strength which he expands each day in his work. The surplus of time, and, if applicable, the surplus of income, becomes available for purposes unconnected with the physical reproduction of labour – for extra consumption, for enjoyment of leisure, and for recreational activities.

The organised working class fought from the beginning not only for higher wages and a higher standard of living, but also for shorter hours and better working conditions.[3] And the labour movement in its educational role also helped the industrial worker to acquire some of the basic skills which would enable him to carry out this struggle, and also to cope with the demands made on his skills and energies by an increasingly sophisticated system of production. As we saw already, the German working-class organisations in particular were from the beginning involved in the education of their members in order to facilitate their emancipation.

2. Cf. D. Mühlberg, 'Anfänge proletarischen Freizeitverhaltens', *Weimarer Beiträge*, 1981 no. 12, pp. 118–50.
3. Even before 1918 trade unions generally included demands for shorter hours in their negotiations. During the last decade before the outbreak of war nearly half of all non-defensive strikes were about the length of the working day or included demands for reduced working hours. (W.H. Schroeder, *Arbeitergeschichte und Arbeiterbewegung*, Frankfurt 1978, p. 196.

The full utilisation of the educational and cultural facilities which the German workers' movement had created was however hampered by the burden of work. In England the organised industrial labour movement had from the beginning fought for the regulation of work and hours; and, as a result of a prolonged agitation, it had by 1847, with the help of middle-class reformers in Parliament, secured a legal limitation of the working day to ten hours.[4]

This measure was not only a significant step on the road of social reform, it was also the first effective success of 'the political organisation of the proletariat into a class'.[5] The success of this agitation was held up to the European labour movement as an example when, in 1864, the First International was established to demonstrate that the proletariat was now to be reckoned with as a political force.[6] But this was not to be, and the German working class had to wait until 1918 before limitations were put on the length of the working day in the famous 'Eight Hour Day' agreement, concluded by the German Trade Union Federation and the representatives of German industry.[7]

The introduction of a limit to the working day, which was soon given legal backing by the government, had been preceded by a long period of agitation and demonstration. This was stimulated by the refounded Socialist International (1889), which, as one of its first acts, proclaimed the first of May as a day of international solidarity in favour of the eight-hour day. The German labour movement was vociferous in support of the May Day demonstrations, although support for demonstrations during the actual day, as against events in the evening, was limited to those workers who were willing and able to absent themselves from work, and trade union support for this was somewhat lukewarm.[8]

The rationale, advanced by the SPD and by the German trade unions in favour of the eight-hour day, was not just to liberate the

4. Formally the Act only applied to women and children; but as they worked alongside men it was, in effect, a limitation of the length of the working day.
5. 'Communist Manifesto', in Karl Marx, *Political Writings* (Penguin Edition, Harmondsworth, 1973), vol. 1, p. 76.
6. Marx wrote in the 'Inaugural Address' to the Council of the International that 'the Ten-Hour bill was not only a great political success, it was the first time that in broad daylight the political economy of the middle class has succumbed to the political economy of the working class'. *Political Writings*, vol. 3, 1974, p. 79 (see note 5.)
7. On this agreement, commonly known as the Stinnes–Legien agreement, see G.D. Feldman, 'The Origin of the Stinnes–Legien Agreement: A Documentation', *IWK* Nr. 19/20, 1973, pp. 45–104.
8. The exhaustive history of May Day celebrations has not yet been written. But see B. Achten, *Illustrierte Geschichte des 1.Mai*, Oberhausen, 1979.

German worker from the bonds of industrial slavery, but to raise the quality of life and permit the sustained and extensive pursuit of education and culture, which in turn would help the worker in his emancipatory struggle. A May Day drawing of 1894 shows the ideal day divided into three eight-hour periods, devoted to work, recreation, and sleep; while a watch made at about the same time actually refers to 'education' in place of recreation.[9]

As it was, the pressure of work lay heavy on the German worker until after the war, adding long hours to an authoritarian industrial discipline. A six-day week and a twelve-hour day were not unusual, and ten hours' labour was common. Only a minority of trades worked shorter hours. And given that mechanisation was, as yet, not very highly developed, and that payment by results (*Akkordlohn*) was widely practised, factory workers, especially those working in heavy industry, were frequently exhausted by their job before the end of their working life. They often had to give up heavy and well-paid work for lighter, less well-paid occupations. The move from owner entrepreneurship to a joint-stock system of ownership led to the emphasis on the 'cash nexus' to the exclusion of everything else. Coupled with a system of payment linked to output, this led to a ruthless exploitation of the individual, and a rigorous weeding out of workers who were no longer fully fit.[10] Only a skilled worker, who managed to rise within the enterprise to a supervisory position, could hope to escape this fate. 'He either turns the corner or he is destined to sink slowly but surely.'[11]

Workers' leisure in the Wilhelmine period must clearly be put in the context of such long hours of heavy work on the part of the male worker, and of the heavy burden on his wife, still largely confined to her role in the household and in the family. Inasmuch as she was also looking after her husband when at home in the evening, her working day may well have exceeded his. If the wife, widowed mother, or unmarried daughter, possibly looking after a widowed father or mother and possibly also looking after siblings, was herself at work, her day would be considerably longer than that of the other members of her family. Unless helped by older

9. Cf. D. Mühlberg *et al.*, *Arbeiterleben um 1900*, Berlin 1983, p. 57.
10. Cf. D. Lande, 'Arbeits und Lohnverhältnisse in der Berliner Maschinenindustrie zu Beginn des 20. Jahrhundert', in *Schriften des Vereins für Sozialpolitik*, vol. 134, ii, pp. 306–484.
11. Cf. H. Herkner, 'Probleme der Arbeiterpsychologie unter besonderer Berücksichtigung auf Methoden und Ergebnisse der Vereinserhebung', in *Schriften des Vereins für Sozialpolitik*, vol. 138, pp. 117–38, p. 127.

children she would undertake all the domestic chores, cleaning, cooking and mending for the family and the home. And this pattern changed relatively little even after the war. A textile worker, mother of four, recorded in 1930 that her day started at 4.30 a.m. and did not finish until after 9.00 p.m. Only at the weekend did most women experience some relief from the drudgery of work and domestic duties.[12]

Given this full absorption through work, and allowing for the time needed for the satisfying of basic needs, investigators of the work and living patterns of skilled industrial workers in Baden before 1914 found that in many cases such leisure time as existed was taken up with 'the mere process of physical regeneration of expended energies'. Thus the free time is either spent in the home 'in a sort of stupor, or, for the male members of the household, in a semi-passive letting oneself go in the pub'.[13]

A study of the Gladbach spinning industry, carried out at the same time, concludes that there was little real leisure. Work was so all-pervasive that answers to questions about the use of leisure showed that those concerned did not really distinguish between mere relaxation and active leisure-time pursuits. The former invariably predominated to such an extent that even purely physical routines, when performed on Sundays – and so, not under any pressure – were looked on as something worth commenting on.[14]

Given the burden of long hours and exhausting work which prevailed right up to the end of the war, we can understand why the eight-hour day was hailed as such a great achievement, and why it was so vigorously defended by the German workers against the attacks by industry which started almost as soon as the agreement had been concluded. Industry had failed to carry out the necessary rationalisations to compensate for the shorter working day, and argued for its repeal or suspension. Factories resorted increasingly

12. See Deutscher Textilarbeiterverband, *Mein Arbeitstag, Mein Wochenende*. Berlin, 1930. There was *some* easing of the burden of domestic work after 1918 as household appliances became more common and as packaged food took some of the strain out of the preparation of meals.

13. Cf. M. Bernays, 'Auslese und Anpassung der Arbeiterschaft der geschlossenen Großindustrie, dargestellt an den Verhältnissen der Gladbacher Spinnerei', in *Schriften des Vereins für Sozialpolitik*, vol. 133, i, Berlin, 1910. (A worker in a spinning works stated that 'on Sundays I sleep late, than I wash myself, get dressed, slowly eat breakfast, and then I slowly smoke my pipe'; and a female worker, when asked what she liked most by way of relaxation replied, 'Oh Jesus, just to sit down and rest').

14. Cf. K. Keck, *Arbeits und Kulturmilieu der Arbeiterschaft in einer badischen Steinzeugwarenfabrik*, Leipzig, 1911: R. Fuchs, *Die Verhältnisse der Industriearbeiter in 17 Landgemeinden bei Karlsruhe*, Karlsruhe, 1904.

to compulsory overtime and to extra shifts; yet compared with the pre-war situation there was a real improvement. The percentage of workers who worked more than 48 hours rose over the years; but we find that by 1926 just under half of all workers covered by wage-agreements were still working 48 hours per week or less.[15] Moreover, a small but growing percentage of workers enjoyed an official working week of under 48 hours – 45 hours or less, which in turn meant a short Saturday, and thus something approaching a full weekend.[16]

And the trade unions began to agitate for a 40-hour week. A leading trade union official argued in a book on the 40-hour week that a reduction in working hours 'liberates hitherto shackled spiritual energies'; a further cutback would improve the content of leisure, and lead to a responsible attitude to work.[17]

The antecedents of today's 'long weekend' had also parallels in the form of very limited workers' holidays. Provision for some paid holidays had been incorporated in a number of tariff agreements in industry; but their use for real holidays away from home was restricted by lack of money. The few mass holidays organised by trade unions and other working-class organisations during the 1920s and in the 1930s were really only used by very well-paid workers. Real mass travel by workers, especially young workers, took the form of hikes. For these the growing German Youth Hostel movement (2,000 hostels in 1924, 4.3 million bednights in 1931) offered cheap overnight stays. And in the ranks of the labour movement itself the Naturfreunde movement, founded in 1906, had by the mid-twenties created its own networks of huts and hostels, which provided cheap accommodation for weekend or holiday stay.[18] In addition the Socialist Workers' Youth and the Kinderfreunde movement, which catered for children and youngsters, regularly set up summer camps for their members. Finally, annual conferences or other national gatherings of working-class organisations and sports events or festivals, such as the national gathering of the Workers' Choral Movement held in Hanover in

15. J. Kuczynski, *Darstellung der Lage der Arbeiter in Deutschland, 1917/18–1932/33* Berlin, 1966. Just after the revolution only 6% of all workers covered by wage agreements worked more than 48 hours.

16. On the eight-hour question in general see G.D. Feldman and I. Steinisch, 'Die Weimarer Republik zwischen Sozial und Wirtschaftsstaat. Die Entscheidung gegen den Achtstundentag', *AfSG*, 18, 1978, pp. 353–439.

17. L. Erdmann, 'Der Wert der Arbeitskürzung, kulturelle Werte', in Th. Leipart (ed.), *Die 40 Stunden Woche*, Berlin, 1930, pp. 116–30.

18. Cf. H. Spode, 'Der deutsche Arbeiter reist' in G. Huck (ed.), *Sozialgeschichte der Freizeit*, Wuppertal, 1980 281–306.

1928 and attended by 50,000, were foci for mass holidays, made possible by cheap excursion trains and free lodgings offered locally.

Thus a shorter working week implied a rise in the physical well-being of the worker and an increase in social opportunities. It did not, of itself, mean a rise in the material standards of living. On the contrary, we find in Weimar Germany that the real wages of most groups of workers were, for most of the period, below their pre-war level. Negotiated wage rates during the 1920s were often above their pre-war level, and actual money wages might even be higher. Real earnings, however, remained for most of the period below their pre-war peak, owing to high prices. Only for a few years after 1928 – and then only for some occupations – did they reach, let alone exceed, their pre-war high points.[19]

The relationship of real wages to the standard of living is however not a linear one. In the assessment of the actual levels of material well-being we must take into account not just the movement of wages and prices but also general social factors relating to the size of the average family, regularity of employment, and social security payments, such as the system of unemployment benefits introduced in 1927. From that year onwards unemployment never fell below a million, and after 1928 it soared, so that in 1932/3 about one-third of the workforce was either out of work or working short time. Thus the actual standard of living is heavily dependent on employment; but on the other hand the standard of living of the unemployed was higher under Weimar than it had been in the Empire. And, taking the concept of social income further, we would have to take account of rises in housing standards, and of other social benefits such as the quality of education and of health care.

To assess in quantitative terms the real, let alone the perceived, level of well-being, and the actual purchasing power of the working-class family, would demand a statistical refinement for which the figures are just not available. We know, however, that the post-war years saw significant demographic changes which affected all levels of society, and not least the working class. The decline in family size, which had hitherto proceeded slowly, was now accelerating.[20] Compared with families of marriages concluded in the early years of the century, those of the war and

19. Cf. G. Bry, *Wages in Germany*, Princeton, 1960.
20. The completed family size of workers' families in terms of children declined from 3.82 for those who married in 1905–09 to 2.76 for the 1915–19 cohort; and in the large cities the decline was even more marked. Cf. J. Knödel, *The Decline of Fertility in Germany, 1871–1939*, Princeton, 1974.

post-war years were significantly smaller, with a corresponding increase in relative family well-being.

In addition there is evidence of some increase in the percentage of married women at work, and of a growth in real terms of adolescents' wages and earnings.[21] The number of married women returned as following an occupation in the Occupational Census of 1925 rose from 2.82 million in 1907 to 3.64 million in 1925. They were unlikely to have all been in employment on the census date, and we don't know how many of them were working class in social terms. We do know, however, that the increase in the figure for all women in occupations between 1907 and 1925 was in part due to a spectacular growth in the number of white-collar workers (that is, officials in the public services and salaried employees), which almost quadrupled during the period, while the number of women manual workers actually declined slightly. This upward trend in the numbers of married women following an occupation continued after 1925, reaching 4.18 million in 1933; but the total for all women remained stationary.[22]

The rise in women white-collar workers was of course only part of a general trend towards salaried employment during this period. This is reflected in the social composition of the membership of the political and cultural organisations of the labour movement. As white-collar jobs were marginally better paid than blue-collar jobs, and as the cultural aspirations of white-collar workers tended to be higher than those of many manual workers, this trend will have affected expenditure on recreation and on cultural activities within the working class as a whole. It probably also gave a fillip to cultural activities in the organisations with which we are here concerned.

In addition to the relatively small number of married women who were working full time there was a significant number of workers' households in which the wife brought in some money from casual work. A budget survey of 2,000 working-class, white-collar, and public-service households found that in just under half the housewife earned some money; but seen as a fraction of the income of the head of the household the amounts were small,

21. An attempt to take all the relevant data into account was made by J. Kuczynski with his concept of the *Nettolohn*. (Cf. Kuczynski, as in note 15.)
22. For relevant statistics see Germany, Statistisches Bundesamt, *Bevölkerung und Wirtschaft, 1872–1972*. The increase in the number of women in employment must be seen in relation to both a somewhat smaller increase in the number of men in employment and a relative preponderance of women as against men in the population, owing to the ravages of war.

exceeding 5% only in the case of households with an annual income of more than 3,600 marks – a figure well outside normal working-class incomes.[23]

To measure perceived standards of living we must go further than the individual income and the social wage. Whatever its political shortcomings, the Weimar state saw itself as a *Sozialstaat*, a 'social state', and this manifested itself not only in respect of social and labour legislation but also in the public provisions in areas such as welfare and education and in support of cultural activities. It showed itself in public buildings and installations ranging from swimming pools to libraries, from schools to theatres. Much of this was due to municipal effort, and this was particularly marked in the case of those local authorities which were controlled by the Social Democrats, generally in alliance with the Liberals or with the Centre Party. Expenditure was not only forthcoming in respect of physical provision, but local or *Land* authorities would also give financial support for various cultural and recreational activities, be they sport or music, plays or museums. In overall terms the public expenditure in these areas may not have been very great; but it had a beneficial effect on the cost of cultural and recreational activities to the members of the working-class clubs and societies.[24]

Quantitative data will not tell the full story, but some figures are indicative of the growth of social provision during the period. Thus the number of pupils per full-time teacher in elementary schools fell from 55 in 1911 to 45 in 1921/2 and to 40 in 1931/2; and there was a similar fall in secondary schools (Mittelschulen). During the same period the number of doctors per 10,000 population increased from 4.8 in 1909 to 7.4 in 1930, and the number of hospital beds per 100,000 rose likewise from around 65 before the war to 90 in the closing years of the Republic. Housing shortage and overcrowding remained; but there was still a marked improvement, as the number of dwellings per 1,000 of population increased from 222 in 1919 to 249 in 1932.[25]

To assess the importance of leisure-time activities for the German working class in quantitative terms is difficult. One of the few

23. Cf. H.A. Winkler, *Der Schein der Normalität. Arbeiter und Arbeiterbewegung in der Weimarer Republik, 1924–1930*, Berlin–Bonn, 1985, pp. 86–7 basing himself on the budget survey referred to below (note 26).
24. Social-democratic cultural organisations were at first reluctant to accept subsidies or to make use of subsidised institutions such as Adult Education Colleges; but the leadership urged them to do so, if only to symbolise that the state was now their state.
25. Cf. the time-series in *Bevölkerung und Wirtschaft* (note 22).

indicators we have relates to family expenditure. The 1927/8 household budget survey referred to earlier comprised 2,000 families in about 60 towns. The statistics reveal that expenditure on education, recreation and amusement averaged *c.* 5% of total current (annual) expenditure, and there is some differentiation in respect of occupational categories – white-collar workers and officials, for example, spending a somewhat larger proportion on the schooling of their children than manual workers.

Expenditure on entertainment was similarly differentiated between occupational groups; but, more significantly, the levels of actual expenditure on leisure-time activities of the three occupational groups overlap, and, if income is held constant, the similarities in amounts and patterns of expenditure between blue-collar and white-collar workers are greater than the dissimilarities. Nor do the statistics reveal many, let alone any very significant, quantitative differences. Thus the share of expenditure on newspapers and books declined in all three groups with rising incomes, although it occupies first place in all categories. And when it comes to entertainment we find that the expenditure on theatre-going and concert-going is higher than that for the cinema.[26]

For working-class households we can make some comparisons with similar pre-war surveys. For the group of 361 families with incomes of less than two thousand marks annually in the German Statistical Office's 1909 survey of low-income families, expenditure in this area averaged 4.2%. But in that survey society membership and trade union dues were included, while in the 1927 survey they are entered separately, averaging 2.0 – 2.4%. The figures would thus suggest a not insignificant increase in workers' expenditure on culture and recreation, without which, one imagines, the expansion in commercial leisure provision and the increase in the activities of workers' cultural organisations in the post-war period would hardly have been possible.[27]

These figures must be seen in relation to the different relative costs of the different types of entertainment, and they don't permit

26. Germany. Statistisches Reichsamt. *Die Lebenshaltung von 2.000 Arbeitern, Angestellten und Beamtenhaushaltungen, 1927/28.* (Einzelschriften zur Statistik, 22[1] and 22[2]), 1928.

27. Cf. Kaiserliches Statistisches Amt, *Erhebung von Wirtschaftsrechnungen minderbemittelter Familien, 1909, Reichsarbeitsblatt,* 2. Sonderheft, reprinted 1981; H.A. Winkler, *Normalität,* pp. 82–90; see also Deutscher Metallarbeiter Verband, *320 Haushaltsrechnungen von Metallarbeitern,* 1913, reprinted 1981. In this connection it is not insignificant that the percentage of household expenditure that went on food declined between 1907 and 1929 from 52% to 45%. L. Preller, *Sozialpolitik,* 1949 edn, Kronberg, p. 159.

conclusions about the pattern of use. What is significant, however, is that a relatively large share of total expenditure on leisure is devoted to sport, dancing and various festivities, and this reflects an expansion in both communal and commercially-produced recreation and amusement. We have a variety of indicators which suggest that during the Weimar years a new attitude to leisure developed. It was no longer seen primarily as relaxation, but conceived as time in which to do something specific.

Not surprisingly, such an attitude developed particularly strongly among young workers, who had now more spare time, and often more spare cash. 'The most beautiful thing in life is leisuretime' and 'when I leave my job at a quarter to five in the afternoon I feel free', are typical comments from Berlin youths at the end of our period.[28] Before the war it was essentially Sunday which afforded the opportunity for relaxation as well as for more purposeful activity. In the post-war period spare time of an evening becomes more important and often jealously guarded, and aspirations in respect of leisure are not restricted to the weekend.

In this connection it emerges fairly clearly that leisure time available is 'social time' rather than a break from work. Thus shop assistants, for example, having a long lunch-break but finishing late in the evening, can use their leisure time less purposefully than the industrial worker clocking off at four in the afternoon. In a survey of 5,000 adolescents in Berlin, shop workers were the group containing the greatest number of those who complained about a lack of spare time – not too surprisingly when we learn that all but 11% of (female) shop assistants finished work at seven in the evening or later. The two-hour break for lunch was for them no compensation for the shorter evening, especially if we bear in mind that 'bedtime' was rather early. Of the groups of young workers in Berlin one-third were in bed by 9.00 p.m., and over three-quarters by 10.00 p.m. Clearly, even under more advantageous conditions in respect of the working day, fatigue and the need for recuperation had not disappeared.[29]

If quantitatively leisure is so highly valued, qualitatively much of it is enjoyment-oriented. As we saw, juvenile wages had risen in real terms during the Weimar period, and a combination of more spending money and more time to spend money led one observer

28. It is significant that the German word for leisure is *Freizeit*, i.e. 'free time', the time fully at the disposal of the individual, in which one feels 'free from the demands of work and of the physical, economic and social demands on (one's time)'. R. Dinse, *Das Freizeitleben der Grosstadtjugend*, Eberswalde, 1932.
29. Dinse, *Freizeitleben* (note 28).

to conclude that 'Earning money and having fun are the two points around which the life of [Berlin] juveniles revolved' in the 1920s.[30] And enjoyment for many, sport apart, is found in the various forms of popular entertainment. Writing no doubt critically, a young socialist worker speaks of the indifference and general lack of concern of the majority of his young colleagues, 'their element is the dance-hall, the cinema, sport and the fairground'.[31]

The convinced and active socialists or communists would inevitably spend a great part of their spare time in work for the cause, be it in organisational activities or in preparing themselves intellectually for the political struggle to which they had dedicated their lives. The young man, who, sharing a bedroom with his parent and siblings, would wait until they had gone to bed 'and then sit down at the table with my books', but goes on to say that 'it is then often too late and my eyes will become heavy with sleep', speaks probably for many organised young workers, but hardly for the majority of working-class youth.[32]

The political dimension of workers' leisure must not be overlooked. Many youngsters were entirely 'privatised' in their spare time, neither belonging to nor identifying with a political or religious movement. And this even in socialist or communist or otherwise politically involved households. The degree of actual involvement with the political culture of the working class is not surprisingly found to be related to the adolescent's occupation or industrial background. It was strongest in modern 'proletarian' trades, for example the metal and building trades, and weakest among the older, largely handicraft-based occupations.[33]

But, extremes apart, the type and character of the leisure-time activities of political and non-political individual workers and working-class families were not strictly separate; nor were the two strictly differentiated in quantitative terms from habits and interests of the petty bourgeoisie or the middle class proper. Common to all was an interest in sport, and general keenness on fitness and outdoor life.

Indeed, if there was one common note in a series of over one hundred essays written by women textile workers in 1928 it was

30. The young worker did not expect to keep his entire wage. He normally paid for his keep or received pocket money from his mother out of his wages. See 'Dreissig junge Arbeiter berichten aus ihrem Leben', *KW*, 1930, nos. 9 and 10.
31. Ibid.
32. Ibid.
33. G. Dehn *Die geistige und materielle Lebensführung der proletarischen Jugend*, Berlin, 1929, pp. 50–8.

that aspect.[34] Gymnastics, swimming, bathing, going for walks and hikes were frequently, but far from universally, linked to membership of and to the activities of labour movement organisations – they were often just family-centred, or undertaken in an informally organised group of friends, or even alone. A 50-year-old trade unionist wrote of her weekend that, 'Saturday is spent with scrubbing and cleaning. On Sunday a walk through the gardens . . . I find that the flowers have never been so beautiful as today – oh the world is beautiful, the sun golden, the sky blue', while an unmarried 39-year-old woman writes 'when I have done my housework I go and join a group where mind and body are looked after, so that capitalism cannot get me down completely'.[35]

For the women involved access to leisure must perforce compete with housework and other domestic chores, and the majority were very conscious of the fact that they did not have enough time to do all they would like to do. Reading, even of the newspaper, was generally postponed to the end of the evening. 'I am ready at half past eight;', wrote a married woman with children, 'then I read the *Volksstimme* or a book from the Textile Workers Library.'[36] For others, the mind (*Geist*) 'is the stepchild, it always has to make do with what is left'.[37]

For many Sunday was the only free day, although married women, or others who looked after children, had a lot to do even on Sundays. As a woman of thirty-three who looked after an elderly mother put it, 'Only the weekend offers some relaxation; then I get out into the beautiful countryside, the only thing which the harassed individual can really call his own, to cleanse myself of the burden of a week's work.'[38]

She, and many others, linked leisure with the political and economic struggle and with work for the party. And the latter, in turn, gradually became for many a personal need. A large number of the respondents to this enquiry were active in the union or in other working-class organisations.

Internal evidence from the women textile workers' accounts suggests that many lived away from the big cities; the enjoyment of nature and of open-air life probably came more naturally to them than it would do to city dwellers. At the same time the full and

34. *Mein Arbeitstag, Mein Wochenende* (n. 12).
35. Ibid. p. 15.
36. Ibid. p.100.
37. Ibid. p. 27. (There is a widespread feeling that 'feeding the mind is as important as feeding the body'.)
38. Ibid.

moving record which this group of industrially organised workers has given us shows also the co-existence and interpenetration of individual and publicly enjoyed leisure.

The majority of these trade unionists, and, one suspects, a great number of the German workers of the period, were, in their after-work activities, neither wholly privatised nor entirely politicised. We cannot speak of *one* overriding pattern of working-class culture, either in respect of everyday life and leisure, or with regard to the politically oriented cultural and recreational activities of the German labour movement. Rural or urban environment, the region and its socio-economic background, skill and craft status, and even religious climate all produce specific leisure patterns within which the individual worker chooses his particular style of leisure.

This shows itself in the cultural institutions which set out to cater for the cultural and recreational interests of the proletariat. We can distinguish between activities which, like workers' sport and workers' music, were geographically widely dispersed, and educational and artistic activities and provisions, like workers' theatre or workers' festivals, which were essentially the product of the cities, and, in particular, of those with strong and well-established political traditions. But even in areas which were the centres of gravity of the German labour movement far from all workers were involved.

But before turning to individual areas of cultural activity we must look at the more general, privately enjoyed but often commercially provided, areas of workers' leisure.

The Working-Class Milieu and Workers' Leisure

The general trend towards shorter working hours and expanding leisure time, and the small but not insignificant and probably rising expenditure on recreation, culture and education which were summarised just now should not lead us to assume that the spare time gained by the worker through his fight for shorter hours was also taken primarily in the form of *public* leisure, that is of commercially or socially provided recreation or edification.

There was, of course, a considerable increase in cultural provision and activities. The cultural and leisure-time organisations of the German labour movement benefited greatly from greater leisure, and from the fact that the pattern of demand, established originally by groups of skilled workers, expanded into other social groups. At the same time the growing commercial leisure-time industries, especially those connected with the media of communication, increasingly attracted working-class support. Some of this is discussed in the penultimate chapter of this book, which looks at film and radio in the context of working-class culture.

All the same, much leisure continued to be spent in the family circle, but such *loci* of leisure as the allotment, the pub, the dance-hall and the fair are also discussed here. The quality of domestic leisure will depend much on the physical environment, housing in particular. The latter affected not only physical well-being and mental health; the cohesion and the ethos of the proletarian family is itself closely linked to domestic circumstances, to the size and amenities of the dwelling. We must therefore look briefly into the character and the facilities of working-class housing and their development.

We know that in the process of industrialisation the working population became increasingly concentrated in the big cities. The latter expanded physically, but did so predominantly on the pattern of tenement blocks – the *Mietskasernen*, literally 'rental barracks', buildings of 4–6 storeys erected generally in a grid pattern, flanking comparatively narrow streets, and often extending backwards through a series of courtyards.[39]

Two to four flats tended to lead off a staircase, which frequently also gave access to a w.c. which was shared by several families. As far as the urban working-class family was concerned housing was, at least in the big cities, almost invariably a small flat – one or two heatable rooms plus a kitchen and possibly a small unheated closet. Few working-class families had larger accommodation, and cottages or terraced housing were unusual except in the countryside or in special settlements put up by factories or mines for their workers.

With such small flats being the rule, and with working-class families often comprising up to 6–10 persons, crowding was frequent and extensive; 3–4 persons' occupation per room was not unusual, and the sharing of beds was common.[40] There was some gradual improvement in the level of occupancy as the progressive effects of continued house-building increased the available stock of accommodation.[41] On the other hand it does not follow that the larger the family, the larger the accommodation; indeed, one way for a growing family to cope with the resultant increasing pressure

39. Cf. W. Hegemann, *Das Steinerne Berlin. Gechichte der größten Mietskasernenstadt der Welt*, Berlin, 1930.
40. L. Niethammer, 'Wie wohnten die Arbeiter im Kaiserreich', *AfSG* 16, 1976, pp. 61–134.
41. Ibid. pp. 86–92.

on the family income was to move to smaller accommodation.[42]

Yet if housing improved somewhat in the early years of the twentieth century, building density grew, at least in the big cities, as the number of small flats increased and as they were developed largely through the 'better' utilisation of plots by means of additional courts, and the utilisation of gardens for building, without any compensatory development to create open spaces and parks.[43] Crowding was further aggravated by the frequent sub-letting of already congested accommodation, which was dictated by economic considerations irrespective of the familial situation. Lodgers were frequent, as were boarders – *Schlafgänger* and *Kostgänger* – and they inevitably intruded on the family circle. Even without this the crowding and sharing must have had a major influence on family cohesion and family leisure. If all rooms were bedrooms and if parents shared rooms and possibly beds with their children, and if family members of the opposite sex were sharing rooms, or even beds, there was neither chance for privacy for the individual nor for the easy enjoyment of communal activities in the home. The lodger merely added an extra, extraneous, element of discomfort.[44] His presence could, however, destabilise the social cohesion of the proletarian family, and even disturb the otherwise harmonious sexual relations of the householders' marriage.

Nor was there in the densely built-up urban working-class quarters a chance to escape from the confines of the home into squares or parks. The enjoyment of nature and of 'the great out-of-doors' in general was only possible at weekends – and it might have been the strongly felt absence of sun and light for the worker confined to the machine hall and the urban slum which drove such large numbers of workers on Sundays into the rural areas bordering the cities.[45]

At the height of the rapid process of industrialisation the proletarian family was anything but a self-contained, protected, and stable institution, where it was easy for members to enjoy happy intimacy. And the family, although usually two-generational, was not the closed nuclear family but what contemporary writers describe as 'half-open', especially where the lodger or boarder

42. Ibid. pp. 90–1.
43. Ibid. pp. 102–9.
44. On the institution of the *Schlafgänger* and the *Kostgänger* see Franz Bruggemeier and L. Niethammer, 'Schlafgänger, Schnapskasino und schwere industrielle Kolonne', in D. Langewiesche and K. Schönhoven (eds), *Arbeiter in Deutschland*, Paderborn, 1981, pp. 139–72.
45. On this see Chapter 11 below.

introduced his own circle of friends and acquaintances into the home.

Nineteenth-century housing, the cause of so much human misery, formed the basis of the housing stock of the Weimar period. To it we must add some public housing of a better standard that had been put up in the immediate pre-war period. And, as the third decade of the century progressed, the effect of the new spate of public housing, built by municipalities and semi-public housing associations, made itself felt. By the end of the decade new (i.e. post-1918) housing accounted for nearly 16% of all housing.[46] The new dwellings, built generally in the form of housing estates at the edges of the towns, or, as in Frankfurt, even further afield, provided generally larger, better-appointed flats. And being more generously planned, with buildings of medium height and lower housing density and with landscaped surroundings, they provided a healthier environment, where 'in sun and fresh air body and soul could recuperate after the nervous exhaustion of the working day'.[47]

The price of these new, and in some respects truly revolutionary, standards, described by the great architect and director of the *Bauhaus* Mies van der Rohe as 'part of the great struggle for a new way of life', was a higher level of rent.[48] In Hamburg the annual rent for a new flat of about 65 square metres was about 700 marks, considerably more than the cost of a small flat in *Altbau* (older) dwellings. In consequence the new flats cannot be described as true working-class accommodation, and their inhabitants were generally drawn from the better-off sections of the working class and from the families of white-collar workers and the lower ranks of the professional classes.[49]

A number of factors taken in combination must nevertheless have been responsible for a general improvement of working-class

46. Cf. F.W. Witt, 'Inflation, Wohnungszwangswirtschaft und Hauszinssteuer in der Weimarer Republik', in L. Niethammer, *Wohnen im Wandel*, Wuppertal, 1977, from which the figures are calculated. Witt gives figures for new constructions and conversions. The figures show that the stock of dwellings in 1932 was 16,541,000, compared with 13,945,000 in 1919.
47. Ernst May in *Das Neue Frankfurt*, 1928, vol. 2, p. 83. On the new housing estates in general, see among others. Thilo Hilpert, *Hufeisensiedlung Britz, 1926–1960*, Berlin, 1980.
48. Ludwig Mies van der Rohe, cited in B.M. Lane, *Architecture and Politics in Weimar*, Cambridge, Mass., 1968.
49. Cf. H. Hipp, 'Wohnungen für Arbeiter? Zum Wohnungsbau und zur Wohnungspolitik in den Zwanziger Jahren', in A. Herzig *et al.* (eds), *Arbeiter in Hamburg*, Hamburg pp. 471–481 Hilpert, *Britz*, (note 47), p. 85.

housing. New accommodation apart, the pressure must have eased
as the result of the decline in family size and the relative decline in
rental cost compared with the cost of working-class consumption
in general.[50]

Smaller families, improvements of dwellings, a decline of crowding, and a widespread disappearance of lodgers and boarders meant
that in contrast to the frequently 'half-open' family before 1914, the
proletarian family of our period was more 'closed'. All this must
have helped towards better family cohesion, and would thus have
given the home a more positive place in family life. From a physical
as well as from a social point of view the 'culture of the home' was
clearly an important part of that element of working-class culture
which belonged to the private rather than the public sphere of life
and leisure.

The relative importance of home-centred family life within the
working class is, of course, difficult to quantify. Given the paucity
of sociological studies we are forced to fall back on material which
is inevitably not fully representative if we wish to attach any
quantitative weight to leisure-time behaviour. Thus Alice Salomon
and Marie Baum's study of family life at the end of the 1920s found
among the respondents great emphasis on those leisure-time pursuits which are centred on the home, and which are at the same
time largely non-intellectual and non-educational in character.[51] Of
26 Berlin workers, mostly skilled labourers or low-level white-
collar workers, only a quarter list activities which were not primarily
domestic or home-related. 'The radio is our only entertainment',
'one loves peace and quiet', 'Sunday is spent with relatives' are
phrases which apply to this group.

Asked about their religion, those who gave information described themselves as Protestants (or occasionally as Catholics), but
admitted in most cases to being inactive. In another sample, containing small towns and villages in Southern and Central Germany,
we find a greater degree of religious activity even among convinced
socialists. And an even greater number of families report regular
celebration of the major festivities of the Christian year (Easter,
Whitsun, and Christmas) in the home, although the last may only
mean better meals and perhaps a decorated table.[52] Religious or
secular celebrations in the home were widely held even in the circle

---

50. Witt, *Wohnungszwangwirtschaft*, p. 406 states that during the period 1924–32 the
average rents of small flats were 16% above those of 1913, while the cost of
living was 41% higher.
51. Alice Salomon and Marie Baum, *Familienleben der Gegenwart*, Berlin, 1930.
52. Ibid.

of social-democratic workers, to judge by the reminiscences of an admittedly small sample of Brunswick workers interviewed in 1980.[53] Workers also engaged in the pursuit of home-based hobbies, such as the breeding of birds and the rearing of rabbits. Hamborn, a mining town in the Ruhr, had in 1909 four clubs devoted to each activity; but these were only eight out of a total of 208 clubs and societies.[54]

By way of an extension of home-centred activities gardening and the cultivation of allotments figure in the life of many workers even in the cities. Cultivation of a plot had always been common among the rural proletariat, especially in the South and the South-West and among the miners of the Ruhr. After the war the allotment (*Schrebergärten*) movement received a new impetus as the result of food shortages and greater leisure.[55] Of the 400,000 cultivators who were organised in the Reichsverband der Schrebergärtner half were manual workers; and in addition many workers rented their piece of land privately, often from the landlords of suburban beer-gardens, who stipulated that the thirsty gardeners obtain their drinks from them.[56] Although the work was mainly done by the head of the household, the whole family could be involved. 'The household would go to the garden already on Saturday afternoon and then on Sunday morning . . . [I also] kept rabbits and they had to be fed every day', a Brunswick worker remembered.[57]

The economic importance of such fruit and vegetable growing and of the keeping of animals must not be overlooked, nor must we forget that workers' leisure was used for all sorts of domestic chores such as repairs about the house, the mending of shoes, and the like. Yet the importance of gardens or allotments was more than merely economic. They had social and indeed community-creating functions, and were seen as liberalising in a purely humane sense, as 'a place where [the worker] could almost be a human being'.[58]

In a similar way, alcohol had a wider function than that of a mere stimulant. During the nineteenth century and well into the next the consumption of alcohol figured largely in the life of the male

53. S. Bajohr, *Vom bitteren Los der armen Leute*, Cologne, 1984, p. 193.
54. E. Lucas, *Zwei Formen von Radikalismus in der deutschen Arbeiterbewegung*, Frankfurt, 1976, p. 94.
55. Erdmann, *Arbeitskürzung* (as in note 17) p. 130.
56. Cf. E. Johannes, *Entwicklung, Funktionswandel und Bedeutung der städtischen Kleingärtnerei*, Kiel, 1955.
57. S. Bajohr, *Vom bitteren Los* (note 53). While male cultivation was customary, we also find that women take up the task as a means of securing an extra income when, after the arrival of children, they are prevented from going to work.
58. Ibid. p. 198.

working class. And drink had a significance which extended into the realm of food and work. Exhausting and often hot work made workers thirsty, and, as water was not always drinkable, and non-alcoholic beverages were not widely available in a commercial form, alcoholic drink was the natural response. Alcohol, mostly in the form of beer, was also widely drunk by the men of the household at mealtimes. It had a nutritional value – though this was not commensurate with its price if compared with that of other foodstuffs – but it was mainly a provider of a spicy and stimulating accompaniment to the rather bland food of the home.[59]

Most significant, however, is the fact that drinking, in bars or beerhalls was for long the principal form of recreation of the German worker. Drink was both a drug and a purveyor of sociability. It assuaged the psychic wounds caused by fatigue and hard work, and it let a worker forget his miserable home and the pressure of domesticity. As a weaver put it around 1912 'deadening work, miserable lodgings, a brood of children deprived one of all pleasure. Capitalism destroys family life, and therefore I go to the pub.'[60] In the group of miners, metal workers and textile workers whose lives and attitudes Adolf Levenstein studied just before the outbreak of the First World War, less than half – and even fewer of the miners – derived all their satisfaction from family life. For them the pub was the principal place of entertainment, recreation, and re-generation.[61]

But the pub was more than a place for the re-establishment of a psychic equilibrium after the ravages of a day's labour and the irritations of factory life and discipline. In the pub those workers who were bent only on recreation met the ideologically committed and politically active workers. The 'local' was the place where men of different occupations and from a wide range of enterprises met and exchanged experiences and views. It thus became a centre for political discussion and a promoter of communal feeling, and hence a focal point for the creation of working-class solidarity. In the view of Karl Kautsky 'without the pub the German working class would have neither a social nor a political life.'[62] Drinking customs

59. Cf. S. Roberts, 'Drink and Working Class Standard of Living', in W. Conze and U. Engelhardt (eds), *Arbeiterexistenz im 19. Jahrhundert*, Stuttgart, 1981, pp. 74–91, who gives the expenditure on alcohol per household as ranging from 4.3% to 5.6%.
60. A. Levenstein, *Die Arbeiterfrage*, Munich, 1921, p. 264.
61. Around 1900 the number of inhabitants per 'outlet' for alcohol in Berlin was 129, and in Leipzig 290.
62. K. Kautsky, 'Der Alkoholismus und seine Bekämpfung' *NZ* vol. 9 ii, 1891,

and the institutions connected with drinking highlight the sexual divisions of everyday leisure in the life of the German working class.

Before 1914 social drinking was essentially a male preserve, a visible expression of the fact that, socialist ideology and belief in equality notwithstanding, belief in male dominance was widespread throughout the German proletariat, and that it extended from the home into the workers' leisure-time institutions.[63]

Drinking habits were to change somewhat after the war, with the expansion of *Volkshäuser* and *Gewerkschaftshäuser*. These establishments, run under the auspices of the local trades union cartel, were a mixture of hostel and clubhouse. They set out to provide communal facilities, especially in respect of eating and entertainment for members. The movement aimed here to provide facilities and comforts which could vie with bourgeois establishments in comfort and attractiveness. The journal *Das Gewerkschaftshaus* declared that 'if the public rooms were furnished and kept so well that colleagues could bring their wives and families for entertainment and relaxation, then the enterprise had served its purpose', but it seems that the 'People's Houses' were generally frequented only by the better-off sections of the working class.[64]

Besides the convivial and the domestic sides of workers' leisure there was always a range of popular recreational activities which tended to involve the whole family, including the popular fête, the fair, and the market, with their various attractions and side-shows, and later the first cinematic performances.[65]

Fairs and fêtes survived in many cities – and, of course, in the countryside – into the twentieth century. Originally often markets, which attracted traders from afar, with some attendant showpeople, they had by our time become venues for popular amusement on a grand scale. The *Kirmess* had everything – roundabouts and rides, booths and shows, food and photography, and soon the travelling cinema. It was a singular event, and it generally occupied a central place in the workers' calendar. It provided an otherwise

---

various pp., p. 107. See also S. Reck, *Arbeiter nach der Arbeit, Sozialhistorische Studie zu der Wandlung des Arbeiteralltags*. Lahn Giessen, 1977. Kautsky was of course also thinking of the pub as a place where the party and other workingclass organisations could meet relatively freely for more formal discussions.

63. Cf. M. Soder, *Hausarbeit und Stammtischsozialismus. Arbeiterfamilie und Alltag im deutschen Kaiserreich*, Giessen 1980, p. 53 and *passim*.

64. *Das Gewerkschaftshaus*, vol. 4, 1929, nos. 1–2.

65. It has been estimated that during the years of the Weimar Republic there were annually some ten thousand fairs with a total of 80 million visitors.

rarely attainable excitement and enjoyment for the mass of the population, and an occasion for more than normal expenditure from many working-class families, who would save up for the event for some time.

The event involved the whole town. On the principal day of the fair factories either closed or found that their workers took the day off or 'went sick'. And apart from the principal *Kirmess* which were held in places like Remscheid and Hamborn, there were smaller fairs in various districts or even in blocks of tenements.[66]

In addition to such peripatetic events we also find by the twentieth century in the big cities permanent amusement parks, such as the one in Nymphenburg near Munich, and, in the 1920s, the Berlin Lunapark. There were also smaller establishments, the *Rummelplätze*, fairgrounds with rides, shooting booths, and beertents, which attracted above all unattached adolescents, and might become assembly places for cliques and street-gangs.[67]

Cultivating human relationships, facilitating contact between the sexes, performing initiation rites into society for the young girl and providing a relief from the humdrum character of the normal working day was the purpose of the '*Vergnügen*'.[68] It was a social which included dancing and entertainment, drink and music, the formal as well as the informal, and was part both of the organised culture and of the informal and the commercial. Many clubs and societies, bourgeois and proletarian, provided such entertainment for their members, often in the form of the annual *Stiftungsfest*, the event commemorating the founding of the organisation. These were generally closed events, but on special occasions non-members might take part.

In any case, these socials tended to follow a general tradition irrespective of class or party. This applied in particular to rural areas, where the village culture might colour even the celebrations of communist organisations. In 'Red Mössingen', a village in Southern Germany of some 4,000 inhabitants, containing both peasants and industrial workers, and with an unusually strong Communist Party, the basis for a successful celebration lay in keeping close to the traditional cultural norms of the village. One

---

66. Cf. Lucas, *Radikalismus* (note 54). Hamborn was one of those cities which had grown enormously within a few decades.
67. Cf. K. Blessing, 'Feste und Vergnügen kleiner Leute', in R. van Dulmen and N. Schindler (eds), *Volkskultur*, 1987, pp. 352–79; Dinse, *Freizeitleben* (note 28); E. Rosenhaft, *Beating the Fascists? The German Communists and Political Violence*, Cambridge, 1983, p. 150.
68. Bajohr, *Vom bitteren Los* (note 53), p. 194.

had to know how to sing a song or how to present a play, and a workers' club might well introduce 'dames of honour' with their escorts in formal dress into the procession, with the young lads wearing traditional costume. Those involved 'had looked on the various elements in the workers' festival as an attempt at the incorporation of the cultural heritage of the village'.[69]

Other socials and dances were non-political and non-organisational in origin. They could even be purely private in character, if a dozen or so workers decided to found a private club and obtain a licence (*Tanzschein*), hire a hall, and organise an event.[70]

But the bulk of the amusements and hops were provided either by the dance-halls in the inner cities, or, especially for the working-class families, by the large beer-halls or beer-gardens in the new working-class suburbs, which normally also provided the venues for the festivities of the organisations of the labour movement. They regularly organised their own events, the numbers of which seem to have gone up with the growth of the population and the expansion of the cities.[71] Thus in 1910 the Hamborn police issued 523 licences for dance-entertainments.[72] The beer-garden and the open-air restaurant at the edge of the city were also centres for families or friends to meet, especially as the growth of urban transport made modest excursions on Sundays possible. They invited families to 'come and brew their own coffee' – charging only for hot water and for the use of crockery.

Workers and their families were at the end of century also making use of certain public facilities for recreational activities which had been created by way of a limited attempt to counteract the evils of industrialisation and of bad housing. Thus the second half of the nineteenth century saw the establishment of the first urban parks – other than royal gardens or deer parks – and the first public baths, as well as the establishment of the first public lending libraries. The end of the period also saw the creation of the modern department stores and the building of the major railway stations, with their concourses. All these provided venues in which the masses could spend some of their leisure time. By the outbreak of war in 1914 an extensive network of leisure-time institutions

---

69. H.J. Althaus *et al.*, *Da ist nirgends nichts gewesen außer hier. Das rote Mössingen' im Generalstreik gegen Hitler*. Berlin, 1982, pp. 131–5.
70. Bajohr, *Vom bitteren Los* (note 53), p. 156. Cf. Lucas, *Radikalismus* (note 54), p. 94.
71. The 1925 Census listed under the general rubric of 'Gaststätten' ('Restaurants') 271 establishments, with 5,835 workers, which were defined as 'Cabarets'.
72. Lucas, *Radikalismus* (note 54), p. 94.

existed, and the period after the war saw major expansions only in respect of cinema (already in existence before the war) and of radio, while in other areas there was expansion without major changes of character.[73] Members of the working class participated in almost all forms of recreational and cultural activities, not counting those which were created specifically for them and were imbued with the ideas and aspirations of the labour movement.

Newer and older forms of commercial entertainment were used relatively heavily by the young workers who, especially in the post-war period, constituted a unique group of consumers within the wider proletarian strata. Not that all adolescents were culturally divorced from their homes. A study of the leisure-time pattern of Berlin youths in vocational schools at the end of the 1920s shows that for a significant number the family circle provided the main outlet for recreational activity. Yet even in this group, composed largely of apprentices with a relatively stable and economically above-average background, more than 10% stated that their leisure was spent away from the family.[74] The adolescent workers of the twentieth century were certainly the first generation with spare cash in their pockets and with the time to spend it. Their expenditure was directed above all at the products of the ready-made and widely publicised new leisure industries, especially the cinema; but they also patronised dance-halls and varieties, and competitive sports events such as football, boxing, and bicycle races.[75]

Some of these activities became more commercialised during the 1920s. More generally, the entertainment industry in the post-war years became more slick and more sophisticated, with the production of bigger events and with a more commercial organisation behind it. Traditional entertainment, from the fair booth to the street and courtyard musicians, did not disappear altogether; but overall the entertainment business became less of a craft and more of an industry. A comparison of the figures from the censuses of enterprises of 1907 and 1925 demonstrates this. Numerically, the industry neither grew nor declined between these two dates – the numbers employed were 87,906 and 83,813 respectively. Yet the figures conceal a marked shift in the character of the world of entertainment. Whereas in 1907 there were still 34,338 enterprises

73. Mühlberg, *Freizeitverhalten* (note 2).
74. *Die Jugendlichen in der Großstadtfamilie*, Berlin, 1930. The sample (1685 young men and 375 young women who submitted relatively unstructured responses) were largely from working-class, and frequently socialist and communist, families, but probably with a greater than normal degree of family cohesion.
75. Mühlberg *et al.*, *Arbeiterleben um 1900*, p. 125.

in the industry, many of them one-man firms, by 1925 the total number of businesses had dropped to 10,665.

A more detailed analysis shows not only an increase in the size of enterprises, but also a shift away from some older types of activity to new forms of entertainment. In 1907 by far the largest category was 'Music and Song', with 27,466 enterprises, in which over 54,000 persons were employed. In 1925 there were only 1,835 enterprises listed under the slightly different heading of *Musikgewerbe* ('the music industry'), and they employed 13,945 persons. At the same time the number of enterprises under the rubric of 'Theatre and Opera' fell from 2,181 to 437, while the number of those employed actually rose from *c.* 17,000 to over 26,000.[76] The commercialisation and modernisation of the entertainment industry, coupled with the rise of the mass media, also helped to popularise new tastes and create wider audiences for new forms of entertainment. A new popular culture came into being in the 1920s, which included such facets as the new fast dances such as the foxtrot, jazz music and the cabaret, gramophone records, and films, and popular magazines had mass audiences of mass consumers. It was essentially city culture, and a Berlin culture above all, appealing neither to an élite nor seeking merely to amuse. Its followers, a critic suggested, stretched right across society 'from the Bank Director to the shop-assistant and from the Film Star to the typist.'[77]

The new mass-culture was more sophisticated, more exciting and more novelty-demanding than the traditional popular culture had been. It was pushed and popularised by a press which increasingly sensationalised events and which gave expression to a personality-cult which fastened very largely on the 'stars of stage and screen' and on the record-breaking champions of the world of sport. In the latter field attention was focused on the highly competitive and the highly visual, thus concentrating on commercialised sport rather than on amateur events. Title-fights in boxing, six-day cycle races, held annually in the Berlin Sportspalast, and, of course, football matches attracted in the region of ten thousand spectators.[78]

76. In 1907 there were in the entertainment industry only 115 firms who employed more than 50 persons. By 1925 the figure had risen to 207, of whom 46 employed more than 200.

77. S. Kracauer in the *Frankfurter Zeitung* of 4 April 1926, quoted in J. Hermand and F. Trommler, *Die Kultur der Weimarer Republik*, Munich 1978, p. 70.

78. Cf. J. Hermand and F. Trommler (note 77) p. 75. Much bigger were the attendances at motor-racing events. At the 1926 German Grand Prix race held

We do not know the total number of those who went to view sports events, nor the proportion who were workers. We know even less about sport's wider public, those who read about it in the newspapers or who listened to sports-reportage on the radio; but sport certainly had a large working-class public. The older forms of mass entertainment continued to attract wide support from workers. It was estimated that in the 1920s some eighty million people visited fairs every season. Circus and variety still enjoyed great popularity, although they were meeting growing competition from newer, faster and slicker forms of commercial entertainment, which, in turn, caused them to modernise their presentation.[79]

The most significant development in the field of commercial leisure after 1918 was obviously the film. The cinema was by all accounts the most popular form of recreation for the masses, and the rapid increase in the number of film-theatres even in working-class districts is evidence of the growing popularity of the film even among workers.

The expansion of the cinema and the significance of the film for workers' leisure and culture is discussed more fully in Chapter 10 on the New Media. In the context of the discussion here I propose to look briefly at the place of the whole of the expanding 'new' and generally commercially provided entertainment in the whole area of the leisure-time activities of the worker and of his family.

It is tempting to see in the change in the pattern of entertainment and leisure and in the advance of the popular media of communication the operation of a kind of *Gresham's Law* by which commercial culture, like debased coinage, drives out the sterling silver of High Culture. There seems however little evidence for this in the decade or so under review here, although it may apply over a longer period. There was, as we shall see, in the 1920s a significant expansion also in the activities of organised workers' culture. It seems likely that what we are concerned with is the expansion of organised leisure activities as such which followed on the reduction of working hours, and to some extent resulted from even a slight increase in the sums available for recreation and culture in workers' budgets. Seen differently, we would be faced with a certain shift from private, unstructured leisure to organised leisure, whether commercially provided or not.

---

on the AVUS racing track in Berlin the attendance is alleged to have been in the region of half a million.

79. Cf. E. Abenstein, 'Alle Tage ist kein Alltag' in *Wem gehört die Welt*, pp. 441–55.

In any case no one pattern of leisure applies throughout the working class. The evening and weekend activities of unorganised young workers in the 1920s, with more spare time and more spare cash than an earlier generation, are more directed at the cinema, the amusement arcade and the dance-hall. The leisure of the rural labourer, cultivating a plot and raising animals, may be entirely devoted to domestic and family-related activities. And while virtually all the respondent workers in the Family Budget survey referred to earlier had some expenditure on entertainment, 40% of households with incomes below 2,500 marks spent nothing on the cinema, while an identical percentage had no expenditure on concerts or theatres.[80]

Figure 2 Leisure-time usage by the working class

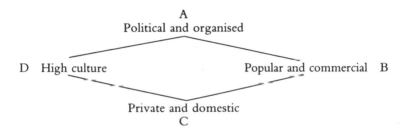

We can represent the types of leisure time usage and enjoyment by the working class in a simplified diagrammatic form as shown in Figure 2 (above).

While individuals may occupy all, many or only one of these positions, certain groups of workers will show a more specific pattern. Thus the women textile workers whose accounts of their leisure were cited earlier tended to move on axis A—C; unorganised adolescents may move along B—C; while the young socialist workers seeking to develop their unique lifestyle, who are described in Chapter 11, will tend to move along a line A—D—C.

80. There is no indication to what an extent the two groups of non-spenders overlapped.

–5–

Workers' Sport: A Million-Member Movement

Origin and Growth of the Workers' Sports Movement

The workers' sports movement is the earliest of the cultural and leisure-time organisations which grew up within the orbit of the social-democratic movement after the repeal of the Anti-Socialist Laws in 1890.[1] It was throughout by far the largest of the workers' cultural associations. At the time of its greatest influence in the years of the Weimar Republic the membership of the dozen or so organisations which since 1912 were loosely federated in the Zentralkommission für Arbeitersport und Körperpflege was equal to the membership of the two parties of the left. The movement's field of activities extended well beyond the circle of party members, and included the whole of the working class – or at least that section of it from which voters for the SPD and for the KPD were recruited. Sport mobilised above all adolescents and younger men and women, principally those who were following skilled or semi-skilled occupations, or who held white-collar jobs.[2]

Originally the workers' sports clubs concentrated on gymnastics, but their scope widened over the years. The expansion and diversification of their activities and the formation of new organisations catering for more specialised interests such as sailing and motor-cycling, not only reflect changing trends in sport as such, but are also evidence of growing affluence in sections of the working class.

As we shall see, workers' sport cannot be fully identified with

---

1. Some gymnastics activities were associated with the Workers' Educational Societies, which had first come into being as early as the 1860s. Cf. V. Schmidtchen, 'Arbeitersport – Erziehung zum sozialistischen Menschen', in J. Reulecke and W. Weber (eds), *Fabrik, Familie, Feierabend*, Wuppertal, 1978 pp. 345–75.
2. It has been estimated that in spite of the mass membership of the workers' sports movement there were as many workers organised in bourgeois sports organisations. In 1923 42% of the membership of the principal workers' sport organisations were under eighteen.

Table 5 Membership of workers' sport organisations

	c. 1910	c. 1928
Arbeiter Turn (und Sport) Bund (1893)	130,000	770,000
Arbeiter Athletenbund (1906)	4,000	56,000
Arbeiter Radfahrerbund 'Solidarität' (1893)	130,000	222,000
Arbeiter Wanderbund 'Naturfreunde' (1895)	7,000	79,000
Arbeiter Schützenbund (1921)	—	5,500
Arbeiter Angler (1921)	—	6,500
Arbeiter Kegler (1912)	—	8,000
Arbeiter Schachbund (1912)	—	13,000
Freier Seglerverband (1901)	—	2,000
Arbeiter Samaritaner (1904)	3,000	43,000
Verband Volksgesundheit (1906)	3,000	15,000
	277,000	1,220,000

Note: Some of the organisations here listed are not sports organisations in the strict sense. They are included because they were affiliated to the Zentralkommission für Arbeitersport und Korperpflege.

'socialist' sport. The movement deliberately refused any formal association with the SPD, and the latter sought only in 1929 to commit its members to carry out their sport activities under the auspices of the Workers' Sport Movement.[3] Politics nevertheless lay at the beginning of workers' sport in the 1890s. But it was a product of the politics of opposition, brought about through an anti-social-democratic attitude on the part of the mainly middle-class members of the Deutsche Turnerschaft, the leading and strongly nationalistic gymnasts' association, which had originally come into existence as the result of the patriotic sentiment engendered by the Wars of Liberation against Napoleon in 1812–13. The leading members of these organisations felt antagonistic to the 'unpatriotic social-democrats' and the 'German Gymnasts' Association', falling in line with the general anti-socialist sentiment prevalent during the period of the anti-socialist laws, expelled individual social-democrats and whole associations.[4] Socialist workers, in turn, felt offended by the anti-socialist attitudes displayed in the ranks of the Deutsche Turnerschaft, and chose to secede. In short, the social and political antagonism between the

3. H. Ueberhorst, *Frisch, froh, stark und treu. Die Arbeitersportbewegung in Deutschland, 1893–1933*, Düsseldorf, 1973.
4. In places with several clubs it was frequently the case that one of them catered for members of the bourgeoisie, one for the lower middle class, and one for the working class. Ueberhorst, *Frisch, froh*, quoting contemporary sources.

classes had by the end of the nineteenth century reached such a pitch that it even penetrated the, on the face of it, neutral area of gymnastics.[5]

Independent workers' sport clubs and societies arose in opposition to the Deutsche Turnerschaft, but they developed initially mainly by way of a break-away of local clubs, which constituted themselves as independent workers' sport societies. Following on such original acts of secession, new local societies were formed in an ever-growing number of places. In 1893 the existing fifty-one individual societies set the seal on the formation of a national organisation under the title of Arbeiter Turn Bund (ATB), which later changed its name to Arbeiter Turn und Sport Bund (ATSB) to take account of the greater range of sports activities it now covered.

The early workers' sport societies generally affirmed their support for social-democratic policies. Indeed, the strengthening of the body was seen not only as a valuable correction to the general strains and the debilitating influences of heavy physical work. Its body-building function was also regarded as a valuable preparation for the class struggle. In the words of the Leipzig worker gymnasts, sport would produce a healthy and resistant body, which even in later years would be capable of withstanding the rigours of proletarian life. Those who took part in sport, and spent their evenings in the gymnasium, did better than if they spent it in the pub. They prepared for the future, because 'the bricks from which the house of the future were to be built should not be rotten or brittle'.[6]

Last, but not least, the ATB fought hard to persuade workers who were organised in the Deutsche Turnerschaft to recognise the anti-working-class character of the latter, and to come across into the working-class camp. By thus emphasising the importance of a class-based organisation outside the strictly political, the ATB contributed to the strengthening of class solidarity. In turn the authorities of the Wilhelmine Empire included workers' sport as an activity against which they should take action whenever possible, and, if the law of associations did not give the means to proceed, the education law could and would be used in an attempt to prevent the recruiting and training of persons under eighteen, or even under twenty-one.[7]

5. Cf. V. Lidtke, 'Die kulturelle Bedeutung der Arbeitervereine', in G. Wiegelmann (ed.), *Kultureller Wandel im 19. Jahrhundert*, Göttingen, 1973.
6. Ueberhorst, *Frisch, froh* (note 3), p. 38.
7. The relevant part of the law relating to private teaching laid down that those involved should be of good character. This clause was used to disqualify social democrats.

Such overt discrimination disappeared after the revolution; indeed state subsidies were available to the workers' sport movement and were widely used. The fast-growing membership of the ATSB – its numbers in 1919 were double those of 1914, and then doubled again during the next decade – show not only the popularity of sport but also the greater leisure, and, possibly, the somewhat greater affluence of the younger members, who formed an increasing share of the membership. Moreover, the movement was now able to overcome its original handicaps, the shortage of halls and gymnasia and the lack of means to purchase and install new equipment. Workers' sports clubs could now use the gymnasia in schools, and other public provisions such as swimming-baths; and, with the help of public funds, they could acquire or construct special sports facilities for themselves.[8]

By the end of the 1920s the organisations of the workers' sport movement could lay claim to the possession of 249 gymnasia and 1,265 sports- and playing-fields with clubhouses attached to them, changing rooms, and so on. They also owned nearly a hundred bathing-places, some with boat-houses, as well as 48 boat-houses on their own, a gymnasium with a swimming-bath attached, two ski jumps, and four regional residential homes. In addition, the workers' cycling clubs owned a bicycle factory, and the Naturfreunde, the workers' hiking organisation, owned some 200 clubhouses, huts, and residential homes in the countryside, where hikers could generally stay overnight, or even spend their holidays.[9] And, last not least, the movement had established a Central Sport Training School in Leipzig, the Bundessportschule with its own, purpose-built, quarters, erected with a 50 per cent grant from the government of the Reich. It regularly organised training courses for officials and athletes.

For the worker-sportsmen above all playing-fields and bricks and mortar had more than a purely utilitarian function. They symbolised the strength of the movement, and they provided not only an anchorage point for their activities but also a concrete focus for the exercise of loyalty and of proprietorial feelings. In rural areas in particular it was easy and not uncommon for the sports club to become the centre of leisure activities, unmindful of the idea

8. Towards the end of the Weimar period a new wave of discrimination can be observed. The right-wing government of Bavaria refused access to public gymnasia and interfered with the organisation of children in the labour movement. (Report of the Landeskartell für Bildung, Sport und Jugendpflege der freien Arbeiterbewegung der Rheinpfalz, 1931.)
9. F. Wildung, *Arbeitersport*, Berlin, 1929, p. 54.

that the solidarity displayed should serve wider political aims and ends. Such societal patriotism (*Vereinsmeierei*) was castigated within the movement and outside it. Fritz Wildung, the General Secretary of the Workers' Sports Movement, criticised those who believed that the 'solution for all social problems could be achieved through the pursuit of Sport, Music, or Drama and who condemned party and trade unions if they would not follow them in their chosen path'.[10] Similar criticism was levelled against the sports movement from without. The political problem with which the workers' sports movement was faced was a dual one. On the one hand, its leaders, who were almost exclusively recruited from those who were strongly committed to social-democratic politics, and who were often active as party officials or as local government representatives, wished to commit the movement to a political role. On the other hand, they were also anxious to maintain the unity and strength of the organisation, which contained a sizeable minority of members who were not committed to the support of a political party or, more importantly, who supported the KPD.

The 'oppositional' members in the workers' sports movement and the German Communist Party were, of course, anxious to secure its support for *their* policies, and, if at all possible, to use it as a springboard for the creation of a 'common front' of proletarian forces ranked behind a revolutionary strategy. On the other hand, sport was the most popular and the most publicly visible of the cultural activities in which the German workers engaged. It was moreover one which obtained support from public funds and assistance at the local and national level, and offered a basis for the expression of commitment to the republican system and the Weimar democracy.

The ideological commitment of the workers' sports movement – discussed further below – showed itself not only in a party-political sense. It was also demonstrated in the way in which actual sporting practices were developed within the movement. Not only might physical and athletic skills be used directly in the service of political action – as in the involvement of worker-cyclists in political agitation in rural areas, which was to earn them such epithets as 'red hussars of the class struggle'.[11] More importantly, the sport ideals and the sports ethos developed within the movement were in many respects opposed to the competition-seeking and record-beating

10. Ibid. p. 32.
11. Cf. Würtembergisches Landesmuseum, *Arbeiterbewegung und Arbeiterkultur in Stuttgart, 1890–1933*, Stuttgart, 1981, p. 46.

spirit fostered by the bourgeois sports organisations. They demonstrate more concretely than we find it in some other branches of workers' culture the desire to create the 'new socialist man', who would show new sensibilities and conform to a new style of life, different from that of the bourgeoisie.

The Ideals and Practices of *Arbeitersport*

The values and goals of sport activities were conceived not only in terms of fitness for the struggle in life and work and of the preparation for the economic and political struggle. More general ideological concepts were brought into the discussion. Physical accomplishments and the aesthetic value of a beautiful or well-developed body were seen not only as valuable in themselves, but, following old humanistic traditions, were equated with general beauty and with education towards humanist ideals. There was an assumption that physical and mental qualities developed in parallel. 'As gymnastics strengthens the individual it makes him better and less selfish, more receptive for generous and noble impulses. It teaches him to love others and by thus bringing people close to each other it also brings nations closer together.'[12]

Fritz Wildung compared sport activities with work; but the latter was oppressive, through the social conditions under which it had to be carried out. Sport was a substitute for the failed work-experience. As physical experience which was freely chosen it could give joy and psychic gratification, and compensate for all that man suffered through work.[13]

General humanist ideals and the basic tenets of socialist philosophy were propagated by the Workers' Sport Journals, or through the medium of pamphlets published by the ATSB. Such ideals were also inculcated through the medium of Mass Oratoria or dramatisations staged before tens of thousands at the great national and international events of the workers' sports movement, the two National Sports Festivals, held in 1922 in Leipzig and in 1929 in Nuremberg, or the Workers' Olympiads, held first in Frankfurt in 1925. They will be discussed below in the context of the whole Festival culture of the German labour movement.

12. *Arbeiterturnzeitung*, 1899 no. 2, quoted in H. Ueberhorst, 'Bildungsgedanke und Solidaritätsbewußtsein in der deutschen Arbeiterbewegung, *AfSG*, vol. 14, 1974, pp. 275–92, p. 283.
13. F. Wildung, '*Vom Sinn des Arbeitersport*', in the *Festbuch* of the first *Arbeiterolympiade*, 1925, quoted in *Die Junge Garde*, Frankfurt, 1981, p. 214.

More germane, because more sport-related and at the same time more immediately educational, were the training practices which the movement developed internally. Workers' sport clearly deliberately set out to suppress the competitive element in modern sport and to encourage the co-operative and the collective element in it – and, through sport, hopefully in life in general. Such sentiments were stated repeatedly. We can find them expressed regularly in the programmes of the annual Workers' Sports Days (Reichsarbeiter-sporttage or RAST). The Altona programme of 1928 spoke of 'the basic characteristics of workers' sport, which was not a vain hunt to beat records. The emphasis was on team achievement, which was a major part of socialist education'; and the Berlin programme, while conceding three years later the fact that there would be 'a noble competition between individuals', stressed nevertheless that 'the principal emphasis would be on mass events . . . the workers' sport movement knows no sport idols, there is only communal effort'.[14]

In spite of a growing personality cult, which had penetrated even the socialist and communist movement, workers' sports organisations sought thus to encourage collective as against personal achievements. At the beginning this sentiment went so far that clubs discouraged giving points for individual performances to gymnasts or recording their achievements, let alone holding contests with prizes, although it knew the role of the *Vorturner*, the gymnast who showed an exercise which the group would then seek to follow. Even at events involving several clubs contests were not permitted at first, although this was changed in 1911; and in 1923 the ATSB introduced an 'order of performance list' in gymnastics, and awarded the title of National Master Gymnast (*Bundesturn-meister*).

Generally the concept of sport and of achievement in sport related to collective performance and group effort; but clubs also sought to bring the 'play instinct' into sport, to foster uncompetitive activities, and to encourage joint family activities.[15] Inevitably the growing emphasis on performance in the world of sport at large gave rise to conflict within the movement and led to secessions, especially of football teams seeking greater support by joining factory sports clubs or by simply turning themselves into factory

14. From the respective programmes. The Altona programme is reprinted in *Arbeiterkultur in Hamburg um 1930*, Hamburg, 1982, p. 202. The Berlin programme, headed *Reichsarbeiter Sport Tag*, contained a preface signed by Adolf Lau.
15. Cf. S. Reck, *Arbeiter nach der Arbeit*, Frankfurt, 1977, pp. 177–9.

teams. Occasionally jobs would be offered to very successful sportsmen by way of inducement to transfer to bourgeois clubs; but the general ethos remained largely unaffected. A minority wished to introduce badges and diplomas, but as late as 1926 the National Assembly of the ATSB affirmed its rejection of all outward signs of competitiveness. Looking back, an activist of the movement confirmed that 'in training, communal achievements remained of supreme importance'.[16]

Pressure towards the introduction of competition was naturally greatest where the outside world put particular emphasis on it. The cult of competitive cycling, which developed during the 1920s, and which showed itself in such mad events as an indoor 'six-day track race', forced workers' cycling clubs into the organisation of competition; but, almost as if to mock the cult of speed racing, they then also staged attempts to show how slowly 100 metres could be covered on a bike.[17]

A greater competitiveness inevitably came into the practices of workers' sport with the growing importance of athletics, including team games. Football was the most popular single activity here, but its competitive character was held in bounds by restricting games to the movement. In the post-war period contests developed in all branches of athletics, and the emphasis on training in respect of specific techniques was no less developed in workers' sports clubs than in their bourgeois neighbours. This introduction of competition and performance was being justified by some with reference to the concept of 'socialist competition' which had been introduced in the Soviet Union. By showing how workers' achievements were nearing those attained by the bourgeoisie, and by thus making competition serve class interests, it was also being made ideologically acceptable.[18]

Not all concerned approved of this development, and they suggested that it was a temporary phase which would give way to a greater emphasis on team sport.[19] In any case, competition was never allowed to develop completely unchecked. Contests were generally held only up to the district level, and there were no prizes

---

16. A former workers' sport official quoted by Schmidtchen, *Arbeitersport*, (note 1). Competition was, of course, also related to the form of sport. Football or running could hardly do without a competitive element.
17. *Arbeiterbewegung. . . . Stuttgart* (note 11), p. 46.
18. Cf. H. Bernett, 'Das Problem einer alternativen Sportpraxis im deutschen Arbeitersport untersuch am Beispiel der Leichtathletik', in H. Teichler (ed.), *Arbeiterkultur und Arbeitersport*, Clausthal-Zellerfeld, 1985, pp. 50–76, pp. 53–6.
19. H. Wagner, *Sport und Arbeiterbewegung*, Berlin, 1931, cited in Ueberhorst, *Frisch, froh*, p. 287.

or medals, but only diplomas – and even these were rejected in 1926, although some written records of performances were often provided on cards.[20] Also, while the ATSB would publish the best annual results attained, the names of the champions were not published. And parallel with individual competitions all sorts of team athletics were staged, such as relays, often over long distances, cross-country running, or group displays with emphasis on style rather than achievement.[21]

The Naturfreunde, founded in Vienna in 1895 and active in Germany since 1905, was probably the most 'intellectual' of the workers' sports organisations. Its basic tenets lay in the belief that the worker was not only suffering social deprivation, but that, as the result of his physical impoverishment, he did not experience joy, that his conditions forced him to be dull and lacking in ability to fight. By exposing him to a regular contact with nature and with the landscape in all its majesty the 'Friends of Nature' movement hoped to remedy this.[22] In this emphasis on a cultural experience the Naturfreunde had more in common with organisations like the Freethinkers than with sports organisations as such, although their network of huts provided opportunities for such sports as mountain-climbing and skiing. Above all, however, it was the practice of *Soziale Wandern* ('social rambling') which was to teach workers not only to understand the landscape in its geological and social configurations, but also to understand flora and fauna.[23] And even more important than the 'learning' aspect of the *Soziale Wandern* was the collectivist aspect of the ramble. It was this which gave it a 'proletarian character', it 'brings into hiking ideas which have their roots in the class-conscious attitude of the working class'.[24]

After the war and the revolution the Naturfreunde experienced a considerable influx, as the ideals of the youth movement stimulated hiking in the workers' youth organisation and as some white-collar and professional workers found their way to the labour movement and helped to swell the ranks of the organisation. And while the young enthusiastically supported the touristic ideals of the Naturfreunde, other pressures sought to bring elements of competition

20. See Schmidtchen, *Arbeitersport* (note 1), pp. 358 and 371.
21. Cf. Bernett, 'Alternative Sportpraxis, (note 18).
22. Cf. H. Wunderer, 'Der Touristenverein Die Naturfreunde, eine sozial-demokratische Arbeiterkulturorganisation', *IWK*, no. 13, 1977, pp. 506–19.
23. J. Zimmer, 'Vom Walzen zum sozialen Wandern', in A. Lehmann (ed.), *Studien zur Arbeiterkultur*, Münster, 1984, pp. 141–73.
24. Ibid. p.164, citing W. Mohr, 'Soziales Wandern', *Naturfreund*, 1930, p. 118.

into the process, for example ski-racing and jumping.[25]

The period after 1918 also saw the rise or expansion of new forms of physical activities, which by their very nature encouraged group enterprise rather than formal competition. New types of sport, such as hiking, and skiing, as well as water sports such as canoeing, were increasingly practised by workers, and were undertaken in groups rather than individually. In swimming, too, communal rather then competitive practices were introduced, such as swimming in formations, figure-swimming, or swimming simply as a family activity.[26]

In Hamburg 20,000–30,000 workers, often with their families, engaged in the various branches of water-sport. Clubs had now easier access to municipal pools; but the Water Sport Club 'Vorwärts' also maintained its own 'Sun and Swim Bath' on the upper Elbe, 23 km above Hamburg. The meadow which they had hired acted also as a camping-place, on which simple huts were later erected. The mostly young sportsmen and sportswomen would paddle their canoes there on Saturday afternoons and spend the night there. Out there they felt themselves to be 'all equal, folk who were keen on swimming and leisure . . . and sport was, after all, the third power, after the party and the unions', as a veteran related fifty years later.[27] Here sport was clearly related to a general desire to escape the dreary urban surroundings of working-class existence and enjoy the 'great out-of-doors'.

Workers' Sport and the Proletarian Community

The workers' sports movement, with well over a million members, engaged in a wide range of activities and meetings, often in the view of spectators and of the wider public, was the most highly visible of the cultural organisations of the German labour movement. But the activities in which *Arbeitersport* was engaged did not only take place in the gymnasium or on the playing-field or the athletics track. Given the strong links of many clubs and organisations with the Social Democratic Party and its branches, sportsmen and women, often in white athletics dress or in black trousers or skirts and white shirts or blouses, took part in demonstrations, or performed at political gatherings or celebrations.

25. Ibid. pp. 164–5.
26. Reck, *Arbeiter*, (note 15) pp. 177–9.
27. *Arbeiterkultur* . . . *Hamburg* (note 14), pp. 194–5.

The disciplined and orderly form in which the athletes participated was not only an answer to bourgeois views of the proletariat as a dangerous and threatening rabble; it also contributed to feelings of strength and self-confidence in participants and spectators alike. At the first Workers' Olympiad in Frankfurt the march-past of sportsmen and women, formed in rows of sixteen, took an hour and a half, and it was clearly a symbolic representation of working-class strength. So too was the performance of the chorus work *Kampf um die Erde* ('The struggle for the world') staged by some 2,000 before an audience of 60,000.[28]

Here and elsewhere workers' sport went beyond its specific field of activities and entered the wider area of workers' culture through its own choral groups, bands and theatre groups. It provided thereby 'points of crystallisation' for organised and unorganised workers.[29] Contacts of this kind were on occasion also created in the halls and clubhouses which workers' sports clubs built in the 1920s. Such foci were of particular importance for the rural and small-town working class. Thus, in the partly industrialised rural districts of Württemberg, a number of *Spielhallen* (indoor sports halls) were built in that period. And although these places owed their establishment to the planning, financing and even direct labour of one or several sports clubs and their members, the provisions which were created served the needs of many socialist working-class organisations and even of communist ones.

Thus the Arbeiter Turn Verein Vorwärts in Steinheim acquired in 1927 a plot for a playing-field and a sports hall, and proceeded to erect a commodious building with a hall which could seat 500, a kitchen with offices, a meeting room, a reading room and a flat for the caretaker. The hall became a centre for political, trade union, and sports activities, an outward sign of working-class solidarity, showing at the back of the platform both a picture of Ebert, the first (socialist) President of the Republic, and another of Lenin.[30] These places were not only places for training and exercise and meeting places for societies. Their function extended to that of '*Gewerkschaftshaus* [Trade Union Centre], Library, place for festivities, Bar, Bowling Alley, Dance Hall, Concert Hall, Theatre', and the like.[31] It extended even beyond those activities customarily

---

28. *KW* 1925, p. 192; Ueberhorst, 'Bildungsgedanke', pp. 285–6; G. Hauk, in *Illustrierte Geschichte des Arbeitersports* (ed. H.J. Teichler and G. Hauk) Bonn–Berlin, 1987, pp. 138–40.

29. *Arbeiterbewegung . . . Stuttgart* (see note 11), p. 38.

30. *Arbeiterkultur in der proletarischen Provinz, 1890–1933*, Marbach, 1983 p. 25.

31. Cf. S. Beck *et al.* 'Spielplatzhallen aus der Weimarer Republik', in Erdmanns-

provided by the labour movement, by providing an informal venue for social intercourse of particular attraction to women, who were traditionally less involved in leisure-time social contacts.

The sports movement was also the most diffuse of the cultural institutions of the working class. In the larger towns and cities most districts would have one or more workers' sport organisations, both general gymnastics and athletics clubs and often specialised organisations for, for example, football or swimming. In the Hamburg area the ATSB alone had, in 1928/9, 144 affiliated clubs with a total membership of nearly 23,000, and with individual memberships ranging from 29 to over 1,200.[32]

Locally the various workers' sport organisations were loosely linked in so-called 'Sportskartelle', to which other organisations, such as the SAJ (Socialist Workers' Youth) were often affiliated. Ties with the youth organisations were particularly close; but the ATSB collaborated also with other organisations in joint activities, especially in the staging of general educational, cultural and entertainment events. Thus in Frankfurt the *Volkschor Union* and the section 'Nord' of the ATSB combined annually at Christmas in the production of a 'Dance and Mime' event, performed before thousands in the Hippodrome.[33]

With the general expansion of its activities the movement also paid greater attention to educational tasks, especially in places where there was a vigorous socialist movement. This might take the form of specific courses – for example, an introduction to the Weimar constitution, which was given by a Hamburg club; or it might take the form of recitation from workers' poets or readings from socialist authors – to be a kind of motto for the particular training session. The movement's central training institution, the Bundesschule in Leipzig, while primarily concerned with physical training, also offered its students lectures on such general topics as sport and socialism.[34]

There is here some evidence of the workers' sports movement's becoming toward the end of the Weimar period a wider cultural movement, occupying a central position in the local community. Yet there are other, countervailing forces at work. The growing emphasis on records and victories in sport, paralleled by an expan-

hausen, Mosbach und Steinheim, *Ludwigsburger Geschichtsblätter* 1985, pp. 104–130, p. 115.
32. *Arbeiterkultur in Hamburg* (note 14), p. 208.
33. *Die Junge Garde*, Frankfurt, 1981, pp. 211–12.
34. *Arbeiterkultur in Hamburg*, p. 189; Schmidtchen, *Arbeitersport*, (note 1) p. 365; Ueberhorst, 'Bildungsgedanke', p. 288.

sion of spectator-sport (boxing, football, cycle-racing) caused some secession of gifted sportsmen and teams from workers' sports clubs into bourgeois clubs and enterprise-based teams.[35] And given the growth of the pro-competition element in sport (which was, at times, even supported by the socialist press) it is obvious that workers, too, increasingly watched general sports events.[36]

The fact that in spite of the growth in the membership of the ATSB and of other workers' sport organisations large numbers of workers, especially young workers, were content to practise gymnastics and athletics in bourgeois organisations, suggests that sport and political commitment did not always go together.[37] On the other hand, the political commitment of the workers' sports movement, discussed below, grew during our period. Much of this was in support of the existing institutions, but from the end of the 1920s onwards the communist movement increasingly sought to mobilise sport for its stance of revolutionary politics. This caused a more marked split in the workers' sport movement than in any other field.

Workers' Sport and Working-Class Politics

As we saw, the workers' sports movement was from its inception involved in discussion about its political role, and this became more accentuated after the revolution, when the legal restrictions under which the organisations had laboured, disappeared. The war-time split of the SPD did not affect the movement immediately, as most of its activities were suspended; unlike the case with the workers' youth movement, there was no split within the sports movement. The young Communist Party too made no attempt to found independent sports and leisure-time organisations, although here, as elsewhere, it sought to influence politics from within. The ideological rift which developed in the political left after the war

35. Schmidtchen, *Arbeitersport*, (note 1), pp. 369–70.
36. Cf. the stimulating article by Peter Friedemann, 'Die Krise der Arbeitersport-bewegung am Ende der Weimarer Republik', in F. Böll (ed.), *Arbeiterkultur zwischen Alltag und Politik*, Vienna, 1986, pp. 229–40.
37. Apart from bourgeois clubs with working-class membership we have working-class clubs which were politically neutral but socially very cohesive, such as the Gelsenkirchen Football Club *Schalke 04*. Cf. S. Gehrmann, 'Fußball in einer Industrieregion, das Beispiel F.C. Schalke 04' in Reulecke and Weber, *Fabrik* (note 1), pp. 377–98. But note that the expansion in the membership of the workers' sports movement in the 1920s was considerably faster than the expansion in that of the Deutsche Turnerschaft over the same period.

had nevertheless repercussions throughout the network of sports organisations, some of which were more radical than others, and sought to commit the movement to a radical left course. As in the wider labour movement, there was a bitter debate on the role of the workers' and soldiers' councils in the process of democratic decision-making, and on the continuation of revolutionary policies in general.

Thus the Berlin workers' sports club *Fichte*, with 10,000 members one of the largest workers' sport organisations in the country, advocated support for the Councils, and caused an incipient split in the Berlin section of the ATSB. The Berlin workers' cyclists too advocated a radical course. Echoing policies of the extreme left they argued that 'a political revolution is only half a revolution, and a workers' cycling club which practises political neutrality has no *raison d'être*. Socialist cyclists should take their stand on their belief in the dictatorship of the proletariat'.[38] This was also an attack, from the left, on the formally neutral stance of the workers' sport movement. The latter had been confirmed repeatedly by the ATSB, and it was expressed in a statement by the Zentralkommission that 'the worker sports movement was consciously socialist, but it was so not in the sense of a specific political party',[39] and the movement also expected that its members would belong to one or the other of the two workers' parties.

This neutrality was not without its critics within the movement and without, and it clearly lost its *raison d'être* with the secession of communist sportsmen and communist-inclined clubs. But even before then there was unofficial criticism from the SPD, who thought that the sports movement should identify more openly and more closely with the institutions of the democratic state, and educate its members in that spirit. As the *Vorwärts* wrote in June 1925, it was strange that the workers' sports movement could not summon up the strength to declare its open support for the republic, together with the whole of the socialist labour movement.[40]

A large section of the movement had, of course, personal ties with the SPD and with the trade union movement. Of the district delegates of the ATSB in 1930, three-quarters were members of the SPD, and 88% were trade unionists, while the rest were mainly

38. From the *Arbeiter Radfahrer* of 1 August 1919, cited in H. Timmermann, *Geschichte und Struktur der Arbeitersportbewegung*, Marburg, 1967, p. 52.
39. *Handbuch der Zentral Kommission für Sport und Körperpflege*, n.d., cited in Van der Will and Burns, *Arbeiterkulturbewegung* in der Weimarer Republik, Berlin, 1982, p. 99.
40. *Vorwärts*, 30 June 1925, cited in Timmermann, *Geschichte*, p. 83 (note 38).

unorganised; and we must also assume that the great majority of the 9,919 local councillors who were organised in the workers' sports movement were social democrats.[41]

Support for the Weimar state and for its institutions was not unrelated to the support which workers' sport received from public bodies. The Zentralkommission was officially recognised as the representative organisation for workers' sport, and it and the local clubs and societies now had claims on public funds, and could use local public sports facilities.

Being thus enmeshed in the political institutions was for many members – almost all of whom were skilled workers and white-collar workers, and did not generally belong to the poorer section of the working class – tangible evidence for the value of the new democracy. The new state was admittedly not the socialist state of the future; but it was a stage in the movement towards it. A writer in the *Freie Sportwoche* declared in 1927 that 'the workers had good reason to publicise the new constitution even more than hitherto and to explain the great changes in the political system that had taken place', and thereby make working-class organisations aware of the need to defend what had been achieved.[42]

As the political situation became more critical the workers' sports press, with its sixty journals and a circulation of several hundred thousands one of the most influential of the propaganda media, increasingly came to support this line. Worker sportsmen, it was argued, had every reason to take up the defence of the Weimar constitution as a matter of concern to them, and to defend democracy against attacks from the right and the left. The movement's engagement in political education was directed particularly at young members, for whom special courses on socialist theory and trade unionism, as well as general cultural questions, were arranged in order to help to create the 'New Socialist Man of Action', the *Sozialistische Tatenmenschen*.[43] It owed much to the activities of the workers' youth movement, who towards the end of our period entered into closer organisational links with the sports movement.

Parallel with this movement on the reformist side the communist section of the membership, generally in a minority, but rather strong in Berlin, Saxony, Hamburg, and the Ruhr, sought to secure the removal of whole clubs as well as of individual members into the organisational framework of the Kampfgemeinschaft für

41. *MdVA*, no. 302 of 1 June 1930.
42. Quoted by Timmermann, *Geschichte*, p. 91 (note 38).
43. Ueberhorst, *Bildungsgedanke*, especially pp. 288–9 (note 12).

rote Sporteinheit ('The fighting front for a red unified sport'), later referred to as Rotsport. Founded originally in 1929, with the paradoxical title of 'Interessengemeinschaft zur Wiederherstellung der Einheit im Arbeitersport' ('Union to re-establish unity in workers' sport'), it was one of the largest of the communist mass-membership organisations, and by far the largest of those in the cultural field. It reached a membership of 100,000, many of whom were, however, not active members.[44]

The communist opposition in the general (social-democratic) workers' sport organisations tended to operate by seeking to secure a majority position in the leadership of the club or among the representatives to district or regional committees or conferences. These would then endeavour to pass resolutions which would be anathema to social-democratic members, and the result would either be the disaffiliation of the organisation or its expulsion by the district or by the central organisation.

In the Ruhr area, where communist influence was particularly strong, the KPD claimed majority support and the secession of many clubs. Their factional activity had secured for them decisive power at district and regional assembly level, and had secured control over local workers' sports cartels. However, after the creation of new 'social-democratic' cartels by the old SPD-based ruling groups of functionaries all communists and sympathisers did not necessarily leave the organisations, which returned to the re-created social-democratic organisational structure.[45]

The leadership of the Ruhr district of the KPD claimed all the membership in the excluded clubs, viz., 7,200, and a further 5,500 out of *c*. 13,000 in the clubs which had remained with the older party or had returned to the fold.[46] What seems clear is that political loyalty and club loyalty were at times at variance, and that however strong the pressure by the KPD and however manipulative its policy *vis-à-vis* the mass organisations, many of those involved preferred to stick to the familiar surroundings and loyalties established in sports-halls and on the playing-fields, irrespective of the politics of the majority of the members. Thus communists would remain in 'social-democratic' clubs – and would be forced to do so in places and areas, especially in the countryside, where there was

---

44. There were no regular statistics, but at the movement's National Conference, held in conjunction with the National Sports Meeting, there were 172 delegates, representing 97,600 members.
45. KPD Bezirk Ruhrgebiet, *Bericht* 1930 (Sektion 'Arbeit in den Massenorganisationen') pp. 185–95.
46. Ibid. p. 189.

often only one, social-democratic, sports organisation.[47] Conversely one would imagine that clubs which had formally moved over to the opposition would continue to contain some socialist members who had long been attached to them.

The Kampfgemeinschaft, like other communist mass-organisations, contained many members who were not fully committed to the cause. Actual party members were clearly in a minority. Thus of the 7,000 or so members of clubs who belonged to the Kampfgemeinschaft in the party district North-West (*Wasserkante*), centred on Hamburg, only 10–15% were estimated to belong to the KPD.[48] In Hamburg itself, red sports organisations claimed in 1932 the support of eighty-five clubs with 5,000 members, while the social-democratic sports groups had a total of 16,000 members – 7,000 less than before the split in 1929.[49]

The strongly political character of the communist sports organisation was in line with the general policy of the KPD which, as we saw, endeavoured to mobilise the resources of the ancillary organisations for the political struggle. General political considerations apart, the party argued, with special reference to sporting activities, that, as capitalist exploitation caused the physical debility of the workers, only political action could put it right. Hence, 'workers' sport must collaborate with the KPD in a "fighting front" to achieve the downfall of capitalist society'.[50]

This concentration on political activity, as against sports events, was assisted by difficulties in actually pursuing athletics and gymnastics. The halls and playing-fields of the workers' sports organisations remained in the hands of the social-democratic clubs, and were not available to the new bodies, which also encountered great difficulties in securing the use of municipal facilities. Not surprisingly, some clubs and teams returned to the social-democratic fold, or even joined bourgeois sports organisations.[51]

A mass organisation such as Rotsport could not maintain the loyalty of its members solely through a political commitment. Sporting activities continued in spite of the difficulties about sports facilities which most societies experienced. Ball-games practices

47. In Saxony the KPD claimed that of 750 local party branches only 250 had sports clubs which belonged to the opposition. KPD Saxony, *Bericht der Bezirksleitung*, 1932, p. 72
48. KPD Bezirk Wasserkante, *Bericht* 1932, p. 109.
49. *Arbeiterkultur . . . Hamburg*, (note 14), p. 206.
50. *Kampfgenoß*, 1930 no. 7, July, p. 20. (The *Kampfgenoß* was the monthly journal of the Berlin Sportsclub *Fichte*.)
51. H. Wunderer, *Arbeitervereine und Arbeiterparteien. Kultur und Massen organisationen in der Arbeiterbewegung (1890–1933)*, Frankfurt, 1980, p. 186.

were maintained most easily, and the communist sports clubs would even play friendly matches against political opponents. They also sought to create new venues. Thus in Remscheid, where communist sports organisations were in a majority, voluntary labour created a swimming pool out of a pond.[52] But Rotsport sought to involve clubs much more in political education and in agitation for the cause. In this view, workers' sport could never do without an education and training based on marxist principles. 'A commitment to the proletarian class struggle and international solidarity . . . the active participation in the struggle against the imperialist war . . . were just as important as sporting principles.'[53]

In practice the effectiveness of political education apparently left much to be desired, and regional party committees complained about this and about the poor sale of the news-sheets which the organisation published in the major areas of activity. Sportsmen and sportswomen, in common with members of other ancillary organisations of the communist party, were mobilised for general demonstrations; they also used sports events for political propaganda. Thus the participants of the Red Sports meeting in Erfurt, the only national gathering of Rotsport, in 1930 marched under a banner inscribed 'Worker sportsmen are the soldiers of the World Revolution'; and in Hamburg the canoes and dinghies of the watersports group carried red flags and the slogan *KPD – Liste 4* on their sails.[54]

Communist sports organisations received support from the young, and as the depression deepened a growing number of these, and indeed of all members, were unemployed. Dues were therefore kept low; and this too restricted the scope for athletic activities. Some of the latter were also serving the purpose of propaganda, as when juvenile footballers organised matches for strikers during the Berlin metalworkers' strike in 1930.[55] At the same time youngsters had to defend themselves against accusations that they were only interested in kicking a ball. 'We are not a bowling club,' a correspondent wrote in *Der Rote Jungsport* 'we seek sport *and* [the political] struggle. With our youthful optimism we shall conquer and secure a Soviet Germany.'[56]

There is little doubt that many communist sports clubs could

52. C.D. Thompson, *The Remscheid Workers' Movement from 1914 to 1945*. Diss. Warwick, 1983, p. 235.
53. *Kampfgenoß*, 1930, p. 95.
54. *Arbeiterkultur . . . Hamburg* (note 14), p. 206.
55. *Der rote Jungsport* (supplement to *Die Junge Garde*) Nov. 1930.
56. *Der rote Jungsport*, Sept. 1930.

arouse such enthusiasm, especially among young and unemployed supporters, and use it to help with athletic and other events. Thus the Berlin sports club *Fichte* (founded 1890), deprived of public sports facilities or forced to pay fees as a result of politically motivated decisions by the municipality, used such help to convert empty premises for sports activities.[57] The hostile measures taken by the SPD-led City Council are symptomatic of the depth of feeling generated by the split in the workers' sports movement; and the resentment of such treatment must, in turn, have strengthened political hostility. The members of *Fichte* took part in political demonstrations and celebrations – even skiers and oarsmen with their gear attended the annual demonstration in memory of Liebknecht and Luxemburg at the Monument in the cemetery in Berlin-Lichterfelde.[58] The politicisation of sport also took on more overt forms. The KPD advocated in just these last years of the Republic some para-military training for communist athletes; but there is little evidence that this was widely realised in the practice of Rotsport organisations. Although the social-democratic sports movement had long upheld the tenets of pacifism, this did not always exclude proposals for a more militant stance in defence of the Republic. Echoing earlier views about the political importance of a well-developed and steeled body and a well-trained physique, Helmut Wagner spoke about a 'rebellion against physical force and the bodily oppression caused by the capitalist system, which would lead to a rebellion against this very system'.[59] The creation in 1931 of a broadly-based paramilitary phalanx against Nazism in the shape of the *Eiserne Front* – the 'Front of Iron' – by the SPD, the Reichsbanner, the social-democratic trade unions, and the workers' sports movement, with its symbol of the Three Arrows to counter the Swastika, attracted wide support from athletes, but failed to stem the tide. With sporadic exceptions there was no active preparation for an armed resistance to the fascist takeover of power.[60]

57. H. Dierker, 'Größter Roter Sportverein der Welt', in Teichler and Hauk, *Illustrierte Geschichte* (note 28), 93–104.
58. Ibid.
59. Cf. M. Scholing and E. Nierhoff, 'Arbeiterbewegung und Wehrsport' in H.J. Teichler (ed.), *Arbeiterkultur* (note 18), pp. 128–41; H. Wagner, *Sport und Arbeiterbewegung*, (note 19), p. 163; E. Rosenhaft, *Beating the Fascists*, Cambridge, 1983, p. 129.
60. Given the isolation of the social-democratic movement and the paralysis of the trade unions in the face of six million unemployed, resistance to the arbitrary dismissal of the Prussian government by Chancellor von Papen would have been a morally significant act, even if it was probably bound to be unsuccessful.

The history of the workers' sports movement presents some of the dilemmas of workers' culture perhaps more clearly than that of any other cultural movement. It was truly a mass organisation, yet spread out over a large number of local and often inward-looking societies, which makes generalisations difficult. Yet the leadership and the body of activists of the majority movement were closely linked to the bureaucracy of the SPD. Given this background it is not surprising to find a fair measure of demonstrative political activity in favour of the SPD and in support of the Weimar Republic – as shown in participation in the festivities of the 'Day of the Constitution', which was widely but not universally celebrated on 11 August. Equally significant, however, is the fact that 'Workers' Sport' and sport for the working class were never identical. It is not only that a large number of workers practised sport outside working-class organisations. But the growing popularity of sport, especially of highly competitive sport, brought out growing numbers of mere spectators and supporters, whom the workers' sports movement could not organise. Finally, the movement could not always reckon on the loyalty of the *Nur Sportler*, those for whom membership in workers' sports clubs was a matter of convenience, not of conviction.

-6-

Workers' Music: Professionalism v. Partisanship

A Column in the Army of the Great Workers' Movement

As this chapter will show, the cultural roots of the German workers' music movement dug deeply into the national cultural tradition. Yet, at the same time, the movement had strong links with other cultural organisations of the working class. Thus the Barmbeck People's Choir had its origin in the choral section of the Adult Education Society (Fortbildungsverein) of this Hamburg suburb. It was founded in 1904, and soon became an independent choir, affiliated to the Deutsche Arbeitersängerbund (DASB), the 'Federation of Workers' Choral Societies', the co-ordinating body for all workers' music clubs. In 1930 it had 700 members, including children's and youth sections. It still exists as the Hamburg Oratorium Choir.[1] The Hamburg Mandolin Orchestra was an offshoot of the local Workers' Water-Sports Society (Arbeiter Wassersport Verein), originally founded in 1909.[2] It played at the latter's social events, or performed at other functions and festivities of Hamburg workers. Both institutions had their roots in the working class or the lower middle class. In 1982 the conductor of one was an elementary school-teacher; the leader of the other was a lighter-man.

It is important to bear such links within the working class and between its cultural institutions in mind if we wish to understand the functioning of German workers' culture and its organisational basis. This applies in particular to music. While the practice of choral singing responds to the musical tastes and aspirations of the singers, the very act of music-making demands an audience; and in the case of workers' choirs this audience was generally linked to a proletarian public and to the social and political activities of the

1. Cf. *Arbeiterkultur in Hamburg um 1930*, Hamburg, 1982, p. 226.
2. Ibid. p. 227. The Workers' Watersport Society members tended towards syndicalism, and did not affiliate to the workers' sports movement.

labour movement. Individual effort and small societies, many with a narrow geographical basis in district or village, were often brought into a wider context through a central association, or, as we have already seen in the case of workers' sport, through co-operation with other sections of the workers' cultural movement.

The development of workers' music in the forty years between the foundation of a formal organisation in 1892 and the destruction of the DASB in 1933 illustrates its role as the musical propaganda arm of the social-democratic movement; it also shows the pressure for increasingly more sophisticated music-making. This, in turn, gave the music performed by workers' choirs a place in public concert life both in their localities and, as visiting choirs, further afield.[3]

The independent organisation of the worker choristers – and initially we are principally concerned with singers – differed from the workers' sports movement in that it did not arise so much as the result of a process of deep political and social cleavage or of deliberate splitting off and dissociation from the principal bourgeois choral music association – the Deutsche Sänger Bund (DSB), or 'League of German Singers', which had been established in 1862.

However, some general ideological factors did come into play to cause the separation of a number of choral societies, including many workers' choral societies, from the DSB.

Local and regional bodies of workers' singers came into being from the 1860s onwards. They were concerned with the cultivation of traditional German folksongs, and, above all, the songs of the German radical movement, and such forerunners of socialist songs as the 'Workers' Marseillaise', all of which were at first sung in unison.

Although 'political', these choirs were generally left unmolested by the authorities, even during the period of the anti-socialist laws, despite the fact that some of them were 'cover organisations' for the proscribed social-democratic associations. Obviously, they adopted many of the trappings – form and ritual – of bourgeois and petty-bourgeois societies, and retained many of these even after the repeal of the penal laws.[4]

The first loose federation of these societies took place in 1892 in the form of the Liedergemeinschaft der Arbeiter Sänger Bünde (literally, the 'song community of worker singers' societies'), with

---

3. Early performances of the workers' choral societies were often looked at as mere entertainment, produced in beerhalls against the background of clinking glasses and conversation.
4. D. Dowe, 'The Workers' Choral Movement before the First World War,' *Journal of Contemporary History*, vol. 13, 1978, pp. 269–96.

the specific purpose of facilitating the publication of songs of an acceptably high musical standard. The Liedergemeinschaft contained 319 societies with a total membership of 9,150.[5] It issued four songs a year, which were approved by a Central Committee out of a much larger total submitted.[6] Locally the societies were loosely integrated in the network of labour movement organisations, but there was a widespread feeling that the societies received little support from officials of the SPD, and that the events arranged by them were given inadequate coverage by the local socialist press; hence the widespread demand for the establishment of a national organ to publicise activities and give advice. By the beginning of the century the movement had grown to nearly 100,000 members, and the individual societies had become stronger. In 1908 it was decided to found a national organisation, in the form of the Deutsche Arbeitersänger Bund.[7] Its journal, the *Deutsche Arbeiter Sänger Zeitung*, was published with a circulation of 60,000 copies.

An additional reason for founding a more powerful national body was to help in defending the movement against interference by the authorities. The workers, we are told, regarded themselves 'as a column in the army of the great workers' party. Its weapons are the jubilant notes of its massed choirs, the songs of freedom, and the political ballad – the *Tendenzlieder*.'[8] Yet there was a great deal of hesitancy about acknowledging this publicly and nationally. The repertoire of the societies was filled not only with rousing political songs. Indeed, the *Volkslied*, plain and simple, took up a great amount of time, as did the songs of the Romantic movement, often based on German folksongs or using texts from them. Even the Workers' Song Books contained many, perhaps a majority, of entirely non-political songs.[9] This was so even in the Weimar period. Thus of the 203 new songs in the DASB book of 290 songs, only 50 were concerned with work and with the struggle and the hopes of the proletariat. Seventy-nine were folksongs, and a further

5. In 1904 it was estimated that just one half of the total membership were actively engaged in singing.
6. During the first ten months the Committee received 67 compositions, and approved only 9.
7. Cf. V. Noack, *Der Deutsche Arbeitersängerbund: Eine Materialsammlung*, 2 parts, Zwickau, 1911, pt. 1 pp. 3–21. A second edition, under the title *Geschichte des DASB*, was printed in 1932 but was apparently never published.
8. Noack (see note 7), p. 4.
9. For workers' songs and song-books see I. Lammel, *Das Arbeiterlied*, Leipzig, 1980; V. Lidtke, *The Alternative Culture*, Oxford, 1985, pp. 103–35, and 'Songs and Politics. An exploratory Essay on *Arbeiterlieder* in the Weimar Republic', *AfSG*, vol. 14, 1974, pp. 253–73.

67 were compositions of old and newer masters.[10]

Political attitudes and declarations confirm this. It was initially proposed to include among their 1908 statutes a clause to the effect that the Association was to operate 'under the exclusion of all political activities', and this was only deleted after protests from local societies. Yet a statute declaring that membership of the Association was open to any society 'committed to the modern labour movement in its social democratic form' was also deleted.[11]

In practice individual societies often had close ties with the local political and industrial organisations of the labour movement. The meetings and festivities of the SPD and of the trade unions, their anniversary celebrations, congresses, and conferences, normally included a musical element, which usually consisted of songs performed by a workers' choral society. The items would include political songs; but they might also include traditional folksongs, ballads and music from operas and operettas – overtures, marches, arias and choruses – all of which figured prominently in the programmes of festivals.[12]

The extent and character of the political commitment of the workers' choirs was to trouble members in the decades to come. Before 1914 this uncertainty found its expression in debates on what was the appropriate attitude for the movement to adopt in the face of hostile police actions against it, and in discussions about the amount of 'risk-taking' which was thought to be justified in this field. Here the movement moved with care. Although Hermann Duncker, who lectured for the SPD and was later one of the principal education theorists of the German Communist Party, argued that workers who joined the choral societies did so to give musical expression to their political feelings, and that the societies should never deny that they were proletarian organisations, the membership at large thought differently.

When, on an appeal against proscription by a lower court, the DASB was confirmed as a political organisation, its Executive noted this with some feeling of relief. They thought that the die had now been cast and that there was now no need to eschew the expression of political sentiment. The delegates to the 1914 Bundestag (the movement's national conference) did not agree with

10. From a chapter on 'Musik der 20iger Jahre', in Institut für Theater-Wissenschaft, Cologne and Kulturamt Kreuzberg, *Die Weimarer Republik*, Berlin, 1977.
11. Dowe (note 4), p. 279.
12. See the analysis and interpretation of festival programmes in Lidtke, 1985 (note 9), pp. 90–101 and Appendix B.

this. A majority subscribed to the view that 'the DASB was today as little "political" as it had always been. . . . Its tasks are of an artistic and cultural nature. What we working men want to do is sing. The workingmen's choral organisation henceforth intends to raise the level of its performance to as near the point of perfection as possible.'[13]

The political quietism of the workers' choral societies in the years leading up to 1914 has been ascribed to the political revisionism which increasingly permeated the SPD in the years leading up to the First World War.[14] It seems more likely that, as Dieter Dowe has argued, the 'depoliticisation' of the workers' music movement was more apparent than real, as such a term assumes a far greater degree of political commitment than had actually existed during the early years. There was always a large number among the membership who were only interested in the musical and convivial aspect of the societies' life. This shows itself in the sentimental names such as: *Alpenröschen, Edelweiß, Harmonie, Liederkranz* or *Waldesgrün*, which many groups had given themselves, instead of names denoting political commitment, which were used by other groups. Moreover, as the movement grew – reaching a membership of nearly 200,000 by the outbreak of war – it absorbed many pettybourgeois and non-socialist elements. This increase in membership, and the admission of women, which brought about a limited growth of mixed choirs, led to an improvement in the quality and sophistication of the music produced. And this in turn increased the movement's impetus to further develop and perfect its art.[15]

The years of the Weimar Republic saw a considerable expansion of workers' music-making. The membership of the association, which during the war had dropped to a mere 16,000, expanded rapidly after 1918. In 1920 the DASB had 230,000 members, and in 1928 440,000, of whom over 300,000 were active members. These figures included more middle-class members and, above all, an increasing number of women.[16] This led to the formation of many more mixed choirs – so-called *Volkschöre* ('people's choirs'), which with the amalgamation of small choirs into larger societies made it possible to undertake the performance of more complex and more difficult works. Also, like the workers' sports clubs, the workers'

13. Dowe (note 4), p. 281.
14. Cf. W. Kaden, *Die Entwicklung der Arbeitersängerbewegung im Gau Chemnitz . . . bis 1933*, Zwickau, 1960.
15. Dowe (note 4), pp. 282–3.
16. Women made up 18% of the membership before the war, 23.5% in 1926, and 32.3% in 1932.

choral societies could now receive financial assistance from the state, co-operate with other music societies, and, above all, have more trained conductors. At first the conductors were mostly teachers, who, as public servants, had generally been debarred from acting as conductors in such 'political' organisations before 1918; but with the expansion of the movement in the 1920s a growing proportion of its conductors actually came to be made up of professional musicians.[17]

This increasing tendency of the local societies to make use of trained and professional musicians in the pursuit of higher standards of performance meant that an increasing number of conductors were not strongly committed politically; nor, as the National Committee of the DASB argued, were they easily to be politicised.[18]

What is equally important is that many of them were clearly musically ambitious, and they set their choirs increasingly more ambitious musical tasks.[19] This, in turn, became an important issue in the political controversy within the movement, as the communist minority wished to break all ties with bourgeois institutions and to reject firmly all political neutralism.

Some of the political controversies within the workers' music movement paralleled those which we observed in the workers' sport movement, and, as in the latter case, they led to the emergence of an opposition group which at first operated within the organisational framework of the DASB, but which after 1929 formed itself into the pro-communist Kampfgemeinschaft der Arbeitersänger, whose activities are discussed below. More interestingly, the problem of political commitment expressed itself at the same time as a problem of musical aspiration, of the standards and aims of musical performance, and of the relationship between musical interpretation treated as an end in itself and music as an activity both expressive and evocative of emotion and of action.

Between 'Music for Music's Sake' and *Kampfmusik*

The workers' choral movement was at first relatively unaffected by

---

17. In 1920 six hundred out of a total of *c.* 1,200 conductors were teachers; by 1930 we find that, of *c.*4,000 conductors, 1,628 were professional musicians.
18. From the discussion at the 1932 congress of the DASB.
19. Cf. K. Rankl, 'Die Aufgaben der Chorleiter im Deutschen Arbeitersängerbund', *DASZ* 1931 no. 1, reprinted in W. Van der Will and R. Burns, *Arbeiterbewegungskultur*, Frankfurt, 1982, vol. 2 Texte, Dokumente, Bilder, pp. 118–23.

the revolutionary upheaval in 1918, and by the political discussions on the left which followed it. Some societies identified with the Independent Socialists, and a minority of members were communists, but the bulk of the membership was not strongly committed politically.[20] Thus, while at the first General Assembly of the DASB after the war, held in Kassel in 1920, some voices were raised in favour of a discussion on the political attitude of the Association, the National Committee declared that it wished to avoid a public debate, and the delegates supported this line. They also rejected a proposal to give greater independence, and hence greater political control, to the regions (*Gaue*) of the Association, but declared that 'the assembly expresses its solidarity with the whole of the working class . . . in its struggle to secure political power'.[21]

The rejection of party-political commitment did not mean that no attention was given to the problem of musical culture and its relation to political commitment. The relevance of the kind of music performed by workers' choirs to the political struggle was widely discussed, and this discussion became increasingly salient after 1928. The discussion centred on two issues. At one level we find an increasing interest among workers' choral societies in the performance of the great choral works of the classical tradition, of oratorios, and even, occasionally, of operas. This was above all music of a religious and sacred character, which ran counter to the political convictions and commitments of many members of the working class. In parallel with this discussion ran a controversy on the function of the *Arbeiterlied*, the radical poem or ballad sung to existing tunes, or, more specifically, set to music by composers with strong roots in the working class. Both discussions emphasise a basic dilemma: whether workers' music should be politically committed, and perform a politicising role, or whether its main function should really be a cultural one.

Political songs occupied a time-honoured place in the repertoire of the worker-singers, and the *Tendenzchöre* made a major contribution to the political activities and celebrations of the labour movement. It was now increasingly recognised that, however rousing the tunes of the socialist *Tendenzlied*, this genre was, in a musical sense, third-rate. With the growth of mixed choirs, there was a natural desire to get away from singing in unison, which had

20. In the late 1920s only one-third of the membership belonged to a political party, and only half were organised in a trade union.
21. Cf. DASB, *Protokoll der Generalversammlung und Geschäftsbericht* 1920; Noack, (note 7), 2nd edn.

become a tradition in a system based, almost exclusively, on performances by male choirs. On the other hand, this practice undoubtedly helped to arouse mass audiences, as it enabled the individual listener to understand the text, and, especially in the highly charged atmosphere of a meeting or a demonstration, to identify with the sentiments conveyed.

An example of this was the music of Gustav Uthmann, an official of the Sickness Insurance Scheme turned self-taught composer, who, before 1914, had put many radical texts to music.[22] These had been at the heart of the choirs' repertoires, but were now held to be musically conservative; the concern with his work, and with similar music, was thought to be a serious obstacle to the musical development of the choirs. But the traditional *Arbeiterlied* was still very much beloved in the labour movement. Over the years it had acquired a hallowed status, and the text and the music, however banal and, often, lacking in revolutionary fervour, probably appealed to the popular tastes of many workers and workers' choirs.

The emotional and symbolic significance of such songs is often little related to the actual text, looked at in terms of its literal content, let alone its literary qualities. The appeal often lies in a heroic-sounding stanza or in a single line which, though possibly expressed in a trite phrase, conveyed an important sentiment for politically committed workers who felt themselves engaged in a crucial struggle. The 'Ballad of Tord Foleson', set to music by Gustav Uthmann, is frequently listed on programmes of workers' festivals and ceremonies. It is the story of a battle between two generations – *Die alte und die neue Zeit* ('old times against new'). There is no indication of what the combatting armies stood for, only a reference to the *Freiheitsbanner*, the standard of liberty, carried aloft by the brave Tord Foleson, who does not relinquish it, though engaged in mortal combat, but rams its shaft firmly into the ground before he himself falls. It is the symbolism of such an act which gives the song its significance. This is summed up in the concluding lines and in their musical annotation. The text reads: 'Und das ist das Herrliche, Große auf der Welt / Das Banner kann stehn, wenn der Mann auch fällt' ('And this is the glorious and great thing in the World / That the Flag can stand erect, though its standard-bearer fall'); and the musical score is annotated 'with great pathos'.[23]

22. Uthmann, who was his own publisher, had composed some 400 songs, predominantly for male choirs. Cf. I. Lammel, (note 9), p. 43.
23. Text and music are reproduced in E. Lucas, *Vom Scheitern der deutschen Arbeiter-*

The leadership of the DASB did not dare to delete such popular songs from its official publications of choral music. This upset the Artistic Advisory Council, who felt that their artistic reputation was at stake.[24] The matter came to a head at the 1926 National Conference in Hamburg, and was resolved by creating the post of 'Musical Adviser' to assist the Council – who, being unpaid, could not be expected to give so much of their time to the work. Walter Hänel, the conductor of the Chemnitz Workers' Choir, was appointed to the post.

The Hamburg Conference also took more positive steps. It resolved to commission new works which 'would meet the ritual and the cultural needs of the proletariat', publish them, and publish more music suitable for choirs of all types, and thereby raise the cultural level of workers' music in general.[25] To provide a new form of 'politically committed' music, technically contemporary and innovatory at the same time, was the task which radical circles within the DASB took upon themselves. They wished to replace the traditional '*Tendenzlied*' with the modern *Kampflied*, the 'song of combat'.

Alfred Guttmann, one of the artistic advisers of the DASB, and an editor of the association's music publications, accepted, albeit reluctantly, the need to keep some of the older *Tendenzchöre*; but he also saw a natural development of workers' music from its role as 'one of the vehicles for the political emancipation of the masses', to its function as 'a movement which fights for the psychic liberalisation of the masses of the workers'.[26] Such a function, he wrote, was performed by all great music, which enabled the hearer to be 'uplifted above the trials and tribulations of the day . . . those who listened to such works sense a breath of the spirit, which unites all those who feel it, in a strange harmony'.[27] That workers could produce such music and that the masses could hear it, was a sign of the cultural progress which the working class had experienced. It is in such a cultural approach to music, as well as in the growing

bewegung, Frankfurt, 1983 pp. 48–52. Lucas comments that the song was sung frequently by the masses who attended the funerals of workers who had been killed in the uprising in the Ruhr in March 1920.

24. Kaden (note 14), p. 245. Alfred Guttmann, one of the musical advisers of the DASB and editor of its collection of choral works, told the conference 'the choirs must be good; do not sing *Kampflieder* which are musically inferior'.

25. A. Guttmann, 'Der deutsche Arbeitersängerbund', *Arb. Bldg.* vol. 1, 1926, pp. 152–3.

26. Kaden (note 14); Guttmann (note 25).

27. Cf. A. Guttmann, 'Die Bedeutung der deutschen Arbeitersängerbewegung', *KW* no. 7, August 1924.

professionalisation of the worker-musicians and of their choirs, that we can find the roots of the preoccupation with performing music from the classical repertoire.

The growing pressure from singers and conductors to get away from the song repertoire, and engage in the production of more sophisticated music, made greater technical demands on the choirs, who naturally wished to progress to the performance of even more difficult works. It also entailed a change in the style of musical performance. The traditional performance of workers' songs tended to relate to inter-society competitions, celebrations and political events. This now also took the form of concerts for a paying public; or, as in Berlin, choirs performed in hospitals, old people's homes and even prisons.

Some of this development gave rise to strong feelings of antagonism. Many societies now performed religious works, and often staged them in churches where no adequate halls were available. In doing so, they offended the sensibilities of many workers, who were a-religious, if not anti-religious. The choice of music with a religious theme was accepted by the leadership of the DASB on the grounds that the great works of sacred music of the classical composers were essentially humanistic in character. It was a case of 'spiritual' music, not of devotional music with a proselytising character. The use of churches, it was argued, was justified because 'the Church, with its organ and its glorious acoustics, was the only place in which beautiful singing could be heard to its best advantage . . . it was the task of the worker singers to cultivate singing as a work of art, and they looked at the church purely as a place for the cultivation of art'.[28] This led to high-quality musical performances – which could, however, have been produced by any bourgeois choir.

Between 1919 and 1932 the repertoire of one local workers' choral society, the Chemnitzer Volkschor und Kunstverein (with nearly 1,000 singers including children, conducted by Walter Hänel) shows concerts of a great range of musical expression, including many modern works; but little that might be considered to display an expressly political character.[29] Among the works performed in Chemnitz during this period were Mozart's 'Coron-

---

28. Cf. Kaden (note 14) pp. 239–40. The decision to hold concerts in churches did nevertheless cause some resignations.
29. Cf. Kaden (note 14), pp. 332–3. The programme of the Chemnitz choir is very typical for the music performed by the large 'People's Choirs' in the great cities. Cf. the supplement to the *DASZ* published on the occasion of the 1928 national gathering of workers' choirs, which gives short histories of three such choirs.

ation Mass', Haydn's 'Creation' and 'The Seasons', Schubert's 'Songs', Mahler's 'Second Symphony' and Bruckner's *Te Deum*, as well as more modern compositions by Humperdinck, Pfitzner and Richard Strauss. At the movement's musical peak works of great sophistication were performed, and mass audiences listened to them – in one such concert a choir of 600 performed the final chorus from Wagner's *Meistersinger* before an audience of 12,000. Smaller choirs would put on less ambitious concerts, but they too would attempt the performance of classical music. Thus on the occasion of its thirtieth anniversary, the workers' choral society *Sängerhorst* (in Ollernhau in Saxony) put on a concert with the following programme:

From Mozart's *Zauberflöte*:
    Bald prangt den Morgen zu verkünden (Female Choir with Orchestra)
    Chor der Priester (Male Choir)

Mozart: Cantata, *Dir Seele des Weltalls* (Mixed Choir, Soprano Solo and Orchestra)

Haydn: *Symphony No. 104* (Orchestra)

From Schubert's *Rosamunde*:
    Overture (Orchestra)
    Aria (Soprano and Orchestra) *Chorus of the Shepherds and Huntsmen* (Mixed Choir and Orchestra)

Weber: Four mixed choirs and Solo Recital from *Precioso*

We would, however, get an entirely erroneous picture of workers' music, if we thought that performances of major classical works were the norm throughout the movement. In general, only the large mixed choirs, the 'people's choirs' of the bigger cities with a strong working-class, undertook performances of major classical works. If only for purely technical reasons, such concerts could not be mounted by the surviving all-male choirs – numerically still in a majority – and would rarely be undertaken by the tradition-bound choirs in small towns or in rural areas.

Thus when the Tübingen workers' choir, *Frohsinn* ('Good Mood'), gave a public concert in the town in the autumn of 1921, we find, not only that the orchestra was under the direction of an ex-Army conductor, but that the songs sung by them were, in the words of the reviewer for the local bourgeois paper, 'carried on the wings of beautiful art', and that there was 'not a sign of the storm of nasty politics'.[30] There were also still frequent musical engagements of the 'concert party' type, with musical recitations and with the choirs performing comic songs. Here music was pure entertainment – often for commemorative events – and indistinguishable from the work of some bourgeois choir at a bourgeois '*Stiftungsfest*'. A great deal of Kitsch and many sugary melodies in the Glee Club tradition were still being performed by workers' choirs at events such as confirmations, *Bierfeste*, and variety-type entertainments.[31]

The strong emphasis which the DASB put on the performance of major choral works shows itself in the programme of the 1928 Arbeitersängerbundesfest in Hanover, the first national gathering of workers' choirs, attended by 50,000 members. This had a series of musical programmes, culminating in nine choral–orchestral concerts given by regional groups of choirs in conjunction with national orchestras and leading soloists. In addition to some of the works listed here in connection with the Chemnitz concerts, there were such difficult works as: Beethoven's *Missa Solemnis*, Handel's *Salome*, Verdi's *Requiem*, and Berlioz's *Damnation of Faust*. Only one concert, the last, performed two works with themes related to workers' experience, Knöchel's *Eiserne Welt*, and Olmann's *Arbeitsauferstehung*.[32]

The concerts received high acclaim even from the bourgeois press, and Siegfried Ochs, a bourgeois conductor and a member of the Musical Advisory Council, praised the concerts and the choirs. 'He knew of no others who put themselves in the service of music with the same enthusiasm and with the same frenzied application. They were really bearers of culture, and the future of mixed choirs in Germany rested with the workers' choirs'.[33] Such praise was no doubt welcome to the leadership of the DASB, who were anxious to prove that working-class choirs were as good as their bourgeois competitors. There was, nevertheless, a growing recognition that music with religious themes was, at least textually, not easily understood by the masses of the German workers.

Bourgeois conductors and the growing proportion of members who were not proletarian by origin would probably not have shared these views, and for some the beauty of great works was

---

30. Cf. B.J. Warnecken and K. Warnecken-Pallowski, 'Arbeitertübingen – Projekt – Bericht über ein Heimatbuch', in H. Fielhauer and O. Bockhorn, *Die andere Kultur*, Vienna, 1982, pp. 261–77, p. 269.
31. Cf. Kaden (note 14), pp. 212 and 228.
32. For full details of the programmes and performers see Noack (note 7), 2nd edn, pp. 240–2.
33. Ibid. p. 170.

such that their performance outweighed all such scruples, and became an end in itself.[34] But the view which was more widespread was that all this was due to the fact that this was a time of transition, and that one had to compromise, until the workers' music movement created its own music, which would correspond to its needs and aspirations.[35] As the *Deutsche Arbeitersängerzeitung* wrote in 1924: 'The music which was cultivated by the proletariat should not sink into a mere aestheticism or just become a social convention, it must show a serious concern with the contents and with the revelation of art.'[36]

The new 'socialist' music – a concept to which many worker musicians subscribed – was expected to follow in the great musical tradition of the 'Mass' and the 'Oratorium'. It was to convey its message textually, as well as musically, and create complex musical works with a socialist content, and with the experience and ideals of the working class in mind. As yet major pieces of music with an ideologically correct message barely existed, and socialist composers of stature were hard to find. Even the two *Tendenzchor* concerts, performed in Hanover, were introduced rather apologetically, since it was recognised that they were musically inferior to the other works which were performed.[37]

To bridge the gap between theory and reality, the DASB sought to commission works 'which would meet the needs of proletarian culture and of proletarian ritual'. The first major piece of *Kampfmusik*, or 'fighting music', was Artur Wolf's *Kreuzzug der Maschine* ('The crusade of the machine'), with text by Lobo Frank, which the DASB issued in 1929. It received its première in Frankfurt's First of May celebrations in 1930. The work was performed as a piece of modern theatre, staged in the style of Erwin Piscator, with the action reaching out from the stage into the auditorium, turning the hall into a machine room. It used projection techniques for texts, and for the reproduction of art by Käthe Kollwitz; the work was staged with the collaboration of Sprechchöre, and dances and rhythmic movements were performed by worker gymnasts.[38] It is clear that the impact of this piece of music, and of others like it, owed much to the presentation, and its message was conveyed as

34. On the influence of bourgeois conductors see Kaden (note 14), pp. 240–2.
35. Noack (note 7), 2nd edn, pp. 148–9.
36. From an article by H. Hartmann-Solingen on 'Musik und Proletariat', in *DASZ*, no. 4, 1924, cited in Noack (note 7), 2nd edn, p. 148.
37. Cf. W. Van der Will and R. Burns, *Arbeiterkulturbewegung in der Weimarer Republik*, 1982, Berlin, p. 109.
38. Noack (note 7), 2nd edn, pp. 189–190.

much by the text as by the melodies.[39]

The DASB published a number of similar modern oratorios, based on texts by socialist or radical authors, including one based on Walt Whitman's poetry; but the new, committed music did not quickly become popular.[40] It was felt that the text and music were often banal and old-fashioned, conveying general messages without giving an answer to current political issues. The subject was discussed at the National Congress of the movement held in 1932, with special reference to the problem of *Kampfmusik*, which was to be the principal theme of the Second National Meeting of Workers' Choirs, which was to be held in Berlin in 1933. There was some criticism, especially by members of the Artistic Advisory Council, of the frequent and ill-defined use of words like 'freedom' and 'equality' in the text of modern oratorios. On the other hand, delegates criticised bourgeois conductors of workers' choirs, because they tended to look at their choirs purely as instruments for the achievement of artistically valuable performances. The leadership argued that it was not easy to 'politicise' the 'I'm only a musician' types who often acted as conductors. There was now a growing recognition that the choirs should respond in their work to the current crisis situation; but it was regarded as equally important to raise the artistic level of the new *engagé* music. Such developments must be based on genuine feeling, and this had not been as obvious in the music as in the texts.[41]

Thus even in the face of a politically critical situation during the last years of the Republic, the DASB showed concern about the artistic standards which it sought to promote in its music. Yet the movement always maintained that great music, 'should not engender feelings of quiescence and reconciliation, but stir its hearers to the depth of their being and cause creative tensions', which would make them politically aware.[42] There was doubt inside the movement how far this ideal was realised.

Communist members in particular, towards the end of the 1920s, sought to persuade the association to adopt a more radical political stance. The communist opposition, at first only very

39. This application of music has strong links with the workers' festival culture which is discussed in Chapter 9.
40. See Van der Will and Burns (note 37), p. 113 for a short list of these new musical works.
41. Cf. the report of the 8th Bundesversammlung, 1932, *passim*, and the report of a speech by Alfred Guttmann on pp. 90–1.
42. *DASZ*, 15 July 1924, cited in I. Lammel, 'Zur Musikrezeption durch die deutsche Arbeiterklasse', in W. Jacobeit and U. Mohrmann (eds), *Kultur und Lebensweise des Proletariats*, Berlin 1973, pp. 212–30, p. 225.

loosely organised, accused the leadership of the DASB of following a 'pro-bourgeois' policy through its co-operation with national music organisations, and by accepting public financial support. They demanded that bourgeois conductors of workers' choirs, and the advisory councils, which had been established in larger centres such as Frankfurt, should be dropped, and that all choirs should be mixed, because 'exclusively male choirs are not compatible with the struggle for proletarian emancipation'.[43] Concerts should have a more specifically proletarian character. Workplace and street choirs should be established to perform in factories, and in the courtyards of tenement blocks, so that political messages could be conveyed through the medium of music. Altogether, musical activities were to be subordinated to the demands of the political struggle; members in Berlin were urged to 'celebrate the forthcoming "District Singers' Festival" under the red flag of the class struggle'.[44]

The Music of Political Dissonance

The communist opposition inside the DASB, at first sporadic and largely rhetorical, began to organise itself in 1929 and 1930. In the purely formal sense, it operated in a similar fashion to the opposition in the workers' sports movement; but, unlike the latter, the communist opposition in the DASB went beyond the sphere of current politics and activities directly related to it, and turned its attention to the pursuit of music-making as such, and the various forms the music itself took. Formally, individual Communist Party members inside the workers' choral societies were organised as *Fraktionen*, which agreed on policies, and tried to use their influence and their voting power to affect the policies of their societies and the decision-making processes of the DASB at local and district level. After the formation of a formal opposition movement in the shape of the Kampfgemeinschaft der Arbeitersänger (KdAS), they endeavoured to secure the affiliation of the individual societies to that organisation, while maintaining their affiliation with the DASB, as long as this was still tolerated.[45]

43. W. Fuhr, *Proletarische Musik* 1928–33, Göppingen, 1977, p. 136, quoting from a resolution passed at the meeting of Music Section at the 1930 Berlin Ifa Congress.
44. Cf. *Ifa Rundschau*, vol. 2, nos. 2–3; resolution of the KPD Kulturkonferenz of the district Berlin-Brandenburg of 15 November 1930, in Bundesarchiv Koblenz, R. 134 vol. 70 fos. 188–90.
45. Cf. *Kampfmusik KM* Nov. 1931 no. 4. The origin and early history of the

The combined strength of the opposition of individual members and individual societies was, however, nowhere powerful enough to enable the opposition to change the policy of their areas or districts. Thus, in the Gau Berlin (Berlin District) in 1930, the opposition could only muster 10 of the 100 delegates to the annual conference. And even in the Rhineland (including the Ruhr), where communist influence was strong, there were, in the same year, only 10 oppositional delegates out of 225. The minority sought to secure the affiliation of the *Gau* to the Ifa, but this was rejected by 136 votes against 63.[46] It was an inevitable result of such moves that the majority expelled the societies which had sided with the opposition.[47]

Until the formation of the KdAS, opposition societies seem to have been organised by the Ifa, who urged them to support the general political line of the KPD. Although the Ifa operated largely at a local level, it also sought to organise cultural societies which were active in a particular cultural field. At a Berlin Ifa conference in March 1930, the 'Sparte Musik' (Music Section), issued a sweeping condemnation of the policy and musical practice of the DASB. 'The penetration of reformism into the labour movement and its development in the direction of social fascism', it declared, 'has transformed the workers' choral societies and the workers' music societies from instruments in the struggle of the proletariat, into venues for philistine entertainment. Choral music and "pure" art, the "neutral" song, have taken the place of *Tendenzmusik*; bourgeois conductors and other bourgeois music specialists, have decisive influence.' Even the new 'radical' musical works fostered by the DASB, were rejected as a sham, which in its texts 'lacked every thread of political realism' and whose music was 'old-fashioned, petty-bourgeois and sentimental.'[48]

When in 1931 the Kampfgemeinschaft was founded, it proclaimed as its aim 'the mobilisation of the whole of the workers'

Kampfgemeinschaft is difficult to disentangle. It was apparently preceded by the Freie Arbeitersängerbund, which, however, did not seem to have had the full support of the Communist Party. (See Massenarbeit oder Sekten – eine offene Antwort an die Mitglieder im Freien Arbeitersängerbund, *KM*, vol. 1 no. 2, March 1930.) The journal *Kampfmusik* was *de facto* the organ of the KdAS; it is a rare and very valuable source for the history of the organisation and for the discussion of workers' music during the years 1930–2.

46. Cf. H. Wunderer, *Arbeitervereine und Arbeiterparteien . . . 1890–1933*, Frankfurt, 1980, pp. 178–81; Fuhr (note 43), pp. 132–7.
47. Ten societies were expelled in Berlin and thirty-nine in the Rhineland. Cf. DASB, *Bericht*, 1929–1932. Not all expelled societies joined the KdAS.
48. Cf. Fuhr (note 43), pp. 136–7.

choral movement for revolutionary politics'. Their anthem was to become a clarion to the masses, 'a call in the campaign against the emergency legislation, against hunger and misery, and against cultural gagging and cultural oppression'.[49] Proselytising among the rank and file of the DASB was, however, not very successful – nor was it apparently pursued with great vigour. It seems that even more than in the workers' sports movement, individual dissenting societies were too keen on their own work and their own musical activities to engage in propaganda among their former comrades, and whole societies decided to pursue their music outside the DASB, without being under great pressure to leave.[50]

The neglect of practical political work was commented on at the Second National Conference of the Kampfgemeinschaft held in August 1932. It was stated that individual members, and whole choirs, had left the DASB to be able to 'paddle their own canoe better', and 'to cultivate revolutionary sentiment among themselves without being disturbed'.[51]

The greater political commitment of the work of these new 'revolutionary choirs' was not unconnected with the policy in respect of conductors, who were now expected to act as much as political functionaries as guides in artistic matters. The great majority of conductors were clearly 'class-conscious co-fighters with the members in the avant-garde of the proletariat, and real comrades of the worker-choristers'.[52] However, the old type of conductor who operated in the DASB survived among some of the choirs; and so did some of the typical DASB musical offerings survive among societies affiliated to the KdAS.

Before seeking to assess the extent of the 'political' in the musical activities of the communist choral societies, we must look at the political and musical thinking which lay behind their enterprise. The assessment of what was the appropriate music for the 'revolutionary' choir touched in some ways on issues which had already been raised inside the DASB. Thus central to the discussion was the place of the song and of the *Tendenzlied* in workers' music. But, while in the DASB the attack on established practice centred on the low musical quality of the established *Arbeiterlied*, the leaders of the Kampfgemeinschaft attacked the traditional music, partly for its lack of revolutionary fervour, as far as the text was concerned, and,

49. Cf. 'Beschluß der 1.Reichskonferenz der KdAS', *KM* 1 no. 5, June 1931, p. 6.
50. H. Wunderer (note 46), p. 181, quoting *Ifa Reichbericht* 1931.
51. Cf. 'Erweiterte Reichsleiterkonferenz der KdAS', reported in *KM*, Sept. 1932, p. 2.
52. Ibid. p. 3.

partly for the way in which the songs were performed.

The established choirs were accused of being preoccupied with the 'beautiful rendering' of the songs, or with the performance of choral music in a 'collective Caruso' style, completely disregarding the crisis and the alleged dangers of war.[53] The Kampfgemeinschaft castigated the petty-bourgeois style of much of the musical activities of the workers' choral societies, commenting adversely on the habit of listening to revolutionary-sounding songs in beerhalls, glass in hand.[54] Hermann Duncker, the KPD theoretician on cultural matters, asked rhetorically in the first issue of *Kampfmusik* 'whether it was really still appropriate to sing "Wer hat Dich du schöner Wald" or perform with modest resignation "Freiheit wir warten Dein"?'[55]

Not surprisingly, the KdAS argued for the rejection of the practice of performing oratoria and other complex choral works, through which the singers sought to shine and receive the admiring applause of relatives and friends, in favour of ideologically based music. Music which existed purely for enjoyment might be sung by the choirs in private; but in all public performances the choir held a responsible and representative position, with an obligation to 'describe the position of the proletariat and prepare it for the emancipatory struggle.'[56]

In general, the opposition rejected the performance of music for its own sake, and opposed the formality of the concert, which they considered to be a bourgeois institution in which the listener is purely passive. Instead, the musical offering should be changed into a vehicle for political education and propaganda, in which the audience should be encouraged to participate.[57] What was more, in order to make their singing politically effective, the revolutionary choirs were urged to perform where workers habitually gathered. At strike-meetings they should sing the 'Song of the Red Trade Union Opposition', and the 'Song of the IAH', and in front of the labour exchanges they should sing the 'Song of the Unemployed'.[58]

53. Cf. E. Meyer, 'Aus der Tätigkeit der Kampfgemeinschaft der Arbeitersänger', in *Sinn und Form* (Sonderheft für Hanns Eisler), 1964, pp. 152–60.
54. *KM*, Nov. 1931, p. 3.
55. *KM*, January 1932. The songs mentioned are particularly blatant examples of texts conveying general sentiments, full of bathos and solemn-sentimental music.
56. *KM*, January 1932, p. 2.
57. Cf. 'Neue Wege und Aufgaben der Arbeitermusik', *KM*, March 1931, p. 3.
58. *Bericht* of the Bezirk Niederrhein, *KM* March 1932, p. 8. Whether and how far such performances actually took place is not clear. A report from Solingen in the same issue had to admit failure to realise these ideas so far.

With such an emphasis, 'singing in unison', which had been rejected by the older movement as old-fashioned and musically unexciting, now achieved a much more positive evaluation. Indeed, it was a widely preferred form of presentation for the kind of musical propaganda in which the choirs of the Kampfgemeinschaft were expected to engage. There was, however, strong opposition to a return to practices which were more suited to the old all-male choirs. The movement preferred mixed choirs on general ideological grounds; but the leadership argued strongly that only by such techniques was it possible to arouse large masses; the listeners can understand the text, and they can be persuaded to sing with the choir; 'the song sung in unison contains the political doctrine; the masses should learn these songs, and carry them into the factories and the Labour Exchanges'.[59]

The bulk of the musical activity in which the revolutionary choirs were engaged was linked to political events, demonstrations and rallies, such as the *Kulturtage* of the KPD and of other communist or communist-linked organisations such as the IAH, the Ifa, and Rote Hilfe. On these occasions the choirs would share a platform with other groups and societies, such as teams producing *Sprechchöre*, or *Bewegungschöre*, or with the troupes of the agitprop theatre, who in turn, also used many political songs in their repertoire. A list of songs and choruses used by the movement was issued by *Kampfmusik*; it contains simple and more complex works, and shows the importance attached to singing in unison. A majority of the songs listed were either composed for one-voice choirs only, or could be produced in such a simplified form.[60] It is also characteristic of the music that, where there was an instrumental accompaniment to the choral compositions, the instruments, other than piano, were mostly a combination of drums, trumpets, trombones, recorders and percussion instruments, which were suitable for music relying on volume of sound and the reproduction of rhythm, rather than the rendering of complex melodies.

The choirs of the Kampfgemeinschaft were encouraged to develop a new style of singing which, in turn, was often linked to a new type of musical composition. Both were frequently the product of the creativity and influence of Hanns Eisler; but other composers and conductors were also at work. Eisler, a committed communist and a pupil of Schönberg, not only composed, but also rehearsed and conducted workers' choirs. He argued that the

59. Cf. *KM* March 1932 and September 1932.
60. For the list see *KM* May 1932, p. 4.

accurate rendering of the text was as important as the performance of the music. Indeed, he suggested that the text should be studied first; it should be discussed by the choir, and the political message of the song should be understood, and, if appropriate, questioned. The choral renderings should be treated as if, like the *Sprechchor*, they were an 'instructor *en masse*', who was speaking to the masses on a specific political theme. With this in mind, the singing must eschew all sentimentality and artificiality, such as the 'murmuring of the basses or the mellow ring of the tenors'. Instead, the song must be delivered 'Coldly, sharply, and with a cutting edge'.[61]

Given such a functional attitude towards music, it is not surprising that the choirs of the Kampfgemeinschaft were not particularly interested in concert-type performance. Rather, they linked their music to acts of political demonstration, or incorporated their songs in revues, or in agitprop theatre. In whatever form, the choirs endeavoured to create audience participation in their singing. Hanns Eisler went so far as to suggest that just to listen to revolutionary songs was only a continuation of the philistine practices which had characterised the old workers' choral societies, which had regarded music as being above party, and had thereby created the illusion that all was well in the world. In the words of a report on the Conference of the 'Enlarged Leadership of the KdAS' in 1932, 'only by persuading the masses to participate in the singing of revolutionary fighting songs would it be possible to activate the masses, and to give them the conviction and the insight which the fighting proletariat needs'.[62] Even singing the old Uthmann songs, which apparently still enthused the masses, was praised; but generally the songs were expected to have greater current relevance.[63]

There is some indication that some of the choirs affiliated to the KdAS continued to sing more complex and more 'artistic' music; but the overt purpose of much of the music performed was the preparation for quasi-political events. For such events, they rehearsed individual songs as well as more complex works of new *engagé* music by Hanns Eisler and other professional musicians, along with works by amateurs.[64] The performances were nearly

---

61. Hanns Eisler, writing in *Kampfmusik* on the correct rendering of *Die Maßnahme*, the musical play which he had produced jointly with Bertolt Brecht as quoted by E.H. Meyer (note 53), p. 157. Karl Rankl, the composer and conductor, advocated similar views in an article quoted by Meyer, and suggested that the music should be subordinated to the text.

62. *KM*, November 1932, p. 2 (from the report of the Erweiterte Reichsleiter Konferenz).

63. *KM* 1931 no. 7, p. 7; and 1931 nos. 8–9, p. 6.

64. *KM*, January 1932, p. 4 and February 1932, p. 4. The journal frequently reports

always interspersed with other items, such as *Sprechchöre*, orchestral pieces, sketches, and recitations, and the events would generally include speeches and political appeals.[65]

The songs themselves were usually of a mixed character, and edited so as to form a *Chormontage*. Such an arrangement might be a mere pot-pourri of songs, or it might be conceived as an entire work. Thus, in Solingen in 1932, the workers' choir *Vorwärts*, performed new pieces by two Solingen workers under the title *Arbeiterleben*.

> 'The work consisted of songs, chorus, recitation . . . and shows the harsh reality of the world of work . . . of bloody sacrifices, and of the treasonable activities of the SPD and of the trade union bureaucracy. At the end it shows the formation . . . of the "red unity front" under the leadership of the Communist Party and of the Red Trade Union Opposition.'[66]

The theoretical discussions and the musical practices of the communist choirs re-focused attention on the role of the song in the labour movement. The *Arbeiterlieder*, the political songs of the social-democratic and communist movements, linked workers' choirs musically with the wider working class. The choirs were, in effect, the music teachers of the proletariat, and they formed popular taste. This applied not only to the melodies but also to the text of the songs and to the sentiments conveyed by the words and by the rendering of the music. In this sense workers' songs not only occupied a central position in the formal political culture, but also helped to lay emotional foundations for basic political ideology.[67]

The great majority of the political and committed songs which were sung throughout the labour movement were new compositions using old or specially written texts; but some of the most popular songs, for example the *Arbeitermarseillaise*, with a text by Jacob Audorf, and first sung at Lassalle's funeral, were based on popular (and generally sentimental) folksongs, or on patriotic songs. Some songs were even used for more than one radical text, the *Wacht am Rhein*, for instance, having six socialist versions. By this device workers' songs utilised the widespread popularity of old

---

on the musical activities of individual choirs.
65. *KM* January 1932, p. 4 and December 1932, p. 6.
66. *KM* 1932 no. 3, p. 8. See also *KM*, Jan. 1932, p. 4 for an account of the performance of a choral work *Solidarität* performed by the Berlin Arbeiterchor for a demonstration by the IAH in the *Sportpalast*.
67. Cf. 'Arbeiter und Gesang', *KW*, 1 June 1925, p. 528.

songs. This would give the new version a quasi-national status; but it created at the same time a symbolic ambiguity, as the well-known tunes must have recalled the traditional texts.[68]

The character of the *Arbeiterlied* ranges from solemn affirmations of ideals and rousing march tunes to songs of mockery and derision. They were sung at meetings, demonstrations, celebrations, marches and strikes, and occasionally even in pubs. Some of the songs were genuine workers' folksongs (*Arbeitervolkslieder*) whose text and music cannot be attributed to any known author or composer, such as the *Leunalied*, a song of lament and solidarity related to the revolutionary fighting around the Leunawerke, the vast industrial complex in Central Germany, in March 1921. Its origin can be traced back to a soldiers' song of the First World War, and it existed in a large number of variants, commemorating workers' struggles elsewhere, before the specific Leuna version was reproduced in a communist songbook in 1925.[69]

Such genuinely 'popular' songs tended to be musically primitive, and they were often regarded as inferior on those grounds. The *Leunalied*, together with five other similar songs, was on its first publication relegated to an appendix of songs 'which were artistically not really valuable' but which had secured their right to be published by their popularity among workers.[70]

It is not surprising that the anonymous workers' songs, such as the *Leunalied* and other 'workers' folksongs' of the period of the post-revolutionary struggles, should have been included in communist songbooks. The latter, rather more than the social-democratic songbooks, put greater emphasis on songs which recorded and celebrated revolutionary sentiments, and on songs sympathetic to Soviet Russia – or even adapted from Soviet songs. In the wider social-democratic music movement political songs had during the later period become generally less prominent. And the songs that were produced and were printed in the songbooks of the DASB and of the workers' sports movement or the socialist workers' youth movement, whose songbook had been published in an edition of 500,000 copies by 1931, were more general in character and more symbolic in language. In the DASB there were also

68. Cf. V. Lidtke, *Alternative Culture*, New York, 1985, p. 127.
69. Cf. W. Steinitz, 'Das Leunalied. Zur Geschichte und Wesen eines Arbeitervolksliedes', *Jahrbuch für Volkskunde*, vol. 4, 1958, pp. 3–52. Steinitz has suggested the formal division of the songs of the labour movement into artificially created *Arbeiterlieder* on the one hand, and the *Arbeitervolkslied*, the working-class folk song, which had a folkloristic origin, on the other.
70. Ibid. p. 51.

attempts to change the text of some songs to express less violent and more generally humanitarian sentiments, and likewise to find new texts for melodies taken from the work of the great composers.[71] In contrast to SPD-linked music communist agitation in the last years of the Republic used more aggressive and more hard-hitting tunes and words. In the songs of the agitprop theatre, whose work will be discussed in Chapter 8, this music was to reach large numbers of workers right across the political spectrum.

The song was clearly the most ubiquitous musical medium to reach the working class, but it was not the only form of music which became popular. Orchestral and choral music increasingly reached workers through concerts arranged by local social-democratic organisations or given by the larger workers' choirs.[72] After 1925 radio was probably the most important vehicle for the popularisation of music, and reached a growing number of working-class listeners. It transmitted much serious, classical and modern music by broadcasting concerts or gramophone records. But it also broadcast much light music, including many of the 2,600 *Schlager* – popular hits of the years 1924–32.[73] Many of these became available as records – a popular tune, such as 'Valencia – my love and your love' sold 500,000 copies, and gramophones and records also began to penetrate to the working-class public.

There is no way of knowing today what workers' musical tastes actually were, but in the last years of our period we find a growing absorption of popular music culture into the culture of the working class.

71. V. Lidtke, 'An exploratory Essay on Arbeiterlieder in the Weimar Republic', *AfSG*, vol. 16, 1974, pp. 253–74 at pp. 264–9.
72. The Mannheim Volkssingakademie gave between 1920 and 1928 eighty major choral and orchestral concerts, many works being given more than once. Cf. an article on the choir in the special supplement of the *Deutsche Arbeitersängerzeitung* published on the occasion of the 1928 Hanover *Arbeitersängerfest*.
73. According to B. Schrader and J. Schabera, *Die 'Goldenen' Zwanziger Jahre*, Vienna (originally Berlin, GDR), 1987, p. 139.

–7–

The Visual Arts in Weimar Workers' Culture

A Red Cinderella

'Visual art is the Cinderella among the cultural subjects with which the workers are concerned'. So Oskar Greiner in the only article which dealt specifically with this subject which I could find in the journal *Sozialistische Bildung* (1929–33), which was published by the National Education Council of the SPD. Greiner went on to say that the German working class was not trained in artistic matters. The party was organising its members for the political struggle, but there was 'no organisation of feeling'.[1]

For the visual arts – though not for music and drama and considered in a formal sense this was undoubtedly true. We can point to relatively few organisations within the wider field of working-class cultural endeavour which concerned themselves primarily with the transmission and popularisation of painting, sculpture and the graphic arts. The place of the visual arts in human culture may be as important as that of the other muses, but this was not reflected within organised workers' culture on anything like a scale comparable to that of the workers' choral movement in respect of music or of the *Volksbühne* in respect of the theatre.

But then the visual arts cannot be reproduced as music or a play can be. They are hence not easily organised for collective practice or experience, as was the case with the representation of the performing arts.[2] Lacking this public image, and lacking within

1. O. Greiner, 'Die bildende Kunst und ihre Bedeutung für das Proletariat,' *Soz. Bldg.*, 1929, pp. 142–7.
2. Although photography was widely practised, and modern printing techniques made the reproduction of works of art in large editions and relatively cheaply possible, the 'aura' of the work of art had not yet disappeared. The museum rather than the cinema was still the place for 'real' art. Walter Benjamin's famous essay 'Das Kunstwerk im Zeitalter seiner technischen Reproduzierbarkeit' was first published only in 1938, and became widely known only after its republication in 1955. Cf. the English translation in Walter Benjamin, *Illuminations*, New York, 1969.

German workers' culture a single promoting agency, it is easy to overlook the extent to which the visual arts were indeed represented in the cultural activities of the working class.

One of the purposes of this chapter is to examine these easily overlooked aspects. Yet what we might describe as the 'educational' aspects of the visual arts is only one symptom of their alleged 'Cinderella''status. There is also the whole question of visual imagination and visual aesthetics as it finds expression in the physical environment of the worker and of his family, above all in the home. Finally we must look at the role of the visual arts in the ideology of working-class culture, and, beyond this, in the political activities of the labour movement. We know that such cultural-ideological discussions and controversies characterised the practice of music and of the theatre during the Weimar period; the discussion of the role and character of the visual arts, although less overt and less public, is every bit as interesting as that in respect of the other arts. This chapter will also attempt to look at this.[3]

There was no natural basis for the development of artistic tastes and of interest in the visual arts in the life of the German workers before 1914. The Social Democratic Party, which welcomed and supported the new workers' leisure-time organisations, and saw them as contributing to the achievement of its political goals, was less openly sympathetic to activities in the arts. Their role was essentially ancillary to the political struggle, and here poetry and music were the arts which were often brought into the sphere of socialist activity. The party generally did not use art – apart from illustrations and cartoons – in its agitation, and the visual arts as such did not figure in the educational programmes which it devised and arranged.[4]

Only here and there, and mainly in places with strong liberal bourgeois traditions, do we find that museum curators and directors of art galleries sought specifically to attract workers as visitors through guide-lectures, or local 'societies for the propagation of

3. Given that the subject matter of this chapter is visual a purely literary presentation imposes certain limitations on the discussion. For some related discussion with illustrative material see the author's 'Bildende Kunst und Arbeiterbewegung in der Weimarer Zeit: Erbe oder Tendenz', *AfSG*, 1982, pp. 331–58; and *Icon and Revolution: Political and Social Themes in German Art*, 1918–1933 (Exhibition Catalogue), Sainsbury Centre for Visual Arts, University of East Anglia, Norwich, 1986.
4. The 'Educational Guidelines' which the SPD had adopted at its 1906 Conference had referred to the need to raise artistic sensitivity through well-designed programmes and brochures and through illustrations, as well as through the publication of reproductions of masterpieces of art.

art' encompassed the working class. In Mannheim, the proposed foundation of a 'Freie Bund zur Einbürgerung der bildenden Kunst' received the support of the local SPD. The success of such an endeavour, wrote the socialist *Volksstimme*, 'would denote power and progress also for the proletariat, and make it an influential force'.[5]

In the Weimar period the concern of the now more powerful and more sophisticated workers' culture movement for the arts, including the visual arts, took on a more positive and formative function. The arts were invested with a significant role in the creation of the 'New Man' – the goal of the (new) socialist culture. The pursuit of the arts was to expand the emotions and to increase aesthetic sensibility. In the words of a speaker at the first conference of the Sozialistische Kulturbund in 1926 'it was essential to shake up people through individual "artistic experiences", to liberate [the worker] from the shackles of his humdrum everyday existence, which brought with it so much psychic stupor and dullness'.[6]

This view of the purpose and function of the visual arts was not shared by all sections of the workers' cultural movement. A more didactic and more political view of their role was held within the communist camp. For the KPD and for cultural organisations linked with it and for some of the artists closely associated with it, paintings, prints and sculpture should not be 'created for their own sake but as a weapon in the class struggle', a view with which the political leadership would not have disagreed.

Before we analyse the wider cultural function of art we must look at the institutions which stimulated the individual worker's interest in the arts, and which set out to form working-class taste.

Workers' Education and the Visual Arts

As before the war, but on a larger scale, workers' educational activities in the field of the visual arts consisted, after 1918, mainly of lecture-type instruction, and, towards the end of the period, frequently of slide-shows prepared and sent out from the SPD's central office, which, in the Lichtbilddienst, had established a special department for films and other visual presentations. The

5. Cf. *Volksstimme* (Mannheim), 23 April 1911. See also E. Howoldt, *Der freie Bund zur Einbürgerung der bildenden Kunst in Mannheim*, Frankfurt, 1982.
6. Leo Kestenberg, 'Die Aufgaben der Kunst', in Sozialistischer Kulturbund, *Sozialismus und Kultur* (Report of the 1926 Conference), Berlin 1927, pp. 38–44.

subjects of these illustrated lectures tended to be popular themes, such as 'Socialism in Caricature' or 'The Representation of Work in the Visual Arts'.[7] Guided tours of museums and galleries also figured prominently. They were generally held specifically for workers on Sunday mornings, and were undertaken by museum staff who, faced with the changed social circumstances after 1918, were anxious to make museums more popular.[8]

There is also evidence that some of the educational and cultural institutions of the working class collaborated with such endeavours. The Leipzig Arbeiter Bildungs Institut, for example, not only organised visits to museums and lectures on art, it also ran a week's tour based on Dresden with art as its theme. This seven-day school combined visits to local monuments with visits to museums and discussions of the art of the nineteenth and twentieth centuries.[9]

In general, however, the social-democratic educational organisations tended after 1918 to leave the instruction and discussion of more general and artistic subjects to the politically neutral Volkshochschulen, while the political movement concentrated on more ideological subjects and on the training of party functionaries. The uptake was limited, but the statistics which we have suggest that workers were as interested in this area as listeners from other social backgrounds.[10]

In this area of liberal education staff usually attempted to relate art to working-class experience, hoping that such an approach would stimulate artistic sensibility and influence creative activity. Workers should be educated to appreciate not merely the 'beautiful', which could so easily degenerate into emotional reactions, or become the basis for a 'flight into the dream world of Kitsch and the satisfaction of desire which we find in the cinema', but also to concern themselves with problems to which they could relate from the experience of their daily lives.[11]

To cite the example of the Leipzig adult education department, we find that they had initially approached the teaching of art-history and art appreciation via such experience-related courses.

7. *SPD Mitteilungsblatt*, 1927, pp. 5–7. The packs contained 50–60 slides with notes for the lecturer.
8. Proposals for a reform in art policy were made in a document by the Museumsbund, *Die Kunstmuseen und das deutsche Volk*, 1919.
9. Cf. R. Kober, *Die Verhältnisse von Leipziger Arbeitervereinen und Vereinen für Arbeiter zur bildenden Kunst . . . von den Anfängen bis 1933*, Diss. Leipzig, 1930, pp. 125–6.
10. V. Engelhardt, *Das Bildungsinteresse in den einzelnen Berufen*, Frankfurt 1926.
11. Cf. Valtin Hartig, 'Arbeiterbildung', *Die Tat*, vol. 18, 1926/7, pp. 250–4.

They then went over to more purely style- or period-based teaching, but found in the end that a general, ideology-oriented course, dealing with themes such as 'What is Art', produced the greatest response from working-class students.

This kind of approach tied in well with the socially critical attitude of most participants. The workers who enrolled in the classes could not easily relate to classical art, and the Volkshochschule was concerned to foster critical attitudes amongst its students. Thus a basic discussion of a theme like 'Kitsch and Trash', (*Kitsch und Schund*) would not seek to stimulate the aesthetic sense; it would rather develop an understanding of the meaning and purpose of form.[12] Men like Hartig hoped that a training in the wider understanding of art would not only lead to the better appreciation of existing art, but that it would also in the end lead to the workers themselves becoming creative.[13] A few institutions also put on courses of practical training in the arts which were particularly appreciated by younger workers.[14] These courses tended to follow from the more theoretical instruction, and there is no suggestion that a vocational element was connected with them.

This was not so in the case of courses in practical art mounted by the Marxistische Arbeiterschule (MASCH), the central educational establishment of the German Communist Party, with branches in the major centres of the party. The principal Berlin institution, and the Leipzig section in particular, began in the late 1920s to give some instruction in drawing and painting.[15] The aim was not to create a proletarian art or to produce amateur artists, but to school the participants for the exercise of visual propaganda. As the *Rote Fahne* wrote in 1930: 'Art was not the main product, but a secondary outcome of revolutionary agitation and propaganda.' Some professional artists emerged from this training; but the 'Worker Artists' (*Arbeiterzeichner*) movement, which sprang from these MASCH classes, was not concerned with art for its own sake or with the development of an individual as a painter or illustrator. It sought rather to demonstrate that great potential artistic forces were already present in the masses of the proletariat. They did not

---

12. P. Hermberg and W. Seiferth, *Arbeiterbildung und Volkshochschule in der Industriestadt* (Leipzig), Breslau, 1932.
13. Hartig (as note 11).
14. F. Grosse, *Die Bildungsinteressen des großstädtischen Proletariats*, Breslau, 1932.
15. In Berlin the teaching was undertaken by 'Durus', i.e. Alfred Kemenyi, a Hungarian political refugee and the art-critic of *Rote Fahne*, and in Leipzig by Alfred Frank, who had trained as a lithographer and worked as an illustrator for the communist press.

wish to develop 'worker-artists with artists' conceit, but politically ever more effectively working revolutionary politicians of the proletariat'.[16]

Both the liberal education in the appreciation of art and the training of workers in drawing were intellectually interesting phenomena, but they involved only small numbers, and thus had no influence on the aesthetic feelings of the masses of the workers. What was more important on the most elementary level here was the attempts to improve taste in respect of furniture, furnishings, and, above all, the pictures and ornaments of the proletarian home.

The Private Art of the Working Class and the Public Art of the Labour Movement

The *Wohnkultur* of the German worker was an inevitably very much poorer imitation of that of the dominant (bourgeois) taste. Pictures and other adornments were generally indistinguishable from those in petty-bourgeois homes, and in strong contrast with the radical political views often held by those who dwelt in them. 'Above the bookshelf with Marx's *Capital* and Kautsky's *Origin of Christianity* we find sugary oleographs, a decadent woman's head, or the "dreary confirmation picture", surrounded by biblical quotations', wrote Valtin Hartig.[17]

In place of cheap ornate furniture, perhaps painted to look like walnut, with plaster decorations, plush-covered sofas, antimacassars, doilies, and dust-catching knick-knacks articles in the workers' press suggested plain, functional furniture and a few simple objects. In place of pictures of elves dancing in the moonlight, or of the huntsman blowing his horn, they should put good reproductions of older or of modern art, possibly with themes relevant to the workers' struggle, or modern artists' prints.

Coloured reproductions or prints were produced in large editions from the end of the nineteenth century. Some were of classical art, a few of modern art; but the majority were specially produced genre scenes which tended to give expression to some banal piece of practical wisdom, or just to show sugary-sentimental scenes. What was completely absent was the modern world of work. Craftsmen's or peasant life appeared only in a romantic halo.[18]

16. 'Durus' writing in the *Rote Fahne*, 8 October and 29 October 1930.
17. Cf. Hartig (as note 11).
18. Cf. W. Brückner, *Elfenreigen-Hochzeitstraum*; Frankfurt, 1974; Brückner, Die Bilderfabrik, Frankfurt, 1973.

Vehicles for the transmission of new aesthetic values and for the formation of visual taste were the exhibitions of original art and of art in reproduction which were regularly put on by local social-democratic organisations, the Kulturkartelle, or the local workers' education committees. Such exhibitions were generally held at Christmas time, and art was shown together with books, toys and other articles suitable for presents. For this potential market socialist and communist publishing houses produced cheap reproductions of traditional and modern art, and the workers' press publicised them through advertisements and editorially.[19]

Among the prints offered by Dietz, a long established SPD publisher, was a Ruysdael landscape, Delacroix's 'Liberty leading the people on the barricades' and Walter Crane's 'Triumph of Labour'. And a Vienna publishing firm advertised in the German communist magazine *Roter Stern* a portfolio of reproductions of Daumier's works 'to make his satirical drawings accessible to the working masses', adding that such prints were 'particularly suited for decorating the home of every revolutionary worker'.[20] Collections such as the Daumier portfolio were however exceptions. It seems that the art which was expected to appeal to working-class tastes was more popular and less elevated or sophisticated.

The illustrations which workers were expected to put on their walls were neither to offend nor to incite. Instead the prints were expected to appeal to the more romantic inclinations of their respective purchasers. It was also suggested that local social-democratic publishers might print local landscapes or townscapes, such as the three portfolios of 'Hamburg Scenes' by J. Mohrt which had appeared originally in the social-democratic *Hamburger Echo*, and which were reproduced separately by its publishers, to be sold at the genuinely low price of 1.50 marks for a set of six.

And at about the same time the women's journal *Frauenwelt* recommended a selection of available reproductions to its readers by linking its choice to the interest of the growing number of hikers among workers, who, the magazine thought, would derive joy from recollections induced by paintings of lakes, moors and mountains. It also recommended reproductions of German romantic paintings by such painters as Schwind, Thoma and Böcklin.[21]

The aesthetics of the workers' domestic environment thus present a confusing picture, extending from the traditional and popu-

19. See photographs of Christmas exhibitions in Berlin in 1922 and 1923 in *Volk und Zeit* of 17 December 1922 and of 23 December 1923.
20. *Roter Stern*, 20 June 1924.
21. Erica Bonte in *Frauenwelt*, 1927, pp. 292–3.

lar in respect of pictures for the home to the results of an advocacy of functional furniture which had links to the *Bauhaus* and the modern movement. This was itself an expression of a belief in greater rationality in social matters. In this view 'only the functional is beautiful'.[22]

The attempts to make the working–class family opt for a modern style of living and choose simple and colourful decorations encountered material as well as emotional resistance. The new functional furniture was normally too expensive for the working-class family, who generally made do with inherited or cheaply bought old furniture. Some young couples, who may have had savings from years of earning before marriage, did go in for modern design, and embraced the tenets of the modern movement. Workers who already had furniture, however old-fashioned, would not normally think of discarding it for modern pieces, although some followed suggestions to 'modernise' furniture by removing the stuck-on ornaments or otherwise making items more simple and functional. But resistance to the new style was not only economic. Many workers apparently found the new style 'too cold and not homely'.[23] Moreover, in the view of a modern writer on popular aesthetics, social factors also influenced working-class views. In their struggle for emancipation workers were naturally and understandably seeking to attain the physical standards of living and comfort so far achieved only by the middle class. The advice to go in for simple design 'must have seemed ironic, because the bourgeois strata did not on the whole live in simple surroundings'.[24]

A somewhat similarly confusing picture presents itself when we look at the public art of the period which is linked to the activities of the labour movement. The fact that we can speak of an art and architecture linked to working-class organisations is in itself a sign of the strength and self-confidence of the movement, as well as of its newly found elevated status. We find that in the discussion on the future of art in the transition from a bourgeois and capitalist society to a socialist one, much was made of the expected rise of 'public art' in the place of art created solely for the enjoyment of a few. Easel painting, thought to have been so closely connected with the rise of that society, would disappear, to give way to mural

22. *Arbeiterkultur in Hamburg um 1930*, Hamburg, 1982, p. 74. The architect Marcel Breuer wrote of the new furniture, which would be 'documents of the outlook on life and of the energy of the now self-confident proletariat' (quoted loc. cit.).
23. Ibid., pp. 84–6.
24. Cf. G. Selle, *Kultur der Sinne und aesthetische Erziehung*, Cologne, 1981, p. 102.

painting and other forms of decoration.[25]

Some buildings in the modernist idiom were commissioned by trade unions and other working-class organisations in the Weimar period, such as the office blocks for the ADGB, the German TUC, in Berlin and Frankfurt, designed by Max Taut, and the *Bundesschule* for trade unionists in Bernau near Berlin, designed by Hannes Meyer, the director of the *Bauhaus* between 1928 and 1930. All these were built in concrete, steel and glass, and their structure and elevation was to reflect only the functions of the building – the design of the trade union school was to be merely 'a plastic expression of its socio-pedagogic function'.[26] But there were also many undistinguished structures for which working-class organisations acted as clients.

The movement's building activity began in the decade before the First World War, predominantly in the form of local *Gewerkschaftshäuser*, which combined the function of a lodging house for travelling journeymen, a restaurant, and social facilities for members, as well as of offices for local trade union branches. Buildings like the Hamburg 'Trade Union Building', built in 1906 and re-modelled in 1913, in the heart of the city, were meant to be an outward representation of the strength of trade-unionism and of its emancipatory struggles. 'A breath of the future wafts through these *Gewerkschaftshäuser*' the *Hamburger Echo* wrote in January 1907. The construction of the Hamburg enterprise showed solidity, through the use of strong and durable materials such as granite, oak and porphyry, and expressed the tradition of the movement with its decorations, which included the heads of Marx, Engels, Lassalle and Liebknecht, as well as a group showing the value of work.[27]

Yet the architecture of the Hamburg building, like that of the one erected in Leipzig at about the same time, like most public buildings of the period, was backward-looking, using pastiches of older styles. Neo-Renaissance in the case of the Besenbinderhof, neo-Norman in the case of the Leipzig building.

25. The *Arbeitsrat für Kunst* had already envisaged this kind of development when it referred in the questionnaire which it circulated to artists of the 'possible abolition of the easel-painting' Cf. Akademie der Kunste, West Berlin, *Der Arbeitsrat für Kunst*, 1980, p. 15.
26. Cf. Hanens Meyer, 'Die Bundesschule des ADBG', in his *Bauen and Gesellschaft*, Dresden, 1980, pp. 63–67, p. 66. The school had an area of 25,270 square metres, and the cost of the whole project was 2.8 million marks.
27. E. Domansky, 'Der Zukunftsstaat am Besenbinderhof', in A. Herzig *et al.* (eds), *Arbeiter in Hamburg*, Hamburg, 1983, pp. 373–86. By the outbreak of war in 1914 two-thirds of the eighty *Gewerkschaftshäuse* were owned by local trades councils, some bought, others specially built.

Yet the creation of public art was a rare phenomenon even within the labour movement. The existence and new construction of buildings, to house activities of parties and trade unions, should have offered much scope for decorative treatment; but few examples of mural painting and other decorations have come to light. None survived, so we have to rely on contemporary photographs to form inevitably somewhat distorted impressions of the forms which this public art took. However, neither Karl B. Völcker's frescos for the Committee Room of the Communist Printing and Publishing House in Halle (1921), nor the murals which Peter Paffenholz created in 1928 for the party's Cologne headquarters, constituted revolutionary departures from existing practices. On the contrary, Paffenholz's apotheosis of the new life in Soviet Russia was a simple, folksy account; and Volcker's series, with its expressionist style and Christian symbolism, is unlikely to have had a widespread influence and appeal. The Leipzig *Gewerkschaftshaus* and the Holiday Centre of the 'Socialist Workers' Youth' organisation also had frescos, those in the former executed by Professor Volter.

Of wider influence were undoubtedly the monuments created in memory of the revolutionary fighters who died for their cause. Leaving aside figures, busts, tablets and steles created in traditional forms, which were put up by workers' organisations, sometimes in quite small places and often stylistically identical with the run-of-the-mill War Memorial, we are faced with three major edifices, the so-called Liebknecht-Luxemburg monument in Berlin, also known as the 'Revolution Monument'; the memorial to the workers fallen in March 1920 in Weimar in the defence of the Republic against the Kapp Putsch; and the monument in remembrance of the dead of the short-lived Socialist Soviet Republic in Bremen.[28]

Given the tendency for the art for the masses to be realistic in character it is interesting to observe that only the last of these was cast in a representational form. The sponsors chose a design by Bernhard Hoetger, a *pietà*-like figure. Originally conceived for a War Memorial, it was executed as a 4.5-metre-high sculpture in red porphyry, and erected in the Waller cemetery in Bremen.[29]

28. On the memorials see R.-P. Baacke and M. Nungesser, 'Ich bin, ich war, ich werde sein. Die Denkmäler der deutschen Arbeiterbewegung in den Zwanziger Jahren', *WgdW* pp. 280–99. An interesting smaller memorial of highly traditional design was erected in Gera to commemorate the victims of the Kapp Putsch. It took the form of a Roman funeral monument, and showed a woman with a child in her arms, flanked by two half-naked youths recessed in a pedimented structure. Cf. *Volk und Zeit*, 21 August 1921.
29. Cf. Baacke and Nungesser (note 28).

The Berlin monument and the Weimar memorial, on the other hand, were abstract and symbolic in character. Not surprising perhaps, as they were the work of architects, rather than sculptors, namely Mies van der Rohe in Berlin and Walter Gropius, then Director of the *Bauhaus*, in Weimar. The latter, an upward- and forward-thrusting crystal-shaped object, was a purely symbolic structure. The Berlin *Revolutions-Denkmal*, also abstract, took the form of an oblong block, twelve metres long, six metres high and four metres deep, and consisted of a series of slabs arranged so as to create sides with protruding and receding surfaces. Not only was it meant to be reminiscent of the *Mur des Féderés* in the *Père Lachaise* cemetery in Paris, where many of the fighters of the Paris Commune were shot in 1871; it was also suitable as a platform for the large demonstrations and gatherings which were held there.[30]

The original scheme for the site had been much more traditional – a wall like that in Paris (and incidentally that of the Kremlin), with a Rodin scuplture in front of it. What caused the change of plan is not clear. However, even given the abstract form of the monument, expressing both masses at rest and in movement, the symbolism of these blocks should not detract from its ritual function as a centre of mass activities and a place of pilgrimage. Together with a Soviet Star and flagstaff and the inscription, 'I am, I was, I shall be' – a quote from Rosa Luxemburg based on a line from a Freiligrath poem with its order reversed – it resulted in a work of art which clearly aimed at influencing the masses and which fulfilled its function as a platform for perorations, demonstrations and displays. 'This monument, with the red flags fluttering in front of it, and with the glowing Soviet Star, should always be a reminder for the struggle, and gather the masses for this struggle, for the organisation of the revolution.[31]

Committed Exhibitions

Yet modern and more challenging and often socially critical art did not on the whole reach the proletariat by this route. This came to it through exhibitions of original art; through reproductions and illustrations in the journals and more specialised magazines which addressed themselves to a working-class readership; and, last not

---

30. The Friedrichsfelde cemetery contained also the graves of Wilhelm Liebknecht, Ignaz Auer, Paul Singer and Franz Mehring.
31. Wilhelm Pieck at the inauguration of the monument on 13 June 1926.

least, through the medium of the political posters which appeared on the hoardings once or twice a year.[32]

The early exhibitions which addressed themselves especially to the German workers owe much to the post-revolutionary groups of radical artists who, as we saw, tended to identify with general socialist goals, which had gained wider credence in the revolution.[33]

These exhibitions were anything but unique events. We can trace a sizeable number of art shows mounted by working-class organisations or by groups of politically committed artists concerned with the popularisation of art within the working class. Some were general art exhibitions, though often showing working-class or politically engaged artists. Most were local events; but some, mostly with a political theme, toured Germany. Their numbers, and such attendance figures as we have, suggest that interest in, and contact with, art, even contemporary and sometimes difficult art, was a relatively minor but not insignificant facet in the cultural life of the Weimar labour movement.

One of the first exhibitions was arranged in 1919 by the Genossenschaft sozialdemokratischer Künstler. It opened in the Berlin West End and then moved to other parts of the city. The exhibition contained works by professionals and by amateurs and, as the *Rätezeitung*, the organ of the Berlin Workers' and Soldiers' Council, wrote, 'it showed that in spite of the considerable political excitement there exists a lively interest in all kinds of artistic questions'. The paper hoped that future exhibitions would show more good and cheap prints, lithographs and etchings.[34]

A few months later the Arbeistrat für Kunst, one of the newly founded groups of progressive artists, mounted a similarly structured exhibition, first in the House of the Proletarian Youth in the Petersburger Straße, and later in bars in Berlin working-class districts. Names of artists were not given; indeed, the organisers chose primarily works which were not by established artists, but paintings and sculpture done by workers themselves. This included some children's art.[35] The exhibition was not primarily conceived

---

32. Between January 1919 and December 1932 most Germans were called on to vote sixteen to twenty times.
33. The attitude of radical artists and of their association to revolution and socialism is discussed in Chapters 3 and 4.
34. *Rätezeitung*, 17 July and 21 July 1919. The paper argued that these exhibitions should bring art into every worker's life, and create a society so suffused with art that no special exhibitions were needed.
35. *Arbeitsrat für Kunst* (note 25) pp. 110–11.

Table 6 Chronicle of exhibitions

Date and Place	Title or Topic
1919 Berlin	Works of Berlin Artists shown in schools in East Berlin
April 1919 Berlin	'The unknown architect', organised by the *Arbeitsrat für Kunst*
July/August 1919 Berlin	Exhibition organised by the *Bund sozialistischer Künstler*
1919 Cologne	Exhibition for working people in the courtyard of the Museum for Applied Art.
1920 April Berlin	Workers' Art Exhibition organised by the *Arbeitsrat für Kunst* in the Petersburger Straße
1920 May Berlin	Exhibition 'Neues Bauen' organised by the *Arbeitsrat für Kunst*
1920 December Berlin	Exhibition of socialist art in the *Vorwärts* Bookshop
1921 March Berlin	Workers' Art in the Petersburger Straße
1922 Düsseldorf	International Art Exhibition in Department Store, Tietz
1924 Berlin	International Exhibition of Revolutionary Artists in the Petersburger Straße
1924 Berlin, etc.	'Große Solidaritätsausstellung', a travelling exhibition of the Künstlerhilfe, organised by Otto Nagel in the Wertheim Department Store
1924 Dresden	Exhibition 'Wir schaffen für Euch'
1924 Leipzig	Art Exhibition organised in conjunction with *Kulturwoche*
1925 Gotha	Exhibition organised in conjunction with *Kulturwoche* showing among others Otto Freundlich, Heinrich Hoerle, Franz Seiwert, and Franz Jansen
1926 Berlin	Exhibition in Department Stores, organised by Nagel
1927 Berlin and elsewhere	Exhibition organised by the Deutsche Kunstgemeinschaft
1928 Berlin	Exhibition 'Kunst und Wirklichkeit' in the Glaspalast in Moabit
1929 Berlin	Exhibition 'Soziale Kunst' in Lichtenberg (organised by the Bezirksamt)
1929 May Berlin	Exhibition 'Kapital und Arbeit' organised by the ASSO in the Europahaus
1929 Leipzig and elsewhere	Exhibition on the theme 'War and Peace' in the Grassi Museum
1930 Hamburg	Exhibition organised by SPD Kulturinitiative
1930 Hanover	Exhibition 'Die Werktätigen in Buch und Bild' organised by the Freie Bildungskartell

Table 6 *continued*

Date and Place	Title or Topic
1931 Berlin and elsewhere	Exhibition 'Frauen in Not' organised by the magazine *Weg der Frau*
1932 Berlin	Exhibition of works by members of the ASSO forcibly removed from the Große Berliner Kunstausstellung in Schloß Charlottenburg
1932 Berlin	'Photomontage' exhibition, organised by the ASSO.

as a political act, but as an attempt at bringing art, and through art beauty, into the life of the working masses. The aim of the exhibition was really 'to help to end exhibitions altogether . . . we do indeed seek to give joy, but it would be really beautiful if this was art, and not an art show. If it was for real, not a peepshow.'[36]

One of the worker-artists who was 'discovered' as the result of the exhibition was Otto Nagel, then still a manual worker and an early member of the Communist Party.[37] He in turn organised exhibitions for workers which circulated in Berlin department stores. One of them, in one of the Wertheim Stores in East Berlin, contained nearly 250 works, nearly all of which were sold.[38]

'Popular Art Shows', like those which Otto Nagel organised in Berlin, had parallels in other cities. They did not necessarily have a political slant, but were more concerned with the transmission of contemporary art and with attempts to persuade workers to buy original paintings or prints. Staged in large stores, and thus seen by many passers-by, their appeal is difficult to assess. Nagel himself estimated the attendances at the four showings of his exhibition in 1926 at 160,000 – a truly remarkable figure. He also recognised that he would not be able to effect a radical re-orientation of the conservative tastes of all those who tended to show the sugary oleograph next to the family photo on the flower-patterned wallpaper. But there was among workers, especially young workers, a section of aesthetically sensitive individuals who preferred artists 'who in their work had established some rapport with the masses'.

---

36. Ibid. p. 111.
37. Nagel painted Berlin workers in a flat, unemotional way, and specialised in composite pictures.
38. Cf. Catalogue of the Nagel exhibition in the Deutsche Akademie der Künste in Berlin (GDR) and E. Frommhold, *Otto Nagel*, Berlin, 1974. See also Otto Nagel, 'Die Lage der bildenden Kunst und das Volk', *Sozialistische Monatshefte*, 1927, pp. 827–30.

He therefore showed in his exhibitions 'exclusively work which could be readily understood by the masses, and with which they had affinities'.[39]

Ideologically committed and often deliberately tendentious and 'political' art was however shown by social-democratic and communist organisations, sometimes even with an overtly political theme. Thus the Künstlerhilfe (the artists' aid organisation) established under the auspices of the IAH, the 'International Workers' Aid' organisation, undertook the publication of two portfolios of lithographs on the themes of 'Hunger' and 'War', as well as of an illustrated pamphlet on the then-threatened eight-hour day. The series were published in large editions, and they were also widely exhibited. Here was art intended to impress a wider public, while yielding profits for the relief of starving workers.[40]

An exhibition, mostly of graphic art, at the Leipzig Kunstverein in August 1924 arranged as part of the first Leipzig 'Workers Cultural Week' sought to show political art in its most general sense. It was also to commemorate the tenth anniversary of the outbreak of war, and it was held in conjunction with the 'Socialist Youth Assembly of Central Germany', for which Käthe Kollwitz had created her famous poster *Nie wieder Krieg* ('No more war'). Among the artists whose work was shown were Masareel, Barlach, Kollwitz, Baluschek, Dix, Sela Hasse, Grosz, Schlichter and Zille. The exhibits were lent by the artists or loaned by local museums. The works shown had been collected especially as examples of 'proletarian art', not as works created by workers but as art which was close to the workers' problems and created 'by artists who had identified themselves ideologically with the cause of the working class' and 'who drew their artistic inspiration from contemporary social problems and conditions'.[41]

In putting on an exhibition of works mostly modern in idiom and often horrific in content, as in the case of Otto Dix's 'War Etchings', the organisers were knowingly taking a risk; and they were surprised and gratified by their unexpectedly great success. Attendances were unexpectedly large, especially among the young. During the twelve days on which the show was open over 3,500 people visited it, and the great majority, we are told, showed very real interest. It was transferred to Halle; but other showings,

39. Nagel, quoted in the catalogue of the exhibition of his *Berliner Bilder*.
40. Cf. article in *Not und Brot* (the periodical of the IAH), no. 29/30, 1924.
41. O. Bauer, 'Die Kunstausstellung der Leipziger Kulturwoche', *KW* 1924, no. 9, p. 148. A list of works exhibited can be found in the Festival Brochure, *Arbeiterkulturwoche und Gewerkschaftsfest*. It is also reproduced in part in Kober (note 9).

requested by many organisations, could not be acceded to because the prints were shown unframed, and local conditions did not offer sufficient security.[42]

In spite of such difficulties special exhibitions were mounted from time to time by social-democratic organisations, as in Gotha, in connection with another *Kulturwoche*. It showed 'the development of a proletarian aesthetic', and how this went upwards from 'being tied to petty-bourgeois thinking, with its emphasis on bric-à-brac and still lifes, via merely critical and accusatory art, to the formative picture of a new life'.[43] In general social-democratic-sponsored exhibitions seem to have been less politically focused, showing 'pure art' as well as art more specifically related to working-class experience. Thus in 1930 in Hanover the Joint Education Committee of the SPD and the unions mounted an exhibition under the title *Die Welt der Werktätigen in Buch und Bild*. This showed works by contemporary left-wing artists like Baluschek, Kollwitz, Grosz and Krain, lent by a local gallery, together with paintings and prints by apparently less committed artists lent by the Deutsche Kunstgemeinschaft.[44]

In the same year the Hamburg SPD put on an exhibition which was conceived essentially in aesthetic terms. The show, held in the Kunsthalle, the city's principal museum, consisted of some works by the *Griffelkunst* group of professional artists, which offered prints on a subscription basis at very low costs, but mostly of paintings and drawings of relatively unknown worker-painters. Employed mainly in printing and the graphic trades, they had little time for the creation of pure art. The exhibition ran under the challenging title of *Trotz alledem!-Kunst* ('Art – in spite of everything!') and it sought to demonstrate how much hidden talent could be found in the working class. Visitors were urged not to judge the exhibits by standards normally applied to professional artists, but to look at the exhibition as a piece of documentation. Its aim was to show 'that together with the economic struggle of the proletariat cultural forces too sought expression'.[45]

A detailed coverage of the thirty-odd art exhibitions mounted by groups of committed artists or by cultural and political organis-

42. A proposal to institute a regular series of exhibitions, made by the *Kulturwille*, came to nothing.
43. W. Lindemann, *Die proletarische Freidenkerbewegung*, (Leipzig) Münster (1926), reprinted in 1980, p. 64.
44. *Soz. Bldg.* 1930, p. 371.
45. From the preface of the catalogue of the exhibition preserved in the Hamburg Bibliothek zur Sozialgeschichte.

ations which I have been able to trace to date cannot easily be achieved, and we know little about contemporary reactions. Not surprisingly, we find a relative plethora of exhibitions showing social and radical art, and of art-shows addressed specifically at working-class audiences in the period soon after November 1918, when the newly formed groups of radical artists were active. We also find that the pace of the exhibition timetable quickens again in the last few years of the republic, when mainly communist political organisations mounted a number of didactic and thematic art shows, and when the ASSO, the Assoziation Revolutionärer Bildender Künstler Deutschlands, founded in 1928, was active in showing the works of its members, either independently or as sections of general major exhibitions.

Thus we find in 1929 an anti-war exhibition, combining art with documentary material, circulating round Germany. It contained, among other works, Otto Dix's great painting 'The Trenches', originally acquired by the Wallraf-Richartz Museum in Cologne, but later rejected under nationalist pressure.[46] And in October 1931, at the height of the campaign against the infamous anti-abortion paragraph 218 of the German Civil Code, the women's journal *Weg der Frau* mounted a travelling show under the title *Frauen in Not* ('The suffering of women'). As the magazine reported, the exhibition not only asserted female suffering in painting and in sculpture, but also demonstrated through large agitational pictures by Heinrich Ehmsen and Werner Scholz 'that the time for lamentation was past' and that working masses had now dedicated themselves to the fight for liberation.[47]

At the end of our period the exhibition of works by members of the ASSO in the centre of Berlin is evidence of the extent to which art and its showing had become almost violently politicised. The works shown in this exhibition had originally hung in the Große Berliner Kunstausstellung in the Charlottenburg Palace. A number of them were removed by the Prussian Ministry of Finance, acting as landlord, because of their alleged open incitement to violence. The group then decided to remove all their works and show them in a separate exhibition. Even there two paintings were removed – this time by the police.[48]

46. Cf. *KW* 1929, p. 12; W. Hutt, 'Die Beteiligung von bildenden Künstlern an den Volksaktionen der 20. und 30. Jahre, *Wissenschaftliche Zeitschrift der Humboldt Universität, Gesellschaftswissenschaftliche und Sprachwissenschaftliche Reihe*, vol. 11, 1962, pp. 223 ff.
47. *Weg der Frau*, no. 6, 1931.
48. See *Magazin für Alle*, November 1932.

The Iconography of the Political Media of the Left

The most important vehicle through which art and visual messages in general, and political and socially critical art in particular, was regularly brought to the attention of a sizeable section of the German working class was probably the socialist and the communist press.

Illustrated magazines for the worker and his family had already existed in the days of the Empire. Social-democratic publishing houses issued the *Neue Welt*, a weekly supplement of a number of socialist dailies; and a satirical magazine, *Der Wahre Jakob* was started in 1884 and continued with interruptions until 1933.[49] The post-war period saw a great expansion of the workers' press. Newspapers apart, journals and magazines were published under the auspices of the two major parties of the left or by sympathetic private publishers. The circulation figures of the major journals ran into tens of thousands, and the most popular, the AIZ (*Arbeiter Illustrierte Zeitung*), reached the half-million mark in its heyday.

Illustrated weeklies apart, other magazines were often also extensively illustrated, and better illustrated, thanks to the spread of offset printing techniques. Newspapers, too, carried illustrations of news items, as well as cartoons and political drawings. The subjects of the illustrations reproduced, the character of the art and of the artists shown, and the relative importance of older and of contemporary art are indicative of what was regarded as significant by editors. Going beyond this, we can draw some conclusions about the general cultural attitudes of the parties and groups which stood behind them. Unfortunately today we know little of the publishing practice, or of the editorial policy, of the vast socialist and communist press, beyond what we can infer from the periodicals and newspapers themselves. We can only look at the aesthetic character of the papers, journals and books as an application of their general ideological approach, and judge the visual appeal of a publication, or the aesthetic profile of a publishing house, as part of the totality of its contributions and style.

Inevitably there was much common ground across the political spectrum, both in respect of contemporary artists, whose work was reproduced, and of the artists of the past who were featured in illustrated articles. The differences in the profiles help us to understand political attitudes, and the imagery conveyed by these popu-

---

49. The *Neue Welt* published only line-drawings. Its readers demanded better illustrations, but the publishers said that they could not afford this.

lar publications must have helped to shape the political culture of the proletariat in its totality and in the two camps into which the German working class became increasingly, and ever more bitterly, divided.

The common ground, in respect of traditional or contemporary visual art, ranged over well-known socially critical artists such as Rowlandson, Daumier, Goya, Steinlen, Meunier and Masareel.[50] It also included pictures relating to work and workers by French realist painters, such as Courbet or Millet.

Individual works such as Van Gogh's 'Potato Eaters', or Delacroix's seminal painting 'Liberty leading the people', received wide recognition and frequent reproduction. Of the German artists of the period, Hans Baluschek, Käthe Kollwitz and Heinrich Zille, who had all taken the German worker and his milieu as their theme, were admired by all sections of the workers' press. The highly charged social and political criticism of George Grosz, on the other hand, can be found predominantly on the extreme left.[51]

Undoubtedly, social-democratic publications drew the circle of the traditional art they considered praiseworthy, more widely. They reproduced Dürer and Rembrandt, and occasionally they also published articles which concentrated on themes such as 'Work', and included examples of other bourgeois artists, men like Leibl with his 'Spinning Woman', or Liebermann with his 'Netmenders'. But their coverage also involved works like Hans Thoma's romanticised accounts of rural life and landscapes, with titles like 'Idyll' or 'Dancing in the Moonbeams', or they reproduced Böcklin's mysterious landscapes. Photographs of contemporary rural scenes, forest and meadows, peaks and valleys, reflecting the changing seasons and Germany's varied regions, grace the pages of *Volk und Zeit*, and must have tended to make their readers take pride in their national heritage, which was put before them for vicarious enjoyment. At the same time, the communist AIZ used the camera not only to draw attention to workers' misery and to proletarian struggles, but its photo montage presented a new art-form often fierce in its imagery and devastating in its criticism.

Even where there was congruity of coverage the journals of the

---

50. Daumier was seen as *the* artist of the revolutionary struggle. The communist *Eulenspiegel* wrote that 'we, the revolutionary proletariat are [his] only legitimate heirs, [we] shall finish the struggle'. (*Eulenspiegel*, vol. 3, no. 3, p. 35.).

51. We don't know whether Grosz was asked by social-democratic magazines for permission to reproduce works and refused it. In general only *Der Wahre Jakob* published some drawings from some artists who also published in the communist press.

two camps often looked at the same artist in a different light. For a social-democratic magazine, Frans Masareel was the portrayer of the sufferings and of the hopes of the industrial proletariat, 'he belonged to the people of tomorrow, not to those who are rich and rest on their laurels, but to the poor, to those who work and who struggle'. 'In his spirit and in his goals he belongs to the revolutionary proletariat.'[52] Yet the communist critic, Alfred Kemenyi ('Durus') wrote that there were shortcomings in Masareel's work, and that it was not sufficiently political. Durus regretted the absence of references to the class-conscious working masses, and to revolutionary cells.[53]

Comparing the two illustrated weeklies, or the satirical magazines such as the social-democratic *Lachen Links* and the communist *Der Knüppel* in their general approach, we are struck by the much greater acerbity and polemical character of the communist publications, compared with the more idealist attitudes conveyed by social-democratic magazines. We have already seen that, for the KPD, art was in the end politically committed and provocative. Satire and merciless criticism was at the heart of that revolutionary art. The 'enemy' was not only the capitalist and the fascist, but also the social-democratic politician; and the hostility of their cartoons must have helped to isolate the communist worker emotionally, while at the same time heightening his political passion.

The social-democratic press, on the other hand, conveyed a more positive picture of the present and a much more hopeful view of the future. Its satire was more humorous and less penetratingly destructive, and it was more balanced by illustrations, many from the pen of Willibald Krain, which concentrated more on the life and struggles of the worker than on the enemies of the proletariat. They often conveyed the impression that strength and determination would ensure victory.[54]

Differences can be seen in seminal issues and their interpretation. The rather sudden death of Friedrich Ebert, the socialist first President of the Republic, provides an example of how ideological differences are expressed in pictorial form. Thus *Lachen Links* put forward a reverential account of the dead leader, and a satirical dismissal of his detractors on the right. The drawing shows Ebert

---

52. F. Rosenthal, 'Masareel', *Die Büchergilde*, 1928, pp. 114–23, p. 123.
53. *Blätter für Alle*, 1930, no. 7.
54. For example, a drawing by W. Krain for the 1924 May Day celebrations shows a well-built young worker standing with his legs apart, the right arm raised, his feet planted on a swastika. The drawing has the caption, 'You will never succeed'.

on his bier, with an angel, complete with wings, approaching it to lay a wreath on his head. At the bottom of the catafalque, doll-like figures of his enemies continue their attack. The feeble drawing carried the inscription 'Not the pygmies' hate, but history will pass its judgement on him'.

Der Knüppel, however, conveyed a radically different message in a drawing by Rudolf Schlichter. While representatives of government and industry pay their respect at Ebert's tomb, the ghost of a dead revolutionary scrawls in blood on the tombstone the word 'Traitor'. Corpses are strewn in the background, and the caption reads '20,000 murdered revolutionaries bear witness'.[55]

Differences between communist and socialist satire can also be observed in stylistic treatment. Biting satire, searing criticism, such as we find in the work of Georg Grosz, often uses the fine line as an instrument. It was in Grosz's own words, 'a thread of Ariadne through the labyrinth of the millions of objects', and also, as the critic put it, 'the thread on which Grosz strings up his subjects'.[56] Contrasted with Grosz's work and with that of other illustrators of communist magazines, the cartoons in the social-democratic press often use softer lines and more painterly techniques. Grosz and artists like him operate by awakening in the reader feelings of revulsion and disgust, while others are more effective in arousing compassion.

The examples of visual art described and reproduced in the press of the left, including trade union journals and periodicals such as *Arbeiterjugend*, which often carried articles on individual artists, performed two functions. They sought to educate workers in the visual arts; but they also made visual statements of political commitment and of appeals to political action. Together with political songs and committed plays they are part of the political culture of the working class and of the parties of the left.

Visual Art and Political Agitation

The most obvious marriage between visual art and the politics of the left occurs of course in the area of political agitation, and in the conduct of political demonstrations and celebrations. Some of the best examples of this art can be found in the political poster and the

55. These cartoons are reproduced in H. Olbrich, *Sozialistische Deutsche Karikatur*, Berlin, 1979.
56. Georg Grosz, quoted in W. Schmied, *Neue Sachlichkeit, Magischer Realismus* Berlin, 1979, p. 46.

illustrative material issued in connection with the celebration of the First of May, which was before the introduction of the pictorial poster after 1918 the principal occasion for the publication of visual exhortation in the form of May Day broadsheets (*Mai-Zeitungen*) and postcards. Their study shows the widespread use of certain styles and iconographical symbols, as well as the differences in the visual treatment of political messages which we just observed.

In general, pre-1914 social-democratic official art, as we find it in *Mai-Zeitungen*, was realistic in style, often exuberant in design, and colourfully pictorial and even sentimental.[57] One of its central symbolic characters was the figure of Liberty. She is both a guide in the struggle and a deity to be venerated. Such illustration often conveyed that almost utopian belief in the imminence of a social revolution which then permeated much of the party.

War and revolution caused a break of the ideological mould, and a split in the tradition of political art. As Gottfried Korff wrote, the pictorial language of the labour movement in the 1920s was now more determined by the questions of the day and by the conflict between the two political wings of the movement.[58]

All the same, we still find in the pictorial May Day message of the SPD some continuation of that older artistic tradition, conveying messages with a calmer, more optimistic air. By contrast the political art of the Communist Party makes greater use of the symbolism of the struggle, and of the serried ranks which fought in it.

On the one hand we have happy throngs, flower-decorated banners, the sun shining above modern factories, a rainbow above the summit just reached by a muscular young worker, and a small troop marching under a gigantic flag with the caption 'Above us the light'.[59]

On the other hand, communist May Day illustrations convey more violence and more action. Masses demonstrate against reaction and against capitalism, heavy boots march, an imprisoned worker breaks his chains, and, Samson-like, shatters the columns of the house, and a sun with hammer and sickle rises in the

---

57. For an analysis of pre-1914 socialist iconography see U. Horn, 'Revisionistische Tendenzen und revolutionäre Haltungen in der Kunst um 1900', *Wissenschaftliche Zeitschrift der Humboldt Universität*, 1985, 1/2, pp. 79–84.

58. G. Korff, 'Rote Fahne und geballte Faust: Zur Symbolik der Arbeiterbewegung in der Weimarer Republik', in P. Assion (ed.), *Transformationen der Arbeiterkultur*, Marburg, 1986, pp. 86–107.

59. The illustrations can be found on the covers of *Volk und Zeit* and in the *Mai-Zeitungen* of the SPD, which are preserved in the Archiv der Sozialen Demokratie, Friedrich Ebert Stiftung, Bonn.

background. A fettered fist breaks loose, and the pygmy-sized enemies of the workers scatter.[60]

This (inevitably subjective) analysis of an area of workers' art could be paralleled and probably bettered by an evaluation and anatomy of the political-poster production of the parties of the Left during the Weimar period. Because here, in the form and symbolism of this agitational device, we are dealing, in effect, with the self-image and the conceptualisation of the enemy which the parties wished to project.[61] Analysed in stylistic, thematic and iconographic terms, and quantified, it should help us to understand the emotive transmission of ideology through art.

The significance of this and of all other kinds of 'applied art' of the period, be it cartoon, poster, banner, leaflet or other print media, lies in their relative publicness compared with the studio art of the period or with the great art of the past, locked away in museums. It is likely that these relatively ephemeral items, viewed possibly only fleetingly, had a much more widespread and more effective aesthetic influence on working-class life and attitudes than the high art of the period.

But we cannot trace such influence in detail, and much of the little which we know about the reception of art by workers during our period relates to expressions of opposition. As early as the immediate post-revolutionary period Berlin workers objected to a series of expressionist posters issued by the government's propaganda agency, the Werbedienst, which appealed to the public to vote in the forthcoming elections to the National Assembly and to support the socialist republic. The workers were opposed to the distortions in the representation of themselves in these posters, to their lack of realism, and to the absence of idealism in the design.[62]

The bitter and highly sophisticated cartoons in the communist satirical magazine *Der Knüppel* came under attack some years later. Some delegates at the KPD's National Conference in 1925 attacked the magazine for being insufficiently concerned with workers. They wanted illustrations which could be more readily understood; and, although the Central Committee deflected the attack, the magazine ceased publication in 1927, to be replaced by *Eulenspiegel* (later *Roter Pfeffer*), which had a more gentle tone.[63]

60. Based on front-page illustrations in the *Rote Fahne*.
61. The number of posters preserved is neither too large to preclude a census-type listing nor too small to preclude analysis.
62. Cf. I.K. Rigby, 'An alle Kunstler: war, revolution, Weimar': exhibition catalogue, San Diego, 1983, pp. 35–7.
63. Cf. KPD 10. Parteitag 1925, *Protokoll*.

These reservations point to the limitations in the workers' appreciation of art, which was inevitably determined by their visual experience and training. The elementary school provided little of the latter, and, as we saw, education in art, let alone art-training, reached only very few adult workers. Hence the majority probably approached art in the same way in which they approached everyday life, looking for the realistic and the familiar. 'If the appeal is not immediate the worker turns away . . . his senses only know the hard reality, his wishes embrace this earth because his cares relentlessly force him into that direction . . . And in art too he looks for the concrete.[64]

It is interesting to reflect that in the art which its press brought before the working class there was virtually no religious art and little abstract art; and we are probably right in assuming that if there had been reproductions of non-representational art they would not have been understood. Certainly suggestions to this effect fell on deaf ears. When the socialist art-critic, Adolf Behne, reviewed one of Otto Nagel's 'Popular Art Shows' he suggested that such social art, such *Elendsmalerei*, should be shown in Berlin's West End stores to educate the bourgeoisie, rather than in proletarian districts which saw the reality every day. Instead the proletariat should be shown 'boldly conceived abstract art, which would be much more revolutionary than the portraiture of social misery'. He was answered by the communist artist, John Heartfield, who wrote that 'even the most adventurous placing of colourful surfaces would not move a dozen workers to act against the rule of capital, let alone persuade them to fire a single shot – and nothing else could be the purpose of revolutionary art.'[65]

It was the latter approach to the visual arts, and, in a way, to all art, which permeated German communism and the policy and practice of its cultural organisations. Not that every work had to have a didactic purpose; but behind artistic manifestations and applications there was the ideal of ideological persuasion, and of the stimulation of political action. The first, short-lived, communist artists' group, the *Rote Gruppe*, put the creation of work in the service of its political ideals as its foremost concern. Its members declared that they were anxious to strengthen the effectiveness of communist propaganda 'through writing, pictorial representation

64. Cf. Adolf Kreiter, 'Was bedeutet dem Arbeiter die Kunst?', in *Arbeiterkulturwoche Leipzig, 1924. Programme*, pp. 12–13.
65. Cf. the articles by Behne and Heartfield, Die *Weltbühne*, vol. 22, 1926, pp. 346–8, 434–5.

and stage design'.[66]

The activities and influence of the more permanent and more effective ASSO, founded four years later, went further. It naturally asked its members to help the political movement with the design and execution of all forms of agitational material; and there is evidence of the effectiveness of this in the creation of banners, placards, posters, and even of three-dimensional objects carried in demonstrations or shown at meetings.[67] In Dresden, where the ASSO was particularly active in the creation of agitational art, members produced and sold, literally for pennies, small woodcuts or linocuts with a strong political symbolism, in pubs and at meetings. And in Bremen the State Archives have yielded up an unexpectedly large amount of agitational material – prints and drawings – produced most probably by worker-artists, though often copied from pattern- and sample-books which had been produced centrally by the KPD or the ASSO.[68] These are examples of the 'revolutionising of the street scenes' which the ASSO had demanded, even if not of the 'beginning of a new revolutionary popular art', as the *Rote Fahne* claimed.

Less public than the spate of agitational art produced largely under the ASSO influence, but politically more significant, was the fact that within the association, but not uninfluenced by the writing and critique of some communist art critics, there developed a new approach to the portraiture of working-class life. In place of art which showed sadness and suffering and exercised a social critique we now find increasingly works which made committed statements, showing the beauty and dignity of working-class life and the virtues of the revolutionary fighter, treated as a heroic figure conscious of his power.[69] 'The worker . . . is portrayed from below . . . not demanding compassion, but conscious of his own strength.'[70] In contrast to the committed art of the KPD we find in

66. Manifest der Roten Gruppe, reprinted in U.W. Schneede (ed.) *Die zwanziger Jahre*, Cologne, 1979.
67. Cf. J. Kramer, 'Die Assoziation Revolutionarer Bildender Kunstler', in *WgdW*, pp. 174–204.
68. Cf. W. Grape, *Aufruf und Anklage. Kunst für die Bremer Arbeiterbewegung*, Bremen, 1983.
69. U. Kuhirt, 'Künstler und Klassenkampf: Zur Geschichte der Assoziation Revolutionärer Bildender Künstler Deutschlands', in *Revolution und Realismus* (Exhibition Catalogue, Staatliche Museen in Berlin, 1979), Berlin (GDR), 1979, pp. 174–204.
70. Cf. H. Gärtner, 'Revolutionäre Programmatik in der Kunst der Dresdner ASSO', in *Entwicklungsprobleme der proletarisch-revolutionären Kunst*, Berlin (GDR) 1977, pp. 170–77, p. 175.

the social-democratic sector of the workers' culture movement a greater separation between politics and art. In the theoretical discussions the arts were accorded a major but educative role. They were no longer just to produce pleasant feeling and 'uplift', but were expected to contribute to the creation of the new socialist man; 'for the proletariat art has a personality-forming function. It must assist in cleansing the worker's instinct and rid him of egoistical attitudes. . . . Art will undertake the function hitherto reserved for religion and morals. It prepares him for the achievement of his great goal, the classless and humane community, by helping to arouse humane and fraternal feelings.'[71]

How the worker was to encounter art, and by what means such a transformation was to be effected, is less clear. No doubt there would be more of the existing pattern of exhibitions and education. However, a formal training in the understanding of art was to be the task of the schools.[72] What mattered for the adult worker was not the art-historical context or the subject of a painting, but the mood which it conveyed and the aesthetic perfection of the created object. Thus in theory the proletariat should make all great art its own; in practice art which would move the masses must be of subjects to which the workers can respond out of their own experience.

One suggestion was that closer ties with the visual arts might be established through a new *Volkskunst* – a folk art which, as in the Middle Ages, would be both an art of the people and a 'popular' art, in the sense of being easily understood.[73] Today, by contrast with the Middle Ages, the separation of life and art meant an enormous loss in feeling, just as the mechanical nature of human production cried out for a compensating beauty. Those who advocated such a development were aware that there was, as yet, no foundation for the creation of a people's art, but noted that the young generation had taken a first step in that direction by creating a lifestyle in which the arts occupied a central place.[74]

The more radical among the social-democratic writers on cultural matters admitted the desirability of a proletarian art, born out of the social experience of the workers. But they also thought that

71. Kreiter (note 64).
72. E. Winkler, 'Bericht über die Kulturwoche (Leipzig 1924)', *Die Tat*, 1924, p. 892 – quoting Leo Kestenberg's lecture on 'Sozialismus und Kunst'.
73. The cultural theories linked with the idea of *Volkskunst* are discussed more fully in Chapter 2.
74. On art and workers' youth see E.R. Müller, *Das Weimar der arbeitenden Jugend*, 1921.

the expression of it must remain individual and unfettered. To demand that this art show a specific *Tendenz* would be crude and lead to a perversion of art. It would be equivalent to 'an aesthetics of the calloused hand', and could lead to vandalism in respect of established art. Artistic creation must preserve its individuality.[75]

We can observe a similar contrast in the field of worker amateur photography. Of all the applied arts this was the only one in which both communists and social democrats were formally organised, the former in the Vereinigung der Arbeiterfotografen and the latter in the Arbeiter-Lichtbildbund. The communist worker-photographers were encouraged to take pictures for the communist press, and their portraiture of proletarian life and work was expected to bring out the internal contradictions of capitalist society and provide visual points of departure for the proletarian struggle. 'We take pictures where ever the life of the proletariat is hardest, where the bourgeoisie is at its most effective', Edwin Hoernle, one of the education experts of the KPD, wrote in 1931. 'We shall raise the fighting spirit of our class by conveying through our photographs, class consciousness . . . solidarity . . . discipline and revenge. Photography is a weapon . . . we, the workers' photographers, are the eye of our class, and we shall teach our class-comrades to use their eyes.'[76]

The aims of the Workers' Photography League were less overtly political. It sought to give technical training, foster a better understanding of the art of photography, *and* to assist in the general expansion of socialist cultural activities through pictures and film. Initially, at least, photography was for them a fine art. Only gradually, and largely as the result of the growing fascist threat, an interest in committed pictures arose even here: 'There was no longer time for snaps of the idyllic birch forest or for autumnal motifs', wrote the journal of the League. Members were encouraged to produce the 'social photo', neither 'genre' nor mere social misery, different in orientation from the didactic-tendential picture; but likewise committed.[77]

The aesthetic problems connected with the photography of an idyllic birch forest or of the depressing queue at a soup-kitchen are the same, but the implication of the statements cited above is that the untutored worker-photographer looked at the former as

75. O. Bauer, 'Kunst und Proletariat', *KW* 1929, no. 1 pp. 2–4.
76. E. Hoernle, 'Das Auge des Arbeiters', *Der Arbeiterfotograf*, 1931, no. 7.
77. Cf. Fritz Heine, *Das Neue Bild*, vol. 2, no. 1, p. 7, and articles on the social photo in that volume.

beautiful and dismissed the latter as a subject not fit for recording. From the political point of view the difference between the two subjects lay in their relative usefulness in terms of the political and economic struggle.

Transferred to a more fundamental plane, the art which was offered to the German workers through the medium of education and exhibitions, or through reproductions in books and periodicals, stretched from 'great and pure art' to art which was to be judged in terms of its use as a weapon in the fight for a better society. As a miner is reported to have said about George Grosz's collection of drawings *Das Gesicht der herrschenden Klasse* ('The Face of the Ruling Class'), 'the dumbest of proletarians will be aroused by these drawings, even those whose feelings are blunted will be goaded into action. Yes, that is what we need – unlimited hate against the exploiters. And Grosz's pictures breathe such hate'.[78]

Such a distinction between types of art and their place in working-class life is in parallel to the controversy between music judged in terms of emotional uplift and aesthetic quality, and music as *Kampfmusik*, to rally the working class through its text and its presentation, discussed in the last chapter. It is also similar to the conflict between the social-democratic *Volksbühne* performing plays for their literary and their entertainment value, and the communist-inspired opposition which demanded plays of relevance and commitment.

In practice there was in the field of the visual arts no organised public and no popular pressure groups, and hence no forum for the discussion of these issues. Nor did the two parties through whose publications and organisations examples of the visual arts reached the working-class public show clearly distinct and separate profiles in respect of the art which they championed. Hence the battle was never joined. We don't even know by whom decisions about contributions and illustrations in the workers' press were taken, or who selected or commissioned election posters or other graphic material for political agitation. As far as the communist press was concerned Alfred Kemenyi (Durus), the art critic of the *Rote Fahne* and a frequent contributor to the magazines and journals, was influential here.

For Durus all art was class-related, and for the working class only such art was relevant as was linked to the political struggle and

---

78. Reproduced from a quotation in A. Stenbok-Fermor, *Meine Erlebnisse als Bergarbeiter*, Stuttgart 1929, in 'Künstler des Proletariats', *Eulenspiegel*, 1931, no. 7.

expected to influence the outcome. He advocated 'a proletarian-revolutionary aesthetic on the basis of dialectical materialism'; to him such a marxist aesthetic was inseparable from communist politics. In opposition to such theories, which would judge art ultimately in terms of its political effectiveness, the art historian and critic Adolf Behne, who was sympathetic to the SPD, defended a pure aesthetics which would judge art by specific attributes, such as colour or form, and the way in which they affect the senses.[79]

The social-democratic presentations did not criticise *engagé* art as such. They approached works of art from a broadly based, catholic point of view; but they tended to exclude all abstract and non-figurative art. The nearest the SPD came to the acceptance of any category of abstract art was in the largely unsuccessful attempts to change the aesthetics of home-making through the replacing of ornateness by functionality. To be simple and functional, eschewing decorations, was a spiritual challenge for some young socialists; but the great majority of workers remained indifferent, if not hostile.[80]

The preference for the traditional, non-functional home, has been linked to a desire for comfort and cosiness; but it has also been ascribed to the wish to show outward signs of 'bourgeois' respectability. The latter is probably related to the way in which workers see themselves and their environment aesthetically as well as socially. Their image of themselves, of their class and of their community must ultimately colour the way in which they look at art and, especially, at the portraiture of the working class.

Chapter 1 presented evidence of aesthetic-cum-moral feelings of aversion by social-democratic workers to the way in which some workers were portrayed in some naturalist novels at the end of the last century. This chapter has also traced a similar critical reaction to the representation of workers in some expressionist political posters in 1919. There was also objection on the left to the critical way in which George Grosz had drawn the proletariat. His workers are mostly shown as sad and miserable figures – miserable, so Grosz argued, because they were the victims of capitalism. But for *Rote Fahne* they failed to show 'the struggle and the heroism of the proletariat'.[81] The workers whom the parties showed in their

---

79. Cf. *Revolution und Realismus* (note 69), pp. 92–4 for extracts from A. Behne, 'Kunst als Waffe' (*Weltbühne*, 1931, pp. 301–4) and A. Durus, 'Die über den Klassen schwebende Kunst' (*RF*, 8 September 1931).
80. Cf. *Jungsozialistische Blätter*, 1922, p. 189.
81. Cf. U.M. Schneede, *Georg Grosz, Leben und Werk*, Stuttgart, 1975, p. 140.

political posters and placards were not depicted as suffering and oppressed; they were almost exclusively strong and confident of victory.

However, the isolated examples of working-class reactions to contemporary art and to visual symbols presented here do not permit generalised conclusions. They can only provide building blocks for a study of the reception of art by the German working class.

The People's Stage and Agitprop:
Two Aspects of Workers' Theatre

The People's Theatre Movement and the Working Class

In discussing the people's theatre movement we are entering new territory. Sport and music were areas of popular entertainment *per se*, and the working class had participated in them for a long time. Not so the theatre. The ideal of a German *Nationaltheater*, envisaged by the writers of the classical period, was never translated into that of a truly *popular* theatre; and there had been virtually no traditional connection between the German working class and the professional theatre.

The only link between the working class and the theatre was in respect of the 'variety' and the 'garden theatre' and other popular show establishments, generally situated in the new suburbs of the growing cities. The attractions of these establishments were as much those of the beer-garden and restaurant facilities which they provided, and which also furnished a substantial part of their income, as those of the theatres themselves. They were thus a place for family entertainment, to which working-class families might repair on a Sunday afternoon. The open-air stage generally offered light artistic fare – musicals, burlesques or cabaret; while the enclosed auditorium of the 'winter' theatre might also offer more serious plays, performed by a resident company, sometimes based on a family of actors, as in the case of the Berlin Rose Theater.[1]

Such amateur companies as we find among the working class in the nineteenth century were generally very simple enterprises, which did not really introduce the workers to the dramatic arts, although they were the forerunners of the amateur-based *Agitprop-theater* which will be discussed later in this chapter. With these exceptions, the commercial theatre remained a middle-class pre-

---

1. Cf. E. Krull and H. Rose, *Erinnerungen an das Rose Theater*, Berlin, 1960; Th. Zantke, *Der Berliner Prater*, Berlin (GDR), 1987.

serve, if only because the price of tickets was too high for working-class audiences.[2]

At the same time censorship and popular apathy prevented the theatre from keeping up with modern ideas and performing the dramas of naturalism and realism which were being written in the last decades of the nineteenth and the first of the twentieth century. In that situation we find that from the 1890s onwards some working-class leaders and left-wing intellectuals sought to break down the barriers of the bourgeois 'theatre-privilege'. They wished to let the working class enjoy the modern stage, and to ensure that contemporary plays, critical of society and of the period, should come to be performed.[3] To do so they wished to replace the commercial theatre by the *Kultur-theater*, the cultural theatre.

The movement which was to make this possible came into existence in the first instance in 1890 in Berlin in the form of the Berliner Freie Volksbühne (The Berlin 'People's Free Stage') and Volksbühne (or 'People's Stage') became the name under which the popular theatre movement spread from Berlin across Germany. The success of the Volksbühne was due to two organisational principles. The first lay in cheaper theatre tickets, through the realisation of mass consumption, and the fixing of performances for Sunday afternoons, a time when most workers were at leisure; the second lay in the bypassing of the censorship. By linking the issue of tickets to the payment of membership dues, and by facilitating both functions through the dispersal of ticket agencies throughout the city, it was possible to play to full houses at charges considerably below those of the commercial theatre. This made these performances, especially those not taken over from commercial theatres but specially produced for the Volksbühne, in effect closed club performances. They could show modern problematic plays, which otherwise would not pass the censors.

The censorship of plays, the only formal censorship which existed under the Empire, was not principally political; it related rather to moral issues and coarseness of expression; but it prevented many plays of modern Naturalism being performed. Nor was the orientation of the Volksbühne primarily political, although the majority of its members were workers – albeit generally skilled workers – and sympathetic to the SPD, if not members of it. The dues and charges were clearly at a level which only better-off

2. Seats in commercial theatres in Berlin in the 1920s were upwards of around three marks.
3. From the programme of the Hamburg Volksbühne, 1920 cited in *Arbeiterkultur in Hamburg um 1930*, Hamburg, 1982.

workers could afford. The monthly membership due was 0.60 marks, and twelve payments gave access to eleven performances. With the cost of the magazine and cloakroom and programme charges this worked out at 0.85 marks per play. During the Weimar period the cost of a visit was 1.50 marks.[4]

The *Volksbühnen* movement was, however, just as much concerned with bringing about a greater awareness of contemporary moral issues and of changes in artistic sensibility. In the appeal for the foundation of a People's Theatre which he published in the radical *Berliner Volkszeitung*, Bruno Wille, a socialist-inclined former clergyman turned *littérateur*, spoke of a theatre which should be the 'source of an enjoyment of art at a high level, of a moral elevation and . . . should provide a strong stimulus to think about the great questions of the day. The plays to be performed should be noble works of art, filled with the spirit of liberty.'[5]

The question of the Volksbühne's political stance was to be a matter of concern throughout most of its history. Already at its first general meeting to discuss its constitution a minority wished to affirm their socialist commitment by proposing that Lasalle's *Franz von Seckingen*, an atrocious but political play, should be given at the inaugural performance. They also unsuccessfully moved an amendment to the statutes, suggesting the substitution of the word 'popular' for 'modern' in a phrase which referred to modern poetry.

From a formal point of view too the political character of the organisation was soon at issue. The police declared the Volksbühne a political association, and, after a series of lawsuits, the status of the association was declared to be political – though not in a party-political sense, but in the more limited sense that their actions were of political consequence. In 1895 the Volksbühne felt more seriously intimidated by the intention of the police to apply censorship to their plays. Opposition to all censorship was deeply ingrained in the political thinking of the German left; rather than submit to it, the leadership first suspended performances and then dissolved the organisation. There was however, much pressure from the membership for the Volksbühne to re-start operations, and the fact that the Neue Freie Volksbühne, which had split off in 1892, did continue in existence with changed rules, persuaded the Freie Volksbühne to do likewise. It tightened up its membership rules, and resumed activities in 1897.[6]

---

4. S. Nestriepke, *Geschichte der Berliner Volksbühne*, vol. 1 (only), Berlin, 1930, p. 166.
5. The appeal was published in the *Berliner Volksblatt* in March 1890.
6. On Bruno Wille and the Neue Freie Volksbühne see H. Scherer, *Bürger-

In its new garb, and with the growing influence of the revisionists in the party and among its leading figures, the Volksbühne pursued a more broadly conceived cultural policy, showing a wider range of plays and not necessarily or even predominantly plays of political or social significance.[7] The Neue Freie Volksbühne, under Wille's direction, had always regarded its task as popular education – *volkspädagogisch* – and the older organisation, which had retained a predominantly working-class audience, now also spoke of the need 'to awaken in the working class a feeling for art', although at the same time it sought to satisfy the more popular taste of a wider membership who 'wish to participate in contemporary culture and to absorb the great values of the past as well as the leisure-time recreational plays of the present'.[8]

The repertory would now include comedy and farce on a larger scale. 'It was colourful and lively, but it was not particularly adventurous, nor did it strike a strong proletarian note.'[9] The number of plays performed which could not have been shown in ordinary commercial theatres was now very small. An experimental theatre, which the Neue Freie Volksbühne started in 1912, was not very successful.[10] Thus the increase in membership led to the accusation that the Volksbühne was really only a 'dramatic soup kitchen' – which its members joined solely in order to obtain cheap tickets to see good plays.[11]

As the organisation grew it had to make concessions to the taste of the great majority of its members, whose views were expressed by its *Ordners*, helpers who acted as ushers and agents, who were recruited from the rank and file of the membership, and who were represented on the governing committee. They criticised satires with anti-socialist sentiments, as well as plays like Strindberg's *The Father*, which they regarded as too obviously harrowing.[12] And looking at the plays which were performed before 1919 we see that whatever its intentions and the rhetoric of its public pronouncements, the Volksbühne pursued, in concrete terms, a policy which turned it into an agent for the transmission of bourgeois cultural

lichoppositionelle Literatur und sozialdemokratische Arbeiterbewegung nach 1890, Stuttgart, 1974.

7. Cf. the very detailed list of plays produced by the Volksbühne in Berlin in H. Braulich, *Die Volksbühne, Theater und Politik in der deutschen Volksbühnenbewegung*, Berlin 1976, pp. 252–83.
8. Gustav Landauer in *Die Schaubühne*, 19 October 1905, cited in Braulich (note 7).
9. Nestriepke (note 4), p. 229.
10. C.W. Davies, *Theatre for the People*, Austin, 1977, pp. 58 and 73.
11. Davies, (note 10), p. 46.
12. Cf. Nestriepke (note 4).

values to a largely working–class audience.[13]

In the year immediately preceding the war, the organisation thus presented a broadly–based repertoire of plays, including light entertainment and operettas. This policy was attacked from within and without by the politically conscious section of the membership and by intellectuals outside it. What was at issue was not only the political play, the *Tendenzstück*, and the directly political role of art, but also the artistic quality of the entertainment that was provided. 'Heinz Sperber', the playwright Herman Heijermans, argued in favour of a policy which would seek to counter the dominant and perverting bourgeois art of the period and of the past by a 'proletarian' art consonant with the sentiments and aims of the socialist working class.[14]

This view was opposed by SPD politicians. Friedrich Stampfer, a journalist on the staff of *Vorwärts*, the SPD's principal newspaper, argued that art should be judged by its quality, not by its provenance, and that the workers had a right to the enjoyment of such little culture as came their way. 'Not conviction makes an artist', he argued, 'but ability', through which that conviction is translated into an artistic form. It was to the credit of the German revolutionary labour movement that it did not seek to destroy older culture, but that 'with loving care it would carry the cultural values of the past over the stream that divides present from the future'. He wished to throw the doors wide open to real proletarian art, which would then be art for all mankind; but he rejected Sperber's belief in the validity of judgements made out of proletarian class instincts, trusting instead in the critical aesthetics of the working class, whose representatives had, after all, directed the affairs of the Volksbühne in that spirit for over two decades.[15]

Although the Volksbühne clearly sided with Stampfer, and incidentally, but hardly accidentally, did not re–elect Sperber to the Council, the issue was to be raised again during the Weimar years, and despite the movement's outward successes, was destined to cause deep rifts within it.

Indeed, after war and revolution, the *Volksbühnen* movement

13. Not all Volksbühne Associations responded fully to popular taste. In Hamburg, where Leopold Jessner produced plays for the local Volksbühne, it was claimed that 'no concessions were made to the desire for entertainment on the part of the mindless, merely effect-seeking theatre-goer'. Hamburg, SPD, Zentralkommission für Bildungswesen, *Geschäftsbericht, 1912–13*.
14. For Heijermans' view see G. Fülberth, *Proletarische Partei und bürgerliche Literatur*, Neuwied, 1972, pp. 127–46 *passim*.
15. Nestriepke (note 4), pp. 190–1.

took a great leap forward. At its most prosperous the National Federation, founded in 1920, had several hundred member organisations and a total membership of 600,000, of which Berlin accounted for nearly a quarter. The Volksbühne in Berlin also had its own theatre, a massive building, free-standing and somewhat heavy in style, and capable of seating 2,000.[16] In addition the organisation leased two other theatres for most of the time, and the Volksbühne was thus capable of mounting plays of its own choice and in pursuit of its own cultural policy. It was understandable that during the war the Volksbühne should have been unable to produce plays of its own, and happy to lease its newly built theatre to Max Reinhardt, whose performances had already been booked previously by them. Less so, that, as the theatre returned to its own management, it should have opened with the premier of Immermann's *Merlin*, a very Germanic play about the Arthurian Legend, written nearly a century earlier and never previously performed.[17]

But this was clearly in line with the artistic conceptions of the theatre's first post-war artistic director, the actor-manager Friedrich Kayssler, appointed in 1918 and described in the journal of the Volksbühne as a German man in the best sense who, without being a chauvinist would naturally give German plays the pride of place which they deserved in a German theatre. His was an aristocratic nature, but he would also 'show a love for the dark upwards-striving masses without which the theatre's most important collaborator could not be imagined'.[18] It is thus little surprising that, in spite of the political upheaval all around it, the general trend of the Volksbühne's policy should be largely a continuation of its pre-war policy. It now proclaimed that it would offer its audiences a catholic selection of modern drama, but would eschew the modish and the desire to be up to the minute. The theatre was prepared to cultivate young talent; but it hoped, above all, to 'have strength and time to show the great dramatic creations from Aeschylus to Gerhart Hauptmann, from Shakespeare to Strindberg, and to express them with a new reverence and offer them to

16. The theatre, designed by Oscar Kaufmann, was fairly traditional in its layout, retaining stalls, circles and balconies rather than adopting an amphitheatre type of auditorium. There were, however, no boxes.
17. Cf. Davies (note 10), pp. 86–7.
18. Cf. H. Scherer, 'Volksbühnenbewegung und interne Opposition in der Weimarer Republik', *AfSG* vol. 14, 1974, pp. 214–51, p. 219. Kayssler held office during the seasons 1918/19 to 1922/3. He was succeeded by Fritz Holl (1923/4 to 1927/8), and by K.H. Martin (1928/9 to 1931/2). Throughout the period Julius Bab acted as *Dramaturg* (Literary Director).

the enjoyment-seeking masses in a pure form'.[19] By producing such plays to the highest possible artistic standards the Volksbühne would contribute to the cultural emancipation of the German worker in parallel with his political and social emancipation, which was allegedly proceeding apace in the new state.

The establishment of the Republic saw the final act of reunification of the two branches of the Berlin Volksbühne, and in Berlin and elsewhere new theatrical opportunities offered themselves to the movement. With a much more open and initially radical and pro-intellectual attitude abroad, the *Volksbühne* movement reasserted its emancipatory and pedagogic role. It 'wished to change the commercial theatre into a cultural theatre' and 'to impart to the working class such cultural values as the proletariat might need in its attempt to emancipate itself; but it did not attempt to be a proletarian theatre in the sense that it would exclude works from its repertoire because they were the products of a bourgeois ideology'.[20]

Thus while the Berlin Volksbühne grew in numbers and in strength during the post-revolutionary period, its artistic policy was at first little influenced by political events. Those in charge thought of the people's theatre movement in terms of a broad cultural movement whose principal aim was to introduce its members to the national cultural heritage. In addition, the Volksbühne, as a theatre with a committed membership, would create a community with a common desire to experience true art.[21] But the concept of the Volksbühne as a *Kunsttheater*, presenting, like other theatres beautiful experiences, rather than as a *Gesinnungstheater*, a theatre of conviction, was to be challenged from within by sections of the membership, mainly the 'Youth Sections', and from without by the protagonists and practitioners of a new and radical theatre, notably Erwin Piscator.

Politics and Artistic Direction

The belief in the role of the Volksbühne as an 'intermediary for the transmission of bourgeois culture', of which the leadership of the Berlin institution was such a strong advocate, was not held

19. Scherer, (note 18), pp. 220–1.
20. *Die Volksbühne – das Theater des Volkes* (Schriften des Verbandes der deutschen Volksbühnenvereine, no. 2), 1920, p. 4.
21. Scherer (note 18); A. Schwerd, *Zwischen Sozialdemokratie und Kommunismus. Geschichte der Volksbühne, 1918–1933*, Wiesbaden, 1975, especially pp. 53–5.

throughout the movement.[22] Opposition to it and to party-political neutrality found expression at the delegate meetings of the *Volksbühnen* movement held annually. Some local *Volksbühnen* societies showed their opposition to the policy of co-operation with public institutions, and, above, all with the Bühnenvolksverband, a bourgeois theatre-club organisation founded in imitation of the Volksbühne. The leadership advocated such collaboration in the name of a community-creating function, which would eventually comprise the whole of the nation, or at least 'the socially and democratically inclined members of all parties';[23] and it was hoped that such collaboration would bring with it concrete benefits in terms of an improved theatre. Oppositional groups rejected this policy, as in their view the Bühnenvolksverband expressed national-ist and religious ideologies; and they also opposed unduly close ties with the public state-supported theatre. Before attempting to create a national community one should concentrate on the creation of the community of the proletariat.[24]

Some of the strongest criticism of the artistic policy of the Volksbühne was expressed in a letter which thirty leading authors and artists addressed to the 1926 meeting of the association. They urged the Volksbühne to further 'the new in art and the contem-porary in drama, and to eschew the merely conventional, tra-ditional and petty-bourgeois'.[25] Arthur Holitscher, one of the signatories, and one of the leading members of the Berlin society, spoke in support of the letter. He noted the absence of representa-tives of the working class from the speakers at the meeting, and urged the return to stronger links with the organised working class, such as, he suggested, had existed in the early days of the movement.[26]

Not that there was much scope for the local Volksbühnen to express political convictions through the medium of dramatic productions. Few had their own theatre or their own theatre companies, so that they generally had to select plays from the established repertory of the local theatres or the opera. Thus while

---

22. Unlike the Berlin Volksbühne, workers' theatre activities in individual cities, and the activities of the Association of local Volksbühnen have as yet not been studied extensively.
23. Julius Bab, cited in Breulich (note 7), p. 136.
24. Breulich (note 7), pp. 136–42.
25. *Die Volksbühne*, vol. 1 no. 13, 1 July 1926. See also 'Der 7. Volksbühnentag und die Arbeiterschaft', *R.F.* 4 July 1926, in M. Brauneck (ed.), *Die Rote Fahne*, Munich, 1973, pp. 226–9.
26. Cited in Breulich (note 7), pp. 141–2.

the Hamburg Volksbühne, which had had an independent organisation during the period 1893–1900, sought to 'do away with the
bourgeois "theatre privilege", and to assist in the production of
modern socially and politically critical plays' it could in practice not
do more than regularly book performances for its 10,000 members
in a number of public and commercial theatres. The decision, in
1930, to create its own theatre came too late. Such 'political theatre'
as existed in Hamburg could only be brought about through the
effort of independent producers, such as Erich Ziegel, or independent actors, such as the members of the short-lived (1932–33)
Kollektiv Hamburger Schauspieler, and, of course, in the largely
amateur *Agitprop* companies such as *Die Nieter* ('The Riveters') and
Das Rote Sprachrohr ('The Red Megaphone').[27] In Cologne the
Volksbühne maintained for a short time its own theatre, the *Theater
des Werktätigen Volkes*, which performed mainly naturalist drama,
and where the emphasis was on artistic quality rather than an
ideological commitment. In any case, the small and declining
membership contained relatively few workers, and the theatre was
forced to close after two years in April 1922.[28]

Only the Berlin organisation offered continuous and extensive
theatre to a large and, even in the 1920s, still largely proletarian
audience; and it provides a case study for the interplay of dramatic
performance and politics. One of the major discussions arose from
the work of Erwin Piscator, who between 1924 and 1926 was a
resident producer at the Volksbühne's principal theatre at the
Bülowplatz. His staging of political plays and political treatment of
plays without a strong political significance laid the fuse for the
critical discussion of the artistic work of the Volksbühne and of its
political commitment.

Piscator's appointment as a guest producer, with the right to
choose his plays, came after he had shown his own brand of
political theatre at the Proletarische Bühne and later at the Zentral
Theater, which he had leased jointly with H.J. Rehfisch in 1923.[29]
His opportunity to produce plays at the very heart of the
Volksbühne movement might be seen as an accolade conferred on
him by a theatre which still paid at least formal homage to the ideals

27. Cf. *Arbeiterkultur in Hamburg* (note 3), pp. 232–48.
28. C. Fischer, 'Das Theater gehört dem Volke', in *Ergebnisse* 2, 1984 (issue on
    Arbeiterkultur).
29. On Piscator's early theatres see H. Goertz, *Piscator*, Hamburg, 1974, pp. 28–34,
    and Chapter 1 above.

of a political stage. Seen in the context of all the plays produced in the Volksbühne over the years, the Piscator plays hardly loom large. Even among the nine plays which Piscator produced only five were of political significance or were accorded a political treatment. It was his production of Elm Welk's play *Gewitter über Gottland* ('Thunderstorm over Gothland') which caused a furore. The Committee of the Volksbühne repudiated the production and Piscator left.

Piscator had sought to shake the Volksbühne out of what he saw as its complacency and its pre-occupation with the artistic standards of the performance, to the detriment of their content and of their ability to act as a springboard for action. Those in charge of the Volksbühne, he argued, thought that they were only concerned with the production of theatre of the highest standards. 'Every-thing cooked in butter' as he remarked caustically. He blamed the solid but unimaginative former trade union officials, who largely ran the organisation as if it was a question of selling groceries, and whose concept of 'art' was that of the 'pure' and the 'elevated', transcending everyday considerations.[30] Thus the Volksbühne, he argued, had failed the working class at a time when it was in need of intellectual and emotional support. With the large financial assets which a membership of over 100,000 had put at its disposal, the Volksbühne could have produced theatre of relevance. But, Pisca-tor went on, the finely honed sword which could have cut the Gordian knot of capitalist contradictions and of its own misery 'hung on the parlour wall, over the plush-covered sofa. For God's sake, children, don't touch. It is an heirloom – what's more, you might easily cut your fingers'.[31]

Gewitter über Gottland, the play causing the controversy, was a historical play, set in the Middle Ages, which described a conflict between the *Hanse* and the Vitalians, a utopian communist group on the island of Gothland. With the help of devices like film and free interpretations, and, above all, by taking great liberties with the text, Piscator put the play into the historical context of a struggle which extended right into the present. And through the device of letting the leader of the revolutionaries, in a filmed prologue, change clothes until he appears in the guise of Lenin, and by the showing of the Soviet Star over the stage at the end of the performance, he turned the play into a modern story of revolution

30. E. Piscator, 'Die Situation der Volksbühne', in his *Das Politische Theater*, Berlin, 1929; and, as facsimile reprint, Berlin, 1963.
31. Ibid.

and of revolutionary leadership.[32]

Here clearly was the political *Tendenzstück*, the play with a political message, for which the youth sections of the Volksbühne had clamoured. Rejecting the idea of the neutrality of art they demanded that the theatre 'should reflect the life and will of the proletariat in its fight for a new social order'.[33] The Executive of the Volksbühne would not accept such criticism. It countered by suggesting that the Youth Groups might consider leaving the organisation. The Volksbühne could not simply equate the 'Volk' (people) in its title with the radical socialist working class. The membership of the movement did not consist exclusively of proletarians, especially outside Berlin. Their task was as before to 'create for the large sections of the population, above the level of party-political dissension, a *community of the wonderful experience*'.[34]

Given its premiss, the leadership of the Volksbühne could not accept a performance of the kind which Piscator had put on in *Gewitter über Gottland*. It described the performance as 'a tendentious political expression and an unjustified transformation . . . the exploitation of the work, in the sense of a one-sided piece of political propaganda . . . had taken place without their knowledge or intention'. This kind of production conflicted with the political neutrality of the Volksbühne.[35]

It is understandable that the directors, good social–democrats as they were, should have recoiled from a performance with so much overt communist propaganda. However, tendentiousness apart, the Volksbühne had increasingly shied away from plays of commitment and concern. Thus they first accepted and later refused to show Toller's *Wandlung*. The production had been originally fixed for the winter of 1925, and then, following the author's reluctant agreement, postponed to March 1926, and finally to November of that year. The play had been postponed because 'it was too radical' and the Executive feared that it would 'drive members away' because it was 'too harrowing'.[36]

32. The critics were united in the view that *Gewitter über Gottland* was a weak play, but that Piscator's production was a *tour de force*. The best account of Piscator's production is in Schwerd (note 21).
33. Resolution of the meeting of the youth sections of 14 March 1927, cited in Piscator (note 30).
34. Georg Springer, a member of the executive of the Volksbühne, writing in the *Weltbühne* of 15 February 1927, p. 462 (emphasis added).
35. Cf. A. Schwerd (note 21), pp. 154–5, n. 168; Piscator (note 30), p. 103.
36. Quotation from a letter by Heinrich Neft, the administrator of the Volksbühne, to Toller, mentioned in the latter's reply to the Directors of the theatre. (Copy in Toller Archive in Akademie der Künste, West Berlin.)

The very success of the Volksbühne in terms of members had clearly hampered experimentation in its dramatic policy. The leadership was no longer interested in educating its members, and was afraid of resignations if its policy was too adventurous. Apparently there was much protest after the showing of works with contemporary political and social themes. Members wished to be left alone. 'Hunger, Revolution, the Class Struggle, Poverty, Corruption, Prostitution – we see it every day at party meetings, at work, in the neighbourhood, or in the home.'[37]

The officials were not prepared to go against such sentiments and, at the same time, risk a loss of members. As the pressure by a minority for more political drama and greater political commitment in the artistic policy of the Volksbühne continued the committee sought to meet this criticism. The Youth Sections, from which most of the criticism had come, were re-named Sonderabteilungen (Special Sections), and thrown open to all members. The sections, *c.* 16,000 strong, demanded a committed theatre, showing 'plays which deal with our problems and questions, which agitate for the cause of the working class, strengthen us in our faith in our cause, and give courage to the daily struggle'.[38] They would not entirely reject classical plays, but would accept only those which in their time had had a revolutionary meaning. The sections urged the Volksbühne to commission plays from authors in sympathy with these aims so that 'a new revolutionary dramatic art should grow'. The authorities were not prepared to go so far; but, in order to meet the demand for a committed theatre, they arranged for special performances at the Theater am Nollendorfplatz, which Piscator had taken over, but refused demands for a change in the repertoire of the Volksbühne itself.

Yet Piscator's own venture showed up the problematic character of a radical theatre which lacked a radical clientele broad enough to guarantee the cost of such productions. The expenses of Piscator's elaborate staging and casting could therefore only be met by subsidies from largely middle-class audiences, which admired the innovative producer but did not agree with the radical politician.[39] Thus after the collapse of the Piscator Bühne the position of the Sonderabteilungen became even more problematic. Piscator was

37. Arthur Holitscher, 'Die Krise der Volksbühne', *Die Weltbühne*, 1927, pp. 377–80, p. 378. Holitscher argued that the Volksbühne, of whose Council he was a member, should follow a radical policy regardless of such criticism.
38. *Die Junge Volksbühne*, vol. 1 no. 1, 1928.
39. Scherer (note 18), pp. 246–8. Scherer describes the situation as one based on a compromise between avant-garde theatre and political avant-garde.

anxious to start a new venture – the Piscator Collective – and the special sections wished to make this the basis of their operation. They sought to create what would in effect have been a Piscator Theatre within the Volksbühne, with a financial guarantee equivalent to a vastly greater membership than the sections could muster, but with independent control over the artistic policy of such a theatre.

The Committee of the Volksbühne could not accept this – neither from a financial nor from an ideological point of view. When the opposition proposed to carry the dissension and discussion from the meetings into the actual theatre performances the Committee struck. In May 1930 it reacted by dissolving the Committee of the Sections (Sonderabteilungen) and expelling its members.[40]

Here was a conflict that went deeper than the policies of a particular producer or the production of specific plays. The Sonderabteilungen had, during the years, moved further to the left, and their official pronouncements increasingly echoed communist policy on the role of the arts and of the theatre in particular. In February 1929 they had started the publication of *Die Junge Volksbühne*, described as a *Kampfblatt für Proletarisches Theater*, a 'fighting journal for a proletarian theatre'. This was edited by Felix Gasbarra, a close collaborator of Piscator.[41] In its first issue it demanded 'a change of guard' at the Volksbühne, condemning the policy of the past twenty years as one of 'aping the bourgeois theatre and following bourgeois aesthetics'. Instead of being a bulwark of the working class it had become a support for the ruling class. It was this policy, not the revolutionary fervour of the few Piscator-produced plays, which had allegedly caused the real loss of membership – from *c.* 90,000 to *c.* 60,000 – that the Volksbühne had experienced.

The opposition wished to create a theatre which based itself firmly on the working masses, which educated its members to fight for socialism, and which would enter the ranks of the modern labour movement. Its aim was not 'art for the people', but a fighting theatre for the proletariat. This approach also envisaged a radical change in the running of the Volksbühne. In place of an admittedly oligarchic structure which gave the 'Ordner', with fifty

40. Cf. Schwerd (note 21), pp. 128–9.
41. The journal described itself as the organ of some members of the section who were working every day in their jobs, and who, without consideration of material reward or personal ambition, felt concerned about the problem of revolutionary art and revolutionary theatre.

per cent of the delegates, the position of a Praetorian Guard, it sought *de facto* control of the administrative and artistic direction of the theatre through the membership at the municipal district level, and the selection of the artistic advisory council through the leaders (*Kulturobleute*) of the district committees.[42]

Once the separation was effected, the politically strongly committed members of the special sections had no option but to secede. Some 4,000, actually a minority of the total membership of the sections, chose the latter course, and formed a new organisation under the name of Die Junge Volksbühne, with Piscator's new theatre venture as its focal point. For this third – and last – venture before his emigration to Russia in 1931 Piscator rented the Wallner Theater in the West End of Berlin.[43] In it he formed the Piscator Kollektiv, a theatrical co-operative in which his power was only that of one member of the whole team. He described it as a 'proletarian-communist theatre', as distinct from his earlier ventures, which he called 'revolutionary'.

The experiment lasted only a year, and, like its predecessors, it could not subsist on workers' audiences alone. The Junge Volksbühne could, of course, not provide an adequate basis for Piscator; and, like all his theatrical ventures, it foundered on the rocks of finance. Even his Theater am Nollendorfplatz had failed, in spite of the large subsidy from the actress Tilla Durieux and her financier husband Ludwig Katzenellenbogen.[44] Piscator was to note with a distinct disappointment that the proletarian masses did not support his theatre 'which from the first day had engaged in a struggle which was of great importance for the proletariat'. Yet he was also forced to admit that at the prices which workers could afford not even full houses could have paid for his expensive productions. For that it would have needed a considerably larger theatre with 3,000–4,000 seats.[45]

Failing either mass support or the provision by a rich political party – which the KPD was not – of large-scale financial subventions – which it would almost certainly not have provided if it had

---

42. 'Ablösung vor', *Die Junge Volksbühne*, vol. 1 no. 1, February 1929. The proposed constitution would have made the manipulation of the election of representatives easier.

43. John Willett, *The Theatre of Erwin Piscator*, London, 1978, p. 121.

44. Cf. Tilla Durieux, *Die Tür steht offen*, Berlin, 1954.

45. Cf. Piscator (note 30), pp. 121–2 and Piscator, *Aufsätze, Reden, Gespräche* (Schriften 2), Berlin (GDR), 1968, p. 54. The communist press, in the shape of *Rote Fahne*, showed a certain scepticism towards Piscator and his theatrical ventures, which were so greatly dependent on bourgeois financial support.

been – it became clear that a formal theatre could not be the real answer to the clamour for a radical, left-wing stage. Only a much more economical, more direct and more tactically political theatre could provide such an answer. In practice, although not historically, this answer was the Agitprop Theatre.[46]

A Megaphone for the Masses

The agitprop theatre group 'Das Rote Sprachrohr' of the communist youth organisation Kommunistischer Jugendverband Deutschlands (KJVD), one of the first and foremost of such troupes, derived its symbolic-sounding name from the red paper funnels which they used as primitive megaphones in their performances. But the name also alludes to the wide dissemination of political views to a large audience, which was the aim of the agitprop theatre movement.

At the height of its operation, around 1930, the agitprop theatre claimed the adherence of 110–120 ensembles, as well as 62 groups linked to the KJVD. On the strength of this figure, and taking the successes of the Dresden group, Rote Raketen, who in 1928/9 gave 50 performances to audiences estimated at 20,000, as a basis, the Central Committee of the KPD concluded that 3,600,000 people must have seen agitprop performances.[47] These figures use what seem to be quite unjustifiable extrapolations – it is unlikely that all theatre groups were as successful as the 'Red Rockets'; but there is no doubt that we are concerned with a genuinely popular movement, which brought its performances right into the heart of the working-class districts and into the political campaigns. During the 1930 election in Berlin nineteen theatre groups performed on 349 different occasions, mostly at open-air meetings and in halls, but, so we are told, not penetrating sufficiently into the factories, where 'the choice of plays is still very limited.'[48]

However closely the agitprop theatre was connected with the

---

46. On the Agitprop Theatre see F.W. Knellesen, *Agitation auf der Bühne. Das politische Theater der Weimarer Republik*, Emsdetten, 1970; D. Hoffmann-Ostwald and U. Behse, *Agitprop*, Leipzig, 1960; L. Hoffmann and D. Hoffmann-Ostwald, *Deutsches Arbeitertheater, 1918–1933*, 2 vols., Berlin, 1972.

47. Report of the Central Committee to the 12. Parteitag of the KPD, 1929, p. 272, quoted in Hoffmann and Hoffmann-Ostwald (note 46), vol. 1, p. 38.

48. Cf. *Ifa Rundschau*, vol. 2 nos. 7–8, p. 60. See also 'Wir Arbeiterspieler des ABTD', *Rote Fahne*, 26 May 1932, reprinted in Hoffmann and Hoffmann-Ostwald (note 46), vol. 2, pp. 342–4.

electoral and the political campaigns of the Communist Party, we must not overlook the fact that looked at in intellectual and historical terms the movement could claim a number of different roots.

Organisationally speaking, the movement drew its strength from the old-established Association of Workers' Amateur Theatre Groups, the Deutsche Arbeiter Theater Bund (DATB), founded in 1909, but with a membership going back into the nineteenth century. Intellectually the movement was influenced by the Russian *Proletkult*, especially after the visit, in 1927, of the Moscow Blaue Blusen, a troupe of the 'Blue Blouses' organisation which had spread across the whole of the Soviet Union. And, last not least, the character of the Agitprop Theatre received a major aesthetic impetus and stimulus from the pioneering theatrical work of Piscator, in particular his work with amateur performers.

The DATB, which under communist direction after 1928 changed its name slightly to Arbeiter Theater Bund Deutschlands (ATBD), must not be confused with the *Volksbühnen* movement. It was essentially an amalgamation of workers' theatre societies, small groups of amateurs who performed sketches, and sometimes shorter plays. They did this in part for their own pleasure and for that of the audience, and, generally, as part of some form of popular entertainment or for the celebrations of organisations of the labour movement.[49]

Amateur dramatic circles, known as *Laientheater*, had existed in Germany since the early nineteenth century, and by the end of the century the total number of such clubs was at least 3,000, and their combined membership was probably in the region of 60,000. With the rise of the Workers' Education Societies the movement spread into the working class, and, as in other areas of leisure-time activities, workers took part in the activities of bourgeois societies.

Until the advent of the Volksbühne these amateur dramatic societies were often the only places where workers made acquaintance with the theatre. Moreover, the fact that the plays performed, even if of low literary value, were generally set in a working-class milieu, meant that the uninitiated and uncommitted workers could generally see themselves in a wider social or historical setting.

Workers active in this welter of organisations, including the societies which federated under the umbrella of the DATB, generally staged one-act plays, comedy sketches, charades and *tableaux*

49. On the workers' amateur theatre movement see U. Hornauer, *Laienspiel und Massenchor, das Arbeitertheater der Kultursozialisten*, Cologne, 1985.

vivants. The last especially were very popular forms of entertainment for events connected with the labour movement, often depicting historical events, such as a series on the life of Lassalle, one of the founders of the social-democratic movement, showing him as a youth, as an orator, and even on his bier. Such evocations, even if sentimental, undoubtedly gave the spectators a feeling of belonging to a historical movement.[50] At times the amateur actors also performed more weighty stuff, serious plays with a political message; but these were generally under-rehearsed and badly presented. The politically committed also tried to bring elements of politics into their acting, and to use the medium of the theatre to provide for members of working-class organisations a political education.[51] During the twenty years before 1914 at least 90 plays of a broadly political character were published.[52] The plays performed could not lay claim to great artistic merit; but, clad in a framework of entertainment, they were not only expected to please the masses, but 'above all to recruit hitherto apolitical workers for the cause of the labour movement'.[53] The unattached and indifferent masses were to be enticed 'away from the dance hall, where they learn bad habits' into the theatre club's venue, 'where they are forced to view the play before the looked-for dancing can commence'.[54]

The political claims of these amateur theatre groups were, however, disputed by the social-democratic leadership, who, after the Education Debate of 1906, were increasingly taking the movement's cultural activities under their wings. They thought that rather low-grade art was produced by the amateur actors, and that much of it was politically irrelevant and of questionable taste and little value. Undoubtedly the stage was a good educational institution, but only if performances were serious and of a high stan-

50. The 'Tableaux Vivants' tradition continued into the Weimar period. Cf. G. Korff, 'Rote Fahnen und Tableaux Vivants. Zum Symbolverständnis der deutschen Arbeiterbewegung im 19. Jahrhundert', in A. Lehmann (ed.), *Studien zur Arbeiterkultur*, Münster, 1984, pp. 103–40.
51. In 1913 *c.* 90% of the members were trade unionists or were politically organised. Cf. P. von Rüden, *Sozialdemokratisches Arbeitertheater*, Frankfurt, 1973, p. 178.
52. P. von Rüden, 'Sozialdemokratisches Arbeitertheater, 1848–1914' in von Rüden and K. Koszyk (eds), *Beiträge zur Kulturgeschichte der deutschen Arbeiterbewegung, 1848–1918*, Frankfurt, 1979, pp. 223–60. These figures were a mere nothing compared with plays with nationalist themes written for the bourgeois amateur theatre companies.
53. Ibid. p. 234.
54. *Die Volksbühne* (journal of the ATBD), 6 March 1909, quoted in von Rüden, (note 51), p. 195.

dard. Dilettantism and poor taste, as displayed by workers' amateur drama societies, was really worse than nothing. False artistic ideals would only have a negative influence on the formation of taste; besides, it was held that the working class had, by now, better means of fighting its political struggle than through dubious 'artistic' ventures.[55]

Moreover, this kind of amateur activity was also regarded as counter-productive, as it was thought to absorb energies which would be better used in the political struggle. Local workers'-theatre societies felt that 'the party as well as the trade unions did their utmost to oppose the work [of the societies]. Even if our societies are being involved in March and May-Day celebrations, they have no opportunity on other occasions to disseminate art and culture' because, in the views of the local Education Councils, they 'lacked the necessary understanding' for the task.[56] It was thus in the cause of a progressive 'people's politics' that a would-be political leisure-time activity was stifled in the name of artistic purity, and in defence of the 'absolute' values of largely traditional art professionally performed. The SPD rejected the DATB because of its low standards; and the latter, minuscule by comparison with the other workers' leisure-time organisations, could not find the means to improve the standards of their theatre groups without outside help.

Attempts at training sessions and courses met with very limited success, and they were not continued after the war. In the 1920s the Association had a membership of *c.* 2,500 organised in a small number of societies. That number only grew when towards the end of the decade agitprop theatre groups affiliated to the DATB, and through such affiliations actually changed the political direction of the organisation, hitherto vaguely pro-SPD. Following on the committee elections of the 1928 national conference the league came under the control of members of the Communist Party, who also took over the direction of its journal *Arbeiterbühne*. This certainly livened things up. Not that the reformed association was to embark on a vigorous new artistic policy – the new ideas of the political theatre derived largely from elsewhere; but the new leadership sought to instil a new political consciousness into the movement. By way of training members the Berlin district of the newly re-formed association put on an eight-day school with the theme 'without revolutionary thought no revolutionary practice'; but the

---

55. Cf. Hoffmann and Hoffmann-Ostwald (note 46) vol. 1, pp. 24–5.
56. Von Rüden (note 52), quoting the *Volksbühne* of May 1913.

theatre itself did not figure prominently in it.[57]

What the agitprop theatre derived from Piscator was not only the idea of political theatre as such, but also ideas about the role of acting and production. Throughout his career Piscator had sought to bring the theatre into the service of politics through the political interpretation as much as through the selection of plays. We saw this in the case of *Gewitter über Gottland*; and we find it again in his interpretation of Schiller's *Die Räuber*, where he switched the emphasis from Karl Moor, the author's hero, to the subversive scoundrel, Spiegelberg, whom he interpreted as a far-sighted revolutionary cast in the mould of Trotsky.

Piscator's inventiveness as a producer was however most in evidence in the techniques of his staging. These included the use of film and of projection and of documentary material in general, so as to give a play as much basis in reality as possible, and to persuade his audience through reason, rather than, by creating a bond of empathy between actor and audience. Indeed, he sought at times to bring the audience into the performance, by placing actors in the auditorium, or by seeking to stimulate a continuation of a discussion on the stage within the audience.[58] Moreover, plays apart, Piscator had also produced more immediately and openly political events, as in his revue-like performances devised and staged together with Felix Gasbara for the KPD in 1924 and 1925. These were the *Revue Roter Rummel* (The 'Red Razzmatazz Revue'), prepared for the December 1924 election campaign, and shown in halls throughout Berlin to large working-class audiences; and the historical revue *Trotz Alledem* ('in spite of everything', the title of a famous appeal by Karl Liebknecht) shown in Max Reinhardt's Große Schauspielhaus for the tenth Party Conference of the KPD in 1925.

Apart from the varied staging and acting techniques used – such as montage, charade, acrobatics, and direct political addresses to the audience – and the extensive use made of authentic historical material, reproduced in words and in pictures, the revues were characterised by their clearly political and didactic orientation. And as the actor was as much as anything else a mouthpiece for ideas,

57. Cf. Asja Lacis, *Revolutionär im Beruf*, Munich, 1971, p. 103.
58. Cf. Willett (note 43), p. 101. Many of the three hundred or so performances of Credé's *Paragraph 218*, staged by the Piscator Kollektiv, which toured Germany, ended in discussions among the spectators. The discussions in the auditorium were not always of a didactic character. There was uproar in the audience during performances of Friedrich Wolf's *Die Matrosen von Cattaro* in the Volksbühne in November 1929.

and as Piscator often dealt in mass scenes, the participants could be amateurs, as were those used in the 'Red Razzmatazz Revue'. Piscator had experimented with amateurs already in his Proletarische Theater – the stage of the revolutionary workers of Greater Berlin – which he opened in October 1920 and which ran for a mere six months before being banned by the police. Amateurs could fill such roles because amateurs would 'cease to be dilettanti because the proletarian theatre . . . seeks the deepening of communist thought, and this cannot be a matter for a profession . . . it is the result of communal striving'.[59] Here was a political discussion in a theatrical form. Acting, scenery, props and music 'nothing was left uncertain, ambiguous, and, hence, ineffectual'. The 'political discussion' which at election times dominates workshop, factory and street, had been turned into a scenic form.[60]

Piscator used the device of the antagonist and the protagonist – bourgeois and proletarian – like *compère* and *commère*, as bases for continuity and for the polarisation of conflict. He also worked through short, snap scenes which sought to include the audience in the dialogue and put the whole into the framework of a political meeting – with the audience interrupting, and ending with a real election speech. In the words of a contemporary observer, of the Red Razzmatazz Revue:

The lights fade . . . Silence. In the auditorium two men quarrel. People take fright. The dispute continues in the central aisle. The podium is lit up, the disputants appear in front of the curtain. They turn out to be workers who discuss their situation. A man in a top-hat joins them. A bourgeois . . . The curtain rises. First scene. Now things are happening fast. Ackerstraße – Kurfürstendamm – Tenement Block – Nightclub. Doorman in blue with gold braid. Begging war-invalid. Pot-belly with heavy gold watch-chain. Matchbox-seller and cigarette-stubs collector. Swastika, *Fehme*-Killing . . . In between film, statistics, pictures. New scene. The begging war-invalid is thrown out by the doorman, people congregate in front of the club. The workers break in, they demolish the place. The public takes part. Hey, how they whistle, shout and rave, exhort.[61]

With his 1924 *Election Revue* Piscator had, in effect, laid down the

59. E. Piscator, 'Grundlagen und Aufgaben des proletarischen Theaters' (*Der Gegner*, 1920/1, no. 4), reprinted in Hoffmann and Hoffmann-Ostwald (note 47), vol. 1, pp. 69–72. It was central to communist thinking about the role and transmission of culture that it ascribed particular power of persuasion to workers who could write from their own experience. Cf. Chapter 3.
60. Piscator (note 30), p. 66.
61. Lacis (note 57), p. 83, quoting Altmeier, *Zur Geschichte des Piscator Theaters*.

main ingredients of the agitprop theatre, the revue as an art-form: the use of speed, key figures as protagonist and antagonist, contrast, conflict, and ultimate victory. Piscator, looking back on it in 1929, saw it as a direct precursor of the proletarian amateur theatre groups that emerged throughout Germany. The Red Revue thus became a permanent element in the arsenal of political agitation.[62]

One of the earliest agitprop theatre ventures was started by the Berlin communist youth organisation. It adopted the expression *Roter Rummel* as a generic term, and spread it as a form of 'entertainment cum propaganda', initially in Berlin but later also in other places. These revues were, at first, used within the organisation; but they soon became part of a general campaign to attract and influence young workers and to draw them away from fairgrounds and other forms of popular entertainment into something that had on the face of it elements of fun and amusement, but also had a definite underlying political content.[63] The performance consisted of short sketches, concentrating on current political issues, treated highly satirically, and using stock figures such as Capitalist, Junker, Public Prosecutor, Priest and General as mouthpieces and as targets of abuse and vilification.

The scenes were interspersed with short, straightforward, political speeches, or else they culminated in them.[64] They were later assisted by slide and film projection, and the addresses to the audience frequently turned into a *Kollektiv-Referat*, a political statement or piece of instruction declaimed by the chorus. The aim of the youth theatre group was 'a political programme full of actuality, which would proclaim the political demands and the basic tenets of the working class'. This emphasis on actuality was very marked in the performances of the Russian Blaue Blusen, who saw themselves as 'Agitators and Propagandists for the building of socialism'. Their theatrical formula was that of the 'living newspaper'. Like newspapers they were very much up-to-date and to the point, and they invited their audience to judge events in a political spirit.[65] The Russian troupes also taught the German communist theatre groups the virtue of the cabaret form, that is of

62. Piscator (note 30), p. 67.
63. Hoffmann and Hoffmann-Ostwald (note 46), vol. 1, pp. 185–6.
64. R. Weber, *Proletarisches Theater und revolutionäre Arbeiterbewegung* Cologne, 1976, pp. 193–4. Weber thinks that sketches and speeches did not really match, but that they were conducted at different levels of reality. However, because of the need for simplification the lecture remained an essential part of the agitprop theatre practice. With the advent of the lecture-chorus it tended to become even more central to the performances.
65. Hoffmann and Hoffmann-Ostwald (note 46), vol. 1, p. 244.

continuous montage of scenes, music, dance, mime and acrobatics. In other words, they put greater emphasis on the visual element, on movement, rhythm and speed.[66]

The Hamburg group 'Die Nieter' ('The Riveters') were founded in the wake of the Russian troupe's visit to the city in October 1927, and the programme and production style of 'Die Nieter', too, owed much to them. They too appeared in uniform dress, and used music (songs) and rhythmic movement; they were sharply satirical, and highly critical of bourgeois theatre and its conventions. The members of the group, six men and one woman, were part-time performers and full-time blue-collar workers, though performing under the direction of Hans Käbitz, a schoolteacher and play-wright. They took their themes from the political issues of the day or from their immediate surroundings, and they gave their shows within the institutional framework of the existing left-wing or communist working-class organisations, adjusting the length and composition of their shows to the occasion:[67]

> Die Nieter treat burning issues of the day . . . the struggle of the Trade Unions and of the Party . . . in short . . . thumbnail sketches, con-nected by the chats of the compère. They will not give a long 'develop-ment of the action', no dramatic dialogues . . . They will not present a naturalist portrait of life in tear-jerking details. Their *métier* is satire, the ironical, if necessary mercilessly sharp and audacious treatment of recent events . . . They seek to convey their views through short accounts which give only the most important and the most urgent points. They aim to make themselves understood by every listening worker – be he ever so tired after the day's drudgery, and they seek to stimulate in the members of the audience judgement, criticism and laughter, biting and mordant laughter.[68]

The agitprop theatre was however not without criticism from within. Contributors to *Arbeiter-Bühne und Film*, the journal of the ATBD, were worried lest the caricature-like characterisation of 'opponents' in the sketches and revues should induce a feeling of disbelief, if not revulsion, at the gross distortion in the treatment of some of their own kind, as when trade union officials and social-democrat leaders were depicted as ogres or as corrupt. At a time when the ATBD adopted the slogan 'To the masses, into the

66. Ibid. pp. 243–6.
67. Cf. 'Wir nieten zusammen die Rote Front' (section on *Die Nieter*) in *Arbeiterkul-tur in Hamburg* (note 3), pp. 232–9.
68. Hans Käbitz, 'Die Nieter' in *Hamburger Volkszeitung*, 28 December 1927, reprinted in Hoffmann and Hoffmann-Ostwald (note 46), pp. 287–92, p. 289.

factories, agitate on the land' there were suggestions of 'oversimplifications' in the presentation of political issues in the agitprop theatre. 'SPD audiences were not impressed by this. They might laugh over the type of the *Bonze* ['stuffed shirt': a trade union bureaucrat] who shuffled across the stage, attaché case in hand . . . but more often they were annoyed and went home.'[69]

Such presentations would not produce a lasting reaction or will to action. What was at one time lively cabaret became frozen in a form which made the characters appear like paper cut-outs. The more rotund the tummy, the bigger the cigar of the capitalist or trade union official, the easier to achieve an immediate impression, but the slimmer the political effect. 'The real task should be to show the *role* of the capitalist, the *role* of the *Parteibonze* [the party hack], in the class-struggle. Form and purpose must correspond. They are in contradiction if the purpose of our agitation is to convert social-democrat workers while we denounce their leaders and make them look ridiculous' without getting down to the basic issues which cause such behaviour.[70]

There was also criticism of the artistic level of the performances as such, which, it was argued, lacked sophistication. Clearly, neither actors nor producers in many of the little troupes could achieve a very high level of expertise. Nor were the texts which they used always very convincing. Only large and well-trained ensembles could hope to work completely independently, being able to adapt, improvise and be creative in general.

For many groups the texts printed in *Das Rote Sprachrohr*, a collection of material published jointly by the Agitprop Department of the party and the KJVD, formed the basis of their activities. And some of the material produced was of the utmost banality, as, for example, the 'conversion scene' printed in the first issue:

FRAU KRAUSE: I agree with Frau Schmidt. I *shall* leave the Social Democratic Party. My life shall henceforth be different.

Here, take my membership card of the SPD and give me straight away an application form for the Communist Party.

FRAU SCHMIDT: Well done, Frau Krause. Our aim should be to fight and make propaganda so that all other class-sisters recognise that the liberation of the working class must be our own work.[71]

69. F. Wolf, 'Schöpferische Probleme des Agitproptheaters', in *Aufsätze über Theater*, (Ausgewählte Werke, vol. 13), Berlin, (GDR), 1953.
70. S. Moos, 'Die politische Lage und die Situation im ATBD', *Arbeiterbühne und Film*, vol. 18 no. 3, pp. 1–5, p. 3. See also R. Weber (note 64) pp. 193–202.
71. *Das Rote Sprachrohr*, no. 1, 1929, p. 29.

Such stilted, unnatural speech was deliberate, as the actors were conceived as stereotypes of political ideas and action; but while the political role of the players and of the performances was possibly even more strongly emphasised – 'the Agitprop troops are active in the service of the emancipatory struggle of the proletariat' – [72] the need for greater realism and greater artistic perfection began eventually to be felt.

> The weakness in the style of performances hitherto adopted had been the abstract way in which general ideas, such as the class struggle, had been depicted. Here the theatre dealt in concepts, like a man in a top hat who carried a sign 'Capital' and said 'I exploit'. It did not show how these concepts arose in the minds of class-conscious workers, nor did it build on actual life experience. This was a fault which had to be rectified.

While such an approach might have been appropriate when the agitprop theatre addressed itself to communist and sympathising audiences it was so no longer at a time when the KPD sought the support of the masses. To do this 'the theatre troupes must get to grips with the whole of man's experience, and see the great general laws of the class struggle in the smallest events of everyday life.'[73]

But the movement was not only intent on mobilising the masses, it was also expected to convert other groups of amateur players to the cause and recruit them to membership in the ATBD. The critics argued that to do so the workers' theatre movement had to show itself more open to the theatrical tradition, even if the tradition was largely bourgeois in character, and reverse the trend to a too-radical rejection of the bourgeois heritage. 'Our artistic method', urged *Rote Fahne* in May 1932, 'does not arise out of an uncritical takeover of bourgeois art, but it cannot develop without a correct application of the bourgeois inheritance in this area.'[74]

Yet the problem was not merely ideological and artistic. The 1931 Bundestag of the ATBD diagnosed organisational weaknesses which pointed in a similar direction. The association had not grown despite all the new ideas; moreover, it was not a focus of loyalty for its members, or its member organisations. This weakness prevented it from playing its full part in the political struggle in which it, like all the other cultural organisations at the side of the

---

72. 'Stoss vor ins Leben', *Illustrierte Rote Post*, 1932 no. 23, quoted in Hoffmann and Hoffmann-Ostwald (note 46), vol. 2, p. 344.
73. Ibid. p. 343.
74. *Rote Fahne* 26 May 1932: 'Die Arbeiterspieler und der ATBD' (article on the 13th meeting of the ATBD).

KPD, was now engaged. In particular, the organisation should attempt to attract to its ranks the newly formed Actors' Collectives, which had established themselves towards the end of our period as an answer to the widespread unemployment in the theatre, as well as other theatre groups outside the agitprop theatre movement.

Underlying this stagnation was the limited attractiveness of a mainly political approach to the theatre, which left little to local initiative and subordinated artistic aims to political ones. By turning ordinary workers into actors, producers, authors, designers, musicians and stagehands, it went further than most social-democratic organisations in bridging the gulf between political conviction and its artistic expression. The members of the agitprop theatre groups were mostly young communist workers, unemployed but enthusiastically devoted to their adopted craft. The best of the troupes were involved virtually full-time in this, travelling by train or lorry the length and breadth of Germany, putting up their 'stages' in halls or in the open, in the courtyards of tenement blocks or at factory gates. Often formally acting as recruiting agents for *Rote Fahne* and other communist papers, or for the party or other communist organisations, they were first and foremost political propagandists. But there was no real involvement of the majority of the members in the running of the troupes and in the creation of plays. The more political the plays, the greater the stress on the message at the cost of the delivery. This led to the prevalence of clichés, and to a torpidity in production together with apathy and resignations by sections of the membership.[75] There is no evidence that the agitprop theatre got out of this crisis, or that the movement, personified in the ATBD, succeeded in mobilising the masses before the advent of Hitler put an end to all such activities.[76]

The agitprop theatre was undoubtedly a popular form of entertainment whose audience must have represented all sections of the working class. The casualness of the encounter and the informality of the performances, together with the fact that generally no entrance-fee was charged (although collections were usually taken) will have attracted many who would not normally go to straight plays. In its sketches and playlets it allows many parallels to be drawn with the popular commercial theatre – cabarets and variety

75. Cf. contributions to the '*Programmkrise*' in the Spring 1931 issue of *Arbeiterbühne und Film*.
76. From the summer of 1932 the association faced the additional hazards of police interference and prohibitions. The organisation, in line with other mass organisations of the KPD, responded by going underground.

performances which included members of the working class among their audiences; but its subjects were mainly political. Finally, the desire to be up to date and topical meant also that the agitprop theatre included many currently popular tunes and dances.

The new commercial theatres, on the other hand, which had developed in the new working-class suburbs, suffered in the 1920s increasingly from the competition of the cinema, of the urban amusement parks and of the expanding field of mass spectator sport.[77] The growing public transport system also permitted more people to find entertainment in the countryside. Thus the Berlin suburban railways enabled some 10,000 visitors, many of them workers, to attend the annual *Volksfest* in the Garden City of Falkenberg. This was started in 1921, and its programmes included all sorts of displays.[78]

In such events, and in the popular mass-entertainment organised towards the end of our period by organisations such as the Reichsbanner and the Universumbücherei, mentioned elsewhere in the book, the performance element was, however, only a minor ingredient. Nor was there in the popular commercial entertainment anything corresponding to the music hall, which was the typical workers' entertainment in Britain at the end of the nineteenth century.[79]

The principal provider of plays for working-class audiences remained the Volksbühne, whether, as in Berlin, performing in its own theatres or arranging for special performances by local companies. The dramatic diet which the 'People's Theatre' set before its members included some light entertainment – popular comedies, farce and operettas. The repertoire nevertheless made some intellectual demands on the audiences, and the subscription charges restricted access financially. The Volksbühne was thus not mass-entertainment in the literal sense, and its scope probably expanded during our period less quickly than those of other forms of popular spectacle and entertainment.

77. Cf. T. Zantke, *Der Berliner Prater*, Berlin (GDR), 1987, pp. 79–87.
78. Cf. E. Abenstein, 'Alle Tage ist kein Alltag. Massenunterhaltung zwischen Kommerz und Kreativitat', *WgdW*, pp. 441–55.
79. G.S. Jones, 'Working Class Culture and Working Class Politics in London, 1870–1900' *Journal of Social History*, 1973/74, pp. 460–510.

−9−

Festkultur: Mobilising the Emotions

Between Tradition and Innovation

The workers' leisure-time pursuits described so far were largely concerned with a single type of cultural activity. They were also, with the general exception of the theatre, largely participant-based. Movements like workers' sport and workers' music addressed themselves primarily to the initiated and the enthusiastic. Only in the 1920s did some of the workers' music societies embark on regular concert series, and it was only towards the end of the Weimar period that the larger sports clubs began to form their own small orchestras and bands and to establish *Sprechchöre* and other forms of artistic activities for appearances in public.

The fêtes and festivals with which this chapter is concerned are not the product of clearly articulated leisure-time interests. They relate rather to the organisational development of the German labour movement and to the salient dates of its historical development. Indeed, in one respect, the festivals of the labour movement echo the general calendar of public events which developed in the nineteenth century. The religious year has always been punctuated by feast-days and holidays, some of which became the occasion for more secular events like fairs. The secular festival is of mere recent origin.

National celebrations in Germany were linked to special occasions or to historical dates. Thus the centenary of Schiller's birth was celebrated in 1859, and that of his death, as we saw, in 1905. Germany's victory over France at Sedan in 1870 gave rise to the annual *Sedanfest*, and the foundation of the Reich on 18 January 1871 was likewise celebrated. Organised labour, often in deliberate contrast, would remember the Paris Commune or, in some places, commemorate the birth of Lassalle.[1] Thus compared with the

---

1. On workers and working-class festivals during the nineteenth and early twentieth century see W.K. Blessing, 'Feste und Vergnügen der kleinen Leute', in R.

internal activities of parties and trade unions and other working-class bodies, which were largely private to their members, the celebrations and commemorations of working-class organisations were related more to the public, outwardly-directed sphere of their activities. Like demonstrations, with which they have some affinity, they were both a means to the mobilisation of the membership, and a vehicle for publicity and persuasion addressed to the rest of the population. At the same time fêtes and festivals had an important social function for members, their families, and the working-class community.

In one sense the *Festkultur* of working-class organisations is as old as the labour movement itself. As in bourgeois communities, the workers' clubs and societies developed and furthered the social side of their activities in spite of political commitment and in spite of their hostility to bourgeois institutions. Thus workers' fêtes and festivities were often indistinguishable from those of middle-class organisations. This tendency was, however, deplored by many leaders of the labour movement and by the officials of the Social Democratic Party and its affiliated organisations, which opposed what they regarded as expressions of philistinism in many of these events. Instead they sought to give the celebrations a more clearly defined political content.

More important and innovatory, however, were the new ideas about a *Sozialistische Festkultur* which were developed during our period. They were as novel and original as anything which the labour movement stimulated after 1918. The new *Festkultur* sought to give a tangible expression to the new ideals about the role of culture within the working class and to the techniques which ought to be employed to create new forms of community and to provide new foci of enthusiasm and loyalty for the working masses. The novelty lay not only in the basic ideas and concepts, but also in the techniques employed. It is in the nature of festival and ritual that they are multi-media in character. This had been so in the old-fashioned and old-established *Stiftungsfest*, the 'Commem' which celebrated the foundation of a society, and which pervaded German bourgeois and petty-bourgeois culture; it was also consciously so in the new traditions which sprang up in the 1920s, and which are discussed here.

---

von Dulmen and N. Schindler (eds), *Volkskultur*, Frankfurt, 1984, pp. 352–79; V. Lidtke, *The Alternative Culture*, Oxford, 1985; P. Friedemann, 'Feste und Feiern im rheinisch-westfalischen Industriegebiet', in G. Huck (ed.) *Sozialgeschichte der Freizeit*, Wuppertal, 1980, pp. 161–85.

The *Stiftungsfest* in the German labour movement was essentially not very different from those which we find in every bowling club or veterans' society. The memorial aspect of the celebrations was largely confined to the *Festansprache* – the oration – and the political to the singing of some of the 'hymns' of the labour movement. The rest was popular entertainment and amusement. Equally significant, and possibly more numerous, were the more 'social' activities, the children's fêtes, the *Waldfest* ('Forest Fête'), or the Christmas or New Year celebrations. They had existed when the German working class began to organise itself, and they continued right to the very end of its independent history. They clearly responded to certain basic needs of working-class life, such as the wish for commensality, for relaxation and for licence. They were also not infrequently influenced by the desire to raise money for the generally under-funded organisations, which could not exist on low membership dues alone. And, in order to make a profit at these events, the organisers had to cater for the public taste at its most popular level. What was needed was a bar, foul jokes, couplets, feeble sketches, raffles, dances and the like. These would attract large numbers of visitors, and some of the things on offer would provide additional income to make up for the generally low prices of admission.[2]

The old type of fête is clearly linked to the low quality of life of the German working class during the period of its industrialisation. It was a response to poverty, physical overcrowding, and the monotony if not the paucity of workers' diets. The fête was a release from humdrum existence, it echoed the festivities of a more earthy rural society where the fête was also a feast, an occasion to gorge oneself, to get drunk, and to throw off the shackles of conventionality and 'let go' in respect of noise, dance and sexuality.[3]

Paul Göhre, a protestant clergyman who had become a social democrat, and who lived for three months as a factory worker in Chemnitz, has given us a detailed and most realistic account of life in the labour movement at grass-roots level at the end of the nineteenth century. He noted that there were workers' fêtes in Chemnitz or in one of the surrounding villages of the textile belt nearly every Sunday. The amusements here were still largely simple and unsophisticated, with games for children, accordion music, target-shooting, a display of curiosities, pole-climbing and dancing to a band.

---

2. Cf. L. Seyler, 'Kritisches zu unserer Festgestaltung', *Arb. Bldg.* vol. 3, 1928, pp. 153–4.
3. R. Wagner, *Zur Theorie der Arbeiterbildung*, Vienna, 1927 p. 56.

Yet while some of the events had a naïve and artless character, others, where the influence of the politically better-trained Chemnitz workers was greater, lacked such naturalness and had a more political atmosphere.[4] And such considerations would also come into play in the more formal and overtly more political celebrations of the German labour movement, such as the commemoration of the First of May and other fêtes of remembrance, like that for the *Märzgefallenen*, the victims of the Revolution of 1848. Demonstrations, banners and speeches notwithstanding, these took on much of the colouring of the *Volksfest*, with decorated floats, tableaux vivants and dancing, not to mention drinking.

Even in the Weimar period, such traditional fêtes, which mixed entertainment with edification, remained important events in working-class life. Anniversary celebrations apart, they addressed themselves generally to all ages and to all interest groups; and even when a workers' sports club or a choral society put on their own festivity, the doors were generally open to the non-affiliated.

Alfred Döblin, physician, novelist and left-wing sympathiser, has described, in one of his essays, such a fête held by a Berlin workers' cycling club in a garden restaurant in the surroundings of the city. It is a critical, even caustic, account; and yet one which shows the basic humanity of working-class festivities:

The fête took place in a clearing in the wood: at the entrance women attempt to sell red paper carnations, on a tree flutters a large Black, Red and Gold flag, (the colours of the Weimar Republic). The members of the cycling club . . . wear red sashes. Nothing happens for an hour . . . Then children in paper hats and with paper trumpets collect sandwiches from their parents . . . Suddenly a man stands up in the middle of the clearing. . . . The children recognise him because he has a black shield over his right eye, and they break into maudlin songs . . . People clap, the children are pleased and continue. Now the time has come for the next distribution of food; but a red-faced man pushes through the crowd and commands silence. A rotund man climbs on the games tables. He begins to speak, he shouts. 'The cyclists are the avant-garde of the working class, but they would let no-one rob them of their love for nature'. As he descends, the red-faced man clambers on the table. He thanks the speaker for his peroration – and he adds that 'to-night there will be a torchlight procession and dancing in the restaurant'.

In the evening the vestibule of the restaurant is full of drinking, talking, laughing people . . . at a long table the cycling champions, wearing decorative sashes, sing *Oh alte Burschenherrlichkeit* – they really do! . . . Three musicians play the newest hits. With variants, because the

4. P. Göhre, *Drei Monate Fabrikarbeiter*, Leipzig, 1891, pp. 98–100.

piano is tuned on B, while the A string of the violin is sometimes G and sometimes H. The people turn about and sweat. Little men and little women drink. More beer appears. At a later hour a speaker pronounces the fête a success. The takings were good. It was possible to convince even the indifferent ones of the power of our ideas'.[5]

Throughout the Weimar period the various working-class organisations of the left continued to cultivate the cultural sphere. There continued to be regular traditional fêtes for children with games and competitions and tombolas, ending with a torchlight procession 'in which the beginning and the end were close together'. Working-class celebrations tended to follow the rhythm of the seasons, with Christmas, the most popular festival of the year, posing special problems for a secular and widely anti-religious movement. Social-democratic organisations often arranged some sort of celebration in connection with the festival, which might even include the distribution of presents. Such celebrations had a predominantly secular character, with songs, sketches and recitations; but they were expected not to offend the sentiments of the majority of the population.[6]

A contemporary observer noted that most of these traditional celebrations were still rooted in bourgeois custom, but that new traditions were being developed, mainly under the influence of the socialist youth movement. As we shall see, these were often merely based on attempts to return to some older folk customs – for instance, in favouring folk-dancing or in eschewing alcohol. They were proclaimed to be the beginning of new socialist lifestyles; but they were not in themselves political. The socialist youth groups would celebrate the coming of spring or autumn or the solstices as watersheds of the yearly rhythm of the seasons, and thus symbolic of the rise and fall of life itself; and, by way of a metaphysical extension, they were also held to symbolise the destruction of the old society and the emergence of the new.[7]

There were, of course, the political festivities proper, May Day and the anniversaries of the salient events and dates of the labour movement, such as the November Revolution or the murder of Karl Liebknecht and Rosa Luxemburg, celebrated in particular

5. Alfred Döblin, *Schriften zur Politik und Gesellschaft*, Olten, 1972, pp. 206–7. (*Oh alte Burschenherrlichkeit* is a students' song, extolling the virtues of the students' fraternities.)
6. *Der Führer*, 1921, p. 123. *Der Führer* was a journal of the SAJ (Socialist Workers' Youth), addressed to youth leaders and helpers.
7. This theme is developed further in Chapter 11 on 'New Lifestyles'.

within the communist movement. We can thus construct a kind of Festival Calendar of the German Left, showing the dates and events which were commemorated by all or by some sections of the movement, and which, as we shall see, illustrate the political aims and the cultural ideals of the two parties, the SPD and the KPD.

Popular Entertainment and Political Commitment

The new *Festkultur* which evolved during the Weimar years was at the heart of the Left's drive to create a workers' culture, but the more popular traditions already sketched out continued to permeate the activities of most working-class organisations. Less 'cultural' and less committed in an ideological sense, their forms were nearer to the everyday leisure-time pursuits of the bulk of the working class.

It seems that at the period of its greatest prosperity the role of celebrations and of festivities in the life of the organised workers and their families increased in size and significance. Thus as the popular entertainment industry grew, so the efforts of social-democratic organisations at least to infuse entertainment and recreation into the normal life of party, trade union, club and society grew as well. Film and slide shows and illustrated lectures became an important part of socialist agitation and of party and union meetings. They often replaced speakers as the principal attraction. Some of this visual presentation was political in character; but we are often concerned with general instruction and even entertainment, which was meant to keep old members interested and attract new ones.[8] This also applied to the activities of socialist women's groups, where it became common to replace the second political part of the gathering by some form of cultural entertainment; and so in Hamburg you could hear 'the young Finnish women, who with their wonderful singing lent true dignity to the evening.'[9] And in Trier the women's afternoons offered 'coffee and cake, as well as an artistic presentation'.[10]

---

8. Cf. *Arb. Bldg.*, vol. 1, 1926, p. 206. For a fuller discussion of the role of film and of the cinema in the German labour movement and in working-class life see Chapter 10 on the 'New Media'.
9. Cf. *Frauenstimme* (Supplement to *Vorwärts*), 20 March 1925. In general see K. Hagemann, 'Frauen in der Hamburger SPD', in A. Herzig *et al.* (eds) *Arbeiter in Hamburg*, Hamburg, 1983, pp. 443–56, p. 447.
10. SPD Unterbezirk Trier, *Bericht für 1927*. p.14.

Table 7 Festival calendar of the German labour movement, 1918–33

Dates and occasion	Event	Organisations participating
15 January, Murder of Liebknecht and Luxemburg	Liebknecht/Luxemburg (later also Lenin) Commemoration	Mainly KPD, occasionally social-democratic organisations
March/April	Spring Festival (*Frühlingsfeier*)	Mainly ancillary organisations of SPD; Socialist Youth Movement
March. Revolution of March 1848. (*Märzgefallenen*)	*Gedächtnisfeier* (Memorial meeting for fallen revolutionaries)	SPD. Rather fallen into abeyance after 1918
May 1	May Day	All sections of Labour Movement. Public holiday in Saxony and Thuringia
21 June	Summer Solstice	Many ancillary organisations of SPD, principally the Youth Movement
Beginning of August	Anti-War demonstrations and commemorations. (Outbreak of First World War)	Most sections of Labour Movement
11 August	*Verfassungstag* (Day of the Constitution)	Official holiday in parts of Germany. Sections of social-democratic movement participated (Arbeitersport, Reichsbanner)
September–October	Autumn Festival (*Herbstfeier*)	As for Spring Festival
7 November	Russian Revolution	KPD (later combined with Anniversary of the German Revolution)
9 November	*Revolutionsfeier* (German Revolution)	SPD, KPD. Public holiday in Thuringia

Table 7 *continued*

Dates and occasion	Event	Organisations participating
November	*Totenfeier* (In Memory of the dead of the War) All Souls Day	Celebrated sometimes by social–democratic organisations
23–24 December	Christmas, Winter Solstice	Many sections of Labour Movement. Celebration of Winter Solstice rare

Even under Weimar the First of May remained the first and foremost of Labour's high days and holidays, although its primary aim, the eight-hour day, had now largely been secured.[11] May Day celebrations had always combined elements of demonstration and agitation, and, ideally, an apotheosis of the ideal of working–class solidarity, combined with elements of abandon and razzmatazz. At the same time, it had lost some of its 'fighting spirit' aspect, at least among the social-democratic working class and their organisation. It was no longer a day which workers demonstratively took off, and the celebrations were now generally held in the evening.[12] Social-democratic ceremonies were 'refined' and 'cultural', combining classical music with the recitation of poetry, which, while vaguely radical and libertarian, did not contain a specific political message, let alone a message about exploitation and the class-struggle; though they did often end in the common singing of *The International*, as we find for example in the programme of the celebrations of the left-wing Berlin Branch of the German Metal-workers, held in the Berlin *Sportpalast*, the largest sports hall in the city:

DEUTSCHER METALLARBEITERVERBAND BERLIN
MAIFEIER 1930

Triumphmarch	Verdi
Overture to 'Rienzi'	Wagner
The Factory Siren (Recitation)	Wendel
Hymn to the Sun	Mussorgski
Address	Alwin Brendel, Chairman

11. The Weimar constitution enabled the German states to make May 1 a public holiday, but only Saxony and Thuringia did so.
12. With the introduction of (paid) holidays in some industries it became possible to take May Day as a paid holiday, and some workers did that.

'Awakening'	Tiessen
Song of Sacred Anger (Recitation)	Barthel
We stand at the glowing fires	Knöchel
The Great Hammer (Recitation)	Barthel
The International (All sing)	de Geyter

The ceremony might be followed by a march through the streets, or by a dance, or a social gathering, with all participants dressed in their Sunday best.[13] Or, in large cities, such as Hamburg, the social-democratic celebrations would be spread over a variety of venues, but would have a more proletarian character, with worker-singers, workers' bands, sports performances and the like.

It was only on Sundays that larger and more varied programmes could be attempted. In many instances the celebrations of the first of May had thus become a casual and perfunctory affair, the execution of which received little preparation. It was not surprising that groups like the Young Socialist Workers, which were more politically and perhaps also more aesthetically committed, objected to such spectacles, and, on occasions, left the common event organised by the party. In a small village, we are told that they moved to the local playing-field, gathered in the village youth around them, and organised games and sang songs embodying the socialist spirit and the sense of community.[14]

The May Day celebrations were, at the same time, the occasion for reunions and for more personal celebrations. 'The grown-ups went into some beer-garden in the Central Park or stretched themselves out on the "Festival Lawn", while the young ones went to the Sprunggarten, and there they sang, played games or danced', a seventy-year-old Hamburg social-democrat is quoted in an interview at the beginning of the 1980s.[15]

Community, commensality, games and gallivanting were among the most common denominators of communal activities in popular leisure pursuits. They showed themselves in many working-class festivities, at least outside the communist orbit. A festival, whatever its political leanings or purpose, was there for

---

13. Cf. 'Die Maifeier', *Arb. Bldg.* vol. 2, 1927, p. 62. It is significant that while the SPD advocated that those taking part in the demonstrations should dress in their Sunday clothes the Communist Party, in Hamburg at least, suggested that workers should turn out in their work clothes.
14. Ibid.
15. Quoted by Helga Stachow '"Festtag, Kampftag": Feste der sozialistischen Arbeiterbewegung', in *Arbeiterkultur in Hamburg um 1930*, Hamburg, 1982, pp. 210–22, p. 217.

people to enjoy themselves. The proposed *Reichsbannerfest* in Gelsenkirchen was to 'spread trust in the Republic among working-class families'; but it was equally important that 'after the hard grind of a week's work the workers should, for "a few pence", be able to be happy for a few hours of relaxation and distraction', as the local SPD newspaper put it.

And the smaller the locality, the more traditional the character of the fêtes which went on under the auspices of working-class organisations. In Tübingen, Christmas and Shrove Tuesday (Carnival) were celebrated, and there were children's fêtes and forest fêtes, held not just as a pure imitation of the festivals of the bourgeoisie, and yet initially not very strongly politically inclined. Only in the later years of the Republic, and under the influence of deepening political conflict, did these events take on a more pronounced political character.[16] This applies equally to events and entertainments which were formally carried out under the auspices of local Sportskartelle, which were generally the most popular of the leisure-time organisations. In Marbach on the Neckar a regular cycle of festivities was soon established: Spring Festival, Masked Ball, Summer Fête, Autumn Festival, and, as a culmination, Christmas celebrations.[17]

The preparations for all this, and for the more sophisticated, more specifically cultural activities with musical and theatrical contributions that followed, made considerable demands on the leisure-time of the participants. It appears as if the sacrifice of time and effort involved was not undertaken for purely political reasons, but by way of an extension of family life. 'In the social, as much as in the sporting club life, the whole family was integrated. Club life was family life.'[18]

Yet whatever the motivation, the effect might well have been more political than was intended. Given the general traditional character of the social and cultural life of workers' clubs in the smaller towns and rural communities, it would be easy to dismiss them as making no contribution to the formation of socialist or communist political consciousness and commitment. That was hardly the case. The political culture here transmitted is an oral culture, political acculturation proceeding by word of mouth and in the setting of social gatherings and of cultural events. In

16. B.J. Warneken and Katrin Warneken-Pollowski, 'Arbeitertübingen', in H. Fielhauer and O. Bockhorn, *Die Andere Kultur*, Vienna, 1982, pp. 261–77, p. 270.
17. Cf. *Arbeiterkultur in der proletarischen Provinz, 1890–1933*, Marbach, 1983.
18. Ibid. p. 20

Mössingen, a traditional workers' village in Swabia, which earned the nickname of the 'red' Mössingen, because of its strong socialist and above all communist organisations, the societies and their festivities, rather than the political parties proper, provided the basis for the local workers' movement – and incidentally the backbone for their unique resistance to Hitler. It was in this setting that 'the workers' cultural facilities and their forms were developed and learnt, here abstract policy was emotionally internalised'.[19]

Whatever its purpose or provenance, the *Arbeiterfest* must clearly be looked at as an agent of communication and socialisation as much as in an educative role. We must also distinguish between verbal and symbolic communication. Some of the popular festival ritual operated at the symbolic level. A harvest festival celebrated in 1920 in the courtyard of a Berlin tenement block, with women in black skirts and white blouses and men in their Sunday best, seems a paradox,[20] but it clearly strengthened that community of tenants – a group which the communist agitprop theatre groups and communist wall newspapers were to address a decade later. And if at a *Mädchenwaldfest* organised by the Berlin Workers' Youth Movement on the theme of 'No more war' girls with wreaths in their hair performed Rounds and Folk-Dances, and if a choir sang 'Press your ear to the ground and listen', it is not obvious that the impression and the resulting commitment created would have been less enduring if the event had been more directly and overtly political.

Those who reported in 1980 on their experience of the demonstrations and celebrations towards the end of the Weimar Republic, which involved thousands and tens of thousands of Hamburg workers, social democrats and communists, stressed the impression created by visual or ephemeral aspects of these events, as well as the pleasure which they derived from meeting old friends. 'On Constitution Day [*Verfassungstag*] things went like that. At night there was the torchlight procession. And you met at the market in Barmbeck, and all the children came, and then the allotment societies and the individual party districts came. And then they built floats, big and small, with garlands and lanterns'. Or, in the words of another veteran, 'On May the first we all assembled in public. One felt more closely linked to the others. Many people met; one was glad to have met again, to discuss things'.[21]

The form and content of these popular celebrations and festivities

---

19. H.J. Althaus *et al.*, *Da ist nirgends nichts gewesen außer hier . . . Geschichte eines Schwäbischen Arbeiterdorfes*, Berlin, 1982, p. 123.
20. Cf. photograph in *Die Freie Welt*, 1920, no. 32.
21. Helga Stachow (note 15), quoting social-democratic and communist veterans.

would clearly vary from occasion to occasion – the more non-specific and secular the occasion, the less political they were. And if we look at more specifically political events we find differences between those staged by the SPD and those put on by the Communist Party.

Communist fêtes had always had a more overtly political and militant character, which increased in emphasis and determination with the years of the Republic and with the growing radicalism of communist policy. The annual *Liebknecht-Luxemburg Feiern*, held in remembrance of their murder in January 1919, to which Lenin's name was added after 1924, had always been highly emotional in appeal and solemn in character.[22]

At the beginning the commemorations did not differ very much from those of similar social-democratic gatherings. Thus the celebrations in Bremen in 1921 commenced with a *Chorus* from Wagner's *Meistersinger*, and included recitations from Herwegh and Freiligrath, poets of the German radical movement of 1848, often included in social-democratic programmes. But by the end of the period this had changed. In 1930 the District Committee of the KPD in the Ruhr sent out a circular demanding that 'the sentimental anniversary celebrations of previous years be replaced by powerful, proletarian and combative events.'[23]

The advice given to local communist organisations drew attention to the importance of creating the right mood and the right environment for such events. Decorations (banners, flags, if possible a bust of Lenin and slogans from his works) should impress the audience. Lighting, too, should create dramatic effects, and it was very important that the celebrations should proceed in a tight and integrated form.[24]

The desire to create an atmosphere of combativeness was generally stressed. In 1931 the communist May Day celebrations included massed choirs, agitprop revues and speeches, and at every event 'the fighting spirit of opposition showed itself'. The traditional character of social-democratic celebrations was, not unexpectedly, denounced by the KPD as petty-bourgeois and reformist. They were, with some justification, accused of being too 'full of solemnity, intoxicated with happiness and far removed from reality'.[25]

22. Ibid. p. 217.
23. Cf. *Bremen Staatsarchiv* 4.65, Bd. 242. The original refers to 'rührselige Toten-feiern'.
24. 'Einige praktische Winke für Agitationsveranstaltungen', *Der Parteiarbeiter*, April 1927, pp. 118–20.
25. 'Ifa Material zur Sonnenwendefeier (1930)'. Copy in Arbeiterliedarchiv, Deutsche

Proposals for socialist celebrations of the summer solstice were criticised as being too full of romantic melody and recitations on themes from nature, culled from compilations prepared by the Free Thought movement. They were contrasted with the KPD's aggressively styled and hard-hitting programmes. The latter used the sun as a symbol for the communist struggle, and produced a series of musical numbers, recitations and *Sprechchöre* which sought to ensure a performance kept at all times at a high pitch of political intensity. Visual and spoken messages were all the time to assail the audience, with banners proclaiming slogans such as 'Religion is the Opium of the People' or *Alles für die Sovietmacht* /('Help Soviet Russia'), and with the chorus intoning: 'Summer Solstice, 1931 – Four Million on the Dole'. All this should proceed without a pause: 'only then will the celebration become a unified whole'.[26]

The communist movement did not create the kind of mass festivals which were organised under Social Democratic Party and trade union auspices in the 1920s; but we can assume that individual members of the party participated in them. Its own mass-events were more directly political, and more rooted in the daily political struggle – as in the revue-type performances of 1924 and 1925 discussed in the last chapter. These, however, were not repeated in later years, and in the highly charged political climate of those years the KPD rejected the idea of the mere festive event. The *Ifa Rundschau* argued in 1932 that there were no grounds for celebrations. 'For us there exists only the demonstration, where we show our resolve to carry on with the struggle.'[27]

We have, however, the beginning of new forms of popular entertainment of the *Volksfest* type, organised by some of the media associated with the publishing enterprises started by Willi Münzenberg. They took the form of fairs, combining entertainment with 'commercial' propaganda for the newspaper or other relevant publications. Thus the Universum Bücherei, a communist book-club, held a *Fest* in the Berlin Sportpalast in 1931. The Book Club showed its wares, and there were visual displays with cartoons, slogans and posters, as well as musical performances and recitations. And in September 1932 the two popular left-wing newspapers started by Münzenberg, *Berlin am Morgen* and *Die Welt am Abend*, organised an event in the *Lunapark* – a permanent amusement complex in the city – under the title *Kampflied und Arbeitersport* ('Songs of Combat and Workers' Sport').

Akademie der Künste, Berlin (GDR).
26. Ibid.
27. *Ifa Rundschau*, vol. 3, nos. 1–2.

Acts of Commitment and Dedication

Festivities and ceremonies for the social-democratic worker were, during the Weimar period, an area of experimentation and of new departures. In the drive of the SPD to incorporate leisure-time activities, and, above all, the arts, into the sphere of socialist activities the attempt to create a new festival culture must rank high. This was at the centre of experiments to improve the quality of life of the working masses and to provide within the framework of working-class organisations a counterweight to the growing commercial entertainment industry.

Leisure had increased, but the boredom and the exhaustion produced by the daily toil of most of the working class, and the strain of life in the big city had not diminished. By way of compensation, it was argued, a 'psychic expansion of the individual' was important.[28] The arts were regarded as particularly suited to the task of ameliorating the quality of life and making it more beautiful. The new workers' festivals, which flourished between 1920 and 1930, set out to combine several of the arts into often grandiose and moving spectacles for mass audiences. The ingredients of the new and highly emotive fare would either come from within the traditional culture, especially literature and music, or they would take the form of oratoria or pageants, songs or dances, produced especially for the occasion. They were often conceived as acts of communion and dedication of a quasi-religious character: 'all that which the believer finds in the Church we should give to socialism in our celebrations.'[29]

The new *Festkultur* was conceived as an event *sui generis*, not necessarily tied to a particular event in the socialist calendar, but expressed in a new kind of festival staged by workers' organisations for the mass of their followers. Indeed, a contemporary writer saw in the new endeavour the precursor of a new kind of 'national festival', analogous with the Festival of Reason established during the French Revolution. He stressed the cult-like aspects, including the torchlit processions of the masses, flowing banners, gymnastics, choirs and choruses and performances by children and young people. Through them 'a new social enthusiasm was to be awakened in the masses, greater and more life-enhancing than the uniformed processions of bourgeois societies with all their pomp

28. Cf. *Sozialismus und Kultur*. Report of the first meeting of the Sozialistische Kulturbund, 1926, Berlin, 1927, especially Leo Kestenberg's lecture 'Die Aufgaben der Kunst'.
29. A. Johannesson, 'Sozialistische Festkultur', *Arb. Bldg.* 1928, p. 183.

and protocol – maids of honour in white dresses' and the like, which workers' organisations used to imitate.[30]

Conceived in this way the festival was to be a catalyst in the formation of the new socialist man. This 'new man' was to be created here and now, and should not depend on first achieving a full socialist society. Valtin Hartig, one of the leading figures in the area of workers' culture and first editor of the *Kulturwille* – the leading journal in this field – saw the contemporary endeavours as contributing to the formation of a new society, for 'whatever was done now [by the labour movement] should be suffused with the thought that it would help to bring about a new society with a new culture'.[31] Such aims were to be realised through two mechanisms, one ideological, the other aesthetic. On the one hand the theme of the events to be staged was to be clearly concerned with aspects of working-class life and with the expectations of the socialist future, which were presented generally in an ethereal and idealised form. On the other hand, the event sought to give the participants a rich and lasting emotional experience through its visual and vocal displays and through the symbolic character of the performances.

In the formal sense this was done by attempting to break down the barrier between the performers and the spectators, and thus producing a shared experience. Behind it, on a more theoretical plane, some people sought to recreate an older, more communitarian culture, akin to what they believed had been the folk culture of the Middle Ages, before the division between artist and spectator or auditor had arisen. 'To create a festival' wrote Max Zelck, the Hamburg educationist, and a creator of the *Jugendweihe* (a form of secular confirmation discussed in detail in Chapter 11) 'means to establish a form which can be the expression of the inner stirrings of the masses.' The new form of festivity was thus to be an event *by* the masses *for* the masses, and on many occasions there were hundreds of performers and thousands, if not tens of thousands, of spectators. Performers and audience were to be physically linked by whirling torches, beams of light, and singing, which was to encompass the whole mass of those assembled. In Zelck's words, 'masses would speak to masses'.[32]

30. Cf. R. Wagner, *Zur Theorie der Arbeiterbildung*, Vienna 1927, reprinted (in part) in J. Olbrich (ed.), *Arbeiterbildung in der Weimarer Zeit*, Brunswick, 1977, p. 77. A photograph of the dedication of a banner of the Workers' Choral Society 'Hoffnung' in Benningen, Swabia, is reproduced in *Arbeiterkultur in der proletarischen Provinz* (note 17).

31. V. Hartig, 'Die Arbeiterkulturwoche', in Leipzig, *KW* 1 July 1924; idem, 'Arbeiterkultur', *KW*, 1 August 1924.

32. Max Zelck, 'Der Kulturwille des Sozialismus', in SPD Hamburg, 25 *Jahre*

And if the performances were not literally a dialogue they should become a symbolic one. The spectator was potentially to be able to feel himself a part of the spectacle. The means for the creation of such empathy were the *Sprechchor* and the *Bewegungschor*, that is the mass-chorus, declaiming and intoning in one or several voices and accompanied by miming. As we saw, the massed chorus had been invested with a central, educative function by the champions of a new workers' culture. It was suggested that the new forms of expression, at the time fairly unique to the workers' festival culture, embodied the common will of the masses and symbolised their strength. Vocal expression and co-ordinated rhythmic movements would, it was thought, stimulate the spectator to sympathise and identify with the display, and thus create a wider community.[33]

These events were generally staged in the open air, in large sports arenas or stadiums or in parks, and it was their mass character which was their most obvious feature. This open-air aspect also determined the form of communication, necessitating short sentences, simple, emotive phrases, and, above all, an emphasis on the visual element to reinforce the dialogue. And while the texts of the festivals have generally survived, and permit analysis in ideological as much as in aesthetic terms, we must turn to contemporary descriptions for a visual impression.[34]

In Magdeburg the 'Festival of the Lake' showed a pageant on the theme of *Flammende Zeit* ('Times of Turmoil'), utilising eighty boats with red torches spread out on the lake; and, as the torches faded, the chorus began to declaim an account of the hard life of the miner. As the chorus ended green lights came on, illuminating gymnasts who expressed in movements the various aspects of physical labour. Thus visually and literarily the sequence of a pageant proceeded in a dialectical fashion, contrasting the sufferings of past and present with the joys of the future, and juxtaposing Capital and Labour.

Towards the end of the 1920s such pageants or ceremonies took place in many large or medium-sized cities. They were often linked with a whole series of events under the heading of a *Kulturwoche* or

sozialistische Kulturarbeit in Hamburg, 1931, p. 15.

33. On the *Bewegungschor* see K. Heilbut, 'Neue Formen proletarischer Festkultur' [Report of a study week in Leipzig], *Soz. Bldg.*, 1931, pp. 205–10, 243–8.

34. Such a literary analysis is not attempted here; but see W. van der Will and R. Burns, *Arbeiter Kulturbewegung in der Weimarer Republik*, Berlin, 1982, pp. 167–232. In a second volume with the same title the authors have reproduced a number of documents, including some *Festspiele*; Jon Clark, *Bruno Schönlank und die Arbeitersprechchorbewegung*, Cologne, 1984.

a 'Festival of Labour'. One such festival took place in Frankfurt in July 1930. As its 'Finale' the organisers staged a grand display under the heading of *Wir sind die Kraft* ('Ours is the Strength') before an audience of tens of thousands.

An account in the *Kulturwille* described the visual effects. The work, written for voice and rhythmic chorus, illustrated the struggle between Labour and Capital in a highly symbolic form. At the beginning, Capital, personified by a speaker in a gold gown, appears, followed by his bailiffs and overseers. He ascends a dais – a golden halo in the background. To the accompaniment of shrill music the servants of Mammon bring their whips to bear on the slaves, who carry bars of gold to build a pyramid. The whippers' shadows appear larger than life on the white backcloth. As the pyramid grows, Capital climbs higher and higher, and declaims: 'I am the power, mine is the strength'. Now the head of Karl Marx appears on the screen. He proclaims the transitory nature of capitalism, and calls on the workers of the world to unite. Then the vast area of the stadium fills with massed columns of workers, each of which congregates round a torch-bearer. The beams of the reflectors criss-cross the dark turf over which they advance. Sounds of war are heard. The capitalist state confronts the masses, who resist and who are victorious. The gold banner on the tower is lowered, and the red flag goes up the flagstaff. The torches are lit. The masses avow their loyalty to the working class and to the trade unions. After a song, sung by the chorus, actors and audience united in the singing of the *International*.[35]

Such spectacles were heavy, and perhaps heady, stuff. As the movement for cultural festivals spread across the country, the discussion of their role also expanded. For the purists such festivals were the apex of socialist cultural activities, and they hoped for lasting effects on the spectators from performances which were to stand out from more humdrum and ordinary cultural events. The Magdeburg 'Lake Festival' was held in conjunction with the SPD's biennial conference, and the report in the *Kulturwille* regretted that it had to be followed by fireworks and, even more, that the day concluded with the 'obligatory social and dance'. Instead, everyone should have gone home with the music and movement still reverberating in their minds, thus strengthening their resolve to embark

---

35. Cf. 'Das Fest am See', *KW*, 1929, p. 168. Among the participants were 200 in the rhythmic chorus, 100 in the voice chorus, 500 singers, 300 members of the *Reichsbanner* Band, 70 athletes and 70 children. The account of the Frankfurt performance is adapted from the account in *KW*, October 1930, p. 194.

on new activities; but 'the best of the impressions created by the festival went down in the usual pyrotechnics and the shuffling on the dance-floor'.[36] The new techniques, above all the *Sprechchor* and the *Bewegungschor*, were given official approval by the Sozialistische Kulturbund, and workshops and conferences were held to discuss how best to improve the necessary skills, which had failed to develop as quickly and as widely as had been hoped.[37]

The belief that the essence of socialist celebrations lay in mass experience and the creation of a collectivity was not universally accepted. Some doubted the need for so much seriousness and intensity in festival culture. They thought that there was 'too much suffering, too much lamentation'. The broad masses, it was admitted, stayed away, and gave their support to the bourgeois entertainment industry, frequenting dance-halls, cinemas and variety shows.[38] Valtin Hartig was not necessarily in disagreement. Building on his belief in the new culture as a return to the organic community of the Middle Ages, he saw the festival as almost self-sufficient and self-legitimating. Its purpose was fulfilled if it made the participants more mature, more relaxed and, in the end, happier. The festival thus had for him a threefold purpose. The restoration of energy, the education towards growing self-awareness, and 'the happy experience of our social existence'.[39]

Some criticised these ceremonies and festivals because they thought that they exhausted their participants with a heavy diet of politics at the expense of the artistic and the emotional. Leo Kestenberg, a senior civil servant in the Prussian Ministry of Education, argued that the socialist movement could already permit itself the luxury of pure enjoyment of the arts for their own sake. The more formal celebrations of socialist organisations, events like the *Revolutionsfeier* or special anniversaries, and the *Proletarische Morgenfeiern* which came into fashion on Sundays in places like Berlin, Leipzig or Mannheim, were in the nature of performances rather than demonstrations. Works by classical composers figured prominently in their programmes. These overtures, symphonies and quartets were interspersed with recitations by professional actors

36. 'Das Fest am See' (see last note). For Otto Wels, the joint Chairman of the SPD, it was nevertheless the unforgettable climax of the conference. See H.A. Winkler, *Der Schein der Normalität*, Berlin, 1985, p. 644.
37. Heilbut (note 33).
38. Cf. *Soz. Bldg.* 1930, p. 215 and A. Kern, 'Neue Festformen', *Soz. Bldg.* 1931, pp. 81–4.
39. Cited by C. Sewell, *A study of the independent social democratic magazine Kulturwille*, Unpublished M.A. Diss., University of Kent, fo. 78.

and with choral pieces from leading workers' choirs; and, of course, by the obligatory speech, which at major events was now often given by Social Democratic ministers, or high-ranking social-democratic civil servants.

These events were meant to be uplifting and soul-stirring. As a report on the *Proletarische Morgenfeier* stated: 'The theatre was lit as for an evening performance. The Kergl quartet performed the Allegro from Schumann's String Quartet in F-Dur. How blessed is such music when it is performed by virtuosi in a circle of like-minded people'.[40] Recitations of poetry on 'Work and War', which spoke of horrors and of suffering, followed, 'but this was contained by a performance of Beethoven's great String Quartet, Op. 18, which led its hearers to the height of emotional ecstasy'.[41]

The programme of the celebrations held on the occasion of the Fortieth Jubilee of the Berlin Arbeiterbildungsschule, reproduced overleaf, is a specimen of the sort of solemn, ornate and slightly pompous events put on by a party which was now involved in the government of the country. In its formality it seems like an official event sponsored by the government itself.

Judged only by the quality of their formal presentation and by the artistic standards attained, such celebrations were acts of affirmation, rather than calls to change society. A party which could now put on performances equal in quality to any that were offered to bourgeois audiences felt that it could take pride in having got so far, and that the events which it arranged 'could now meet the most advanced and sophisticated tastes.'[42]

The *Festkultur* practice which we find in the various organisations of the German labour movement during these years did not, of course, always correspond to the ideal patterns which a few enthusiastic and committed individuals proposed and projected. In the smaller towns and in the countryside in particular it was difficult to achieve reasonably high standards of performance.[43] And, standards apart, the generally unsophisticated tastes which continued to prevail in the German proletariat meant that petty-bourgeois patterns of entertainment continued to prevail in many celebrations and festivities of working-class organisations.

At the other extreme we have, especially during the early years of the decade, the influence of the socialist youth movement, whose

40. *Volksstimme* (Mannheim), no. 323, 29 November 1926.
41. Ibid.
42. SPD, Unterbezirk Hannover, *Geschäftsbericht . . . für das Jahr 1928*, 1929.
43. Proletarische Festgestaltung, *KW*, 1928, pp. 182–3.

40 JAHRE ARBEITERBILDUNGSSCHULE BERLIN
Sunday 11 January 1931 at 11 o'clock
in the Chamber of the former Prussian
Upper House, Berlin, Leipziger Straße

PROGRAMME

Festmarsch	L. van Beethoven
Prologue (from a speech of Wilhelm Liebknecht at the Inaugural Meeting)	
Sinfonie C dur (Adagio, Allegro assai)	J. Haydn
Begrüssung der Gäste by Alexander Stein, Chairman of District Committee for socialist Education	
Frei treten wir zum Singen an	Ottomar Gerster
Die Wissenschaft und die Arbeiter Oration by Staatminister Adolf Grimme	
Staatsekretar Heinrich Schulz, Chairman of the Central Council for socialist Education	
Karl Litke, Member of the Reichstag, Second Chairman of the Berlin SPD	
Sonnenhymne	Modest Mussorgski
Sinfonie C dur (Menuetta Finale)	J. Haydn
Deutsche Hymne (Sprechchor)	Heinrich Lersch
Weckruf	Heinz Tiessen

desire to seek an enhanced sense of community and novel collective experiences made them see in the festival in particular an expression of their ideals. This culminated in the celebration of the summer solstice, in the romantic elements of which 'there were mixed-in a commitment to the present and the will to a re-shaping of life in the future'.[44] Social democrats, who had generally rejected established religion, were nevertheless seeking in such festivals not only a cultural, but also a quasi-religious experience, because this would serve to release the emotional energies of the masses. This in turn would demand new forms of celebration, different from the way in which such events were conducted by the 'demoralised bourgeoisie'.[45]

44. *Arb. Bldg.* vol. 1, 1929, p. 76.
45. Hamburg SPD, *Bericht der Landesorganisation* . . . 1927 and 1928, p. 169: 'Leitsätze zur Festkultur'.

We have seen already how the desire to create a secular ritual found expression in the *Proletarische Feierstunden* – a form of non-religious celebration held on Sunday mornings as a substitute for church services; and the institution of a system of secular confirmation, in the form of the *Jugendweihen*, will be discussed in connection with new socialist lifestyles. The *Jugendweihe* stood at the beginning of adulthood, and was to commit the young to socialism.

Yet the festival as such was in danger of becoming an obstacle to the political struggle. By seeking the highest standards of artistic expression, by 'giving the oppressed and the disadvantaged all that was beautiful, true and good on this earth' the social-democratic cultural movement deliberately sought to anticipate what might otherwise be attainable only through the political struggle.[46]

In doing so, and in emphasising the form and quality of performance of the festival as much as its content, and by stressing emotional experience and aesthetic qualities rather than political direction, the *Festkultur* had an integrative role. It sought to enrich the personal life of the participants; and it may thus have contributed to the relative quiescence of sections of the German working class in the face of threats to the fabric on which this culture was built.[47]

46. *Vorwärts*, 1928, quoted in C. Rülcker, 'Arbeiterkultur und Kulturpolitik im Blickwinkel des Vorwärts, 1918–1928', *AfSG*, vol. 14, 1974, pp. 115–55.
47. For a stimulating discussion of this subject see D. Langewiesche, 'Politik, Gesellschaft, Kultur. Zur Problematik von Arbeiterkultur und kulturellen Arbeiterorganisationen in Deutschland', *AfSG*, 22, 1982, pp. 359–402.

The New Media and the
Parties of the Left

Rise and Scope of the New Media

Taking up themes developed earlier, this chapter looks again at individual and largely privately-enjoyed leisure. But while our discussion of the 'culture of everyday life' in Chapter 4 concentrated on informal and comparatively uninstitutionalised forms of leisure, the 'New Media' of film, radio and press discussed here are technically complex and often highly structured forms of enterprise. Moreover, the popularity and the mass-consumption aspects of the new media stand in sharp contrast to their centralised production. Because of this, and because our knowledge of the popular reception of film or radio, of listening patterns, visual communication and literary tastes is limited, this chapter concentrates on the new media in their political context.

The advance and growth of new techniques of communication must be seen in the general context of an entertainment industry which during these years increased in size and sophistication. The number of men and women working in this area began to rise only with the economic recovery after 1924 but the number of enterprises declined sharply in the years after 1907 largely as the result of a reduction in one person and very small firms. As far as the film, the largest of the new entertainment industries, is concerned, we find that while the industry does not even figure in the 1907 census it employed nearly 23,000 people in 1925. Of these, 18,135 worked in 2,808 film theatre enterprises.[1]

Film and radio are at the heart of the new techniques of mass-communication, but new forms of publishing are also important in the context of the labour movement. The first moving pictures became commercially available around 1900, and radio as a public medium only after the First World War. It was during the later part of our period that the scope of publishing by working-class organ-

---

1. Cf. *Statistik des Deutschen Reich*, vol. 213, p. 43; vol. 413, p. 78; vol. 453, part i.

isations or by enterprises associated with the labour movement expanded and took on new forms. The first two became very important as providers of recreation and purveyors of news and information for workers. At the same time, they became a powerful influence on public opinion. This influence resulted from the immediacy of the impression which the new techniques made possible, and from the economic and institutional forces which stood behind them.

The power of broadcasting was derived from the monopoly position that the state had conferred on the companies, and, in the last resort, from the state itself, which supervised them.[2] The cinema, on the other hand, was not similarly controlled; but while the ownership of the film theatres was widely distributed, the production and distribution of films was mainly in the hands of large enterprises, especially the UFA film studios and production company, which later became part of the right-wing newspaper empire controlled by the nationalist politician, Alfred Hugenberg.

The German labour movement was initially hostile to some of the new media, especially to the film. It looked at the cinema as an instrument for mere recreation. Indeed, it was held that the film transmitted false values and distracted the workers from their real tasks. The hours spent in 'mindless' radio-listening or movie-watching would be better spent in activities which improved the mind, or indeed in political activity. Yet at the heart of the criticism was the awareness that the productions of the two media did not reflect the interests, ideals and aspirations of the working class.

This negative attitude towards the new media, especially to film, changed only gradually and with a growing awareness of their potentially powerful role in political education and in the agitation of the parties of the Left. Thus both the SPD and the KPD sought to create or import films which would be in tune with their aims. Both criticised the scope and content of radio programmes, and demanded that this public service should be more widely representative of the views and interests of the working class. As the editor of the social-democratic journal *Arbeiter Bildung* wrote in 1926 'one may argue about the real value of film and radio, but there is no denying that they are highly suitable for exerting influence over the masses. Our enemies make great use of this fact, and we therefore must not adopt an entirely negative attitude. On the contrary, radio

2. Overall control of broadcasting was exercised through the *Reichsrundfunkgesell-schaft*, a holding company for the individual networks with majority sharehold-ing vested in the *Reichspost*.

and film must be put into the service of our cause'.[3]

The struggles to exploit the new media for the political aims of the Left are important politically. They reflect the respective cultural policies of the two parties. While the Communist Party saw independent provision under worker control as the only solution, the SPD believed in the possibility of bending institutions like broadcasting to serve its own ends. This policy had some limited success. At the party's biennial conference in 1931 Heinrich Schulz, now a member of the party's executive, expressed a cautious optimism, and urged 'collaboration [with the broadcasting companies] whenever this was possible by all relevant organisations'.[4]

In spite of the parties' criticism working-class enjoyment of radio and film does not seem to have abated in our period; but as listening and viewing was generally private and individual its character, its extent and influence is not well documented. The popularity of these media is an important corrective to the picture of workers' culture seen from the angle of the organised cultural activities of the German labour movement. On the other hand socialist- and communist-inspired developments in some of the new media and the Left's activities in film and publishing are evidence of an enterprise and originality which contributed to the whole of Weimar culture. Beyond this, individuals and organisations of the left, and especially social democrats, sought to influence the development of the new media culture by supporting new forms of communication which they regarded as innovatory and progressive. They wished to stimulate the opportunities which broadcasting offered for radio-documentaries and radio-drama, believing them to be both educative and less amenable to distortion than other broadcast forms. They also favoured the *Kulturfilm*, the documentation of historical, artistic and scientific themes in visual form, which would widen the horizons of the working-class audience.[5]

A Neutral or a Committed Ether?

Of the public and universally accessible leisure-time institutions the radio was the youngest; but it was also potentially the most powerful, able to penetrate into every household and to be used as

---

3. *Arb. Bldg.* 1926, p. 200 (from a speech at the First Conference of the Bezirksbildungsausschüsse).
4. SPD Parteitag 1931, p. 253.
5. Cf. S. Marck, 'Rundfunk, Kultur und Arbeiterschaft', *Soz. Bldg.* 1929, no. 9, pp. 257–60.

something approaching quite closely to the nature of a public-address medium. Starting from a very low level of activities the wireless reached millions, including a large section of the working class, by the end of the republican period. Public broadcasting in Germany commenced in 1923, and the licence fee was two marks a month, the equivalent of about twice the hourly wage of a skilled worker, and of approximately two or three visits to the cinema. In addition there was the cost of subscribing to one of the programme magazines, priced at between 90 pfennigs and two marks a month. By April 1925 there were more than 750,000 subscribers, and the figure virtually doubled within a year. The number of subscribers rose to 3 million in 1930, and to over 4 million in 1932. The potential audience increased even faster with the evolution of the loudspeaker and the possibility of better sound-amplification through the valve-based receiver. By the beginning of the 1930s the total radio audience was estimated at 15 million.[6]

Broadcasting in Germany was subject to state control, and the state's influence was extended by measures passed in 1926 and 1932. When the Nazis came to power it was easy for them to take over broadcasting and turn it into a major and most effective weapon of propaganda. From the beginning, however, broadcasting was undertaken by public companies in which the state held a share. The stations were organised on a regional or Land basis, and they were required to be politically neutral, and forbidden to broadcast party political programmes or show ideological leanings. At the same time the radio was expected to act in the service of the state and to disseminate government views, in obvious contradiction of its theoretical neutrality. As Professor Schubotz, the Director of the *Deutsche Welle*, the nationwide radio established in 1926, told his colleagues shortly afterwards 'the radio performed official and semi-official functions, and the state must have scope to express its views and ensure that views hostile to the state do not find expression'. The broadcasting companies 'would act foolishly if they were to put any obstacle in the way of the state'.[7]

To ensure this political neutrality the companies were controlled by supervisory boards (Überwachungsausschüsse) composed of a representative of the Reich government and delegates of the *Länder* in whose territories the station broadcast. On paper the boards

6. Cf. W.B. Lerg, *Rundfunkpolitik in der Weimarer Republik*, Munich, 1980, pp. 113 and 526. See also E.K. Fischer (ed.), *Dokumente zur Geschichte des deutschen Rundfunks und Fernsehen*, Göttingen, 1975. There was a relative decline in subscriptions in 1932.
7. Cited in H. Pohle, *Der Rundfunk als Instrument der Politik*, Hamburg, 1955, p. 151.

were only concerned with programmes in areas other than art, science and liberal education; and as news broadcasts were not produced by individual stations but centrally provided, this might have given them relatively little scope to exercise their role as pre-censors or as retrospective critics. In practice, however, the distinction was hard to maintain and, news and reportage apart, plays and even transmissions of outside events, including celebrations and ceremonies, might become subject to censure, especially if the event emanated from the left. Talks, especially those by politicians, were subject to scrutiny and possible prohibition, and most companies were particularly restrictive when it came to programmes dealing with left-wing thought and policy.[8]

In spite of this the SPD – though not the Communist Party – did not oppose the concept of broadcasting as a public-service institution which assumed a mantle of political neutrality. Inasmuch as the party was often represented on the supervisory boards it could not object to their legal powers, which could extend to interference with programmes. The SPD believed however in a less strict definition of political neutrality, which would not lead to the exclusion of all political and ideological aspects from the programmes. Its view was that political neutrality meant 'the representation of all intellectual tendencies and ideologies in relation to their strength in society'.[9]

This view slowly gained ground, and the scope for political discussion widened after 1928 – a move which was probably not unconnected with the formation of a Centre-Left coalition government with the Social Democratic politician Hermann Müller as Chancellor. In these last years of democratic government the broadcasting companies embarked on some political discussion programmes (always excluding the KPD); and they were encouraged in this policy by government statements, such as that of the Minister of the Interior, Carl Severing, who declared that 'listeners should gradually get used to listening to the expression of points of view which differ from their own, provided that they were put

8. Lerg (note 6), pp. 374–7 gives a list of the original appointees to the Supervisory Boards. A total of 30–40 persons were responsible for the political supervision of broadcasting throughout Germany. They were not fully independent, but held their position as delegates of the Reich or of one of the German States. An example of how this quasi-censorship was exercised in Hamburg is given in *Arbeiterkultur in Hamburg um 1930*, Hamburg, 1982.
9. From the reply of the Central Education Council of the SPD to demands made by the *Arbeiter Radio Bund* for a wider scope for broadcasting to working-class audiences, reproduced in P. Dahl, *Arbeitersender und Volksempfänger . . .*, Frankfurt, 1978, p. 52.

forward in a fair and factual manner'.[10] Both government and broadcasters were now anxious to develop wider and more critical understanding of the political issues of the day and thus to strengthen support for the democratic state.

Leaving out the provision of news and the disputed role of political discussion, the aim of broadcasting was from the beginning to bring culture, education and entertainment to listeners, with special emphasis on the former two and on the provision of programmes of a high standard. Hans Bredow the 'Radio Commissioner' (*Rundfunkkommissar*), whose influence extended further than his formal position as the Chairman of the Board of the national wireless holding company, saw the task of radio as 'to satisfy equally the most cultivated and the most simple tastes . . . [it should] approach ideological issues with great care . . . and carefully avoid party-political issues. At the same time it should be up to date, varied and of a high artistic level.' In practice much of broadcasting provided light fare, and one spoke of the *Unterhaltungsfunk*, chat-shows and 'pop'-type music, but the radio also performed an important role as a populariser of 'High Culture'. This applied above all to serious, classical music; for all those, especially workers, with little opportunity for regular concert-going, 'it was the wireless which [had] opened up a whole branch of art'. This also applied to a lesser degree to drama, and to the newly developed radio play, which gave great scope for experimentation.[11]

German Social Democracy saw in radio a potentially great force to the good, which, being in the public domain and ideally amenable to public influence and pressure, should be more responsive than the essentially capitalist medium of the cinema. The ideals of the party, and its identification with education and the arts, made it stress the cultural role of broadcasting, over which it could hope to exercise some control through the network's Cultural Advisory Committees (Kultur-Beiräte) on which the SPD was often represented.[12]

The SPD's criticism of broadcasting policies was directed at the companies' failure to involve the working class and its representatives directly in programmes which would cater for their needs and use their language. The party, and, more specifically, the socialist radio fans, the Arbeiter Radio Klubs (later Arbeiter Radio

---

10. Pohle (note 7), p. 62.
11. Cited in Pohle (note 7) from a lecture by Bredow in February 1928; F. Scherret, 'Proletarischer Rundfunk', *Arbeiter Jugend*, 1930, vol. 22, pp. 156–8.
12. On the *Kulturbeiräte* see Lerg (note 6), pp. 394–403.

Bund or ARB) which had grown out of groups of wireless hob-byists into a cultural pressure-group, sought to direct the radio more towards the needs and interest of working people.[13] An example of this was the demand for the broadcasting of *Arbeiter-feste*, and the production of special programmes for the major annual celebrations of the labour movement, such as May Day or the anniversary of the Revolution.[14]

Social-democratic broadcasting policy also aimed at the intro-duction of regular services along the lines of the *Proletarische Morgenfeiern* as an alternative to broadcasts of religious services, so as to cater for the needs of agnostics and atheists. The SPD, however, rejected demands for special workers' radio, advocated by some workers' radio clubs. It wished to strengthen the role of the state in broadcasting, and to educate workers to be 'demanding listeners in a cultural as well as in a technical sense'.[15]

This rather evolutionary approach was not entirely shared by the workers' radio movement. Although still largely concerned with technical matters, and with the construction of wireless sets, among its aims was 'to make broadcasting serve the cultural aspirations of the working class'.[16] The *League* originally stood close to the SPD; but it drew members from all sections of the working class, and was thus subject to radical and communist pressure. Indeed, the Berlin section of the movement was under communist leadership until its expulsion by the pro-SPD leader-ship of the movement in 1928.

The more strongly politicised and vocal sections of the Workers' Radio League advocated a much more independent broadcasting policy for workers and the direct control of the programmes by working-class organisations, as well as a much greater emphasis on the broadcasting of writings by socialist and working-class authors. The party's line was less radical. The SPD recognised that radio programmes were biased in favour of conservative, nationalist and at times militarist views and sentiments, and that this tendency was less the result of action by administrators and producers than due to the intervention of the controlling committees. These, the party said, were either biased or so afraid of controversy that they censored everything controversial, so that the programmes had

13. From the reply of the SPD's General Education Council (see Dahl, note 9).
14. From the resolution of the *Reichsbildungskonferenz* of the SPD, cited in W. Bierbach, *Rundfunk zwischen Wirtschaftsinteressen und Politik*, Diss. Münster, 1980. (Also as book, Frankfurt, 1986).
15. Dahl (note 9), p. 58.
16. From the Statutes of the Arbeiter Radio Klubs cited in Dahl (note 9), p. 154.

become irrelevant for the workers.[17]

Carl Severing justified the operation of a system of internal censorship because Germany had not so far reached the necessary degree of tolerance to allow uncontrolled broadcasting. Radio listeners had to be educated to be tolerant of the views of others, and until this was achieved censorship would continue to be necessary.[18]

Social-democratic tactics *vis-à-vis* the broadcasting system relied on trying to exert pressure on the organisation through its membership of the relevant committees or through people active in the media. Such a pressure-group policy, which worked *within* the system, was frequently frustrated by the party-political and ideological neutrality which prevented the representation of workers' problems in as far as they were related to economic and political issues. Thus when, after prolonged pressure by the SPD, the West German Radio (WERAG), in common with a few other stations, instituted a series of 'Hours for the Worker' (*Arbeiterstunden*) the Director of the company, Hardt, was anxious to defend himself against possible bias. He said that the station had acceded to the request only after prolonged examination. The task of broadcasting was to bridge social differences, not to deepen them, and this programme was 'to bring from the world of the worker that which united all – humanity'.[19]

A list of the broadcasts shows that they were either talks or readings from workers' autobiographies or of other literature, and that we are largely concerned with historical or artistic themes. There were some talks on housing or legal matters, but none that dealt with burning contemporary issues. Some of the participants in the programmes were connected with the trade unions or other labour-movement organisations, but there is no suggestion that the series as a whole was a forum where issues which currently concerned workers could be discussed.[20]

By contrast to the political line of the SPD that of the KPD was

17. Arthur Crispien in the Reichstag debate of 23 March 1928, cited in Lerg (note 6), p. 366.
18. Carl Severing, speaking at an *Arbeiterfunktag* in Berlin in 1930, cited in Dahl (note 9), p. 57.
19. Bierbach (note 14), p. 366. See also *Arbeiterkultur in Hamburg* (note 7), pp. 267–8 for an account of the 'Hours for the Workers' in the programmes of the North German Broadcasting Station.
20. Cf. Bierbach (note 14), p. 367. Dieter Langewiesche thinks that the scope of these series was agreeable to the trade unions, who were looking at them in terms of their educational programmes. See his introduction to the reprint of the *Gewerkschaftszeitung, 1924–1928*, Bonn, 1988.

almost entirely antagonistic to the existing broadcasting system. Formally, this found expression in the Freie Radio Bund Deutschlands (FRBD), founded in 1929 following the expulsion of the Berlin section of the ARB. The FRBD concentrated more on producing a regular and sharp critique of the existing programmes, and on the organisation of listening circles for the German-language broadcasts of Radio Moscow. These assembled in the flats of members, and their scope was restricted by the limited availability of multi-valve receivers.

The communist fight against the wireless was increasingly carried out on the plane of political demonstrations. The party was rightly aggrieved that it was refused broadcasting time for the Reichstag elections in the summer of 1932, and the 'Free League' organised protest actions against the *Rundfunkreaktion* under the slogan *Rundfunk frei für Liste 3* ('Make the radio free for List 3' – the KPD list). They hoped to mobilise a 'common front of all working-class radio listeners' in a fight against a system which was hostile to them, while utilising the agitation at the same time in the on-going electoral struggle.[21]

Looking at the attitude of the labour movement to broadcasting as a whole, we find at one extreme a demand for an ideologically based radio. This was expressed most vocally by the Communist Party; but it was a view which at one time was shared also by sections in the Workers' Radio Clubs, and it could been met only by a separate wireless station. At the other end of the spectrum, represented largely by those concerned with trade union education, broadcasting was to help in the dissemination of knowledge for the worker. In one sense this was an extension of the adult education system; but it was also conceived in terms of the special information needed by workers for their jobs and careers.[22] In the middle was the majority view of the SPD, which sought to tilt the balance of broadcasting more in the direction of subjects of interest to the working class or representing socialist culture. This assumed the basic neutrality of the system, at a time when a more forceful propagation of the ideals of social democracy might have been indicated.

21. *Arbeitersender*, 28 October 1932, quoted in Lerg (note 6), p. 514. See also H. Wunderer, *Arbeitervereine und Arbeiterparteien* Frankfurt, 1980, pp. 182–3.
22. Cf. D. Langewiesche, 'Kompetenzerweiterung und Bildung. Zur Bedeutung der Bildungsarbeit der Gewerkschaften in der Weimarer Republik', (Introduction to the reprint of the *Gewerkschaftszeitung*, 1924–28), Berlin–Bonn, 1984, pp. 11–30, pp. 28–9.

The Cinema – Creator of Illusion or Weapon for the Revolution?

Of all the recreational activities in which German workers and their families engaged outside the home cinema-going was probably the most popular. During the 1920s millions of workers regularly went to the 'flicks', and paid between 50 pfennigs and one mark for a seat, depending on the size and location of the film theatre.

The rise of the film as mass entertainment dates back to the years before the First World War. Initially a mere curiosity, shown in movable, tent-like structures at fairs or markets, or installed in larger public houses, the cinema became more permanent in the years immediately before 1914, when the first purpose-built cinemas also came into being.[23] The pre-war and war years saw a considerable expansion in public viewing, and by 1918 there were 2,300 cinemas with some 800,000 seats. Ten years later these figures had risen to over 5,000 'film-theatres', with 1,940,000 seats.[24] During that period the German film industry produced an average of 250 films a year – a total of 2,300 between 1923 and 1932.[25] Estimates suggest that in 1926 one and a half to two million people went to the cinema on an average day, and 800,000 of these were thought to be workers.[26]

The habit of regular film-going was essentially a feature of city life – rural areas had relatively few cinemas. By and large the workers were attracted to the many suburban cinemas, which tended to change their programmes twice weekly. The large picture-palaces in the city centres were rarely visited by workers and their families. Hamburg, for example, had in 1930 seventy-two cinemas with 50,000 seats, not counting theatres in Altona, which included the *Reeperbahn* entertainment area which served the two cities. The average size of the cinemas was therefore about 700 seats; but the number included the gigantic UFA Palast, with 2,667 seats, as well as 'flea pits' with just over 100 seats. In 1929 there were an estimated 14 million visits to Hamburg cinemas, or 13 visits per inhabitant.[27]

A contemporary observer reported that he 'ascertained repeatedly that even on the finest summer Sunday afternoons a large cinema in a Berlin working-class suburb was already full to over-

23. R. Pabst (ed.), *Das Deutsche Lichtspieltheater*, (place unknown), 1926.
24. *Arbeiterjugend*, 1931, p. 40.
25. Ibid.
26. INPREKOR, 1926, no. 7, p. 165.
27. *Arbeiterkultur in Hamburg* (note 7), p. 298.

flowing at 4 o'clock in the afternoon'.[28] Cinema-going was probably more popular among workers who were politically unattached
and generally uninterested in politics. For this section of the audience, who frequently read neither book nor newspaper, the cinema
created illusions and satisfied dreams:

> the visit to the cinema was (often) the only occasion when they gained
> impressions and stimuli beyond the events of their everyday lives. The
> cinema is the only place where they can obtain more comprehensive
> views of the world . . . The young proletarian woman learns through
> the cinema to venerate those Olympian heights where the stars show her
> how to attract love and gain money, drive in motorcars, dance and wear
> beautiful clothes for ever.[29]

The contrast between social reality and the film-generated dream
world was greatest for the working-class housewife and the young
working girl who could not hope to apply any of the 'lessons' of
the romantic film idols. If she tried she would only estrange herself
and her feelings from her proletarian background, without being
able to imitate the lifestyles which the moving picture conjured up
before her eyes.[30] The criticism levelled against films was thus
based as much on moral considerations as on political ones. It was
connected with an attitude which thought that purely recreational
leisure-time pursuits were less valuable than the purposeful and
educational ones.

Before 1914 film production was largely involved in the creation
of humorous and entertaining short films, a series of which made
up a cinema programme. Many of the later full-length films were
merely seeking to entertain, and such films, it was argued, gave no
lasting benefit to the viewer. For Klara Zetkin, an ardent champion
of culture and art for the working class, 'the cinema robbed the
worker of precious leisure hours.' It destroyed valuable energy
which should be devoted to the struggle for the liberation of the
working class. At least three-quarters of regular film-goers should
not be there, but 'at political or trade union discussion, or taking
part in socialist educational activities.'[31]

Such a view seems exaggerated and excessively critical; but in
general the initial attitude of organised labour to the film as enter-

---

28. R. Weimann, 'Vom Film', *Der Führer*, 1929, p. 53.
29. E. Kramer, 'Politische Filmkritik', *MdVA*. 1 March 1928, pp. 4–5.
30. Alice Lex, 'Die Frau und der Film', *Arbeiterbühne und Film*, 1931, no. 5, p. 12.
31. Klara Zetkin, 'Gegen das Kinowesen', *Der Sozialdemokrat*, 11 December 1919,
    cited in Toni Stooss, 'Erobert den Film, oder Prometheus gegen UFA & Co', in
    WgdW, 482–525, p. 494.

tainment was negative, and continued to be so in the early years of the Republic. The SPD was particularly concerned about the harmful influence of the cinema on working-class youth. Before the war the party had been equally disturbed by the pernicious influence of trashy literature, the so-called *Schundliteratur*, and it had agitated for some control.[32] After 1918 they worried about the danger of the trashy movie. In 1919 the Berlin 'Committee to combat *Schundliteratur*' staged a large demonstration against bad films, in which social democrats participated; and the Hamburg Lichtspielausschuß also sought to protect the young against films considered harmful. In Magdeburg a meeting representative of all political parties unanimously adopted a resolution urging the reintroduction of film censorship.[33]

Films were also attacked on moral grounds, these attacks showing at times a bigoted and philistine streak, reminiscent of the debate on the content of the *Neue Welt* in 1896.[34] When after the war a film with the title 'Dangers of the Streets' was thought to paint a rather attractive picture of prostitution, the *Proletarier Jugend*, the organ of the youth section of the USPD, urged warning and boycott.[35] The existence of prostitution, it pointed out, was not the fault of the prostitute but of the capitalist system. The young workers were urged to keep their eyes open. '. . . look around you and see how they seek to pervert you. No comrade should support such capitalist vehicles for the expression of power. Enlighten your brothers and sisters who still queue in front of the cinema about the aims and consequences of the capitalist film.'[36] In a more positive vein the journal of the youth section of the Metalworkers' Union regularly published lists of recommended films and of films which should be avoided.

The argument against commercial films often went further than an attack on their moral character. The major charge was directed at their tendency to show the world in a rosy light, and to offer the viewer, and especially the oppressed and impoverished worker, a vicarious satisfaction. Moreover, the political left saw the commercial film as a weapon of ideological persuasion.[37] It transmitted

32. For the original attempts by the SPD to counter the influence of inferior literature on working-class youth see G. Fülberth, *Proletarische Partei und bürgerliche Literatur*, Neuwied and Berlin, 1972, pp. 114–19.
33. *Arbeiterjugend*, 1919, p. 251. Film censorship was reintroduced in 1920.
34. On the *Neue Welt* debate see Chapter 1 above.
35. There were other films which claimed to serve the purpose of sexual enlightenment, but were, in effect, subtly voyeurist.
36. A. Oelssner, 'Augen auf', *Proletarier Jugend*, 1920 no. 5, p. 3.
37. In 1932 the UFA, then under the control of the Hugenberg Konzern, resolved

bourgeois values and a conservative, nationalist interpretation of history, and frequently extolled the virtues of militarism disguised as patriotism. 'The style of the German film of the 1920s', wrote *Der Querschnitt durch 1922*, 'is the style of the old Empire, a blown-up pomposity. From *Pharaoh's Wife* to *Fredericus Rex*, one continuous *Siegesallee*'.[38]

Against this view we must put a more positive assessment of the medium of the film which had already begun to be expressed before the war, and which gained ground in the years after 1918. In this view the SPD should encourage a critical understanding of the new medium in its working-class audience, support good films, set about establishing a workers' cinema and embark on the production of films consonant with its ideas and values for proletarian viewers.[39]

Not to do so, a writer was already arguing before the war, would leave this powerful instrument in the hands of other political groups, who would use it for their own political ends.[40] Speaking concretely, the pro-film lobby suggested that cinema criticism should be a regular feature of the social-democratic press, so that workers would learn to approach films critically. The party and the trade unions should also install projection facilities in the new social centres, the *Gewerkschaftshäuser* and *Volkshäuser*, and fit out mobile cinemas.[41] According to this argument, not all commercial films were bad, and there was great scope for the 'Film-Drama', which, it was hoped, would bring serious literature to the masses in film form.[42]

After the Revolution the SPD began to see the need to create its own films, and, more importantly, to acquire good films for hire. This policy led to the establishment of a film-distribution agency, the Film und Lichtbilddienst, which was attached to the central party organisation. On the other hand the protagonists of the film acknowledged that the workers could not exert any real pressure on either film producers or distributors or cinema-owners to improve the quality of films made or shown. Although the working class

---

to stop producing entertainment films and concentrate on the production of national, viz., nationalistic films. Cf. Stooss (note 31), p. 520.

38. Cited in Stooss (note 31), p. 520. *Pharaoh's Wife* and *Fredericus Rex* were popular films. The *Siegesallee* in Berlin celebrated Germany's victories and victorious generals.
39. F. Forster, 'Das Kino Problem und die Arbeiter', *NZ* 1913/14, vol. i, pp. 482–7.
40. S. Drucker, 'Das Kino Problem und unsere Gegner', *NZ* 1913/14, vol. i, pp. 867–72, 907–12.
41. Drucker (note 40).
42. Forster (note 39).

constituted a significant section of the total cinema audience, it could not be mobilised as a pressure-group to force local cinemas to change their programmes. The parties of the left came therefore to accept the idea that they had to go their own way in the production and showing of films more in line with their views and policies.

The socialists took the first steps in the direction of a 'Workers' Cinema' by creating a system of mobile cinemas. They were first used in the 1928 election, and showed only party propaganda films. Later the SPD provided more general film entertainment through the medium of the party's film-hiring agency, which made available films of higher quality and with a progressive message, as well as shorter documentaries and films with cultural themes.

The SPD's own film production was restricted by lack of finance and by the limited availability of expertise. The SPD sought to create films with a 'republican and socially progressive spirit', and it hoped to extend their appeal to the whole of the working class.[43] It also produced a few longer films through the medium of small independent film-producers, who used mainly amateur actors.[44]

To help in the creation of a new type of cinema a number of left-wing radicals, social democrats and communists founded in 1928 the Volks-Filmverband (VFV) the 'People's Film Society', which they hoped to turn into a cultural mass movement. Starting from the recognition that the importance of the film was greater than that of any other art-form, because of its potentially large public and its correspondingly greater influence, the society set itself the task of 'organising the broad masses of working-class cinema-goers and educating them to critical understanding of the film'. The Society admitted that the cinema was bound primarily to fulfil the need for relaxation and amusement, 'but [it] believed that amusement need not be identical with trash, and that relaxation need not mean spiritual impoverishment'.[45] The VFV believed, without adducing any evidence, that large sections of the working class were dissatisfied with the existing bourgeois films; their aim was to mobilise this dissatisfaction and to strengthen the demand for the working-class film.

43. S. Nestriepke, 'Die technischen und kulturellen Möglichkeiten des Films' in Sozialistischer Kulturbund, *Film und Funk* (Proceedings of the *Sozialistische Kulturtag*, 1929), Berlin, 1929.
44. In 1930 the stock of films available for hire contained only six full-length feature films. The majority of the films were shorts of less than 300m in length.
45. From the 'Foundation Appeal' of the *Volksfilmverband* reprinted in G. Kühn *et al.* (eds), *Film und revolutionäre Arbeiterbewegung*, 2 vols, 1975, vol. 2, pp. 236–7.

Strictly speaking the organisation was a federation of local societies, and it was the Berlin body, the first and largest, which gave
its name to the whole movement. At the beginning there were
branches in Hamburg, Frankfurt, Breslau, Dresden and Darms-
tadt. By 1930 there existed 14 VFV branches throughout Berlin,
and a total of 30 local societies in the rest of the country.[46]

The national association never achieved the hoped-for mass
following. They aimed at a membership of 200,000, and thought
that this would have made it possible for them to produce their
own films and exercise real influence on the commercial cinema. A
larger membership might even have permitted the establishment in
Berlin of a 'West End' type of cinema for the première showing of
progressive films. But this was not to be. The few thousand who
joined came by and large from the two parties of the Left, although
the organisation also secured support from the ranks of the radical
intelligentsia. Thus Heinrich Mann figured as the President of the
Volksfilmverband, and the local honorary committees contained
mostly bourgeois radicals.

Having failed to become a mass-movement the Volksfilmverband now thought of itself as a *Kampfgemeinschaft* to combat the
exploitation of the masses through the 'deceitful, inartistic and
reactionary film'. The more strongly political, and largely pro-
communist, members now recognised that the fight against the
reactionary film also meant 'to agitate among the masses and direct
the fight energetically at the low level of want of the broad
masses'.[47] The VFV attempted to unleash a mass-protest against
films like *Alt-Heidelberg*, which glorified life in the student fraternities, and the militarist *Fredericus Rex* series. It spoke out against
the bias in the allegedly neutral newsreels.[48]

The organisation failed to create such a critical-combative climate of opinion in the working masses. It remained, in effect, an
association of film clubs, 'a society of cinema fans which sold cheap
tickets for progressive films to its members'.[49] Local groups of the
VFV tended to arrange regular series of 'Film Evenings', in which
'progressive' and original, mostly foreign, films were shown.
Apart from Russian films they were, however, commercial productions, and although they were thought to be free from the bias
of much of the German film industry, they were not necessarily

46. Stooss (note 31), note 109.
47. 'Das 2. Jahr', *Volk und Film*, 1929, no. 3.
48. Franz Höllering, 'Eroberung des Films', *Volk und Film*, 1928, nos. 3 and 4, pp.
   4–5, no. 5, pp. 3–4.
49. 'Das 2. Jahr', *Volk und Film*, 1929, no. 3.

films with a social content.[50] Thus the practical work of the Volksfilmverband during its short existence was not very different from the practice of many working-class organisations which during the last few years of the Republic increasingly put on film shows for their members or as part of campaigns to boost membership. Thus in Berlin there were in January 1929 fifty-two such film shows.[51]

The Volksfilmverband presents a number of interesting features. It united in one organisation communists, social democrats and bourgeois radicals who were genuinely interested in the cinema and critical of current trends in commercial film production. The impetus for its foundation, and the driving force behind it, was largely communist, and the editor of its journal, *Volk und Film*, was Franz Höllering, a close collaborator of Willi Münzenberg. These groups were little concerned with the aesthetic and broadly cultural aspects of film which moved middle-class members. They did not seek the cultivation of the 'good bourgeois film' practised within the VFV. As in the field of music, communists wished to promote the *Tendenzfilm*, the committed movie, which would stimulate political action.[52]

At the end, the communist view prevailed in the VFV. The early assertion that there were large number of dissatisfied viewers who were only waiting for a better and more wholesome diet proved illusory. In contrast to a viewing policy based on aesthetics the communists in the organisation demanded a more active, and, if necessary, a more forceful policy against the bourgeois film and in favour of a committed cinema. This was to be not merely cultural but a basis for political action and demonstration, as in the case of a mass meeting in Hamburg in October 1929 in which Eisenstein, the creator of *Battleship Potemkin*, spoke. With the economic crisis the VFV too found itself in a crisis situation. It had to discontinue the publication of *Volk und Film*, which was amalgamated with the journal of the Workers' Theatre League, and the organisation eventually became absorbed in the communist Ifa organisation. As its film section its practical activities were now directed increas-

---

50. Films shown by the Hamburg VFV in 1939, when it was already under communist direction, included Stroheim's *Gier nach Geld*, Mittler's *Jenseits des Stroms*, Protasanov's *Kellner aus dem Palasthotel* and Eisenstein's *Kampf um die Erde. Arbeiterkultur in Hamburg* (note 8), p. 316.
51. Das 2. Jahr (note 49).
52. For an account of communist views and policies within the VFV see H.M. Bock, 'Brüder zur Sonne zur Freiheit. Kino, Film und Arbeiterbewegung' in *Arbeiterkultur in Hamburg*, (note 8), pp. 297–316, especially pp. 312–16.

ingly at general political protest and at the task of mobilising grass-roots support for a more aggressive policy of demonstrations against cinema-owners who showed nationalist or militarist films with the object of forcing them to show 'proletarian' films. Such mass-actions were meant to go beyond the aims of a cultural policy, and by their appeal to the unorganised to raise revolutionary consciousness; but the section also wanted to assist in film-production by the workers themselves. The aim was the *Agitpropisierung* of the proletarian film, to make films analogous to the agitprop theatre.[53] Given the economic situation and the cost of film-making, even using eight- or sixteen-millimetre film, such a policy could hardly succeed.

The development of the Volksfilmverband illustrates the different approaches to the cinema of the social-democratic and the communist movements. For the social democrats the bourgeois film was in the last resort to be judged by its artistic and aesthetic qualities, and they believed in the possible reform and improvement of the cinema through the production of films of a better quality and by a more positive attitude on the part of the film industry to working-class aspirations. Siegfried Nestriepke, the administrator of the Berlin Volksbühne, thought that 'the truly artistic will always enrich our knowledge of people and of life [and] the ideologically-conditioned attitudes of the artists do not matter'.[54] The films which the SPD produced concentrated largely on the activities of social-democratic organisations, portraying, for example, life in the socialist workers' youth, whose hikes and camps provided photogenic backgrounds. Alternatively, they featured the achievements of the party, as demonstrated in the institutions created by the labour movement, or established by governments or municipalities as a direct result of working-class pressure.[55] Only a few feature films were produced under social-democratic influence.

The Communist Party, in contrast to the SPD, rejected the whole system of bourgeois film production. This was not only because of the alleged tendentiousness of the individual capitalist film. The KPD believed that because of its economic basis, the bourgeois film industry could only produce films of a low artistic

53. Cf. Bock (note 52); K. Senda and H. Lüdecke, 'Agitpropisierung des proletarischen Films', *Arbeiterbühne und Film*, 1931, no. 5, pp. 8–10.
54. S. Nestriepke (note 43).
55. For a list of films available from the SPD *Lichtbilddienst* see G. Kühn *et al.* (eds), *Film und revolutionäre Arbeiterbewegung*, 2 vols, Berlin, 1975, vol. 2, pp. 462–7.

value.[56] 'Whoever controls film production, controls, in effect, the ideology of the great masses of the population,' the communist critic Axel Eggebrecht wrote in 1922.[57] In the place of the bourgeois film the KPD wished to put the proletarian film, whose object was primarily to educate and to commit the viewer, although for aestheticians and film critics, like Bela Balasz, it had also to be a work of art and had to provide entertainment for a large section of the working class.[58] The realisation of such a programme was not easy. The KPD too produced shortish documentaries and used them in its campaign; but the economic depression halted this development, and proposals to use film extensively for political propaganda, advocated by the party after 1930, came to nothing. The Ifa slogan of the *Agitproprisierung* of the film remained a slogan, except inasmuch as it related to attacks on bourgeois films.

The production of full-length films presented immense difficulties; but it is here that issues of political aesthetics emerge. For the communist movement the problem of presenting films with the right kind of tendency to working-class audiences was partly solved by importing Soviet films, especially those produced under the auspices of Meshabprom, the Russian section of the International Workers' Aid organisation (IAH) and distributed through Weltfilm GmbH, a subsidiary of the German IAH, which was directed by Willi Münzenberg. Among Meshabprom productions were documentaries on the achievements and the suffering of the Russian people which were to help with fund-raising for relief work in the Soviet Union.

Münzenberg, who was also the head of the major communist publishing empire, wished to create in the film 'a weapon in the arsenal of agitation and propaganda of the communist party'. Weltfilm arranged the German distribution of such films as Eisenstein's *Battleship Potemkin*, and later his *October* as well as Pudovkin's *The Mother* (based on Gorki's novel) and his *Storm over Asia*. To supplement imported Russian films, which circulated both as general releases and more especially for working-class audiences, Münzenberg founded the Prometheus film company to produce German proletarian films. Beginning with a sobering and saddening social reportage on the famine and the suffering in the Waldenburg mining area, the enterprise went on to produce more

---

56. W. Münzenberg, *Erobert den Film*, Berlin, 1925, p. 10.
57. Stooss (note 31), p. 495.
58. B. Balasz, 'Der reaktionäre Film', *RF* 10 October 1922, reprinted in M. Brauneck, *Die Rote Fahne*, Munich, 1973, pp. 175–77.

politically challenging films, culminating in two classic proletarian films, *Mutter Krause's Fahrt ins Glück* and *Kuhle Wampe*.[59]

Mutter Krause is a widow who barely manages to feed herself and her two unemployed grown-up children from her wages as a newspaper deliverer. When her son helps her to collect the paper money he spends it in the pub. Unable to replace the money he attempts a robbery, bungles it, and is arrested. The daughter considers prostitution, but draws back at the last moment. For the honest and upright Mother Krause there is only one way out: suicide. Only the daughter finds a positive answer to her misery. She meets Max the class-conscious worker, and joins him in a communist demonstration.

The intimate setting and the concentration on individual fates in this film is not very different from the character of the social-democratic feature film *Lohnbuchhalter Krempe*. This is the story of a wages clerk who loses his job because of the mechanisation of the payroll accounting, and whose daughter marries below his status aspirations for her. He too commits suicide, and the film ends with shots of a demonstration which marches up to the Reichstag, calling for work. Thus the ending of this and of other social-democratic films shows 'a lack of perspective, or rather its conversion into a general humanistic formula or the call to vote for the SPD.'[60]

Kuhle Wampe, subtitled *Wem gehört die Welt?* ('To whom does the world belong?') although it has individual, identifiable characters, deals much more with broad social forces and a didactic theme. Produced by a collective whose most prominent members were Bertolt Brecht, Hanns Eisler and Slatan Dudow, the Director, it is a film of the suffering *and* the struggling proletariat. It begins with an unsuccessful chase by unemployed young workers in Berlin after a vacancy. He returns to his family, and, after a row with his father, commits suicide. The family, long in arrears with its rent, is evicted and settles in the permanent camping place *Kuhle Wampe*. There workers are seen both in a boozy maudlin engagement party

59. On Münzenberg see B. Gross, *Münzenberg, eine politische Biographie*, Stuttgart, 1967; F. Raddatz, *Erfolg oder Wirkung. Schicksale politischer Publizistik in Deutschland*, Munich, 1972; R. Surmann, *Die Münzenberg Legende*, Berlin, 1983.

60. Stooss (note 31), p. 507. The ending of another social-democratic film is similar. *Brüder* (Brothers) has the Hamburg Dock Strike of 1896/7 as its theme. It shows how a worker becomes involved in the strike, how he mobilises others. His own class-consciousness is strengthened and his recognition of the enemy is made concrete. Yet in the end all we are left with is a general sentiment of how even this unsuccessful strike awakened enthusiasm in thousands who might otherwise have remained apathetic. See Stooss p. 510 for an account of this film.

(presaging a 'shot-gun' wedding which does not take place) and in disciplined athletics performed by thousands of worker sportsmen, pointing up the solidarity which is symbolised in this display. And, in place of the demonstrations of the earlier films, *Kuhle Wampe* ends in a dialectical discussion among the passengers on a crowded journey home, occasioned by a newspaper report about the burning of coffee in Brazil. To the mocking question 'who will change the world' the answer is 'those who do not like it as it is'.[61]

Mutter Krause and *Kuhle Wampe* were films which satisfied the political demand for the visual representation of the dialectical tensions in working-class existence at the time of the depression. *Kuhle Wampe* especially was, with its crowd scenes, also a pioneering work in an aesthetic sense; but these or similar proletarian films could not furnish an answer to the needs of workers for distraction and entertainment. Nor could a limited number of Russian films fill the gap.

The cinema industry was fed with a constant stream of entertainment films from the dream factories in Hollywood and Babelsberg – the home of the German UFA film company; and the films produced under communist or social-democratic auspices, which totalled only a few dozen feature films or major documentaries, hardly made an impact. The German industry had of course produced some major films – mostly using expressionist techniques; but the great majority of commercially produced films were shows of glitter and of 'happy endings'.

Even the pure entertainment film, however, might have artistic merits, as did some of the great comic films of the era of the silent film. The labour movement had acknowledged the importance of the cinema as the theatre of the masses; but communists especially looked at the film primarily in terms of its political message and of the values which it conveyed. They did not look at the film as a work of art, or accept the relative innocuousness of some degree of vicarious satisfaction. There was a failure to understand what it was in the medium that 'made large numbers of ever so class-conscious comrades go and see the most foolish and stupid military and *Alt Heidelberg* type of film'.

To change the character of the commercially-produced German film would have demanded extensive consumer resistance. This could probably only have been brought about via a major educational and propaganda campaign in the working class; and this

61. Cf. *Kuhle Wampe oder Wem gehört die Welt?* (text and production notes), Frankfurt, 1969.

was not attempted. Moreover, it would have demanded a more sophisticated approach to film its positive role as mass entertainment than the strongly moralistic or exclusively political approach which generally prevailed in the labour movement.[62]

Old Media in a New Garb

Among the media of instruction and entertainment of the German workers we must not forget the oldest and most ubiquitous medium, the printed word. Newspapers and books, their publishers and purveyors, played a salient role in the organisation and utilisation of workers' leisure and in their self-education. In Germany, as elsewhere in industrial Europe, self-education helped to create successive generations of working-class leaders. Wenzel Holek, a one-time unskilled worker, described this process in an article with the telling title *Wie ich mich emporlas* – 'How I rose through reading'.[63] Although Holek hardly refers to the press, the socialist newspaper was from the beginning of the greatest importance for the political education of the German working class. Perusing the paper after a long day's work was often the only regular reading of the industrial worker. In addition, the politically committed worker might have bought one or the other pamphlet or book on political, economic or social subjects, issued in large editions by the SPD or by one of the other social-democratic publishing houses.[64]

Workers and their families might also obtain other reading, mostly of cheap fiction, through purchases of serial novel or adventure stories sold by itinerant traders, and hence known as *Kolportageromane*.[64] Most importantly however, organised workers

62. Cf. H. Siemsen, 'Arbeiterschaft und Kino' *Klassenkampf*, 1927, vol. 1 no. 1, pp. 23–4 and vol. 2 no. 3, pp. 81–2 (quote on p. 82).
63. *Der Bibliothekar*, vol. 3, 1911, pp. 357–61; K. Keck, *Arbeits und Kulturmilieu der Arbeiterschaft*, Leipzig, 1911, p. 31.
64. It was estimated that before 1914 the *Vorwärts* Bookshop, effectively the publishing house of the SPD, produced annually 1.6 million books and pamphlets. Other social-democratic publishers had some 800 titles in print. Prosperous and active local party organisations, such as the Hamburg SPD, had their own publishing programmes. Cf. E. Drahn, *Zur Entwicklung und Geschichte des sozialdemokratischen Parteibuchhandels*, 1913; SPD Hamburg, *Annual Reports*.
65. For the *Kolportageroman* see R.A. Fullerton, 'Creating a mass book market in Germany', *J. of Social History*, vol. 10, pp. 265–83; H.J. Steinberg, 'Workers' Libraries in Germany before 1914', *History Workshop Journal*, no. 1, 1976, pp. 166–80; D. Langewiesche and K. Schönhoven, 'Arbeiterbibliotheken und Arbeiterlektüre im Wilhelminischen Deutschland', *AfSG*, vol. 16, 1976, pp. 135–204.

would generally have access to the Arbeiterbibliotheken, set up in large numbers by individual trade unions or by local trades councils between 1890 and 1914. These libraries were conceived primarily in educational terms; but the extensive statistical material which we have about their stock and their users' reading habits suggest that workers' reading tended towards fiction and other popular literature. Workers' libraries continued their activities after 1918 – some 2,000 collections still existed in 1931, but workers turned increasingly for their reading to the communal libraries (Volksbibliotheken) set up by the municipalities. These were by and large the traditional institutions for working-class reading and for the provision of literature for education and enjoyment as they existed before 1914. We must now consider how in the period after the war, and in the period of the democratic republic, some of these media changed, and how others were created.

The socialist press was a powerful weapon of socialist and general enlightenment, but it did not reach the whole of the social-democratic masses. After the repeal of the anti-Socialist law in 1890 socialist newspapers grew rapidly in numbers and in readership. In 1912 there were 89 socialist newspapers, with a total circulation of 1,478,000. Newspaper readership was, of course, larger than circulation; yet of the total social-democratic electorate in that year of over 4 million a substantial number must have made do without a paper or read the popular bourgeois press, the so-called *General-Anzeiger Presse*.

Social-democratic newspapers were from the beginning highly politicised and rather tedious in style, and made no concessions to the ordinary reader's desire for 'human interest' reading or even for general local news. The newspapers were slow in news coverage, and 'replaced variety, the alpha and omega of the modern newspaper, by their thoroughness in respect of what they covered'.[66] After the revolution the mighty social-democratic newspaper empire experienced a crisis. The split in the labour movement meant that the newly founded communist dailies and the papers which the Independent Social Democrats took with them now competed with the old papers. After the split of the USPD in 1922 between those who joined the KPD and the majority, who returned to the SPD, there was a further realignment of the press.

Even more serious for the formation of a socialist public opinion was the fact that the growth in trade union membership after the

---

66. Cf. K. Koszyk, *Zwischen Kaiserreich und Diktatur. Die sozialdemokratische Presse, 1914–1933*, Heidelberg, 1968, p. 29.

war was not reflected in circulation figures. In 1922 it was estimated that only some 100,000 of Berlin's 800,000 trade unionists read a socialist or a communist paper.[67] Equally damaging was the economic effect of inflation and the scarcity and high price of newsprint, all coming at a time when there was a great need to modernise and replace plant in order to compete with the bourgeois press. Economic pressure thus forced a re-organisation of the social-democratic press, and this provoked a re-thinking of the aims and contents of the papers. Yet local party representatives, hitherto solely responsible for their publications, were anxious to preserve the primacy of the papers' political and educational functions, while the SPD's national leadership and many of the journalists argued that if the press was to attract more readers it must change its character and widen its appeal.

The first step towards a more modern socialist press, and one with an improved circulation, came with the reluctant acceptance of advertising, although local Pressekommissionen (the supervisory boards for the individual papers) continued to agonise over the contents. In 1925 the SPD set up the Konzentration A.G. to act as a central holding agency and a central purchasing agent, and as auditors of the financial performance of the local newspaper publishers.[68] The agency distributed loans and subsidies and insisted as a condition that the newspaper receiving them should respond to the taste of the vast masses of workers for less political and more entertaining papers. Papers should reduce their political content in favour of more news and more material which related to the worker's daily environment in the locality and in the region, and should provide more stories and more pictures. 'It was essential to depoliticise the local-provincial part, polemicise less, and chat more.'[69]

The new editorial policy and the improved appearance of the papers managed to boost circulation figures. After the end of the inflation the circulation of social-democratic newspapers rose to 1,090,000, and it reached its post-war peak with 1,300,000 copies in 1929 – not surprisingly below the pre-war total of 1,500,000, in view of the split in the labour movement. The number of papers also rose to over 200, but largely as a result of a growth in the number of local editions of established papers. Individual regional

---

67. Ibid., quoting *Die Freiheit*, 22 August 1922, which probably meant subscribers.
68. Cf. Konzentration A.G., *Unsere Betriebe, 1890–1925*, Berlin, 1925.
69. Wilhelm Sollmann at a meeting of the *Verein Arbeiterpresse*, the organisation of social-democratic journalists. Sollmann was a leading journalist, and at one time Minister of the Interior of the Reich.

papers, however, only rarely reached their pre-war maximum, and there was a great variation in the density of newspaper coverage. At best the circulation figures of social-democratic newspapers represented 7.05 copies per 100 people; at worst they reached less than one per cent of the population.[70]

In the widening and popularising of newspapers the *feuilleton* played a significant part. If before the war the discussion still centred on the quality of the literature in that part of the papers' output, its major theme during the Weimar years was the need to attract and retain readers. With the motto 'good and beautiful is what pleases [the reader]' the press sought to boost circulation figures and to prevent its politically not very strongly committed readers from deserting the paper; and this was seen as the paramount task of the growing band of literary editors.[71]

There is, of course, no way to ascertain which kind of literature readers of the social-democratic press preferred; one can only report the discussion within the SPD and among journalists about the principles which should underlie the selection. Before 1918 the underlying criterion was that the works of the imagination should underpin and supplement the political-ideological part of the paper.[72] We unfortunately lack a 'genre' type of analysis of the works which were serialised before the war and after the revolution, but there is evidence that before 1914 newspapers did indeed give some preference to the great historical-social novel. After the war the novels and stories were generally less weighty in character, and included more love stories and family novels. There were also a number of works with a local slant – *Heimatsromane* – and the literature reprinted in the bourgeois press and that which was offered by social-democratic newspapers became more alike.[73] In contrast, the communist press was inclined to print more *engagé* literature. Unlike the social-democratic press the communist newspapers – much more tightly controlled from the centre – were initially not seeking to enlarge their circulation beyond the circle of party members and committed adherents. In 1923 the KPD had 34 daily newspapers, of which 19 were the principal papers, and the rest only local editions. Their total circulation reached 395,000 in

---

70. The highest concentration of socialist newspaper coverage was in Saxony, the lowest in East Prussia.
71. K. Zorges, *Sozial Demokratische Presse und Literatur . . . 1876–1933*, Stuttgart, 1982, p. 108.
72. Ibid. p. 182.
73. Ibid. pp. 205–7.

the mid-1920s, but in 1929 it was down to 210,000.[74]

Like the social-democratic papers the communist press had an identity problem. The discussion on the 'Workers' Correspondents' showed how dissatisfaction with the dull and arid diet with which the communist newspapers fed their readers caused the press to mobilise its readers to report regularly about current issues at their workplace or their domicile. In this way in the mid-1920s the communist press sought to become more sympathetic to its readers; but, given its aims, it could hardly hope to become a genuine popular press. Any leavening of the character of the newspapers had to take place within a clearly-defined framework. It was assumed that the fact that readers and correspondents shared a similar background would make the latter's contributions more convincing, and thus lead to the establishment of a new type of press. The underlying assumption of the *Arbeiter Korrespondenten* movement, of a considerable degree of 'identity' in the experience of author and reader, was also applied to the *feuilleton* of the communist press.[75] The serialised novels in, for example, *Rote Fahne*, were not all expected to demonstrate the application of marxist dialectics and revolutionary theory; but the literature selected was to have a bearing on the current political situation. A reprint was generally accompanied by commentaries and explanations designed to 'integrate the work into the context of actual daily events'.[76] A list of novels which were serialised between 1920 and 1932 shows a mixture of bourgeois novels which exposed the capitalist system or satirised bourgeois society and militarism (Sinclair's *Petroleum* and Hasek's *Schweijk*) and social reportage novels, like Marchwitza's *Sturm auf Essen* or Crede's *Frauen in Not*, dealing respectively with the Ruhr under French occupation and with the problem of unwanted pregnancies.[77]

Even if the circulation of the social-democratic and the communist press fell far short of reaching all those who supported the two parties, the newspapers had a major influence on the working-class public. They remained, moreover, in spite of all innovation, primarily vehicles of political information and education. The rest of the workers' press, including the illustrated magazines and some of the special supplements of the daily papers, provided more

74. For a comprehensive bibliography of the communist press see C. Hempel-Küter, 'Die Tages und Wochenpresse der KPD', *IWK*, vol. 23, no. 1, pp. 27–46.
75. Brauneck (note 58), p. 31.
76. Ibid. p. 35.
77. Ibid. pp. 30–5 gives a list of fiction published in *Rote Fahne*.

information about the phenomenon of working-class culture. These publications related more directly to the everyday life and leisure of the worker and his family. Circulation figures for this section of the workers' press are difficult to come by, but probably a not insubstantial minority subscribed to such weekly or fort- nightly publications, some of which were aimed at a female readership.[78]

Of general importance as cultural magazines were the two illus- trated weeklies, *Volk und Zeit* and the *Arbeiter Illustrierte Zeitung*, generally known as AIZ. *Volk und Zeit* was the supplement of a large number of social-democratic newspapers. It appeared from 1919 until 1933 in several regional editions, which, while substan- tially identical, carried local material and adverts. It combined the character of an illustrated news magazine with that of an entertain- ment medium, offering also a limited amount of instruction. Its political message came to the fore in the frequent title-page draw- ings, marked by a realistic and at times a slightly romantic style. With these they conveyed a general message of hope and optimism over the realisation of their political ideals. In retrospect this mess- age seems strengthened by the general appearance of the paper, which was characterised by a high standard of photography and layout and by the frequent publication of photographs of the beautiful landscapes of Germany.

These illustrations can either be read simply as examples of the high artistic standards which characterised the paper, or, and more convincingly, they can be seen as a way to show aspects of the national heritage which the working class was now making its own. Similar sentiments are conveyed in the illustrated articles on some of the great artists of the past, or in the reproductions of their work which were published fairly regularly in the paper during its first year. Although some of the paintings reproduced have 'work' or 'industry' as their themes, or were politically inspired, many were printed as examples of the 'great art' which now formed part of the workers' heritage. The acceptance of the wider cultural tradition can also be seen in the way in which *Volk und Zeit* dealt with Christmas. Until the onset of the depression we regularly find rather uncritical photographs of the traditional secular symbols of the festival.

The communist AIZ was originally the magazine of the IAH, the

78. A description of many of the cultural and literary journals published by the SPD, the trade unions and other socialist organisations is given in F. Hüser, 'Literatur und Kulturzeitschriften der Arbeiterbewegung', in *Arbeiterbewegung, Erwachsenenbildung, Presse. (Festschrift für Walter Fabian)*, Cologne, 1977.

Workers' Aid Organisation, with an original title of *Sowjet Rußland im Bild* ('Soviet Russia in pictures'); and throughout its existence (1925–33) it was published independently of the communist party organisation by Willi Münzenberg's publishing empire. Much more than *Volk und Zeit* it sought to combine entertainment and instruction with political propaganda and education, and its character was also much more focused on reports from working-class life, ranging from sport to strikes.[79] Global political events found little coverage; but much space was devoted to reportage from the Soviet Union, often shown in a rosy light. At home part of its photographic coverage came through pictures taken by the group of worker photographers, the Arbeiterphotographen, who often produced intimate and realistic pictures of the minutiae of proletarian life.

The AIZ also published practical hints on domestic and house-hold matters, notes on games and puzzles, and a special children's section, all as part of its self-imposed task to act as a mouthpiece of the exploited and the fighting masses.[80] As a counterpart to this attempt at a portraiture of working-class life, its interpretation of events was more consistently political, and it sought to turn 'the everyday conscience of the worker into a revolutionary conscience'.[81] Such commitment came out most clearly in the many emotionally highly charged and strongly political title-pages of the AIZ, carrying drawings and photographs, especially after 1930, when John Heartfield became a regular contributor. His photomontages showed an uncompromising hostility to the bourgeoisie, to fascism, and frequently also to the SPD. They operated through the analysis and dissection of realistic and factual photographs and their re-combination and juxtaposition in a new and revealing context to provide new interpretations and new insights and contribute to the political education of the reader.[82]

Of the other popular magazines published by the parties of the Left those which addressed themselves to women, for example *Frauenwelt* (1924–33) and *Weg der Frau* (1931–3) are of particular interest. Unlike earlier publications, such as the social-democratic *Gleichheit*, edited by Klara Zetkin, these were not political journals.

79. On the AIZ see H. Willmann, *Geschichte der AIZ*, Berlin, 1974; G. Ricke, *Die Arbeiter Illustrierte Zeitung*, Hanover, 1974.
80. AIZ vol. 10, p. 193, quoted in Ricke (note 79), p. 73.
81. Ricke, quoting the AIZ, p. 79.
82. On photomontage see above all the books on John Heartfield, especially E. Siepmann, *Montage: John Heartfield*, Berlin, 1977; R. Maerz, *John Heartfield, Der Schnitte entlang der Zeit*, Dresden, 1981.

They were women's journals published by the socialist and communist movements respectively, which dealt with the domestic problems of working-class women as much as with the stimulation of leisure-time interests.

The social-democratic *Frauenwelt*, whose circulation reached the 120,000 mark, sought to combine serious cultural writing with advice on domestic issues. It took it for granted that the working-class woman had not much time or opportunity to read books or visit the theatre and cinema; and the magazine sought to satisfy her thirst for knowledge and show how much beauty there was in the world. 'Many of our best artists' Toni Sender, the newly appointed editor wrote in 1928, 'are moved by your fate and by the fate of our class, and you don't know each other.' She regarded it as her task to bring these two groups together. At the same time, the magazine wished 'to accompany its readers into their daily lives, make their daily chores easier and help them to make their home more beautiful and to simplify their household duties'.[83]

The communist *Weg der Frau* also aimed to be a popular magazine, combining entertainment with advice on the management of the home. This included hints for the making of clothes; but the proposal to issue an edition which also included dressmaking patterns like those which appeared already in the *Frauenwelt* was not realised. Judged by the character of the advice offered both magazines addressed themselves to women who had, in working-class terms, a relatively high standard of living; but the cultural part of *Weg der Frau* aimed a somewhat lower level of sophistication than the socialist women's magazine, which was more elaborately produced and illustrated, and, unlike *Frauenwelt*, it did not serialise novels.

In general the content of *Weg der Frau* was more political and more oriented towards political questions of particular interest to women. It also organised the circulating exhibition *Frauen in Not*, in which the problem of abortion was a central theme. *Frauenwelt* repeatedly published examples of art and literature which dealt with problems affecting women from a political point of view; but the paper also published much on female themes which had no specific political stance, and whose appeal was purely humanist.

Magazines and newspaper *feuilletons* were not the sole sources for working-class educational and recreational reading during the years

---

83. From the 'Letter to her Readers' by Toni Sender published in *Frauenwelt*, March 1928, p. 102. See also Sender's autobiography, *Memoirs of a Rebel*, London, 1940.

of the Weimar Republic. There was then, as earlier, book-borrowing and book-buying by workers. Some buying took place through the commercial booktrade and through itinerant book-dealers; but probably more important was the growing number of political bookshops. The SPD Parteibuchhandlung – the party bookshop – had branches in many places, while others were established by local social-democratic papers. Thus Hamburg had in 1930 seven bookshops run by the SPD paper the *Hamburger Echo*.[84] In addition there were two communist bookshops in Hamburg; but the KPD operated normally through a system of *Kolporteure*, who sold mostly party literature in factories and on housing estates.

What was novel and important, however, was the establishment during the period of economic recovery of a number of book-clubs for working-class readers. These were set up under the influence of trade unions, of the SPD, and, a little later, of the Communist Party. The first book-club was the Büchergilde Gutenberg, established in 1924 under the aegis of the printing trade union, and consequently distinguished from the outset by a high standard of book-production. At the same time the social-democratic publishing house Dietz promoted the Bücherkreis, and in 1926 Willi Münzenberg started the Universum Bücherei with his publishing firm *Neuer Deutscher Verlag*. All three organisations charged a membership fee of around one mark a month, for which the members received a book a quarter, as well as a magazine.

From the beginning all three book-clubs stressed their political commitment and their desire to assist in the creation of a new working-class culture; but the early publications of both Büchergilde und Bücherkreis did not really bear this out. The Büchergilde set out to publish 'books that give pleasure' and are 'full of good spirit and good to look at'[85] while the Bücherkreis 'wished to disseminate among its members work which will remain of permanent value for the working people of our time'.[86] The original emphasis of the two non-communist organisations was on the publication of good books of a high literary standard at a low cost, and there was as yet no strong ideological commitment. *Vorwärts* found no fault with this approach. For the central organ of the SPD the book-clubs were 'an important cultural factor' because they attempted 'to publish books by older and contemporary authors' and to 'do so in

84. *Arbeiterkultur in Hamburg* (note 8), p. 143.
85. M. Bühnemann and T. Friedrich, 'Zur Geschichte der Buchgemeinschaften der Arbeiterbewegung in der Weimarer Republik', in *WgdW*, 1977, Berlin, pp. 364–97, p. 368.
86. Ibid. p. 374.

a highly perfect form, and thus demonstrate what a really good book should look like'.[87]

With the advent of a new generation of editors the two socialist book-clubs began, however, to show a more radical profile. Under its new editor, Erich Knauf, the guild set out to be 'not just a community [of subscribers] . . . but the realisation of the cultural aspirations of the working class', and Karl Schröder, who took over the management of the Bücherkreis at about the same time, called it 'a tool in the service of the great socio-cultural movement of socialism'. It should become 'the axe and the swinger of the axe'.[88]

Schröder sought above all to cultivate what he called 'proletarian literature' in contrast to the 'workers' literature' (*Arbeiterdichtung*: poetry written by workers) which the SPD had traditionally, but somewhat uncritically, favoured.[89] The latter, Schröder argued, implied only that the literature, primarily poetry, was written by someone from a working-class background, and often concealed writing with a nationalist flavour. Schröder wished to replace it with a 'proletarian' literature which would be firmly rooted in the experience of working-class existence. 'The new social novel', he wrote, 'must give a comprehensive picture of the period, and this can only be written out of a deep-rooted recognition of the class character of our epoch.'[90]

Schröder was not too successful in his desire to find literature with a working-class milieu, and he had to include books which did not carry a socialist message. He could realise his intentions better in the columns of the Bücherkreis magazine than in its book production.[91]

The regular publishing activities of these two book-clubs continued to contain a great deal that could not really be described as socialist literature. This applies especially to the Büchergilde Gutenberg, which even in its second and more radical phase published the collected works of Goethe, Schiller, Dickens and Dostoevsky, as well as serious modern novels or travel literature, all of which were not particularly political in their orientation. The

87. *Vorwärts*, 13 January 1925, cited in C. Rülcker, 'Arbeiterkultur und Kulturpolitik im Blickwinkel des *Vorwärts*', *AfSG*, vol. 14, 1974, p. 139.
88. Bühnemann and Friedrich (note 85), p. 375, quoting the journal of the *Büchergilde*, 1931; *Bücherkreis*, vol. 2, no. 1, 1930.
89. On workers' poetry in Germany see C. Rülcker, *Ideologie der Arbeiterdichtung, 1914–1933*, Stuttgart, 1970; *KW* 1926, p. 239.
90. Schröder cited in H.H. Müller, *Intellektueller Linksradikalismus in der Weimarer Republik*, Kronenberg i.T., 1977, p. 76.
91. On the magazine see Bühnemann and Friedrich (note 85), pp. 377–8.

Bücherkreis, too, included general educational literature and re-portage, written without specific ideological commitment.

The history of the Universum Bücherei, the only communist-inspired book-club, published by Münzenberg, has some parallels with that of the other book-clubs. Its programme addressed itself to the 'progressive men and women of our age', to whom it wished to bring German and foreign literature 'which would be welcome in the name of progress and culture'.[92] Initially it did not develop a complete publishing programme of its own, but also took many titles from other publishing houses for distribution among its members. In 1929 the Universum Bücherei changed its character into a more fully proletarian book-club. This showed itself less in the character of the publications distributed to members than in the attempt to politicise the membership. The book-club's journal, *Magazin für Alle*, became more strongly political in content, and publicised political activities for members as well as for non-members, who after 1931 could purchase the magazine for a nominal price of 10 pfennigs. They were invited to meetings and demonstrations and to cultural and agitational events, such as the 'Festival of 100,000' in the environs of Berlin.[93]

In its publishing programme the Universum Bücherei, like the others, included editions of major authors, such as Zola, as well as educational works. Yet more than any other book-club it also assiduously cultivated the specifically political and ideological literature of the left. Its monthly journal discussed everyday politi-cal issues, unlike the other two journals, which dealt more with general literary and artistic issues.[94] By 1932 the Universum Bücherei had reached a membership of some 40,000, compared with 45,000 for the Bücherkreis and 85,000 for the Büchergilde Gutenberg. Allowing for family involvement, the total number influenced by the workers' book-clubs may have been up to half a million. This is admittedly small compared with the readership of the workers' press, let alone the regular voters for the two parties of the left, or compared with the two bourgeois book-clubs, which claimed 200,000 and 600,000 members respectively.[95] Yet in terms of a mass circulation of high-quality literature, produced in an

92. The Universum Bücherei also had a highly prestigious and not exclusively communist Advisory Council, which included Albert Einstein, Käthe Kollwitz, Upton Sinclair and Helene Stocker, the Liberal feminist.
93. Cf. *Blätter für Alle*, vol. 3, 1928, no. 3.
94. Bühnemann and Friedrich (note 85), pp. 392–3.
95. For the membership figures of the two bourgeois bookclubs see Bühnemann and Friedrich (note 85), p. 391.

attractive form, mainly to workers without a tradition of book-buying, we are faced with a significant intellectual, social and economic phenomenon.

From the beginning the German labour movement had shown a strong belief in the power of the printed word. This is evident from the vigorous development of socialist publishing, in the rapid expansion of the social-democratic press after 1890, and in the vast output of books, pamphlets and agitational literature which poured from the socialist presses.[96] Compared with the pre-war period the development of socialist and communist political publishing in the Weimar period was less spectacular. As far as newspaper circulation was concerned it seems that a kind of saturation point had been reached by 1914. After 1918 the circulation figures of workers' newspapers, including the new communist dailies, did not really make any inroads into the growing circulation figures for the cheaper, more easily digestible and more sensationalising tabloids, many of which were published by the Scherl publishing house which was under the control of the nationalist politician Alfred Hugenberg.

Indeed, in view of this competition it is significant that, even after allowing for the deliberate policy of making the social-democratic press more readable, the newspapers of the SPD and of the Communist Party remained so serious and so strongly political in character. This applies also to the new weekly magazines and illustrated papers and to the cultural periodicals which were established in the 1920s. They included the more specialised journals of the socialist and of the newly founded communist youth organisations and of other journals of the ancillary organisations of the parties, including the workers' cultural organisations, which expanded during this period. All these were swelling the number and circulation figures of the workers' press and increasing the amount of literature which would regularly reach the families of organised workers.

By contrast the volume of socialist and communist book publishing reached only a minority of workers. Its significance lay in the broad range of the literature brought out. Before 1914 the output of the social-democratic Dietz Verlag and of the *Vorwärts* Party Bookshop was almost solely concerned with political books and pamphlets, including socialist classics. Apart from this there were only some socialist plays and socialist songs, as well as a series

96. Cf. B. Emig *et al.*, *Literatur für eine neue Wirklichkeit*, Bonn–Berlin, 1982. (This is a bibliography of the Dietz Verlag and of the Buchhandlung *Vorwärts*.)

of booklets on matters realing to health and hygiene.[97] Taking the three book-clubs described earlier we now find publications covering a wide range of subjects, both older and modern literature, some less demanding works, and relatively little that could be described as purely political. The literature destined for the politically committed worker represented a catholic spectrum, and not a narrow selection based on a purely party-political outlook.[98]

Apart from the quality and the catholic selection offered to members of the workers' book-clubs, the books were produced to a high standard of printing and design. This signals a new concept of working-class book-ownership, which would hardly have been possible a generation earlier. Book-buying, however, is not book-reading. For the great majority of workers in the Weimar years the admittedly very limited studies which we have suggest that reading, as measured by the pattern of loans made to working-class readers, seems to have been concentrated very largely on light, recreational reading.

97. For the freedom to print socialist publishers and editors suffered frequent imprisonment before 1914; and communist newspaper editors continued to be sentenced to terms of imprisonment even in the 'liberal' Weimar Republic.
98. Cf. Archiv der Sozialen Demokratie (Friedrich Ebert Stiftung), *Die Buchgemeinschaften der Arbeiterbewegung in der Weimarer Republik, ein Bestandsverzeichnis*, Bonn, 1982. See also Wieland Herzfelde, Der Malik Verlag 1916–47. (Catalogue of an exhibition at the Deutsche Akademie der Künste), Berlin (GDR), 1967.

–11–

New Lifestyles and the Labour Movement

Towards a Socialist Culture of Everyday Life

'A socialist culture of everyday life', a writer on socialist education wrote in 1927,

> should counteract bourgeois customs and philistine tastes in such things as furniture and dress and the conservative conventions of human intercourse. There should be an end to the non-proletarian ceremonials of the churches . . . Away with the wedding-ring and the widow's veil and with ear-rings and bangles . . . Landscapes and pictures of the life of the proletariat belong in the working-class home. Respect and comradeship, not subservience and deference in human conduct is what socialists demand even in love. Simple dresses should envelop proletarian women, who should be able to demand the recognition of their personal attributes even without glittering baubles.[1]

Implied in this appeal is the recognition that the proletariat had not yet created adequate new lifestyles, and that workers and their families still widely followed the mores and customs, forms of behaviour and tastes which prevailed in the middle and lower-middle classes. Indeed, many leaders of the SPD in its early years were themselves drawn from the middle and petty-bourgeois strata. In addition, the growing party and trade union bureaucracy, journalists, and the like, though modestly paid, were yet able to move out of the industrial working class and to establish for themselves a lower-middle-class type of existence. Robert Michels has described the *embourgeoisement* of these groups, and ascribed the loss of revolutionary fervour in the SPD to this phenomenon.[2]

Whether or not this is the case, we do not find in the early years

1. From R. Wagner, *Klassenkampf um den Menschen*, Vienna, 1927, reprinted in part in J. Olbrich (ed.), *Arbeiterbildung in der Weimarer Zeit*, Brunswick, 1977, p. 57 (abridged and slightly re-arranged).
2. Cf. R. Michels, *Political Parties*, London, 1915 (translated from the first German edition of 1909 in 1915, and reprinted in 1966).

of the social-democratic movement any deliberate attempt to wean the party away from bourgeois mores and conventions. We have only to look at photographs of party conferences and demonstrations, with their black-suited, black-hatted and tie-wearing masses, to find evidence of how far bourgeois dress had influenced at least the more well-to-do workers. Nor did the concept of working-class emancipation, central to socialist beliefs, imply initially a rejection of bourgeois personal lifestyles analogous to their opposition to the economic and political power of that class. Party programmes generally steered clear of subjects which might touch on questions of personal morality and of pronouncements about the moral character of a future society. And where they do make statements, as in respect of religion, the party sought to make it clear that religious beliefs and observances were entirely matters for personal conscience.[3]

If, especially after 1918, new lifestyles became more widely practised in the German labour movement, this was due above all to three types of influence which will be discussed at length in this chapter, namely those of the youth movement, of atheism, and of the bourgeois *Lebensreform* ('reform of life') movement.

As we have seen already, the general discussion of workers' culture brought up proposals for new forms of cultural activities and events which tended to produce new rituals or adapt existing ones, as in the celebrations for New Year's Eve. In place of the bourgeois tradition, widely copied by the working class, of seeing the New Year in with drinks and fireworks, some working-class organisations, such as the Leipzig Arbeiter-Bildungsinstitut, developed the custom of performing Beethoven's Choral Symphony, with its concluding appeal to the spirit of fraternity. This custom was instituted because 'the hour demands . . . that only great and community-creating works shall be played'.[4] Christmas celebrations also came into that category, although they are an example of how difficult it was to change the character of this traditional festivity.

Pressure for change and pressure for new lifestyles and for new, proletarian, traditions, as against old bourgeois and in part religious ones, came from some working-class organisations whose aims and interests were especially oriented in this direction, such as the

3. The texts of the major SPD programmes and declarations are translated in S. Miller and H. Potthoff, *A History of German Social Democracy*, Leamington Spa, 1986.
4. See H. Wiegand, 'Die Sylvesterfeier des Arbeiterbildungsinstitut in Leipzig', *KW* 1932, from which the quotation is taken.

atheist socialist-proletarian *Freidenker* ('Freethinker') movement, and the youth movements of the respective political parties of the left, whose activities and influences in this area are discussed in the next section. Another influence in the direction of a reform in lifestyles came from general, and, originally at least, bourgeois reform movements, in particular those devoted to abstinence and teetotalism and to nudism.

The abstinence movement within the working class was at first only a general but widely shared sentiment that drink was an evil from a moral as well as from an economic point of view. Later a socialist anti-alcohol movement was organised in the Arbeiter Abstinenten Bund (1903–33). Its influence on socialist ideas was greater than might have been predicted from its few thousand members, and abstinence was widely practised in the Naturfreunde and throughout the socialist youth movement, and was influential among worker athletes. The Arbeiter Abstinenten saw anti-alcoholism as a part of a general drive towards a new 'food culture', which eschewed nicotine and other stimulants, and suggested less meat-eating and a more 'natural' life.[5]

Nudism too was seen by its exponents as part of a general move in favour of a natural, and for some also a libertarian, lifestyle. In its bourgeois form it often had certain eugenic and racial components, and it wished to stimulate the erotic as against the merely sexual, which, nudists thought, was actually stimulated by the curiosity engendered by female dress.[6] Within the labour movement nudism was propagated by the section for 'proletarische Lebensreform und Freikörperkultur' within the pro-social-democratic Verband Volksgesundheit. While the group aimed above all at health and fitness another sub-group of the Verband, the Bund für sozialistische Lebensgestaltung: Freie Menschen approached the matter more from an ethical and political point of view.[7] Hence at the time of the split in the workers' sports movement the Bund allied itself with the communist sports club *Fichte*. Members saw the fight for nudism as a part of the general struggle. They thought that the training of the body, which would make it a more efficient tool in the proletarian struggle, was carried out better if done in the nude.

5. H. Wunderer, *Arbeitervereine und Arbeiterparteien . . . 1890–1933*, Frankfurt, 1980, pp. 48–51.
6. W.R. Krabbe, *Gesellschaftsveränderung durch Lebensreform*, Göttingen, 1979, pp. 98–105.
7. Approximate translations are: 'Section for the Reform of Proletarian Lifestyles and for Nudism' of the 'League for People's Health' and 'League for Socialist Lifestyles: Free Men and Women'.

Nudism was also a challenge to the moral hypocrisy of the bourgeoisie, and the fight against bourgeois morality was seen as part of the fight against bourgeois political and economic power.[8]

The number directly or indirectly involved in the socialist nudism movement has been estimated at 60,000.[9] Most of them were members of the youth movement and men and women athletes, and their practice of nudism is associated with sport, above all swimming, and with organised and spontaneous camping, practised increasingly around Berlin and some other big cities as unemployment gripped the working class.

The overall significance of these new departures, which are discussed in greater detail in this chapter, does not lie in the numbers affected by them, but in the extent of the innovation and in the way in which the new customs complement some cultural activities of the socialist and communist movements.

New Rituals for Old

In the search for new lifestyles for the German proletariat and in the attempts to instil a new consciousness in the individual the *Freidenker* (Freethinkers) movement occupied an important place. Although atheism and anti-clericalism go back a long way in the development of European thought, and although socialist thinkers very often combined their socialist ideology with a rationalist attitude towards religion, the formal organisation of Free Thought in the German labour movement began only in the twentieth century. Not that Christianity had traditionally a strong hold on the German working class. Agnosticism was widespread, both as a way of thinking and as a largely unreflective attitude, throughout the industrial working class which identified with the social-democratic movement, especially in the Protestant parts of the country. The churches themselves were hostile to the socialist labour movement, partly in reaction to the latter's rationalism, and partly because of the general link between organised religion and the bourgeoisie. Religious socialism, as an intellectual tradition, arose only in the 1920s, and remained a minority movement.

A survey of workers' views and attitudes undertaken just before the First World War shows that over half the miners, metal

---

8. J.R. Becher, Kurt Kläber, Fritz Rück (eds), *Kampfgenoß, ein Buch für die proletarische Jugend*, Berlin, 1929, pp. 40–1.
9. Krabbe (note 6), p. 150.

workers and textile workers asked for their views said that they did not believe in God, and less than one-fifth expressed a positive attitude. Depending on the trade, between 3.9% and 7.3% of those asked had actually formally left the church; and others claimed that they would have done likewise if they had not been afraid of opposition from their families or concerned that their children would be discriminated against at school. Thus while anti-religious views were common in the labour movement before 1914 the number of workers actually organised in the Free Thought movement was small, and many of those who adhered were more interested in the cremation facilities and the death benefit which often went with membership than in the propagation of a rationalistic philosophy. Thus the Berlin Verein der Freidenker für Feuerbestattung ('Association of Freethinkers for Cremation') was founded in 1905, and was primarily concerned with the propagation of cremation. Membership was initially linked to secession from the church; but this requirement was dropped when it was found that numbers stagnated. A little later, in 1908, a number of local societies formed the Zentralverband deutscher Freidenkervereine ('Union of German Freethinker Societies').[10]

After 1918, however, the Freethinker movement grew fairly rapidly. In 1914 the Zentralverband had only 6,500 members; but by 1929 this figure had risen to around 100,000, and by 1932 membership had reached 153,356, while the whole of the proletarian Freethinker movement had some half a million members by the mid-1920s. The immediate concern of the movement was the propagation of agnosticism and atheism and agitation against organised religion, including the advocacy of formal withdrawals from the churches (without which the membership of a specific denomination, universally imposed at birth, remained an obligatory administrative categorisation).[11] The latter campaign, and the parallel agitation of the Communist Party in favour of resignation from the churches, was quite successful. Withdrawals from the religious communities averaged 200,000 a year in the 1920s. Only 10–20% of these were due to movement from one denomination to another.[12]

---

10. A. Levenstein, *Die Arbeiterfrage*, Munich, 1912, pp. 323–53; cf. Wunderer (note 5), pp. 56–67.
11. Cf. H. Wunderer, 'Freidenkertum und Arbeiterbewegung', *IWK*, vol. 16, no. 1, 1980, pp. 1–33, p. 7.
12. Cf. J.C. Kaiser, 'Arbeiterbewegung und organisierte Religionskritik Proletarische Freidenkerverbande im Kaiserreich und in der Weimarer Republik', Diss. Munster, 1979, p. 526. Not all resignations, of course, were by workers.

The Free Thought movement did not, of course, limit its activities to the religious sphere. The *Freidenker* wished to replace religious tenets and values with general ethical ones, and to create new secular institutions in place of the old sacral ones. Their thinking extended beyond rationalist ideas and new communal practices to the wider area of workers' culture and conduct. The *Freidenker* claimed to have a historical role 'to respond to many of the cultural and educational needs of the proletariat, especially the forms and conventions of the everyday life of the community, in a form consonant with the teaching of Marxism'.[13]

We have already seen how the movement sought to respond to the needs for new ritual to replace religious cults through the creation of new forms of celebrations, such as the *Proletarische Feierstunden* conceived as a substitute for the Sunday church services. More specifically, the Free Thought movement was concerned with the establishment of new customs and new ceremonials to celebrate and commemorate the various stages of life and the salient social acts of individuals and their families. In the place of Christian baptism the *Freidenker* wished to establish *Kinderfeiern* with speeches, recitations and music; and, while most working-class marriages were contracted only in Registry Offices in any case, they sought to institute a new non-religious ritual to celebrate the concluding of a marriage bond, but had difficulties in finding an appropriate form for this.[14] Above all, they were the earliest protagonists of the *Jugendweihe*, which was to replace the Christian confirmation with a secular ceremony commemorating the passage from childhood to adulthood.

Of the other stages of the human life-cycle the *Freidenker* movement was particularly concerned about events related to death and the commemoration of the dead. They advocated cremation instead of burial, not only in order to symbolise the secular as against the religious, but for social and hygienic reasons. They argued that the more mobile society of the twentieth century and the dispersal of families over the country prevented the regular tending of graves, and also affected acts of remembrance associated with burial and cemeteries. As a substitute the Freethinkers advocated the introduction of the *Totenfeier* and of secular meetings of remembrance. The emphasis of this ritual was on the roots of the deceased

13. From the programme and theses of the Gemeinschaft proletarischer Freidenker (Leipzig), cited in W. Lindemann, *Die proletarische Freidenkerbewegung – Geschichte, Theorie und Praxis*, Münster, 1980, pp. 50–1.
14. Cf. H. Waldmeier, 'Kultische Feiern', in C. Schweitzer and W. Künneth, *Freidenkertum und Kirche*, Berlin, 1932, pp. 282–90.

in the working-class community. In place of hymns the congregation would sing socialist songs and 'The International', and the halls where such ceremonies were held were to be decorated with flags, busts and pictures. Language and dress were supposed to give expression to the solidarity which existed within the movement.[15]

The *Freidenker* sought to replace traditional Christian festivals with new secular rituals, and they endeavoured to substitute the celebration of the winter solstice for that of Christmas. Their influence in this area was limited. As the most secularised of the traditional festivals, Christmas was widely celebrated in the German working-class milieu, and various socialist organisations regularly organised in early December fairs and exhibitions where books and other presents could be bought. Youth groups, too, organised the distribution of gifts among their members – sometimes these were given anonymously. Yet a picture in *Volk und Zeit* shows that even in these celebrations, Christmas trees and candles are usually present.[16] Even if individual families did not feel positively inclined towards the festivities, the pressure to conform was strong.[17] And so was the pressure for some form of common celebration of Christmas among working-class organisations. Such limited evidence as we have suggests that the programme of many socialist celebrations was a mixture of general pacifist elements, a celebration of the conquest of darkness, and the performance of Christmas music and of old folksongs.[18]

Given the strength of traditional sentiment socialist youth groups were warned not to be too revolutionary in their celebrations. Too radical a reform would offend many people unnecessarily. The tenor of their celebrations should not be iconoclastic, but it should be tender and intimate with a light-hearted note.[19] Contrasted with this, the attitude of the communist youth organisation was more antagonistic and uncompromising. *Die Junge Garde*, the weekly paper of the communist youth organisation, told its readers that 'no working-class child may sing the pious Christmas songs, all children will sing fighting songs instead . . . they must put an end to the fairy tales of the Christmas tree and join in the fighting front of

15. Lindemann (note 13), p. 65.
16. *Volk und Zeit*, 15 January 1924.
17. A. Rode, 'Weihnachten', *KW*, 1930, pp. 226–7.
18. Cf. the Programme of three Christmas celebrations in Altenburg (copies in the *Arbeiterliedarchiv* M 16, 17, 18). The most daring departure from the family Christmas seems to have been the Soviet Star, made out of branches and decorated with candles.
19. *Der Führer*, November 1924, p. 115.

revolutionary children'.[20]

As the membership expanded, and as the level of secessions from the churches grew, the Freethinkers felt optimistic about the future. 'We are on the road to victory, our spring will come' wrote Walter Lindemann in 1926.[21] The Communist Party, which, as we saw, had succeeded in splitting the movement, used the section in sympathy with it as the spearhead of its cultural campaign. Its anti-religious agitation became more pronounced in the process, but there is little evidence that the *Freidenker* secured support for their more specific reform proposals. At the same time the SPD, to whom the bulk of Free Thought still professed allegiance, began to advocate a more conciliatory attitude towards religion. At the party's national conference in 1927, Rudolf Hilferding, the keynote speaker, urged greater tolerance *vis-à-vis* religion; and the 1929 conference passed a resolution confirming the view that religious beliefs were matters of private decision.[22]

The general ideas of the Freethinkers made them sympathise with a variety of new forms of living, such as nudism and vegetarianism, and with the search for greater sexual freedom; and such ideas also gained support in the social-democratic movement. Above all, the Freethinkers wished to be involved in the new *Festkultur*, in which they saw a major manifestation of a new community spirit. Those who organised such events were often also active *Freidenker*, but apart from the organisation of the *Proletarische Feierstunden* and the celebration of the *Jugendweihe* there is little evidence of the direct involvement of the movement in the organisation of cultural activities.

The *Jugendweihe* was the most interesting and potentially most significant of the ceremonies and festivities which were linked to new beliefs and new lifestyles, and which came into being with the expansion of the labour movement. It was a popular institution in the big cities; in places like Hamburg and Leipzig one-fifth or one-quarter of all those leaving elementary school might take part – a percentage which exceeded the percentage of the politically organised even in these major centres of the labour movement. Formally organised by socialist teachers who were often connected with Free Thought or with the Frei-religiöse Gemeinden or, especially in communist celebrations, by the 'Proletarian Freethinkers' the ceremony was held in the schools which the youngsters had

20. *Die Junge Garde*, 15 December 1929 (ex Bundesarchiv 134, vol. 70, fo. 80).
21. Lindemann (note 13).
22. SPD Parteitag 1927 *Protokoll*, pp. 170 ff.; Parteitag 1929 *Protokoll* pp. 75 ff.

attended, or, for large groups, collectively, in central halls or, as in Berlin, in the Prussian State Theatre or in the Sportpalast. Its outward form was one which was 'staged' for those undergoing the rite of moving towards adulthood; and the organisers sought to create for it a solemn and elevating atmosphere. With good music, rousing choruses, and an address – generally by a teacher – and a token of remembrance, mostly in the form of a book,[23] the ceremonies were outwardly not very dissimilar to a religious confirmation. The songs of the labour movement replaced religious hymns, and the *Sprechchor*, pronouncing beliefs and intoning responses, replaced the service. But the ethos of the *Jugendweihe* was entirely different.

The Leipzig *Jugendweihe*-ceremony of 1929 may be cited as an example. It was held in the Alberthalle, and it centred on a play which used various media – movement, chorus, film and straight performance.

> To the strains of the organ the youths entered. A solemn adagio of violin and organ was followed by a short address. Then came the play *Und Licht auf der Straße* ('Let there be light on the road'). The stage shows a street with factory and department store. Children play in the street. A boy and a girl enter. They look for their first job. A conversation about their experience and their future follows. They leave, the lights fade. A film shows life in the factory and in the store. The two children return – they have found work. Factory and store close, and the workers and shop assistants speak to their future comrades. The film comes on again. It shows fashionable luxuries, the alien, hostile world. A group of young workers appear behind a red flag. Now the film shows life in the Kinderfreunde youth organisation, mass demonstrations and *Arbeiterfeste*, to the accompaniment of the songs of the proletariat. The father of the new factory worker speaks of the past, of what has been achieved and of what still needs to be fought for . . . All sing a socialist song. Youths march up and form a lane, down which the two children leave the hall.[24]

In the confirmation the confirmand vowed that he would be a good and obedient Christian, while the working-class child who

---

23. I have traced fifteen titles of books which appear to have been given as presents at *Jugendweihen* or recommended for the occasion. They were mostly published between 1925 and 1930, some in more than one edition. These publications suggest that for a few years at least there was a considerable demand, and hence that there must have been a sizeable number of participants in this rite. The Dortmund Institut für deutsche und ausländische Arbeiterliteratur has a good collection of this literature.

24. From 'Die Leipziger Jugendweihe', *KW* vol. 6, 1929, p. 97 (slightly adapted).

underwent the ceremony of the *Jugendweihe* was made to feel that he was now entering on his life as a worker, loyal to his class and responding to the demands of the working-class struggle. Thus embedded in the music, recitations and grouped displays there was often an act of dedication in which the young were exhorted to be 'loyal sons and daughters of the toiling masses. Your fathers put their trust in you that you will join them in their struggle and that you should always put the interest of your class before your own interest.' And while the children linked arms with their neighbours they were told that 'in this struggle you are nothing if you are not standing by each other. Solidarity is strength, solidarity ensures victory, solidarity should be your watchword.'[25]

Although at the beginning the *Jugendweihe* ceremony was shared by socialists and communists, there soon developed a fair amount of discussion and differences between the parties, and even within the SPD camp. Some saw in it a humanist religious ceremony, while others thought more in political and possibly even militant terms. Parents often thought that the ceremony should, above all, be 'beautiful' – solemn and enthralling – viz., as much like a church ceremony as possible, with the children in formal dress. Educationists, on the other hand, often wished for the creative participation of the youngsters, so that the whole would become more like a dialogue between the generations. Dress should be as colourful as possible, so that 'the secular and the life-affirming should be symbolised in the dresses worn'.[26] In the SPD especially it was suggested that the event should have more spontaneity and more gaiety, and that the children should engage in a play whose aim was to show communal effort, not a high level of artistic performance, in line with the character of the young generation. It was more important to interest the children than to move their parents to tears.[27]

While in the social-democratic movement there was thus a trend towards a more child-centred and educative ceremony, the Communist Party, who often preferred to have a 'School-leaving Celebration' (*Schulentlassungsfeier*), were increasingly concerned to give the celebrations a more specifically political content. The *Jugendweihe* celebrations organised by the pro-communist proletarian Freethinkers in the Berlin Sportpalast in 1931 commenced with

25. Cf. E. Altenberg (ed.), *Feste der Jugend*, Waldenburg, 1929, p. 23.
26. Cf. Paul Ströbel, 'Ratschläge für die Jugendweihe', *Soz. Bldg*, no. 1, 1929, p. 56; Walter Zeiler, 'Unsere Jugendweihe', *Soz. Bldg*, no. 4, 1932, pp. 14–17, p. 15.
27. Cf. R. Lohman, *Die Jugendweihe*, (Schriften des Zentralausschuß für sozialistische Bildungsarbeit), Berlin, 1923; *KW*, vol. 6, 1929, p. 97.

'The International', and right at the beginning a speaker told the young that they were members of an oppressed class exploited by the capitalists, who used the authority of the state against the proletariat, supported by the churches. Interspersed with revolutionary songs, a 'giant puppet theatre' showed the figures of the reactionary forces, and the school-leavers vowed 'to give their all, their blood and their life, for the struggle of their class.'[28]

A similar message was conveyed by the anthology *Kampfgenoß*, published by the Communist Youth International, and probably used for *Jugendweihe* celebrations. Printed on the flyleaf was the message 'to remember the imperialist war, fought in the interest of your exploiters and oppressors, and to realise that all wars would cease with the destruction of the cursed capitalist order . . . hence you should become a class-fighter.'[29]

Youth Movement and 'Youth Culture'

In no other section of the German labour movement do we find as much concern and as much discussion of new lifestyles and new forms of communal living as in the socialist youth movement. The movement organised young workers aged 14–18 within the social-democratic organisation, and had its national leadership appointed by the Party Executive. Attempts to organise young workers had started already at the beginning of the century. Social-democratic youth organisations were formed at a number of places by older members, starting in Mannheim in 1904, and two co-ordinating organisations were formed in North and South Germany soon afterwards.[30] Originally sponsored by the party and by the trade unions and under the auspices of local Jugendausschüsse and of a 'Central Agency for Young Workers' (Zentralstelle für die Arbeitende Jugend) the unions created, after 1918, their own youth organisations, catering for a potential membership of around half a million young trade unionists, while the Sozialistische Arbeiterjugend ('Socialist Workers' Youth') achieved a certain measure of independence.[31]

28. Waldmeier, (note 14).
29. See J.R. Becher, Kurt Kläber, Fritz Rück (eds), *Kampfgenoß, ein Buch für die proletarische Jugend*, Berlin, 1928.
30. The two organisations were the Verband junger Arbeiter und Arbeiterinnen (South Germany) and the Vereinigung der freien Jugendorganisationen Deutschlands (North Germany). They amalgamated to form the Verband der arbeitenden Jugend Deutschlands.
31. D. Prinz and M. Rexin (eds), *Gewerkschaftsjugend im Weimarer Staat*, Cologne,

Out of the chaos of the immediate post-war period a new and much more independent socialist youth organisation arose, as well as youth organisations of the newly formed Communist Party, first known as the 'Communist Workers' Youth' (Kommunistische Arbeiterjugend – KAJ) and later as the 'Association of Communist Youth', the Kommunistische Jugendverband – KJV. The Workers' Youth of the SPD was reunited with the 'Socialist Proletarian Youth' (Sozialistische Proletarier Jugend) of the USPD, the Independent Social Democrats, to form the 'Socialist Workers Youth', Sozialistische Arbeiterjugend – SAJ. Its membership was, in most cases, committed and keen, and by background and occupation represented the better off and mostly politically organised section of the manual working class and the white-collar sector of the population.[32]

Before 1914 the youth organisation of the SPD was primarily concerned with education; but members increasingly also wished to discuss the burning political issues of the day, and to have greater control over their own activities. This had led to tension between often very radical young workers and a reformist bureaucracy; and during the war a substantial section of the members sided with the opposition to the official SPD policy, and went over to the USPD. Apart from radicalism and pacifism another trend and complex of ideas began to show itself after 1918. This was the set of ideas and practices of the *Jugendbewegung*, the predominantly bourgeois youth movement, founded after 1900, whose ethos and special lifestyle began to permeate the thinking of socialist young workers.

The *Jugendbewegung*, exemplified in the Wandervogel organisation, stressed youth's right to lead its own life, and their opposition to the lifestyle and mores of the generation of their parents, which they regarded as philistine and moralistic. The movement opposed the 'artificiality' of bourgeois social life, rejected its formalities of dress and ceremonial and was opposed to alcohol and tobacco and to all other artificial stimuli. On the positive side the members sought to develop self-expression in personal conduct, while at the same time attaching a high value to personal relationships and to the establishment of community ties. They sought to get close to nature in their personal lives, and hence put great emphasis on

---

1983, p. 27.

32. For example, of thirty-nine girls who in 1924 attended a residential course in Burg Tannich, the central educational and holiday establishment of the SAJ, half were white-collar workers. Cf. *Arbeiterjugend*, October 1924. See also C. Bondy, *Die proletarische Jugendbewegung*, Lauenburg, 1922, pp. 28–9.

outdoor activities, rambles and camps, and on the revival of the folksong, folk-dancing and other folk customs. Cultural activities were important to them, and the arts particularly so.

These reformist and cultural innovators influenced the young workers through their publications as well as through direct contact. Friedrich Erfurth was, in 1919, a young bank clerk in Mannheim, and an enthusiastic member of the Arbeiterjugend. 'There were', he relates, 'two members who had come to us from the Wandervogel and were enthusiastic supporters of the ideals of the *Jugendbewegung*. They really brought life into the organisation. They both played instruments, guitar and lute, and they persuaded others to buy instruments and taught them to play . . . We danced reels . . . and there were lectures on communal institutions, like the Kunsthalle, as well as lectures on the history of the labour movement.'[33]

Within the workers' youth movement there was, on the whole, less emphasis on conflict between the generations, but otherwise there was considerable borrowing of the outward symbols of the bourgeois youth movement. Their dress was chosen to show variety and personal style, with open-necked shirts in place of collar and tie, shorts and loose-fitting garments, or skirts and blouses. Sandals rather than boots were worn, and, while girls might dress up with hand-made buckles or hand-made metal brooches, glitter or make-up was taboo.[34]

It was axiomatic for the Arbeiterjugend, though not always for their bourgeois contemporaries, that both sexes should belong to the same organisation and share in all activities. Given the widespread acceptance of stereotyped roles for men and women in the working class, such comradeship and co-education, based on equality and on the mutual esteem and respect of the sexes for each other, was far from universal; and uncouth behaviour and foul language, so common on the shopfloor, was much resented. 'Our workers' youth organisation seeks an education for purity and beauty; but what is the good of it if in the factory we are exposed to the coarse jokes and unseemly behaviour of our older colleagues.'[35]

33. Quoted by F. Steinbach, *Mannheim, Erinnerungen eines halben Jahrhundert*, Mannheim, 1984, p. 283.
34. Some groups also wore badges. The Bochum Workers' Youth had such a badge, which, executed in silver, red and blue, showed a young man, his hair blowing in the wind, climbing a mountain peak while gazing at the 'blue flower' which symbolised the yearning of the poets of the German Romantic movement. Cf. F. Osterroth, *Die Zeit als Jugendsekretär des Bergarbeiterverbandes in Bochum, 1919–1924*, Bochum, 1983, p. 13.
35. *Der Führer*, no. 3, 1921, p. 35.

Photographs of the period show us boys and girls mixing freely on walks and at rest in wood or meadow, and the casual appearance of such groups when on rambles is a significant feature of the workers' youth culture of the early 1920s. It contrasts strongly with the disciplined military bearing of more authoritarian youth movements then and later.[36] In their gymnastics and athletic activities they put great emphasis on team spirit and on group activities.[37] Walking tours and camping holidays were by all accounts the most community-forming and the most valued of all the activities of the movement. In and through them the young workers found that they could best express their personalities. They enabled members to get to know each other, and the shared experience of the landscape and of camping provided the opportunity for social contact with other local groups and with youth from other towns.

> They marched with joy in their hearts to the beautifully situated rocks in the Nero Valley to celebrate the summer solstice. Who of the many thousands will forget those hours. . . . or our beautiful songs, sung by thousands and alternating with hymns of freedom from the Wiesbaden Workers' Choral Society . . . In the middle of the splendidly situated spot gigantic flames shot upwards . . . Those were sacred hours, it was a socialist act of devotion.[38]

The emotional impact of the new style of leisure on the young workers involved was considerable. From the tenement block and the grey and noisy city he, or she, was transposed into a wide landscape, exposed to sun and wind, and able to establish bonds of comradeship through communal walking, singing and dancing.

> He experienced for the first time the joy of marching along while songs rose to the very tops of trees . . . he let himself be drawn into the circle which danced the old reels . . . he felt that he was part of nature like a bird or butterfly . . . he realised that for the first time he had found himself and knew what it meant to be young.[39]

The perceived importance of these activities is seen in the programmes of regional or national gatherings of the SAJ, in which thousands of young workers participated. Even at these formal

36. A series of such photographs covering the first post-1918 *Arbeiterjugendtag* in Weimar in 1920 is reproduced in Osterroth, (note 34).
37. 'Wir lieben den Sport', *Arbeiterjugend*, 1930, p. 196.
38. *Die Junge Garde. Arbeiterjugendbewegung in Frankfurt am Main 1904–1945*, Frankfurt, 1980, p. 67.
39. Osterroth (note 34), p. 11.

events opportunities for rambles and games existed. The programme of the Third Workers' Youth Days in Nuremberg in 1923 shows this:

1. Republican manifestation and celebration of the 'Day of the Constitution' (*Verfassungstag*).
2. Demonstration – March through the City.
3. Festivity in the Municipal Theatre. Film *Über den hohen Bergen*.
4. Morning Ramble. Festival of Youth.
5. Games.
6. Torchlight Procession.

Next to the importance put on rambles and other group-related physical activities and on exercises, games and dances, was the emphasis which the movement put on culture and, above all, art. The latter was not seen as part of political activity, but as a way to enrich the mind and to widen the young worker's experience. Culture was thus not viewed in ideological terms, and art was seen as much in terms of its form as of its content – a part of daily life, not a weapon in the political struggle. Music was expected to move and grip the listener, and to be enjoyed irrespective of the words of a particular choral work.[40] Yet art was in no way a matter for mere entertainment, it was a supreme vehicle for the formation of the personality, 'a ring of fire in which we can cleanse our new inner man and from which, strengthened and matured, we can step out into the world'.[41]

The ways in which this goal could be achieved included evenings devoted to art education, reading or watching educational films, and visits to concerts, plays or museums.[42] In addition there were also more individual and personal ways of living with art and beauty. The magazines of the workers' youth movement published poetry, and the Arbeiterjugendverlag published a series of books of poetry by worker poets, as well as books on art and music.

The SAJ's view of culture was not very different from that generally propagated by the party at large; but culture was given greater emphasis, to the exclusion of other aspects of workers' leisure-time activities. Leaders of the movement, like Erich Ollenhauer and Max Westphal, repeatedly stressed its importance. Ollenhauer

40. Heinrich Deist in *Der Führer*, 1925, p. 41.
41. *Der Führer*, 1921, p. 100.
42. For a detailed report of what youth groups were expected and encouraged to do see M. Westphal (ed.), *Handbuch für sozialdemokratische Jugendarbeit*, 2nd edn, Berlin, 1930, pp. 58–63.

spoke of the need to lead members 'into the sunny uplands of our cultural ideals', and Westphal wrote that youth 'seeks to create a new communal life and aspires to a new culture'.[43]

The first practical demonstration of the movement's search for culture and of the belief in its community-creating function was the first *Reichsjugendtag*, held in Weimar in August 1920. The choice of location was a deliberate and symbolic attempt to identify the movement with the new state, whose constitution had been created in Weimar, and which, in the view of one of the organisers, 'had united the spirit of the Paulskirche with the basic philosophy of the labour movement'.[44] And the link with the classical heritage, which Weimar expressed, had also been uppermost in their minds when choosing the venue.

The proclamation of the event had expressed this by speaking of Weimar as 'the Bethlehem of German culture', and it called 28 August, the day of Goethe's birth, chosen for the arrival of the delegates, 'the holiest date of that great cultural period of our people'.[45] Partly by design, and partly fortuitously but genuinely, the events appeared to demonstrate the reverence which the participants felt for that heritage.

Speeches and symbolic actions expressed the commitment to what was seen as the humanist tradition of classical literature. The young workers, assembled at the monument to Goethe and Schiller, decorated the statue with a laurel wreath with the inscription 'To the eternally young from the German workers' youth' and Erich Ollenhauer spoke of the young workers' dedication to the poets. 'They had experienced the tribulations of the life of the proletariat, but inside them there lived the spirit of Goethe and Schiller'.[46]

In the heady and hopeful intellectual and emotional climate of the early Weimar days the young and not so young, who had come there from all over Germany, probably genuinely believed that the new state would solve the economic and political problems against which the SPD had fought for so long. Theirs was now the task of creating a new and higher culture. At the beginning of this road they saw themselves as 'the heirs of the gigantic intellectual work of Marx and Engels; in us Heine, Mozart and Beethoven survive . . .

43. Ollenhauer quoted in H.A. Winkler, *Der Schein der Normalität. Arbeiter und Arbeiterbewegung in der Weimarer Republik, 1924–1930*, Berlin–Bonn, 1985; M. Westphal in *Vorwärts*, 9 May 1928.
44. J. Schult, *Aufbruch einer Jugend. Der Weg der Arbeiterjugend*, Bonn, 1956, p. 132.
45. 'Aufruf zum Reichsjugendtag', *Arbeiterjugend*, 15 May 1920.
46. Erich Ollenhauer, *Reden und Aufsätze*, Hanover, 1964, p. 28.

we have made folksongs and folk-dances our own, and through our rambles we have sunk deep roots in the true national consciousness'.[47]

The spirit of Weimar clearly had elements of a cultural nationalism as well as of a political quietism, because it seemed to romanticise communal experience, and because it tended to foster the emotions at the expense of the intellect and of critical judgement. The cultural activities which the movement supported most strongly were those which gave scope for individual expression, an *Ausdruckskultur*, to use the term of the period. Critics feared that a preoccupation with issues linked to lifestyles, especially with such things as the 'correct' dress and with games, dancing and ceremonies, threatened to become ends in themselves rather than pursuits which, however pleasant, should be subordinated to the political struggle.[48] The Arbeiterjugend, they argued, did not seek 'some vague community of the whole people, but the community of the proletariat, and, by securing economic and political power, to do away with all classes'.[49]

This stress on lifestyles was not universal throughout the movement. Individuals and local groups, especially those which had come mainly from the youth organisation of the Independent Social Democrats, were not in sympathy with the heavy emphasis on form and culture. They saw the SAJ as an essentially political movement, which should concern itself with ideological clarification and with the daily political struggle. Some groups wished to go even further, and to make the discussion of current political issues a central activity, thereby exercising a direct influence on socialist policies. The leadership of the SAJ regretted what they regarded as an undue politicisation of youth – and feared the threat of opposition to the leadership of the SPD. They drew a distinction between attempts to put politics within an educational framework, which they accepted, and a concern with concrete issues of policy, which they rejected.[50]

The majority of the youth groups continued on a broadly cultural course of activities; but the emphasis on new lifestyles declined with the end of the 1920s. Thus after 1929 the casual and

47. J. Schult, cited in E.R. Muller, *Das Weimar der arbeitenden Jugend*, 2nd edn, Berlin, 1923, pp. 54–5.
48. W. Rüdiger, 'Weimar, Ein Rückschritt', *Arbeiterjugend*, February 1921, pp. 41–5.
49. K. Korn, 'Der Geist unserer Bewegung', *Arbeiterjugend*, February 1921, pp. 23–4.
50. *Die Junge Garde* (note 38), pp. 92, 113–14.

individualistic dress of members was replaced by a sort of uniform of blue blouses with red cravats, held together by a ring with the letters SAJ. Members marched in formation rather than in casual groups, and instead of guitars, lutes and violins they were now accompanied by a 'band' of drums, pipes, trumpets and timpani. The purpose of their rambles was no longer merely enjoyment – instead they often ended in political demonstrations. And in a similar way the plays which the young used to perform were now chosen for their political message, and not purely for enjoyment.[51] In the 1930s the political controversies and political fights became more bitter, and, as unemployment among young workers increased, the play-like character of many youth activities gave way to more purposeful political action. The last national gathering of the SAJ in Frankfurt in August 1931 had as its slogan 'Against Fascism and War. For Democracy and Socialism'.

The workers' youth movement had lost some of its romanticism and its a-political, if not anti-political, aestheticism; but it did not abandon its broad cultural and educational objectives. The SAJ retained to the end a central belief in the importance of cultural pursuits and in the ideal of the 'New Man', the socialist personality which could be created in advance of a socialist society.[52] This line, which the adult leadership continued to propagate, led to some secessions; but, unlike in the case of the Jungsozialisten, the organisation of some 18- to 20-year-olds whose fierce opposition to the party leadership led to their dissolution, the SAJ stayed together.[53] Probably more than any other social-democratic organisation it continued to believe in the Weimar Republic and in the possibility of realising the socialist goals of the SPD on the foundation laid by the Weimar constitution. As the journal *Arbeiterjugend* wrote in 1930, à propos the tenth anniversary of the meeting in Weimar, 'today we are convinced, as we were in 1920, that the road to socialism lies via democracy. We do not see democracy as the ultimate goal; but it is a fundamental pre-condition for the victory of socialism.'[54]

51. There is no comprehensive history of the Workers' Youth Movement. For a discussion of some of the political issues and the controversies over political action see F. Walter, 'Jugend in der sozialdemokratischer Solidaritätsgemeinschaft', *IWK*, vol. 23, pp. 311–76.
52. Cf. 'Weimar als Wegweiser, Ins zweite Jahrzehnt unseres Verbandes', *Arbeiterjugend*, vol. 22, 12 December 1930, pp. 265–6.
53. On the Jungsozialisten see R. Lüpke, *Zwischen Marx und Wandervogel. Die Jungsozialisten in der Weimarer Republik 1919–1931*, Marburg, 1984.
54. 'Weimar als Wegweiser', (note 52). A slogan which was at that time advanced by the Left of the SPD, and which also found an echo inside the youth

The Limits to Reform – Sex and Family Life

In their way Proletarian Freethinkers and the Workers' Youth Movement were each looking for new forms of sociability and better human relations. They wished to establish new ceremonials to replace old customs, opposing what they saw as religious obscurantism or bourgeois hypocrisy. Many of the lifestyles which the organised young workers developed were novel, but they did not fundamentally challenge established mores and morals, especially in the one area where such a challenge would have been truly revolutionary – namely that of sex, marriage and the family.

The contemporary discussion within the parties of the left of what was somewhat coyly referred to as the *Intimsphere*, was curiously restrained and conducted on a fairly abstract plane. Neither the existing *Sexualnot* – the sexual problems arising out of relatively late marriages, which were postponed because of economic pressures and shortage of housing, nor the social and health problems linked to a vast volume of unwanted pregnancies, and the consequential frighteningly high number of illicit and often medically harmful abortions, led to radical changes in traditional thinking.

This applies also to the youth movement. Here the attitude fostered in regard to sexual relations contained a fair measure of puritanism. As we saw, the *Ausdruckskultur* showed itself in part in the dress adopted. Traditional female dress, and fashion in particular, were seen as attempts to hide some of the natural forms of the human body while exaggerating others, thus creating illusions, manufacturing disguises in order to titillate human sensuality. Bourgeois dress, it was argued, stimulated erotic feelings, while the 'reform dress', developed in Hamburg, and consisting of a simple gown, worn with bare legs and sandals and without any make-up, aimed in contrast at an anti-sensual, if not puritanical, appearance.[55]

The co-educational character of the workers' youth movement posed questions about the relationship between the sexes, especially during puberty. The SAJ encouraged education in sexual matters and urged their free discussion. It recommended books of sexual instruction like the famous and frank 'Bub und Mädel' ('Boy and Girl') by the Berlin physician Max Hodann; but it approached the general problem of juvenile sexuality, contraception, marriage and the family with circumspection and in a conservative spirit.

---

movement, was 'Demokratie das ist nicht viel, Sozialismus ist das Ziel' ('Democracy, that is not much, We want Socialism as such').
55. Cf. 'Ausdruckskultur im Hamburger Jugendbund', *Arbeiterjugend*, 1920, p. 218.

The socialist youth movement argued that sexual intercourse before marriage was not necessarily unnatural if practised without the intention to have children; but it emphasised that it must be done responsibly, and in the context of a loving and enduring relationship. It was better to prevent conception than to produce children irresponsibly or to resort to abortion; but the movement never preached anything remotely approaching 'free love'.[56] Members of different sexes were expected to be considerate to each other and to establish comradely rather than erotic relationships. Pairing-off was tolerated, but it does not seem to have been the norm.[57] 'Members of the SAJ would tend to tie themselves down only at 18 or 19 and marry only around 25', which was the norm during that period.[58]

Reminiscences and later interviews suggest that the influence of new mores and of new lifestyles practised by the post-war generation of young workers was often deep and lasting.[59] There is evidence to suggest that the freer and more egalitarian attitude which prevailed in the youth movement influenced their subsequent marriages and family life in the 1920s and early 1930s.[60] The relationships stressed mutual esteem as well as love, and partners often embarked on joint or separate work in the labour movement. A commonly used word was *Kameradschafts-Ehe*, the 'marriage of comrades', sustained by egalitarian beliefs. 'We lived like brother and sister' one woman reported some fifty years later; and for another it was only natural that 'as long as we were both

56. P. Bernstein, 'Die Enzyklika des Papstes über die Ehe', *Arbeiterjugend*, 1931, pp. 118–20. (This was one of the few articles on this subject in the long run of the journal.)
57. An article in *Der Führer*, the periodical for the group leaders of the SAJ, maintained in 1921 that puberty was not so much notable for the awakening of erotic feeling as for being the period 'when the body prepares itself for its most beautiful and important task: motherhood and fatherhood.' *Der Führer*, 1921, p. 88.
58. Maike Bruhns, 'Bauvolk der kommenden Welt', in *Arbeiterkultur in Hamburg um 1930*, Hamburg, 1982, pp. 170–86, p. 177; P. Lang, 'Mein Mädchen und mein Familienleben', in *Arbeiterjugendbewegung in Frankfurt, 1904–1945*, Frankfurt, 1978, pp. 140–2.
59. See the reminiscences and documents collected from former members of the SAJ and of other left-wing youth organisations in Frankfurt and published in *Arbeiterjugendbewegung in Frankfurt, 1904–1945*, (note 58). See also recollections quoted by K. Hagemann, 'Wir jungen Frauen fühlten uns wirklich gleichberechtigt . . .', in W. Ruppert (ed.), *Die Arbeiter*, Munich, 1986, pp. 64–79.
60. See K. Hagemann, '"Der Sozialismus fängt im Hause an". Familienalltag in sozialdemokratischen Milieu' (unpublished paper for the Conference on Working-Class Culture in Britain and Germany, Lancaster, March 1988).

working and were politically active the household jobs were shared. . . . In our marriage we did not talk much about equal rights, one did not have to talk much about that, one just does it, and this is the way one lives in a family.'[61]

These reports were however generally from families where the husband was in relatively well-paid and secure employment, and which had a small number of children whose care was a central task of the parents. They often lived in modern homes, and by background and upbringing they identified with the working-class movement and were often active in it. They are unlikely to be typical of the bulk of working-class families. The full partnership marriage was, in our period, probably the exception, practised by some of those who had been through the workers' youth movement or were active in the women's movement.

On the other hand, the ideal of the small nuclear family had by the 1920s been widely accepted in the working class and was often realised in practice, as is shown by the course of the declining birthrate, especially after the war. Behind it stood the realisation that economic conditions demanded a limitation of the size of the worker's family. Yet the ideal of the *Kleinfamilie* still assumed that the proper and natural role of the working-class wife was that of mother and housewife. She was expected to find fulfilment in her duties in child-bearing, child-rearing and home-making. And in this she should be supported by the state. Indeed, the SPD argued that social policies should be oriented specifically towards the needs of mothers and children.[62]

Underlying this concept was the assumption that the social role of the working-class wife, like that of all women and wives, was as much sexually specific as was that of the man in his role as breadwinner and head of the household. Conversely, there was only a low value attached to women's work, let alone a woman's career, unless economic circumstances forced her into it.

Significantly this view was apparently widely shared by German working-class men. A survey carried out by Erich Fromm in 1929, but only published in 1980, asked a sample of workers questions about their attitudes to the employment of women and of married women in particular. Depending on political orientation, between 66% and 93% of respondents approved of single women working; but the approval rate was much lower for married women. Only

---

61. Hagemann (note 60), pp. 22–3.
62. Hagemann (note 60).

13% of social-democratic workers wholly approved of this, and even among communists the figure was only 36%. These attitudes were clearly a 'decisive test of emotional attitude to the independence of women'.[63] It is thus not surprising that the attitude of the SPD towards female emancipation and sexual freedom was ambiguous. The party had fought for equal rights for women on the political and on the legal plane, and this attitude found expression in votes for women and in other provisions of the Weimar constitution.[64] It did not, however, include equal treatment of women in respect of work and a career, and, while social-democratic opinion accorded women equality in the sexual sphere, the SPD also sided with the traditional view that the sexual roles of men and women were best played out within a lifelong monogamous marriage and the family life resulting from it.

The customary 'dual standard' of sexual behaviour, which expected marital faithfulness from women but permitted men a much greater latitude in sexual matters, was condemned; but so was unrestrained sex.[65] There was support for contraception; but the SPD did not make it an issue for wide public discussion or policy. For *Vorwärts* monogamy, and within monogamy, relative chastity was the preferred mode of conduct. As far as the young were concerned the paper was even more certain that restraint and compensatory physical activities were the appropriate form of behaviour.[66]

The *Frauenwelt*, the SPD's popular women's magazine, discussed issues like marriage and family life, and even, though usually only in very general terms, the questions of contraception and abortion. Here even women writing for women adopted on the whole a rather conservative attitude. The paper agreed that at least in capitalist society, and under conditions of considerable deprivation, the size of a family had to be restricted; and while chastity was not

63. E. Fromm, *The Working Class in Germany. A Psychological and Sociological Study*, Leamington Spa, 1984, p. 168.
64. In practice women's status left much to be desired even under Weimar. Cf. R.J. Evans, *The Feminist Movement in Germany, 1899–1933*, London, 1976, pp. 246–7.
65. Therese Schlesinger, 'Ist unsere Jugend verderbt? Frauenstimme', Supplement to *Vorwärts*, 19 February 1925.
66. *Vorwärts*, 19 September 1925, cited by C. Rülcker, 'Arbeiterkultur und Kulturpolitik im Blickwinkel des *Vorwärts*', *AfSG*, vol. 14, 1974, pp. 115–56, p. 132; *Vorwärts*, 23 May 1928, cited by Rülcker, 'Arbeiterkultur', p. 133, from an article on co-education. A leading official of the workers' sports movement, Karl Schreck, suggested at the 1929 Conference of the SPD that if you gave the young good opportunities for athletics and encouraged rambles these 'would push back these dark urges'. SPD Parteitag 1929, *Protokoll*, p. 247.

necessarily undesirable, the paper recognised that it was bad for a marriage. The answer lay in contraceptive practices, not in abortion; and it was hoped that a richer and juster society would obviate the need even for that.[67]

It is interesting and significant that contraceptive advice and agitation was directed almost exclusively at women; and the methods most commonly advocated were those which women could apply.[68] Propaganda for birth-control and assistance to working-class women was undertaken by a number of organisations which operated mainly in the big cities, notably the Gesellschaft für Sexualreform, and later also the Reichsverband für Geburtenreglung und Sexualhygiene. They were assisted by a few left-wing doctors, who lectured and gave practical advice at centres where devices were also available. They issued leaflets and booklets for instruction, and published journals with an estimated circulation of about 100,000. The factors which motivated these largely middle-class inspired bodies were related to social amelioration, and even to issues of eugenics; they were less concerned with sexual freedom and women's control over their own bodies, and we naturally know little of their effectiveness, especially among proletarian women.[69]

That large families might be undesirable as such, irrespective of the economic situation, is not acknowledged; but there is some awareness of the value of a career for women and of the way in which careers conflict with a woman's role as wife and mother. For most contributors to *Frauenwelt* woman's dual role as wife and mother is assumed to be the normal and desirable state. At the same time they often underplayed the sexual element in marriage. Puritanism had now swung to its opposite, argued a contributor, and this had not brought with it greater joy but an enormous amount of suffering, bitterness and disappointment. Sexual discipline might be looked at askance, the argument continued, but it was really the source for spiritual and psychic forces which were culturally creative.[70]

It is perhaps not surprising that the SPD did not develop a

---

67. *Frauenwelt*, 1930, p. 201. A more specific article on contraception by Hedwig Schwartz appeared in October 1927 under the title 'Geburtenregelung'. The survey comes to rather pessimistic conclusions about the practicability of the various methods.
68. Primarily the diaphragm and the cervical cap.
69. Cf. A. Grossman, 'Satisfaction in Domestic Happiness. Working Class Sexual Reform Organisations', in M. Dobkowski and I. Wallmann (eds), *Towards the Holocaust*, Westport, 1983.
70. Cf. Grete Wels, 'Die Kameradschaftsehe', *Frauenwelt*, 1929, pp. 202–3; Judith Grünfeld, 'Mütter und Töchter Wandlung der Geschlechtsitten', *Frauenwelt*,

libertarian answer to these problems; but neither did the KPD despite its early rhetoric. The Communist Party gave strong support to the agitation against the infamous anti-abortion paragraph 218 of the Criminal Law which developed towards the end of our period. Indeed, the party tried to make the campaign its own. It saw in the sexual question a useful vehicle to mobilise support among women, and it supported campaigns which under the heading of sexual politics and proletarian sexual reforms also spread knowledge about contraception and offered advice and assistance in this field.

The SPD, which advocated reform rather than abolition of the anti-abortion law, was less wholeheartedly involved in this agitation, although the party acknowledged that this was a burning issue in the women's sections.[71] On the other hand, the KPD was careful not to attack the basic assumptions of existing sexual morality too vigorously. The party did not support the *Sexpol* movement of Wilhelm Reich and his small circle, which sought a revolutionary change in sexual relations, although Reich himself was a member of the party. His theories and proposals aimed at the liberation of the sexual act from social conventions, and he sought to make this the basis for a political appeal. Communist activities in this area, while gaining some mass support, were conservative in their aims, because they did not seek to change existing attitudes fundamentally, while Reich's movement, although revolutionary in its implications, lacked an organisational and political base, and therefore did not have much practical impact.[72]

Social-democrats and communists, including members of the proletarian women's movement, seem to have largely adopted traditional views on marriage and family life. Such a view was even shared by so eminent a leader of working-class women as the left-wing radical social-democrat, and later communist, Clara Zetkin.[73] Indeed, it was in part the radicalism of the economic and

---

1929, pp. 249–51. A speaker at the 1929 Conference of the SPD criticised the fact that agitation among women focused almost exclusively on this area. In his report (SPD Parteitag 1929) he declared that when he got to a branch and suggested that they should mobilise support among women the answer was almost invariably that they should organise a meeting about *The Paragraph*.

71. See also K. Hagemann, 'Politik war Männersache – Die Frauen kämpften anders', in *Arbeiterkultur in Hamburg*, (note 58), pp. 145–68, especially pp. 146–54.

72. On Reich and the *Sexpol* movement see P. Robinson, *The Freudian Left*, London, 1969; E. Chesser, *Salvation through Sex*, New York, 1932.

73. Cf. J.M. Quartaert, 'Feminist Tactics in German Social Democracy, 1890–1914', *IWK*, vol. 13, 1977, no. 1, pp. 48–65.

social policy of the left which caused the negative features of actual sexual relationships and of family life to be seen simply as the results of the workers' oppression and poverty. The evils of large families, and of married women's being forced to go out to work, would disappear in a better economic and social order. Thus, in a historically significant episode in 1913, when two socialist Berlin physicians urged working-class women to carry out a *Gebärstreik* (to refuse to have any more children), the party leadership rejected the proposal, arguing that social problems must be solved through political action.[74]

On a more emotional plane the act of motherhood was widely accepted as the climax of women's fulfilment of their natural role, and this view was in all probability widely internalised by women themselves. Even 'emancipated' working-class women, who were politically active at the side of their men-folk, were so in a largely subordinate role, and their political activities were often in specifically 'female' fields (for instance, welfare).[75] The more libertarian attitude to sex and marriage which developed in sections of the German working class in the train of the general movement for the reform of lifestyles, under the influence of the workers' youth movement and of other specific pressure-groups, was constrained by the character of the general thinking which permeated the labour movement. This related the emancipation of the working-class woman to a largely sex-specific set of roles, with the maintenance of the small family, with the wife in the role of mother and housewife, as the dominant model.

In general the workers' cultural organisations, with their broad popular base, acted as 'transmission belts' between the traditional political organisations of the labour movement and the *Alltagskultur* of the working class.[76] This applies also where the organisations sought to foster new lifestyles and new forms of social intercourse. Here, however, the link was often fragile, and subject to strains as

74. Cf. U. Linse, 'Arbeiterschaft und Geburtenentwicklung im Kaiserreich', *AfSG*, vol. 12, 1972, pp. 205–71, at pp. 244–9. See also E. Kleinau, 'Über den Einfluß bürgerliche Vorstellungen von Beruf, Ehe und Familie auf die sozialistische Frauenbewegung', in *Frauen in der Geschichte*, IV, Düsseldorf, 1983.

75. Cf. A.E. Freier, 'Dimensionen weiblichen Erlebnis und Handelns innerhalb der proletarischen Frauenbewegung', in *Frauen in der Geschichte*, III, Düsseldorf, 1983, pp. 195–215. The principal field of women's activity in the SPD was the Arbeiterwohlfahrt ('Workers' Welfare'), which in 1930 had 114,000 members ('helpers').

76. Cf. A. von Saldern, 'Arbeiterkultur-Bewegung in Deutschland in der Zwischenkriegszeit', in F. Boll (ed.), *Arbeiterkultur zwischen Alltag und Politik*, Vienna, 1986, pp. 29–70, p. 53.

the new ideas and the new mores came into conflict not only with established forms of behaviour within the working class but also with traditional thinking in the labour movement. This applies above all to the Social Democratic Party; but we find evidence of it also in the communist camp.

Although many of the ideas for the reform of the everyday way of life of individuals and of families originated in middle-class reform movements, they were often in opposition to established bourgeois mores and morals, and were denounced by the church. In its rhetoric the political labour movement had declared its hostility to bourgeois society. This should have made it receptive to such reforms, and nowhere more so perhaps than in the field of sex and family life in the working class, burdened with too many children. But this was the case only to a limited extent.

The reasons for this can be found partly in the conservative attitudes in the SPD in matters of moral conduct, and in its unwillingness to offend sections of its membership and support – that is, the reasons were similar to those for the party's neutrality in religious matters after 1918.[77] More importantly, socialist ideology saw the solution of issues pertaining to human conduct, and to the social problems of the time, largely in institutional terms. Within the SPD the belief in the pre-eminence of economic factors and of economic solutions was widespread. Problems of personal life-styles, such as attitudes between the sexes, were not really considered to be a matter for the operation of some kind of moral public opinion within the working class. It was expected that they would be solved once economic and social institutions had been reformed and the material conditions of the working class had been improved. In any case, the structure and organisation of the working-class parties, with their extensive bureaucracies, neglected life and opinions at the base. Workers had little scope to articulate their hopes and their fears at the level of residence or workplace.[78] And although the Communist Party at the end of our period concentrated its organisation increasingly on cells in factories and housing blocks, this concentration was to serve political rather than communal ends.

77. In a related sphere, namely religion, the Görlitz Programme (1921) of the SPD stated that 'Religion is a private matter, a question of inner conviction, not a party matter.'
78. Von Saldern (note 76) cited the absence of worker participation in the management of new housing built in close connection with the labour movement, and the lack of consultation with workers over agreement on the rationalisation of work practices between unions and management, as examples of the remoteness of the organisation from the base.

The more powerful and more efficient Social Democratic Party of the Weimar Republic was increasingly involved in questions of day-to-day politics and administration. Yet it was less capable of establishing itself as a community which created fraternal bonds among its members, as it had done in the period when it was operating in a more hostile world. People spoke of a 'loss of utopia'. Whilst the party organisation was now less of a cohesive force, the cultural organisations increasingly took on the role of fulfilling such functions. Cultural Socialism, as we saw, was in some measure to anticipate the socialist society of the future. And nowhere more so than where the pursuit of cultural goals was combined with the practices of new lifestyles.

Conclusions

Let us now look at German workers' culture in perspective. The cultural movements and institutions which came into being barely a hundred years ago existed only for less than half of this period. Together with the whole of the German labour movement, they were brutally destroyed within a few months of the Nazi accession to power in January 1933. But while the parties and trade unions re-started life soon after the defeat of Adolf Hitler's 'Thousand Year Reich', the whole network of cultural institutions, with a few permanent and some temporary exceptions, was not brought back to life.

The fact that such successful organisations as Workers' Sport and Workers' Music were not re-established after 1945 gives cause for reflection. It signified a widespread belief, within the resurrected Social Democratic Party, that the socialist ghetto, with which working-class cultural life and practices had been identified for so long, was a matter of the past. Thus, as far as sport was concerned, the SPD had already resolved in 1946 to throw its energies behind the plans for a new independent national sports organisation, though it hoped that social democrats would guide the new organisation from within.

The decision not to resurrect specific working-class cultural institutions also owes much to the new, post-war, belief among social democrats that the future of the party lay in its role as a *Volkspartei* – a people's party, rather than a class party. Ideologically and organisationally, the party should now be able to appeal to all sections of the population; and the socialist sub-culture was conceived as an obstacle to this development. The 1959 Godesberg programme of the Social Democratic Party finally re-created the party on a new humanist and liberal basis, and as a party which was to be fully integrated in the national community.[1]

To assess the historical significance of German workers' culture

1. For the English text of the Godesberg programme of the SPD see S. Miller and H. Potthoff, *A History of German Social Democracy from 1948 to the Present*, Leamington Spa, 1986, pp. 274–87.

against the background of the new socialist thinking, and of the wider social developments of the post-war world, I must end on a speculative note.

The cultural institutions and organisations which the German working class had created before 1933 were a monument to the seriousness of purpose and willingness to dedicate time and effort to the betterment of their class manifested by a very large number of individuals. Given the size and strength of these movements, it still seems surprising that they were not re-started after the fall of Nazism. In this situation we are bound to ask whether, considered in retrospect, there were not other reasons which would have made the disappearance of the largely class-based and ideologically rooted cultural practices discussed in this book inevitable.

One such reason is the expansion of commercial entertainment. As we saw, the provision of commercial recreation through the medium of film and radio had made growing inroads into working-class leisure activities even before the end of our period. They had moreover developed further in the following decade – witness the improvements in the quality of the sound film and in the reproduction of broadcasts. Before 1933 the cultural organisations of the working class had not been able to arrest the desire for this type of popular entertainment. Nor had they been able to utilise the interest in radio or cinematic entertainment for activities under their auspices, let alone to provide visual or broadcast entertainment imbued with the ideology of the labour movement, at a really significant level.

For Dieter Langewiesche, a percipient and sympathetic historian of working-class culture in the Weimar Republic, this failure implied 'that the hitherto successful endeavours by the labour movement to incorporate new developments in the cultural sphere, had come up against their limits'.[2] Projected a generation or so on, these reflections would suggest that the cultural institutions of the working class would in any case have been unable to meet the challenge of the ever greater volume of commercial leisure time facilities which had been created in the industrialised countries of the West in the years since the Second World War.

Parallel to this development we have, of course, the vast increase in affluence and the growth in leisure activities which took place nearly everywhere in the industrialised countries. During the past three to four decades workers have achieved rising living standards

2. Cf. D. Langewiesche, 'Politik, Gesellschaft, Kultur. Zur Problematik von Arbeiterkultur und kulturellen Arbeiterorganisationen in Deutschland nach dem ersten Weltkrieg', *AfSG*, vol. 22, 1982, pp. 359–402, p. 402.

on a scale never dreamt of before the war. Coupled with the reductions in the length of the working week and with the widespread introduction of a longer weekend and of paid holidays, this laid the foundation for new privately enjoyed and increasingly privately styled forms of leisure.

This expansion makes it plausible to suggest that the practices of the workers' cultural organisations, which had been conceived in terms of groups and of collective activities, and had sought to anticipate some communitarian ideals already within capitalist society, were really only a transitory phenomenon on the road of the working class from a culture of poverty to a culture of affluence.

The affluent workers of today may remain collectivists in their political or their economic affiliations and actions; but they will believe themselves to be acting as individualists in the expression of their tastes and preferences as consumers. This choice includes above all the goods and services which make up their recreational, cultural and other forms of leisure-related consumption. They might even feel encouraged in their emphasis on the freedom of choice – including the freedom not to conform – by the widespread espousal of libertarian principles in contemporary socialist thinking.

Yet these conclusions can themselves be challenged, on the grounds that they lack another historical perspective. They do not make allowance for possible developments and changes in the character of that German workers' culture which was so suddenly cut short in 1933. Given the inherent strength of this culture, a potentially different political development might have falsified projections made on such general grounds.

The years between 1924 and 1929 had seen expansion and innovation in these cultural activities, and this might well have continued into the next decade. With the onset of the depression there was a general slowdown, and cuts in public expenditure which hit cultural activities particularly hard. The depression also sharpened the conflict inside the left, and politicised communist cultural activities. Without it, the attempts inside the KPD to mobilise workers' literary and artistic talents, innovatory in themselves, might well have developed more independently, and produced more original work, instead of being forced into channels whose course was dictated by tactical considerations. A growing affluence might also have led to a further expansion in the provision of literature for workers which had started with the book-clubs during the 1920s.

On the other hand, but for the advent of authoritarianism and of the breakdown of the democratic system, social-democratic cultural policy might have moved into a more pluralistic direction, such as the party had accepted in adult education and was advocating for broadcasting, whereby more independent but democratically controlled institutions would provide education and culture for working-class audiences.

Finally, but for the experience of fascism, the communitarian practices and ideals, which were so central to the organised workers' culture, might appear to us today in a more positive light. The *Sprechchor* and other mass-based techniques, developed for the workers' festival culture, contained elements later used in Nazi rallies and ceremonies. The fact that the mass indoctrination then practised was to lead later to mass extermination has made us aware of the inherent danger of such techniques. Labour-movement experiments sought to make art more politically committed; under other auspices similar techniques would make politics aesthetic, and lead to ceremonials and cults which inhibited rational judgement.[3]

Recent experience of political mass movements has shown again the importance of symbolic acts and of emotional appeals. They contain the danger of irrationally-based politics, and help fundamentalist doctrines. On the other hand, the mobilisation of political support through the mechanism of the market-place, analogous to the politics of consumers' choice, is not necessarily more rational if the persuasive and emotionalising techniques of the mass media are brought into play.

The model presented by the cultural movements of the German working class, democratically controlled, based on common leisure-time interests and pursuing common and evolving cultural goals within a broad ideological framework, may still have some relevance in an age of commercialised mass-culture.

3. The concept of the *Aesthetisierung der Politik* is generally linked to Walter Benjamin's essay on 'The Work of Art in the era of its technical Reproduction', originally published in 1938, but available in book form only since 1966. It can, however, be found already in a short article by 'Durus' in the *Rote Fahne* of 8 October 1930.

Select Bibliography

Bibliographies

Archiv der Sozialen Demokratie (Friedrich Ebert Stiftung), *Die Buchge-meinschaften der Arbeiterbewegung in der Weimarer Republik. Ein Bestands-verzeichnis*, Bonn, 1982

Barhausen R., *et al.*, compilers, *Arbeitersportbewegung. Ein Bestandsverzeich-nis der Bibliothek der Sozialen Demokratie* (Friedrich Ebert Stiftung), Bonn, 1981

Emig, B., *et al.*, *Literatur für eine neue Wirklichkeit* (Bibliography of the publications of the Dietz Verlag and of the Buchhandlung Vorwärts), Bonn–Berlin, 1982

Hempel-Küter, C., 'Die Tages und Wochenpresse der KPD', *IWK*, vol. 23, no. 1, pp. 27–46

Herzfelde, W., *Der Malik Verlag*, Berlin (GDR), 1967 (an illustrated bibliography with an introduction)

Hüser, F., 'Literatur und Kulturzeitschriften der Arbeiterbewegung', in *Erwachsenenbildung, Arbeiterbewegung, Presse. Festschrift für Walter Fabian*, Cologne, 1977

Klotzbach, K., *Bibliographie zur Geschichte der deutschen Arbeiterbewegung, 1914–1945*, 3rd, enlarged edn, Bonn, 1982

Koszyk, K., and G. Eisfeld, Die *Presse der deutschen Sozialdemokratie*, Bonn, 1980

Lidtke, V., 'Recent Literature on Workers' Culture in Germany and England', in K. Tenfelde (ed.), *Arbeiter und Arbeiterbewegung in vergleich-ender Sicht*, Munich, 1986, pp. 137–78

Workers' Culture: Contemporary Books, etc.

Engelhardt, V., *An der Wende des Zeitalters. Individualistische oder sozialisti-sche Kultur?*, Berlin, 1925

Franken, P., *Vom Werden einer neuen Kultur*, Berlin, 1930 (repr. Munich, 1980)

Herrmann-Neisse, M., *Die bürgerliche Literaturgeschichte und das Proletariat*, Berlin, 1922 (repr. in F & R, pp. 64–86)

Kampfmeyer, P., *Arbeiterbewegung und Sozialdemokratie*, Berlin, 1921

Kulturkartell der modernen Arbeiterbewegung, *Sozialistische Kultur und*

Bildungsarbeit, Frankfurt, 1929

Liebknecht, W., *Wissen ist Macht – Macht ist Wissen*, 1872 and later editions (modern edn by H. Brumme, Berlin (GDR), 1968)

Lindemann, W., *Die proletarische Freidenkerbewegung. Geschichte, Theorie, Praxis*, Leipzig, 1926 (repr., Münster, 1980)

Man, H. de, *Der Sozialismus als Kulturbewegung*, Berlin, 1926
—— *Zur Psychologie des Sozialismus*, Jena, 1926, rev. edn, 1927 (English edn as *The Psychology of Socialism*, London 1928)

Olbrich, J. (ed.), *Arbeiterbildung in der Weimarer Zeit* (contemporary documents and readings), Brunswick, 1977

Radbruch, G., *Kulturlehre des Sozialismus*, Berlin, 1927, and 1949

Schulz, H., *Politik und Bildung*, Berlin, 1931

Sozialismus und Kultur, Bericht der Tagung des Sozialistischen Kulturbundes, 1926 Berlin, 1927

Steiger, E., *Das arbeitende Volk und die Kunst*, Leipzig, 1896

Wagner, R., *Klassenkampf um den Menschen. Menschenbild und Gesellschaft*, Vienna, 1923

Will W. van der, and R. Burns, *Arbeiterkulturbewegung in der Weimarer Republik, vol. 2, Texte, Dokumente, Bilder*, Berlin, 1982

Winkler, E., 'Bericht über die Kulturwoche' (in Leipzig), *Die Tat*, 1924, pp. 892–902

Wittfogel, K.A., 'Zur Frage einer marxistischen Aesthetik', *Linkskurve*, May–November 1930, rcpr. in *Aesthetik und Kommunikation*, 1971, no. 3

Zur Tradition der deutschen sozialistischen Literatur, 4 vols, Berlin, 1979, vol. 1 *Eine Auswahl von Dokumenten, 1926–1935*

Workers' Culture: Contemporary Periodicals

Arbeiter Bildung, 1920–2; 1926–8 continued as *Sozialistische Bildung*

Arbeiterbühne, 1926–30 (formerly *Volksbühne, Zentral organ für die Interessen des deutschen Arbeitertheaterbundes* continued as *Arbeiterbühne und Film*)

Arbeiterbühne und Film, 1930–1

Arbeiter Illustrierte Zeitung, 1925–32

Arbeiterjugend, 1909–33

Arbeiter Turn Zeitung (later *Arbeiter Turn und Sport Zeitung*), 1893–1933

Büchergilde (published by the Büchergilde Gütenberg), 1925–33

Bücherkreis, 1924–32

Deutsche Arbeiter Sängerzeitung, 1907–33

Eulenspiegel, 1928–31

Film und Volk, 1928–30

Frauenwelt, 1924–32

Freie Welt (supplement to *Die Freiheit*), 1918–22

Die Front (Journal of the ARBKD), 1928–31

Der Führer. Monatschrift für Führer und Helfer in der Arbeiterjugend, 1918–1932

Ifa Rundschau, 1929–32
Die Junge Volksbühne, 1929
Kampfgenoß. Zeitschrift für proletarische Geistes und Körperkultur, 1926–1932
Kampfmusik, 1929–32
Knüppel. Satirische Arbeiterzeitung, 1924–7
Kulturwille, 1924–33
Lachen Links. Das republikanische Witzblatt, 1924–7
Die Linkskurve (published by the BPRS), 1929–32
Magazin für Alle (Journal of the Universum Bücherei) 1929–32
Das Neue Bild. Zeitschrift zur Pflege von Film und Foto, published by the Arbeiter Lichtbildbund) 1930–1
Die Neue Welt, 1883–1914
Die Neue Gesellschaft, 1905–7
Neue Zeit, 1883–1921
Sozialistische Bildung (continues *Arbeiterbildung*) 1929–32
Sozialistische Monatshefte, 1897–1933
Sportspolitische Rundschau, 1928–1933
Volk und Zeit, 1919–33
Volksbühne. Zeitschrift für sozialistische Kunstfragen (published by the Verband der deutschen Volksbühnenvereine, formerly *Freie Volksbühne*, 1897–1933
Volksbühne. Zentralorgan für die Interessen des deutschen Arbeitertheaterbundes (continued as *Arbeiterbühne*), 1914–1920
Weg Der Frau, 1931–2

Workers' Culture: General

Arbeiterjugendbewegung in Frankfurt, 1904–1945. Material zu einer verschütteten Kulturgeschichte, Frankfurt, 1978
Arbeiterkultur in Hamburg um 1930, Hamburg, 1982
Arbeiterkultur in der proletarischen Provinz. 1890–1933, Marbach a.N., 1983
Assion, P. (ed.), *Transformationen der Arbeiterkultur*, Marburg, 1986
Boll, F. (ed.), *Arbeiterkultur zwischen Alltag und Politik*, Vienna, 1986
Emig, B., *Die Veredlung des Arbeiters. Die Sozialdemokratie als Kulturbewegung*, Frankfurt, 1980
Feidel-Merz, M., *Zur Ideologie der Arbeiterbildung*, Frankfurt, 1983
Feilhauer, H., and O. Bockhorn (eds), *Die Andere Kultur. Volkskunde, Sozialwissenschaften und Arbeiterkultur*, Vienna, 1982
Heidenreich, F., *Arbeiterbildung und Kulturpolitik. Kontroversen in der proletarischen Zeitschrift Kulturwille, 1924–1933*, Berlin, 1983
Juttner, W., *et al.*, *Geschichte der Arbeiterbildung bis zum Faschismus*, Hanover, 1983
Kocka, J., 'Arbeiterkultur als Forschungsthema', *Geschichte und Gesellschaft*, 1979, pp. 5–11
Langewiesche, D., 'Politik, Gesellschaft, Kultur. Zur Problematik von

Select Bibliography

Arbeiterkultur und kulturellen Arbeiterorganisationen in Deutschland nach dem ersten Weltkrieg', *AfSG*, vol. 22, 1982, pp. 359–402

Lehmann, A. (ed.). *Studien zur Arbeiterkultur*, Münster, 1983

Müller, E.R., *Das Weimar der arbeitenden Jugend*, Berlin, 1921

Petzina, D. (ed.), *Fahnen, Fäuste, Körper. Symbolik und Kultur der Arbeiterbewegung* Essen, 1986

Ritter, G.A., 'Workers' Culture in Imperial Germany', *Journal of Contemporary History*, vol. 13, 1978, pp. 165–89

Rüden, P. von (ed.), *Beiträge zur Kulturgechichte der deutschen Arbeiterbewegung, 1848–1918*, Frankfurt, 1979

Rülcker, C., 'Arbeiterkultur und Kulturpolitik im Blickwinkel des *Vorwärts*', *AfSG*, vol. 14, 1974, pp. 115–55

Saldern, A. von, 'Arbeiterkulturbcwegung in der Zwischenkriegszeit', in F. Boll (ed.), *Arbeiterkultur zwischen Alltag und Politik*

Studemann, E., and M. Rector (eds), *Arbeiterbewegung und kulturelle Identität*, Frankfurt, 1983

Stuttgart, Württembergisches Landesmuseum, *Arbeiterbewegung und Arbeiterkultur in Stuttgart 1890–1933*, Stuttgart, 1982

Tenfelde, K., 'Anmerkungen zur Arbeiterkultur', in W. Ruppert, *Erinnerungsarbeit*, Opladen, 1982, pp. 107–34

Will, W. van der, and R. Burns, *Arbeiterkulturbewegung in der Weimarer Rcpublik*, Berlin, 1982

Wunderer, H., *Arbeitervereine und Arbeiterparteien. Kultur und Massenorganisation in der Arbeiterbewegung, 1890–1933*, Frankfurt, 1980

'Alltagskultur' and Workers' Leisure

Althaus, H.J., *et al.*, *Da ist nirgends nichts gewesen außer hier. Geschichte eines Schwäbischen Arbeiterdorfes*, Berlin, 1982

Bajohr, J., *Vom bitteren Los der kleinen Leute*, Cologne, 1984

Dehn, G., *Die geistige und materielle Lebensführung der proletarischen Jugend*, Berlin, 1929

Deutscher Textilarbeiterverband, *Mein Arbeitstag, mein Wochenende*, Berlin, 1930

Dinse, R., (ed.) *Das Freizeitleben der Grosstadtjugend*, Eberswalde, 1932

Evans, R.J. (ed.), *The German Working Class, 1888–1933. The Politics of Every Day Life*, London, 1982

Fromm, E., *The Working Class in Germany: A Psychological and Sociological Study*, Leamington Spa, 1984

Geiger, Th., *Die soziale Schichtung des deutschen Volkes*, Stuttgart, 1932

Huck, G. (ed.), *Sozialgeschichte der Freizeit*, Wuppertal, 1980

Jacobeit, W., and U. Mohrmann (eds), *Kultur und Lebensweise des Proletariats*, Berlin, 1973

Kuczynski, J., *Darstellung der Lage der Arbeiter in Deutschland, 1917–1932/33*, Berlin, 1966

Select Bibliography

——, *Die Geschichte des Alltags des deutschen Volkes (vol. 5, 1918–1945)*, Cologne, 1982 (originally pub. Berlin (GDR), 1982)

Leipart, Th. (ed.), *Die 40 Stunden Woche*, Berlin, 1931

Levenstein, A., *Die Arbeiterfrage*, Munich, 1912

Mooser, J., *Arbeiter in Deutschland, 1900–1970. Klassenlage, Kultur und Politik*, Frankfurt, 1984

Mühlberg, D., 'Anfänge proletarischen Freizeitsverhalten', *Weimarer Beiträge*, 1981, no. 12, pp. 118–50

—— et al., *Arbeiterkultur um 1900*, Berlin (GDR), 1983

Niethammer, L. (ed.), *Wohnen im Wandel. Beiträge zur Geschichte des Alltags in der bürgerlichen Gesellschaft*, Wuppertal, 1977

Reck, S., *Arbeiter nach der Arbeit. Sozialhistorische Studie zu den Wandlungen des Arbeiteralltags*, Lahn-Giessen, 1977

Reulecke, J., and W. Weber (eds), *Fabrik, Familie, Feierabend. Beiträge zur Sozialgeschichte des Alltags im Industriezeitalter*, Wuppertal, 1978

Ruppert, W. (ed.), *Die Arbeiter. Lebensformen, Alltag und Kultur*, Munich, 1986

Salomon, A., and M. Baum, *Familienleben der Gegenwart*, Berlin, 1930

Soder, M., *Hausarbeit und Stammtischsozialismus. Arbeiterfamilie und Alltag im deutschen Kaiserreich*, Giessen, 1986

Sport

Bernett, H., 'Das Problem einer alternativen Sportpraxis im deutschen Arbeitersport untersucht am Beispiel der Leichtathletik', in H. Teichler (ed.), *Arbeiterkultur und Arbeitersport*, Clausthal, Zellerfeld, 1985, pp. 50–76

Friedemann, P., 'Die Krise der Arbeitersportbewegung am Ende der Weimarer Republik', in F. Boll (ed.), *Arbeiterkultur zwischen Alltag und Politik*, Vienna, 1986, pp. 229–40

Schmidtchen, V., 'Arbeitersport – Erziehung zum sozialistischen Menschen?', in J. Reulecke and W. Weber (eds), *Fabrik, Familie, Feierabend*, Wuppertal, 1978, pp. 345–75

Teichler, H. (ed.), *Arbeiterkultur und Arbeitersport*, Clausthal, Zellerfeld, 1985

—— and G. Hauk (eds), *Illustrierte Geschichte des Arbeitersports*, Berlin, 1987

Timmermann, H., *Geschichte und Struktur der Arbeitersportbewegung*, Diss. Marburg, 1987

Ueberhorst, H., *Frisch, froh, stark und treu. Die Arbeitersportbewegung in Deutschland, 1893–1933*, Düsseldorf, 1973

——, 'Bildungsgedanke und Solidaritätsbewußtsein in der deutschen Arbeitersport Bewegung', *AfSG*, vol. 14, 1974, pp. 275–92

Wagner, H., *Sport und Arbeitersport*, Berlin, 1931

Wheeler, R.F., 'Organised Sport and Organised Labour. The Workers' Sports Movement', *Journal of Contemporary History*, vol. 13, no. 2, 1978, pp. 191–210

Wildung, J., *Arbeitersport*, Berlin, 1929

Wunderer, H., 'Der Touristenverein Die Naturfreunde, eine sozialdemok-ratische Arbeiterkulturorganisation', *IWK* no. 13, 1977, pp. 506–19

Zimmer, J., '*Mit uns zieht die neue Zeit*'. *Die Naturfreunde, zur Geschichte eines alternativen Verbandes in der Arbeiterkulturbewegung*, Cologne, 1984

Music

Dowe, D., 'The Workers' Choral Movement before the First World War', *Journal of Contemporary History*, vol. 13 no. 2, 1978, pp. 269–96

Eisler, H., *Musik und Politik. Schriften, 1924–1948*, Berlin (GDR), 1973

Fuhr, W., *Proletarische Musik, 1928–1933*, Göppingen, 1977

Kaden, W., *Die Entwicklung der Arbeitersängerbewegung in Gau Chemnitz bis 1933*, Zwickau, 1960

Lammel, I., *Das Arbeiterlied*, Leipzig, 1980

——, 'Zur Musikrezeption durch die deutsche Arbeiterklasse', in W. Jacobeit und U. Mohrmann (eds), *Kultur und Lebensweise des Proletariats*, Berlin (GDR), 1973, pp. 221–30

Lidtke, V., 'Songs and Politics. An Exploratory Essay on *Arbeiterlieder* in the Weimar Republic', *AfSG*, vol. 14, 1974, pp. 253–73

Meyer, E.H., 'Aus der Tätigkeit der Kampfgemeinschaft der Arbeiter-sänger', *Sinn und Form (Sonderheft für Hanns Eisler)* 1964, pp. 152 64

Noack, V., *Der deutsche Arbeitersängerbund. Eine Materialsammlung*, 2 parts, Berlin 1911; 2nd edn as *Geschichte des Arbeitersängerbund*, printed but not published 1932

Steinitz, W., *Arbeiterlied und Volkslied*, Berlin (GDR), 1965

——, 'Das Leunalied. Zur Geschichte und Wesen eines Arbeiterliedes', *Jahrbuch für Volkskunde*, vol. 4, 1958, pp. 3–52

Visual Arts

Akademie der Künste (West Berlin), *Der Arbeitsrat für Kunst, 1918–1921*, Berlin, 1980

Baacke, R.P., and M. Nungesser, 'Ich bin, ich war, ich werde sein. Die Denkmäler der deutschen Arbeiterbewegung in den Zwanziger Jahren', *WgdW*, pp. 280–99

Domansky, E., 'Der Zukunftstaat am Besenbinderhof', in A. Herzig *et al.* (eds), *Arbeiter in Hamburg*, Hamburg, 1983, pp. 373–86

Geller, R.H., *Die politische Zeichnung der Laien. Arbeiterzeichner der KPD*, Bad Honnef, 1984

Grape, W., *Aufruf und Anklage. Kunst für die Bremer Arbeiterbewegung*, Bremen, 1983

Grosz, G., and W. Herzfelde, *Die Kunst ist in Gefahr. Ein Orientierungsver-such*, Berlin, 1925 (repr. in Schneede, *Die Kunst der zwanziger Jahre*, pp.

136–7)

Herzfelde, W., *Gesellschaft, Künstler und Kommunismus*, Berlin, 1921

Howoldt, E., *Der freie Bund zur Einbürgerung der bildenden Kunst in Mannheim*, Frankfurt, 1982

Kliemann, H., *Die Novembergruppe*, Berlin, 1969

Kober, R., *Die Verhältnisse von Leipziger Arbeitervereinen und Vereinen für Arbeiter zur bildenden Kunst*, Leipzig, 1970

Kramer, J., 'Die Assoziation revolutionärer Bildender Künstler', *WgdW*, pp. 174–204

Kuhirt, U., 'Die Arbeiter Zeichner Bewegung', in W. Jacobeit and U. Mohrmann (eds), *Kultur und Lebensweise des Proletariats*, Berlin (GDR), 1973

Kunst als Waffe. Die ASSO und die revolutionare bildende Kunst der Zwanziger Jahre, published by the Parteivorstand der Deutschen Kommunistischen Partei, Nuremberg, 1973

Lane, B.M., *Architecture and Politics*, Cambridge, Mass., 1968

Olbrich, H., *Sozialistische deutsche Karikatur, 1848–1978*, Berlin (GDR), 1979

Revolution und Realismus. Revolutionäre Kunst in Deutschland, 1917–1933, (exhibition catalogue), Berlin (GDR), 1978

Rigby, I.K., *War–Revolution–Weimar. German Expressionist Prints, Drawings, Posters and Periodicals from the Robert Gore Rifkind Foundation*, San Diego, 1983

Rinka, E., *Photographie im Klassenkampf. Ein Arbeiterphotograph erinnert sich*, Leipzig, 1981

Schneede, U.M. (ed.), *Die Zwanziger Jahre*, Manifeste und Dokumente deutscher Künstler, Cologne, 1929

Selle, G., *Kultur der Sinne und aesthetische Erziehung*, Cologne, 1981

Wem gehört die Welt. Kunst und Gesellschaft in der Weimarer Republik (exhibition catalogue) Neue Gesellschaft für Bildende Kunst, Berlin, 1977

Theatre

Braulich, H., *Die Volksbühne. Theater und Politik in der deutschen Arbeiter Bewegung*, Berlin (GDR), 1976

Davies, C.W., *Theatre for the People*, Austin, 1977

Hoffmann, L., and D. Hoffmann-Ostwald, *Deutsches Arbeiter Theater, 1918–1933*, 2 vols., Berlin, 1972

Hornauer, U., *Laienspiel und Massenchor*, Cologne, 1985

Knellessen, F.W., *Agitation auf der Bühne. Das politische Theater der Weimarer Republik*, Enmschetten, 1970

Lacis, A., *Revolutionär im Beruf. Berichte über proletarisches Theater*, ed. by H. Brenner, Munich, 1971

Piscator, E., *Das Politische Theater*, Berlin, 1929 (reprint, Berlin (GDR) 1963: trans. as *The Political Theatre*, New York, 1978)

Select Bibliography

Scherer, H., *Bürgerlich-oppositionelle Literatur und sozialdemokratische Arbeiterbewegung. Die 'Friedrichshagener' und ihr Einfluß auf die sozialdemokratische Kulturpolitik*, Stuttgart, 1974

——, 'Volksbühnenbewegung und interne Opposition in der Weimarer Republik' *AfSG*, vol. 14, 1974, pp. 214–51

Schwerd, A., *Zwischen Sozialdemokratie und Kommunismus. Zur Geschichte der Volksbühne*, Wiesbaden, 1975

Die Volksbühne – das Theater des Volkes (Schriften des deutschen Volksbühnenvereins no. 2) Berlin, 1920

Weber, R., *Proletarisches Theater und revolutionäre Arbeiterbewegung*, Cologne, 1976

Wolf, F., 'Schöpferische Probleme des Agitproptheaters' *Aufsätze über Theater. (Ausgewählte Werke*, vol. 13), Berlin (GDR), 1953

Zentker, T., *Der Berliner Prater*, Berlin (GDR), 1987

Festkultur

Altenberg, E., *Feste der Jugend*, 1929

Blessing, W.K., 'Feste und Vergnügen der kleinen Leute', in R. von Dulmen and N. Schindler (eds), *Volkskultur*, Frankfurt, 1984, pp. 352–79

Clark, J., *Bruno Schönlank und die Arbeitersprechchorbewegung*, Cologne, 1984

Heilbut, K., 'Neue Formen proletarischer Festkultur' *Soz. Bldg.* 1931, pp. 205–10; 243–8

Hornauer, U., *Laienspiel und Massenchor*, Cologne, 1985

Lohmann, R., *Die Jugendweihe*, Berlin, 1923

Stachow, H., '"Festtag, Kampftag"' Feste der sozialistischen Arbeiterbewegung in *Arbeiterkultur in Hamburg um 1930*, Hamburg, 1982, pp. 209–22

Will, W. van der, and R. Burns, *Arbeiterkulturbewegung in der Weimarer Republik*, Berlin, 1982, pp. 167–232

Zelck, M., 'Der Kulturwille des Sozialismus' in SPD Hamburg', *25 Jahre sozialistisch Kulturarbeit in Hamburg*, Hamburg, 1931

Film, Radio, Press

Bausch, H., *Der Rundfunk im politischen Kräftespiel der Weimarer Republik, 1923–1933*, Tübingen, 1956

Bierbach, W., *Rundfunk zwischen Kommerz und Politik. Der Westdeutsche Rundfunk in der Weimarer Zeit*, Frankfurt, 1986

Dahl, P., *Arbeitersender und Volksempfänger. Proletarische Radiobewegung und bürgerlicher Rundfunk*, Frankfurt, 1978

Korte, H., *Film und Realität in der Weimarer Republik*, Frankfurt, 1980

Koszyk, K., *Zwischen Kaiserreich und Diktatur. Die sozialdemokratische*

Select Bibliography

Presse, 1914–1933, Heidelberg, 1968

Kühn, G., *et al.*, *Film und revolutionäre Arbeiterbewegung in Deutschland, 1918–1932*, 2 vols., Berlin, 1975

Lerg, B., *Rundfunkpolitik in der Weimarer Republik*, Munich, 1980

Lüdecke, W., *Der Film in Agitation und Propaganda der revolutionären deutschen Arbeiter Bewegung, 1919–1933*, Berlin, 1973

Reinken, L., *Rundfunk in Bremen, 1924–1974*, Bremen, 1975

Ricke, G., *Die Arbeiter Illustrierte. Gegenmodell zur bürgerlichen Illustrierte*, Hanover, 1974

Sozialistischer Kulturbund, *Film und Funk* (proceedings of the Sozialistische Kulturtag in Frankfurt, 1929), Berlin, 1929

Stooss, T., 'Erobert den Film, oder Prometheus gegen UFA und Co.', *WgdW*, pp. 482–525

Willmann, H., *Geschichte der Arbeiter Illustrierte, 1921–1938*, Frankfurt, 1974

Literature

Albrecht, F., and K. Kändler, *Der Bund proletarisch-revolutionärer Schriftsteller Deutschlands, 1928–1935*, Leipzig, 1978

Bühnemann, M., and T. Friedrich, 'Zur Geschichte der Buchgemeinschaften der Arbeiterbewegung der Weimarer Republik', *WgdW*, 1977, pp. 364–97

Burns, R., 'Theory and Organisation of Revolutionary Working-Class Literature in the Weimar Republic', in K. Bullivant (ed.), *Culture and Society in the Weimar Republic*, Manchester, 1977, pp. 122–49

Fahnders, W., and M. Rector (eds), *Literatur im Klassenkampf*, Munich, 1971

Fülberth, G., *Proletarische Partei und bürgerliche Literatur*, Neuwied and Berlin, 1972

Hagen, W., *Die Schillerverehrung in der deutschen Sozialdemokratie*, Stuttgart, 1977

Klein, A., *Im Auftrag ihrer Klasse. Wege und Leistungen deutscher Arbeiterschriftsteller*, Berlin, Weimar, 1972

Langewiesche D., and K. Schoenhoven, 'Arbeiterbibliotheken und Arbeiterlektüre im Wilhelminischen Deutschland', *AfSG*, vol. 16, 1976, pp. 135–204

Möbius, H., *Progressive Massenliteratur? Revolutionäre Arbeiterromane, 1927–1932*, Stuttgart, 1977

Rohrwasser, M., *Saubere Mädel, Starke Genossen. Proletarische Massenliteratur*, Frankfurt, 1975

Rülcker, C., *Ideologie der Arbeiterdichtung, 1914–1933*, Stuttgart, 1970

Schmitt, H.J. (ed.), *Die Expressionismusdebatte. Materialien auf einer marxistischen Realismuskonzeption*, Frankfurt, 1973

Simon, E., 'Der Bund proletarisch-revolutionärer Schriftsteller und sein Verhältnis zur kommunistischen Partei Deutschlands', in A. Klein (ed.), *Literatur der Arbeiterklasse*, Berlin, 1974, pp. 119–90

Zorges, K., *Sozialdemokratische Presse und Literatur. Empirische Untersuchungen zur Literaturvermittlung in der sozialdemokratischen Presse, 1876–1933*, Stuttgart, 1982

Index

Name Index

Index of Institutions and Organisations

Excluding references to the German Social Democratic Party (SPD) and the German Communist Party (KPD)

Index

Index

Index